A Practical Introduction to Literary Study

James S. Brown
Bloomsburg University

Scott D. Yarbrough
Charleston Southern University

PEARSON

Up

Library of Congress Cataloging-in-Publication Data

Brown, James S. [date]
    A practical introduction to literary study / James S. Brown, Scott D. Yarbrough.
        p. cm.
Includes bibliographical references and index.
    ISBN 0-13-094786-5
    1. English literature—History and criticism—Theory, etc.   2. American literature—History
and criticism—Theory, etc.   3. Literature—History and criticism—Theory, etc.
I. Yarbrough, Scott D. [date] II. Title.

PR21.B76 2005
    808—dc22

                                                            2004060044

VP/Editor in Chief: Leah Jewell
Acquisitions Editor: Vivian Garcia
Editorial Assistant: Melissa Casciano
Executive Marketing Manager: Brandy Dawson
Marketing Assistant: Mariel Dekranis
Senior Production Editor: Shelly Kupperman
Permissions Coordinator: Ronald Fox
Manufacturing Manager: Nick Sklitsis
Prepress and Manufacturing Buyer: Brian Mackey
Cover Design: Robert Farrar-Wagner
Cover Art: Comstock Production Department/Comstock Images

This book was set in 10/12 Palatino by GGS Book Services, Atlantic Highlands, and was printed and bound by Phoenix Book Tech. Covers were printed by Phoenix Book Tech.

For permission to use copyrighted material, grateful acknowledgment is made to the copyright holders on page 334, which is considered an extension of this copyright page.

Pearson Education LTD.
Pearson Education Singapore, Pte. Ltd
Pearson Education, Canada, Ltd
Pearson Education—Japan
Pearson Education Australia PTY, Limited

Pearson Education North Asia Ltd
Pearson Educación de Mexico, S.A. de C.V.
Pearson Education Malaysia, Pte. Ltd
Pearson Education, Upper Saddle River, NJ

10 9 8 7 6 5 4 3 2 1

ISBN 0-13-094786-5

✃ Contents ✄

ᦔ Preface ᦕ

As English professors with large teaching loads at small colleges, we have had the opportunity to teach a considerable number of literature courses at every level of college education, from first-year introductory courses through graduate seminars. Although many of our sophomore students may have been exposed to the rudiments of literary study as first-year students, it has become apparent to us that a good many students seem to have difficulty retaining what they have learned about critical reading, analytical writing, and research and documentation methods into their second-year literature surveys. We have also begun encountering transfer students from schools that do not require literature and composition courses for first-year students. Such students have upon occasion been thrust into college-level literature courses where they are expected to read critically and analytically, to write thoughtful and concise papers of literary analysis, and to perform competent literary research. These expectations are difficult enough to meet for sophomores who have had the benefit of first-year instruction in literature but exceedingly difficult to meet for students like the transfers we noted or students who have exempted their first-year class through placement exams.

At the same time, like many other professors, we have become somewhat dissatisfied with many standard first-year literary texts. Although some of the pedagogical apparatus included in such texts is very fine, often the anthology of included works doesn't live up to the sections on writing. Similarly, several excellent anthologies seem to contain very little in the way of useful pedagogy. A text containing very good notes on critical theory, for example, may contain nothing on Modern Language Association (MLA) documentation. Finding supplemental texts that let us teach literature from a variety of anthologies and primary sources while at the same time not sacrificing any of the pedagogy proved quite difficult. We have also had problems in finding texts that were suitable for students who were still learning to read critically and to write analytically or who needed to be refreshed on the fundamental rules of literary research before being asked to make use of theory in a paper.

Our goal in this book, then, is to provide a practical guide for students entering literary study. This text is intended as a supplementary text for survey of literature courses and is written and designed to be useful and accessible for the undergraduate student. We have particularly focused on sophomores and on first-year students who are taking courses that use literature anthologies or other texts without pedagogical apparatus.

A Practical Introduction to Literary Study begins by focusing on critical reading and the literary canon and introduces students to the tools, terms, and methods they need for discussing literature. It also contains chapters on practical research methods, on understanding criticism and using it in papers, and on MLA documentation. We have also included a brief overview of critical theory that should prove useful in courses designed for introducing new upper-division students to the English major. We have used **boldface** to indicate important literary terms throughout the text that are defined in the glossary at the back of the book.

Although *A Practical Introduction to Literary Study* does include a small number of readings to help illustrate various points throughout the text, this book is not intended to function as an anthology or to replace any of the excellent anthologies instructors use in their classes. Instead, we have for the most part chosen short, commonly taught or relatively straightforward texts in order to facilitate classroom instruction. The readings have been kept to a minimum because the text is intended to be supplemental to other literature texts; we realize that instructors may often wish to choose alternative works to teach the lesson at hand. Some readings are incorporated into the chapter for the convenience of the instructor and students; others are contained in Part Six of the book.

Above all else, this book is intended to be understandable and useful to the beginning student as well as to the more advanced student. We have included Thinking Exercises throughout the book that instructors may assign if they wish; these exercises are tailored to provoke further thought in students who are learning how exciting and stimulating literary studies can truly be.

ACKNOWLEDGMENTS

We gratefully acknowledge the help and input of the following reviewers for this book: Cheryl M. Clark, Miami-Dade Community College; Maria A. Clayton, Middle Tennessee State University; Genevieve B. Coogan, Houston Community College; Lezlie Laws Couch, Rollins College; Gary Davis, Miami-Dade Community College; Donna J. French, Valencia Community

College; Kate Gray, Clackamus Community College; Bryon Lee Grigsby, Centenary College; Loren Gruber, Missouri Valley College; H. George Hann, Towson University; Kimberley Harrison, Florida International University; Ana A. Hernandez, Miami-Dade Community College; Keith Higginbotham, Midlands Technical College; Jeffrey Hornburg, Miami-Dade Community College; Beth Howells, Armstrong Atlantic State University; Betty Huford, Glendale Community College; Joe Kelly, College of Charleston; David Kirby, Florida State University; Erica Koss-Smith, San Diego State University; Scott A. Leonard, Youngstown State University; Gay Lyons, Pellisippi State Technical Community College; Price McMurray, College of Charleston; Barbara Nightingale, Broward Community College; Daniel Pinti, Niagara University; Anne H. Southard, Okaloosa Walton Community College; Rebecca Steinberger, College Misericordia; Bradley J. Stiles, Clackamas Community College; Myron Tuman, University of Alabama; Victor Uszerowicz, Miami-Dade Community College; Ryan G. Van Cleave, University of Wisconsin–Green Bay; and Ralph F. Voss, University of Alabama.

Furthermore, we would like to acknowledge the help and support of our colleagues in the English Department and Foundation Studies Program at Charleston Southern University: Nancy Barendse, Nancy Canavera, Nancy Drago, Carol Drowota, Anne Hawkes, Dawn Leonard, David Phillips, Clay Motley, and Tunis Romein. We also appreciate the support of the Dean of Humanities and Social Sciences, Don Dowless, and Provost A. K. Bonnette. We are especially grateful to CSU student Faith Bafford for permission to use her essay.

We also appreciate the excellent guidance we have received from the people at Prentice Hall, including Carrie Brandon, Brian Buckley, Leah Jewell, and particularly Vivian Garcia, Shelly Kupperman, and Judy Kiviat.

Finally, we would like to dedicate this book to the students with whom we have enjoyed discovering and rediscovering literature each semester; we also dedicate this book to our families, who have endured the long process involved in its writing: Deanna Gast, Michelle and Jessica Brown, Leigh and Marie Yarbrough, and our helpful and supportive parents.

James S. Brown
Scott D. Yarbrough

᭧ 1 ᭡

Literature and the Literary Canon

One of the first things we do in any of our literature courses, regardless of the course's level, is write this question on the board: *Why do we study literature?*

Just as you'd think, this question invites a number of answers reflecting various levels of thought and multiple tones. They range from the casual joking answer ("Because the catalog requires us to take this class") to somewhat more thoughtful responses like "Literature broadens the mind and teaches us new ideas" or "Literature teaches us about our culture."

All these claims can be true. Almost all college students are required to study at least *some* literature. And certainly, literature can broaden our scope and present us with new perspectives and concepts. Furthermore, most literature reflects something about the culture that spawned it. One learns a lot about aspects of ancient Greek beliefs and culture, for example, by studying the *Iliad*.

Although the question seems straightforward, *Why do we study literature?* is quite tricky to answer. It is slippery because it contains a hidden question that represents a value judgment on the part of the reader.

The hidden question is *What is literature?* What does the word *literature* actually imply or mean?

For the purpose of most literature courses you'll take in college, the term *literature* means far more than just "writing." Many kinds of writing don't qualify as literature. For instance, you wouldn't expect to read menus, manuals to DVD players, or your college's catalog as texts in your Introduction to World Literature course. Nor, for that matter, would you expect to read current newspaper editorials, previews of new fall television programs from *TV Guide*, or your instructor's personal letters. Although it is not beyond the realm of possibility that such selections may be offered for college literature courses, they would be the exception rather than the rule.

Consider this: when you visit a bookstore, notice how the management has divided the fiction section into various **genres** (or more accurately,

1

subgenres of the fiction genre) like science fiction, mystery, and romance. In addition to these, there may often be either a general "fiction" section or possibly even a "literary fiction" area. Some bookstores have a "classics" section. So who decides whether a particular novel is "literary" or a "classic," and what criteria are used?

We can't speak for bookstores, though we suspect that a decisive factor for them might be inclusion on local school reading lists. For the purposes of literary studies at the college level, a work of "literary" writing—whether it's a novel by Tolstoy, a poem by Emily Dickinson, a play by Samuel Beckett, or a piece of creative nonfiction by Joan Didion—has been judged by a large consensus of readers, authors, scholars, critics, and teachers to have literary merit. In older texts, this merit may sometimes be determined by their historical value. For example, although John Smith wasn't a particularly gifted writer in the way that Shakespeare was, his *General History of Virginia* is often taught in Early American Literature courses because of the portrait it paints of the Jamestown settlers. Generally speaking, most writing judged to be literary and thus a part of what is referred to as the **canon** is so classified because of some combination of its perceived **aesthetic** and cultural value. Because it relies on such shifting, subjective, and potentially political standards, however, the process of canonization is problematic in the extreme.

In that the canon has a tremendous influence on the choice of works included in literature courses and thus shapes our very idea of what literature is, it's important that you are aware of how a work or author becomes canonized. Remember that everything you read in college for classes has been chosen by someone else or, more likely, by a series of people: the various readers who first valued the text, the critics and scholars who helped sustain interest in the work, the editors who chose it for their anthologies, and the teacher or panel of teachers who selected it for your class. Understanding the process of how something gets chosen helps you better understand your class as well as the aesthetic and cultural value of the literature you are reading.

As any dictionary will tell you, "aesthetic" value means value attributed to an art form because of its artistic beauty. In terms of literature, this may apply to the wordcraft and mastery of language that the author employs. Or perhaps the work is a departure from all literature that has gone before it, like James Joyce's *Ulysses*; perhaps the work of literature tells a moving story that comments on and possibly even helps change the culture around it, like Frederick Douglass's *Narrative of the Life of an American Slave*. Possibly the work has been immensely influential for later authors, as shown by the burgeoning growth of American **free verse** in the wake of Walt Whitman's *Song of Myself* or the marked expansion of **magical realism** following the rise to popularity of Gabriel García Márquez's *One Hundred Years of Solitude*.

Another risky measuring tool for ascertaining the importance of a given literary piece is its actual or expected longevity. That is to say, will this story (or poem or play or essay) last? Will people be reading it in fifty years? A hundred? In addition to the numerous other merits of their work, history alone testifies to the literary significance of writers like Dante and Shakespeare; their influence on the generations of writers who have followed them is undeniable. A nineteenth-century writer like Emily Dickinson is a comparative newcomer, yet she is still far enough removed from our own time that we can perceive and begin to understand the magnitude of her influence on later writers. In the case of contemporary writers, however, the canon is much more fluid with respect to literary influence and reputation.

The "canonicity" of a work depends, then, on the perception of readers that it is culturally or aesthetically important. Their opinions are judged and revised over the passage of time. But the literary canon is not created in a vacuum. Rather, it affects and is affected by changing political climates, social change, and economics. It's safe to assume that a canonical work deserves attention and study, but the exclusion of a work from the canon in no way suggests the opposite.

As we stated before, there are problems with this selection process. First of all, during all but arguably the last few decades of literary history, women authors were often not taken seriously and not accorded proper attention and respect by a literary establishment largely dominated by men. All persons of minority status faced the same prejudicial system. To paraphrase the English novelist Virginia Woolf's point, how are we to know which women among Shakespeare's contemporaries might have been his equal if English culture of that day had afforded them a chance? Although writers like Jane Austen might have been popular, they often weren't accorded the respect they were due. Likewise, very few African American writers were able to see their works published before the twentieth century, largely due to slavery and the inherent racism of the culture that either perpetrated or tolerated it. In each case, the problem is even more insidious than one realizes at first glance: women who were denied education and told from childhood that serious literary work was for men only had not only to overcome other people's prejudices but their own internal ones as well. Before the American Civil War, it was considered wrong in many areas of the slave states to educate a slave; Frederick Douglass's monumental feat in creating his slavery memoir is even more impressive when you realize that he taught himself to read and write while living in a society that denied him the right.

Longevity, as we have said, is a major issue in canon formation. But how are we to decide if a work is to be long-lasting if it's only a few years old? We can be reasonably sure that works that win major awards may stand the test of time, but this isn't always true. And besides, some great writers are never recognized by their contemporaries, only to be embraced years later: Herman Melville, author of *Moby-Dick*, enjoyed only minor success during his own lifetime, but his work rose to posthumous prominence in the 1920s. Correspondingly, many works that are greatly valued during an author's life slowly fade from the canon with the passage of time.

Furthermore, even an apparently established canon continues to change due to shifting societal values. As we said before, a glance at the nineteenth-century canons in Europe or America would have shown them to be inappropriately weighted toward white male writers. In recent years, the literary canon has tended to reassess itself constantly; writers who were once considered important are no longer taught to many students, while writers previously ignored due to the skewed canon politics of their day have been retroactively included.

One of the best examples of this is the American writer Kate Chopin, who published the early feminist novel *The Awakening* in 1899. The novel deals with a woman, Edna, who has been more or less forced into an unfulfilling marriage by the strict social standards of the 1890s South. Driven by her love for another man, Edna slowly begins severing bonds with her family and decides to strike out on her own. Chopin doesn't make it easy for the conventional reader of 1899 to identify with Edna. Edna doesn't leave her husband because he beats her or is cruel to the children (although he is a distant and self-centered father who thinks raising the children is Edna's job). The novel is an indictment of society more than of any one person, and because of this, the literary establishment judged the novel harshly. The negative reactions of many critics and reviewers caused *The Awakening* to fade quickly from sight.

In the 1960s, however, as feminist concerns became more common in the American consciousness, *The Awakening* was rediscovered and reevaluated. Chopin's novel (as well as several of her short stories) has been a staple of American Literature courses ever since. It has been retroactively fitted into the canon and serves a useful purpose. The literary critics and scholars who defined the canon at the time of its release and who denied the importance of *The Awakening* were perhaps also declining to acknowledge the initial beginnings—even an "awakening"—of a societal concern with women's issues and gender equity that Chopin recognized. Now, however, Chopin is a well-established part of the canon.

Many professors, scholars, and critics are engaged in constant "canon wars," endless debates over which writers should be included and which authors should be left out. You shouldn't let the fluidity of the canon and the resulting disputes trouble you; rather, be excited that you live in a time when such choices are debated and when gender and race are not the obstacles to inclusion they once were (although, as always, one could argue that our culture still has a long way to go). Be prepared to evaluate a work of literature based not only on its reputation but also on its intrinsic aesthetic qualities and cultural significance.

So then, what is literature? As we have seen, some would answer that question by saying that literature is written work of significant aesthetic or historical value, and some would say that literature is written work that has been entered into the literary canon by the great number of scholars and readers and critics who have deemed the work worthy of study and appreciation. Each of these methods of determining literature has its merits. However, we would contribute the following notion: works of literature are written works that demand and reward active, critical, and careful reading.

THINKING EXERCISES

1. Can you think of any literary works you've studied in college or high school that seem to be part of the literary canon? Make a list of them. Why do you think these works are considered important enough to be part of the canon?

2. Have you studied any that you think aren't part of the canon? Why do you think these texts were assigned to you?

3. Have you studied any texts presented as part of the canon that you think should be removed from it? If so, why should those works be removed?

4. Can you think of any works of literature you may have read that are worthy of inclusion in the canon? Why do you think they should be included? Do you think these texts will stand the test of time?

☙ 2 ☙

Challenges to the Canon

2.1 POPULAR FICTION

As we have pointed out, one set of challenges to the canon has come from readers who question the long-standing exclusion of voices outside the cultural mainstream of the day. At the same time, we can also question the exclusion of certain types of writing. Often the students who are the most avid readers outside of class are the ones who are most disappointed with the reading list of a college literature course, since many popular writers are excluded. Why aren't their favorite popular authors on the syllabus? What separates "literary writing" from other kinds of writing?

One primary difference is that because writers of literary fiction and verse aren't aiming simply to entertain their readers (although that may well be one of their hopes), their stories and poems are almost always more complex than nonliterary works. The literary writer wants to challenge readers and to force them to engage their intellect. Literary writing requires active reading rather than passive reading. Popular or escapist writing often doesn't want to confuse a reader or make that reader work too hard; demanding reading doesn't always help a reader relax. Rather, it often calls for hard work on the reader's part. Escapist reading is usually (again, there are many exceptions) more passive.

Consider the difference between a novel like *Frankenstein* (first published in 1818) by Mary Shelley and the horror and science fiction novella *Who Goes There?* by John W. Campbell (1938). Although Hollywood has greatly simplified Shelley's book in its various adaptations, the original novel is about far more than a monster running amok. It is about a man's attempts to usurp the powers of God and nature. The text asks that the reader consider whether Victor Frankenstein's lack of responsibility and immense pride bring about the destruction of all he loves. Furthermore, the novel gives rise to a multitude of questions and discussions regarding the roles of men and women as creators of life and caregivers and has been the subject of numerous feminist articles and debates. Although the novel could possibly be read simply for the thrills any horror text would offer, it asks more of a reader: it asks to be read by an active, seeking, searching mind, and it rewards such a reading with layers of significance and insight.

Campbell's *Who Goes There?* tells of a small group of isolated Arctic explorers who discover an alien spaceship encased in ice. As they attempt to thaw the craft, they are attacked by a deadly, shape-shifting extraterrestrial creature. The alien entity can reproduce itself asexually, and the men understand that if they don't stop the creature while it is isolated in the Arctic, it may be able to inflict horrific damage on their world.

Had he chosen, the author could have used this plot and setting to address issues of identity, isolation, paranoia, and human interaction. But Campbell doesn't digress very far down any of these avenues. His goal in the novella is to scare and thrill you, and he does these things very well. He does not, however, make you think beyond the plot, nor does he ask you to question assumptions or perspectives you take for granted. *Who Goes There?* requires relatively passive reading from its reader. It's probably significant that the film adaptations of Campbell's novella, the 1951 film *The Thing from Another World*, directed by an uncredited Howard Hawks, and John Carpenter's 1982 version, *The Thing*, are both able to remain much truer to their source than film versions of Shelley's *Frankenstein*. The literary qualities that make her novel a classic are much harder to translate to the screen, but they are the qualities that mark the difference between literature and popular fiction.

THINKING EXERCISES

1. Make a list of books you've read and enjoyed that you think would be qualified as "escapist," written primarily to entertain readers. Are they mysteries, science fiction, historical romances, fantasies, westerns?

2. Do you think any of the books on your list would be worthy of study in your literature class? Which ones? What makes them worth considering?

3. Pretend you're an instructor of a college-level literature course. You've decided that you want to include noncanonical escapist novels on your reading list. Draft a memorandum to the head of your department arguing why one of these novels should be included.

2.2 THE BOUNDARIES OF POETRY

In poetry, the distinction between literary verse and escapist verse is even more apparent than it is in fiction. Much nonliterary verse takes the form of song lyrics or simplistically rhymed poems written for children. Less ambitious verse often seems to focus on rhymes and to convey simple platitudes or stories. Literary poetry draws on a wide variety of literary devices such as **imagery**, **metaphor**, and **symbols** to convey more complex ideas. Occasional books of poetry published by pop stars and other celebrities aside, most published poetry attempts to strike a literary tone.

Of all the literary forms or genres, poetry is probably the hardest one to define. While we can debate whether a story is literary or nonliterary, or even fact or fiction, we generally know whether or not it is a story at all. The same is true of drama. Poetry, though, can be a little more challenging to define. Many people would probably point to **meter** and **rhyme** as identifying qualities of poetry, and until the advent of **free verse** in the mid-1800s, these structural elements would have been fairly accurate indicators. Today, however, although much poetry does use traditional structuring devices like rhyme and meter, much of it does not. The apparently vague distinction between what is and is not poetry is reflected in other art forms as well. For the past fifty years, annoyed parents have declared of their children's choice of musical entertainment, "That's not music," although these parents would be hard pressed to offer a working definition of what music *is*. And according to a Reuters news story from October 2001, the British artist Damien Hirst created an "impromptu installation" at a West London art gallery by arranging empty beer bottles, dirty ashtrays, coffee cups, and other party leftovers. The next morning, a cleaner discarded the entire work of art as trash, saying, "I didn't think for a second that it was a work of art. It didn't much look like art to me."

So what is the difference between a pile of trash and an "impromptu installation"? Between paint spattered on a wall and a painting? Between William Carlos Williams's poem "This Is Just to Say" and a note left on a refrigerator door? These questions can be approached from at least two different perspectives. One way of answering them would be to point to the intention of the sculptor, artist, or poet. An *accidental* pile of trash *is not* art, but an *intentional* arrangement of trash *is* art. A child who leaves peanut butter handprints on a wall is not creating a work of art, but an artist who blows paint through a straw at a canvas is. An e-mail reminder of an upcoming meeting is not a poem, but Williams's plain-language poem about having eaten the last of the plums is—because it is intended to be a poem.

This brings up one of the major issues in current **critical theory**: how do we know the intentions of the creator of a work of art? In the 1954 work *The Verbal Icon*, W. K. Wimsatt Jr., aided by M. C. Beardsley, coined the term **intentional fallacy** to describe the practice of evaluating a work of art based on the artist's explicit or perceived intention in creating it. If we accept the basic claim that identifying an artist or poet's *true* intentions is virtually impossible (or at least very difficult), then we realize that it becomes more profitable to consider "art" or "poetry" as a method of reading or interpretation.

Students who find reading poetry to be a difficult, almost foreign task might benefit from considering a form of poem they encounter nearly every day: the song lyric. As the word itself suggests, *lyric* was originally used by the Greeks to describe a poem that was the expression of a single speaker (or singer) with musical accompaniment on a *lyre*. Today the term **lyric poem** refers to a short poem, generally nonnarrative, that creates the impression of coming from a single speaker. Thus literary history justifies the comparison of poems and songs: poems, like language itself, existed in oral form long before being written down. The transmission of poetry was inseparable from performance.

In spite of their common origins, song lyrics and poems are not identical genres. Not all song lyrics make worthwhile poems, and not all poems benefit from being sung. Edwin Arlington Robinson's poem "Richard Cory" suffers only mildly in translation to the Simon and Garfunkel song of the same name, but T. S. Eliot's masterpiece *The Waste Land* would probably fare much worse. Approaching from the other direction, only songs with substantial lyrics can be fruitfully analyzed from a literary point of view, and even then, the careful reader will eventually be faced with the fact that song lyrics and poems, though they may share many qualities, are essentially different kinds of art.

The reason for this distinction is obvious, but it bears mentioning: the way we read poetry is fundamentally different from the way we hear music. In general, song lyrics are simpler and more direct than poems because listening is necessarily more linear than reading. When we listen to a song on the radio and miss a word or a line from the song, it's impossible to rewind and listen to a particular passage again; even with a recording, it's inconvenient and jarring to do so. For a song to be effective, the listener must be able to apprehend at least a portion of it on first hearing. Many song lyrics are highly nuanced, but our enjoyment of the song is not necessarily contingent on our understanding of those nuances. Instead, listeners are more easily influenced by the quality of the music and of the singer's voice, and—increasingly since the advent of music videos—by the appearance or persona of the artist. As Roger Daltrey of The Who sings in their song "Join Together": "It's the singer, not the song, / That makes the music move along." Song lyrics rely on more than the words for their effect, and our understanding of a song's lyrics is inseparable from our attitude toward the music or the persona of the artist. In contrast, consider William Butler Yeats's lines in "Among School Children": "O body swayed to music, O brightening glance, / How can we know the dancer from the dance?" With poetry, our understanding of the poet's persona frequently originates in the poem, rather than vice versa. While the lyrics of a song are just one component of its overall presentation, poetry depends solely on the more subtle nuances of language for its power. For most of us, reading a poem means rereading it; after we have attempted to identify the poem's basic subject and theme, we go back through it in an attempt to see how all of its component parts work together.

One of the exercises at the end of this section will ask you to compare a poem of the sort you'd find on greeting cards to more literary poems. We wrote this as an example of greeting card poetry and intentionally didn't aim too high. However, even if "I Love You Because . . ." doesn't work well as a poem, does this mean that it doesn't belong on a greeting card? Perhaps the opposite is true. We don't expect the recipient of a greeting card to spend a long time poring over the meaning of the poem on the card, so ambiguity—a common rhetorical device in literary poetry—would be inappropriate. Though the card may be cherished for years to come, the sentiment of the verse needs to be clear from the very first reading. And despite the fact that purchasers of these cards may spend hours agonizing over their choice, remember that each verse will be sold hundreds, even thousands, of times and given to people who may or may not even read the whole poem. The gesture itself of giving a greeting card is generally more meaningful than any ideas expressed by the verse printed on it. Although we may poke fun at the kind of poetry you find on greeting cards, such verse has its place and serves its function.

The problem arises, of course, when readers bring the expectations appropriate to greeting card verse to their reading of poetry. Unlike greeting cards, which we frequently read at a glance even as we eagerly unwrap the accompanying gift, literary poems do not necessarily reveal themselves to a superficial, casual reading. Neither are they, like the gift, to be torn violently open or instantly, thoroughly, and permanently unwrapped and comprehended. The best way to appreciate a poem is to devote yourself honestly to the task of appreciating it. Read it slowly and carefully, paying attention to the various meanings of its words and also to the sound of the poem itself. When you read poetry, you can't expect to understand it fully the first time you read it or the tenth; the best poems keep working on you every time you revisit them.

THINKING EXERCISES

1. Do you like poetry? Why or why not? If you do, what makes a poem good to you? What makes you dislike a poem? Can you make a list of what you consider good qualities and bad qualities for poems? Are rhyme and meter important to you? Is imagery or other poetic language? Theme?

2. Consider the following greeting card verse. Do you think this verse succeeds as a poem or not? What do you consider its weakest points?

I Love You Because . . .

I love you because you care,
Because you share your world with me.

I love you because your eyes
Do not disguise the beauty that lies within you.

I love you because your heart
Is a part of me, and mine is a part of you. . . .

I love you because you are you.

3.   Compare this poem to any one of the other poems you'll find in this book. Create a checklist using the qualities you defined in response to Exercise 1. Which poem is more successful? Why?

2.3   TELEVISION AND FILM AS DRAMA

Although America's most popular forms of narrative entertainment—television and movies—fall into the category of nonliterary drama, **drama** as a literary genre is ever more removed from the average reader's experience. This is tragic—pardon the pun—because plays are some of the most vibrant and significant works of literature in existence. Some might even argue that a play can convey an understanding of the culture in which it is produced more effectively than any other literary genre. Certainly plays like *Antigone* and *Oedipus Rex* tell us about ancient Greece more eloquently than almost anything else could; and one can hardly think about Renaissance England without thinking about the plays of Shakespeare, in spite of the fact that many of his best-known plays were frequently set in other times and places. The ideals and values of twentieth-century America are simultaneously preserved and scrutinized in plays like Arthur Miller's *Death of a Salesman* and Eugene O'Neill's *Long Day's Journey into Night*. All of these plays are at once firmly grounded in their particular epochs and yet somehow remain timeless. Many who love *Romeo and Juliet* have no idea where or when the play is set. For scholars and advanced members of the audience, it may be interesting and important to realize that it's set in Verona, Italy, several centuries ago, but the story itself transcends its setting. Even more than poetry and fiction, drama seems to draw on **archetypes** to touch the audience's imagination deeply, directly, and permanently. Why, then, don't people read plays?

Actually, it's a trick question. When we talk about the impression a play makes on its audience, we are usually not talking about its readers. Most plays, after all, are written to be performed, not to be read. There are some exceptions to this, of course; some plays would be impossible to produce as written. Others, called **closet drama**, are written expressly to be read rather than performed. Still, most plays in print are nothing more than words, mostly **dialogue** and stage direction, with some description and analysis occasionally supplied by the author. The play as we remember it after witnessing a performance is much more than that: the physical presence of the actors, the live vocal inflections that simply cannot be reproduced on the page or in electronic media, the visceral response we experience by being in the same room with a live person who is shouting, weeping, or laughing.

When we're watching a play, we feel that anything could happen because we are seeing it *as it's being performed*, not afterward.

In spite of the power and energy frequently associated with the live performance of plays, movies and television enjoy much greater mass popularity, and indeed, even beyond convenience, they have plenty to offer that no stage production could. Many colleges and universities offer courses or whole programs devoted to the study of television and film, and we agree that these media are worth studying. And we're not just talking about the film classics that rank alongside the greatest works in any genre (*The Maltese Falcon, The Wizard of Oz, Citizen Kane,* and the like); we're talking about whatever special-effects-laden blockbuster is playing at the local cinema. For better or worse, it's probably safe to say that more people will see the next installment of the *Star Wars* saga on its opening weekend than will read James Joyce's *Finnegans Wake* from cover to cover from the date of its composition until the extinction of humankind. At the same time, the merits of a work of art are not dependent on its commercial success.

Narrative film and television are, after all, forms of drama. Many of their conventions originate in stage drama. The **asides** and **soliloquies** of Shakespeare's plays become the voice-over narration of films like *Apocalypse Now.* The chorus of his *Henry V* becomes the intrusive narration of Matthew Broderick's character in *Ferris Bueller's Day Off.* On television, many shows (situation comedies in particular) are presented essentially as stage plays, set in rooms with the **fourth wall** removed. We never see the view from behind the bar in *Cheers* or from Archie Bunker's well-worn chair in *All in the Family,* any more than we see the view from Juliet's balcony in a stage production of *Romeo and Juliet.* Of course, many interesting television shows challenge and defy these conventions; the camera can do many things an audience cannot, and more innovative efforts stretch the limits of the media. Still, by and large, film and television are the direct descendants of stage drama, and a convention has to be established before it is defied.

When professors and critics extol the virtues of plays over the more common forms of dramatic entertainment, it's not because they don't enjoy movies and television; nor is it because they don't respect them as art forms. Reservations with these forms of entertainment lie in the fact that they need not be studied to be experienced. They encourage passive viewing rather than active analysis. It would be hard to deny that most television appeals strictly to the lowest common denominator. Innovative, groundbreaking shows either die young or learn to conform to the needs of a viewing public that uses television as a mild, legal narcotic.

THINKING EXERCISES

1. Many people will claim that the original novels are always better than movies made from them. Do you think this is true? Can you think of any

films you like more than the original books? If so, why did you like those films more?

2. Can you think of films that have what you would consider "literary" qualities? What would those be? Do you think these films could or should be studied in literature courses? Why or why not?

3. Can you think of television dramas and comedies that you believe demand critical and active viewing? Do you find this kind of show more rewarding than others? Why or why not?

❧ 3 ❧

Why Read Literature?

3.1   THE HABIT OF CRITICAL THINKING

As should be clear by now, we believe that the study of literature can teach you about a culture, enrich you, and encourage you to consider this multifaceted and amazingly complex world of ours from a variety of viewpoints. Literature can help you put things into perspective and make you see your life in a new way. Well-crafted words, whether spoken in the theater or read in a story, memoir, or poem, are themselves as worthy of our attention as dance, painting, sculpture, or architecture.

Here, however, we'd like to focus on the fact that the study of literature is *useful*. As many educators and scholars have pointed out, literature doesn't occupy the role in education that it once did, and as a result, the joys and benefits of active literary reading are unknown to many otherwise highly educated people. There are, of course, many reasons for this phenomenon. Changes in the higher education system since the Second World War probably account for it in large part. The study of literature seems inevitably to find itself at odds with the other, apparently more pressing vocational and professional demands of many university programs, even many English programs. The democratization of higher education—by no means a bad thing!—means that more people go to college for more different reasons. Many of the most popular majors available to college students today did not even exist fifty or sixty years ago. The downside, though, is that the role of the arts in general in today's college education is a lot smaller than it probably should be.

The liberal arts model of higher education, in which a college education is intended to produce well-rounded individuals, has largely yielded to a professional certification model in which a college degree constitutes credentials for employment in a given vocation. Obviously, most people would consider the study of literature to be more relevant to the liberal arts model than to the professional certification model. We disagree with this common wisdom. The skills students must develop to do a good job of understanding and writing about literature will be of great benefit in nonliterary studies and professional training as well. The students' ability to engage in critical thinking is an essential requirement for reading literature—and for comprehending it well enough to write about it intelligently. Critical thinking will help you regardless of whether your major is physics, accounting, sociology, secondary education, or English. Critical thinking skills can and probably should be applied to just about anything you run across in and out of the college classroom.

Critical thinking, in the case of literature, becomes *critical reading*. Critical in this context doesn't mean that one is attempting to find faults in a given text. Rather, the term implies that a given reader or student takes nothing for granted. Everything in the text (or problem or scenario) is analyzed, piece by piece, carefully weighed, and carefully considered. What are the implications of this element? Why was this placed here? What purpose does this serve?

Although most of our discussion of critical thinking skills has focused on the literary arts, we're sure that the phrase "critical thinking" has come up in other facets of most students' lives. Certainly, most college disciplines try to encourage analytical thinking, and countless academic conferences have devoted time to discussing how critical thinking skills can be fostered not just in literature classes but across the disciplines.

We believe that developing the ability to solve problems through critical analysis should be one of the primary goals of a college education, regardless of whether one subscribes to the liberal arts or professional certification model. In fact, it is the ability to respond to situations that one has not previously encountered that marks the difference between education and training. Training conditions someone to behave a certain way in response to a certain stimulus. Education prepares someone to think critically in order to identify and solve problems. It is true that only a few of those who learn how to engage with literature will spend their lives performing literary analysis in academia. For them, the work they perform in literature classes prepares them directly for their future careers. For the majority, literary analysis can be considered aerobic and strength conditioning for the mind as well as a significant way to access the cultural heritage of human civilization. The appreciation of literature can be its own reward.

THINKING EXERCISES

1. Can you compare reading a difficult poem, story, or play to solving a problem in one of your other classes? In math? In biology or chemistry? In accounting?

2. Which do you consider to be the point of a college education: to be trained for a profession or to be well rounded in areas like the arts, mathematics, and sciences? Or do you think both approaches are equally valuable? Do you think your choice of a major affects your belief in this instance?

3.2   CRITICAL THINKING AND POPULAR TASTES

Even though we're talking about skills that are useful not only for analyzing literature but also for solving problems in all areas of life, our focus here is on literary analysis. Earlier in the book, we addressed the relationship between popular literature, music, and film and their highbrow counterparts. What all of this talk about the relationship between popular culture and literature and the usefulness of critical thinking skills comes down to can be summed up in a single word: *taste*—or in less culturally loaded terms, *discernment*. *Taste* is a word that usually comes up when somebody is accusing somebody else of not having it; by the time students reach college, they will surely have tired of hearing these accusations levied at them by instructors, school boards, and the like. Some self-appointed arbiters of taste will apparently not be happy until they hear opera music blasting from car stereos and dorm windows across campus; they seem to expect students to give up commercial television entirely in favor of the more cultured fare available on public television and the artsier cable networks. They won't be happy until college dramatic productions are filled to standing-room-only capacity while the football stadium bleachers are empty, until no movie in color without subtitles is screened at the campus theater.

Granted, we're representing an absurd extreme of a culturally snobbish attitude. It does seem to be ironic, however, that so many of those who complain about the closing of the American mind are themselves rather closed to various cultural phenomena that at least partly represent the current state of the American mind. It's probably safe to say, though, that most literature professors would like to foster the development of discriminating tastes in their students. Though it may sound old-fashioned, we believe that the development of discernment really should be one of the goals of a college education. Imagination is one of the principal attributes that differentiates humans from animals, and courses in the arts expose students to the best products of artistic imagination our species has to offer. The goal of a literature course is not to alter students' tastes so that popular writers like John Grisham or Danielle Steele are driven out of business. Rather, one of the goals of a literature class is to open a new world to students, a world that is challenging, exciting, and demanding.

Furthermore, it may be that learning about various arts—literature, dance, painting, theater, or others—will enhance students' appreciation for the components of popular culture that they've always enjoyed. That is, if you learn to apply critical thinking to various aspects of your academic life, it's only natural that sooner or later this process of critical thinking will become automatic and spill over into your consideration of television shows, comic books, pop songs, newspapers, acts by stand-up comedians, advertisements, and even television commercials.

A by-product of using critical thinking in your everyday life might be a change in your tastes or, perhaps a better way to say it, the development of greater discernment. Obviously, you are not necessarily a lost soul just because you prefer music videos to ballet. Even so, the development of discerning taste should mean that you are able to tell a good music video from a bad one, and ideally, eventually, a good ballet from a bad one. Earlier in this chapter, we hinted at ways critical thinking skills could be applied to popular forms of entertainment such as pop music, movies, television, and best-seller fiction. The ability to identify quality is applicable in all genres.

While the development of critical thinking skills will almost certainly lead the student to explore more subtle and more complex forms of entertainment and edification, the development of discernment does not necessarily mean saying goodbye to the pleasures of the popular media. It is possible to enjoy *Ace Ventura: Pet Detective* while still understanding why other, more critically lauded films like *His Girl Friday* (1940) might be considered superior to it.

Neither we nor your instructors are asking you to give up whatever pleasure you take in escapist literature, popular music, blockbuster movies, or television in general. We only ask that you recognize that it's not so much what you read, listen to, or view; it's how passively or actively you're reading, hearing, or watching. The practiced critical thinker can find interesting issues in nearly any creative expression. Even something as remote from the college literature classroom as professional wrestling can merit analysis. There is, of course, a narrative plot in wrestling—an archetypal battle between good and evil forces that accounts in large part for its popularity, even among viewers who believe that all matches are faked. And there are certainly economic and psychological factors at work in the marketing of professional wrestling. Though we fervently hope otherwise, analyzing issues like these, far from being a waste of time, may well give more relevant insight into the state of America today than a handful of doctoral dissertations on Thomas Pynchon.

Like any other skill, critical thinking improves with practice. It is, furthermore, the most important life skill most college students will learn. Everything should be subject to analysis: politicians' campaign promises, infomercials, the evening news, anything that is heard, read, or experienced. The ability to separate the gold from the dross is an essential quality for anyone who would confront contemporary life.

THINKING EXERCISES

1. Consider ways that critical and analytical thinking can contribute to every-day activities in your life. (For example, don't football coaches use critical thinking to develop an offensive game plan most likely to take advantage of a defense's weaknesses? Don't mechanics have to think critically to properly diagnose what's wrong with an automobile?) Write a list of non-academic responsibilities and pursuits that occupy your time that either require analytical thinking or could benefit from analytical thinking.

2. As you continue through this text, you'll learn more about reading analytically. Think of ways to apply these analytical skills to some work of popular media culture. After watching an episode of a popular television sitcom, ask yourself, what was its central point? What devices did the show use to convey this point?

❧ 4 ❧

The Act of Reading

4.1 TEXT AND SUBTEXT

If we agree that one of the more useful definitions of literature pertains to the ways in which a written work is approached—that is, works are "literary" if they reward intense reading, scrutiny, or literary analysis—the importance of reading critically is obvious. Being told to do something and knowing how to do it are two different things, however. We teachers of literature are sometimes guilty of presuming that students have been taught how to read critically in earlier classes. Even worse, we sometimes assume that students have just picked up the requisite skills by watching how we go about presenting interpretations of texts during class discussions. Most people don't learn by watching, however; they learn by doing. The issue becomes further complicated by the fact that today's high school English teachers are loaded down with large classes and varying duties that seem to have little to do with the study of literature. They're often called on to teach word processing or journalism, even if their primary training is in other areas. So some students graduate from high school without having taken an active part in a literary discussion and without having much opportunity to write critically about literature.

As we noted earlier, one of the first things readers have to do when approaching a literary text—whether it's fiction, drama, or poetry—is to realize that the author is very often trying to get something across to the reader that isn't entirely obvious. In the case of fiction, it is sometimes not difficult to assume that the author has something in mind other than the resolution of the plot, because the plot in itself is pedestrian or simple. Ernest Hemingway's "Hills Like White Elephants," for example, tells the story of a couple having a discussion at a train station in Spain. Their conversation almost heats up to the point of argument but never quite gets there; at the end of the story, the man carries their baggage to the other side of the station. That isn't much of a plot, but of course, the story is about far more than just an argument. Likewise, James Joyce's "Araby" is about a boy who has a crush on an older girl. The boy tells her that he will buy her something at the bazaar. When he arrives at the bazaar, however, he decides not to buy her anything. Again, the plot alone accomplishes very little; again, there is far more going on in the story than an outline of the plot or even the surface narration of the story will convey.

The parts of a given story, work of drama, or poem that need no elucidation, that are obvious to any careful reader, are known simply (obviously, even) as the *text*. If you can grasp the basic plot, setting, and character motivation of a story or play, you can be said to understand the text. If you can read a poem and more or less understand the sentiment behind it and the point it makes, you comprehend the text. For example, the text of the narrative poem "My Last Duchess" by Robert Browning (see section 9.4) is relatively easy to grasp. A rich Italian nobleman, the Duke of Ferrara, is seeking a new wife; the text of the poem is his monologue to his prospective father-in-law's representative as he explains all the shortcomings he found in the character of his deceased former wife. It's almost as if he's saying, "The Ford truck I bought had this transmission problem, so I don't want to find the same problem in my Dodge minivan." Readers who only comprehend the surface text, however, without reading more into the narrator's nature and the images and symbols in the poem, are probably going to miss the point altogether: the duke is by nature controlling and vindictive, and he quite possibly gave an order that resulted in his wife's death.

What about the essential elements that lie beneath the surface of the text? What about the themes and levels of meaning that are implied or gestured toward through use of symbol, metaphor, imagery, and the like? What of that current of implicit purpose designed to carry you toward certain objectives, that students and teachers will often call the "underlying meaning"?

We're talking about **subtext**, of course. *Subtext* is one of those ubiquitous terms that suffer from vague definitions although teachers and students use it all the time. Generally speaking, however, the subtext is the web of underlying points or themes (since a given work of writing may have multiple points or themes) that is implied in a work of literature rather than stated baldly in the text. References within a work to its subtext may be quite obvious, or they may be so subtle that the implied theme is obscure to all except those most skilled and knowledgeable readers.

You shouldn't confuse subtext with *moral* or *message*. Both of these terms are value-charged; they imply fables that teach us lessons (and obviously so, for the most part) or, even worse, after-school television specials that are meant to impart a platitude that will help the young teen caught up in the show's melodrama (for example, "drinking and driving is very bad" or "unprotected sex can lead to pregnancy"). In either case, literary works that impart a clearly identifiable and unequivocal moral often do so at the expense of art. Although much great literature may implicitly espouse some moral or ethical stance, it is not usually intended to teach its audience how to live better. For instance, an important theme of Alice Childress's play *Florence* (included in Part Six) is cultural identity, but few would argue that the story's most important function is to dictate to its readers how to view themselves in the context of their own race, nationality, and gender. The story raises these questions and points at answers, but it does not attempt to impose directly on its readers' behavior.

Subtextual meaning, then, may be more idiosyncratic or subtle; in fact, it may not carry a lesson (as such) at all. The boy in "Araby" merely learns that growing up can be painful and that we're capable of being our own worst enemies during the process. Neither he nor the readers are given a self-help manual that will guide them through puberty with a whole and unscarred heart, and the narrator does not intrude with a moral at the story's conclusion. For that matter, subtextual information is often meant to do no more than help readers develop a deeper understanding of a given piece. We can still appreciate the poem or play without comprehending it on every level it reaches. For example, the audience of Susan Glaspell's short play *Trifles* (included in Part Six) easily grasps that the suspect, Mrs. Wright, killed her husband; the audience even understands why the other two women in the play (Mrs. Hale and Mrs. Peters) decide not to help the County Attorney and the Sheriff uncover a key piece of evidence. If the audience members are able to read critically, however (or in this case to watch actively and critically), then they notice the introduction of a birdcage into the play and realize that in some respects, Mrs. Wright has also been caged in her life of cold and ordered domesticity. Their understanding of the play is not contingent on their having recognized this literary **symbol**, but it *is* enriched.

Why make use of subtext in the first place? If one of the goals of good writing is efficient communication, why doesn't literary writing want to spell everything out to a reader? If an author wants to write a poem about a famous duke who was a jerk and possibly abusive to his wife, why not write a poem that begins with "Once there was a duke / Who was famous and who was also / A real jerk to his wife"? Well, for the same reason that a novel that deals in some way with racism, like Harper Lee's *To Kill a Mockingbird* or Richard Wright's *Native Son*, speaks more to some of us than a local news documentary about racial profiling in law enforcement. It affects us at a different level. In literature and film, the **theme** or "underlying meaning" is generally secondary to the craft of the art that presents it, which is usually not true of local news broadcasts.

A work of literature that strives too earnestly to offer some commentary on the human condition may end up being **didactic** or preachy (just like those after-school television specials) and as a result may turn readers away. A successful poem or story or play, however, can make even the oldest and most banal story seem fresh and new and can somehow still offer new insights. Reduced to its simplest terms, *Romeo and Juliet* is about teen love and the value of forgiveness. Nevertheless, there's a world of difference between Shakespeare's tragedy of star-crossed lovers and an episode of *7th Heaven* that conveys the same message. *Romeo and Juliet* reflects greater craft on every level: the characterization is more sophisticated, and the stakes are larger as Tybalt kills Mercutio, Romeo kills Tybalt, and the lovers kill themselves, bringing peace to the horrified, warring families. The language throughout the play reflects Shakespeare's amazing ear for poetry and the spoken word.

At the same time, readers must realize that even simple texts may be read critically, although (paradoxically) this is an even more complicated endeavor. Many newer and more sophisticated styles of criticism and critical theory use popular texts in order to focus on **cultural studies**. A novel like Margaret Mitchell's 1936 blockbuster *Gone With the Wind* may have been primarily intended to entertain its audience with a romantic story of the Old South, but readers can also draw conclusions from it about race relations and women's rights in the New South of the 1930s. Some may even argue that the immensely popular film *Titanic* is as deserving of serious critical analysis as more obscure works based solely on the number of lives it has touched.

THINKING EXERCISES

1. Think of some literary work—a poem, play, or story—you've had to read this semester. Do you think that the work in question actually contained a "subtext"? Were you able to distinguish it? Did class discussion help your understanding of a possible subtext?

2. Do you prefer reading works that don't immediately reveal themselves and that challenge you, or do you prefer works that are more easily understood on the first reading? Why do you think you prefer the one you prefer?

3. In earlier Thinking Exercises, we asked you to note films and television shows and popular books you've read that might be worthy of literary study. Can you think of various kinds of subtexts those works might contain? Are the subtextual themes and implications in those works obscure or obvious? Write down what you think some of those works might be trying to accomplish on a subtextual level. Also, write down why you believe what you do about the various subtextual inferences.

4.2   SEARCHING FOR CLUES

Writers often make interesting choices in the construction of their works that signal that something is going on beyond the obvious, and the more experienced reader learns to look for these choices. Of course, just as there is a danger in concentrating too much on the surface of a piece of literature and missing its subtext, there is also a danger in examining it so deeply that we start seeing things that just aren't there.

Consider Edgar Allan Poe's short story "The Purloined Letter." The story is famous for any number of reasons. Published in 1844, it was one of the first detective stories (it provided the blueprint that later authors like Arthur Conan Doyle would follow closely), and its tale of a letter that is hidden in plain sight but missed by those searching for it because they assume it must be secreted away has become a useful metaphor for many of us, teaching us to not always address problems in the same old tired ways. Rather, one must be prepared—as the cliché would have it—to "think outside the box." "The Purloined Letter" is not just about recovering a stolen letter, however; on some levels, the story is also about how one should read.

In "The Purloined Letter," the police inspector reports that not only has the **antagonist** Minister D—— stolen the letter, but he also knows that he was observed doing so. The detective, Dupin, says to his compatriot and the inspector, "Here then . . . you have precisely what you demand to make the ascendancy complete—the robber's knowledge of the loser's knowledge of the robber." By this he means that since the thief knows that the police will be looking for the letter (a matter they have to handle subtly rather than openly, due to the letter's delicate political nature), he will have taken special means to hide the letter cleverly.

Similarly, sophisticated writers will often seek to enrich and complicate their works because they assume a certain willingness to work on the part of their readers. Active, critical readers should consider themselves as a kind of literary detective. The readers must approach the text with open minds, actively searching for clues, striving to get to the bottom of the challenge presented them.

As we stressed earlier, some texts—like some mysteries for detectives—will be simple, open-and-shut cases. Others, however, may be "whodunits" that present a number of obstacles to the reader. As we have already seen, one danger is the problem of misjudging a work and finding clues where there aren't any. Another common error (also discussed later) occurs when one approaches the text in the way that the police in "The Purloined Letter" approach Minister D——'s theft, with a mind too narrowly focused, open to only one possibility rather than many.

Detectives working to solve a mystery have any number of weapons in their arsenals, of course. They have years of experience and training as police officers before being promoted to detective. They have forensic specialists who work for them and perform tricky tasks like fingerprint identification, hair and fiber analysis, and DNA matching. They can draw on national databases maintained by agencies like the FBI to help them in their investigations.

By the same token, very experienced readers have it easier in some regards than those who haven't read as widely. They may find it easier to recognize allusions to other texts, historical incidents, or classical mythology (T. S. Eliot, for example, makes an enormous number of such references in his poem *The Waste Land*). These readers recognize common **tropes** and familiar **metaphors**, are more practiced at developing various interpretations for a given work, and may be more experienced at reading and comprehending complicated and often jargon-heavy criticism.

However, just as the observant amateur sleuth in mystery fiction frequently beats the police to the solution, one doesn't have to have a master's degree in English to learn to read critically. Any reader can consider a text in a careful, attentive manner, searching for elements that stand out and eventually add up in a way that informs the reader's understanding. No two readers can possibly approach a work of literature from identical perspectives, and a great part of the joy of reading comes from learning to see a poem, novel, story, or play in a new context or from a different perspective. Every work you have read becomes part of the context from which you approach literature.

Whether you are yourself a creative writer or whether you write only when compelled to do so by school assignments, you know that writing is all about making choices. You decide what your message is going to be, you decide which reading audience you are going to address, and you decide what style and level of language are appropriate for that audience. To a great degree, you even decide how you are going to seem to your readers: Are you going to sound friendly or antagonistic? Knowledgeable or ignorant? Aloof or engaged? As a writer, you make these choices either tacitly or explicitly; either way, though, you will be held to them as if you had made them consciously.

As readers, we must remain aware that we do not have direct access to what the author meant, only to what he or she said; the process of reading is the process of creating a plausible interpretation based on the evidence at hand—in other words, the text. When reading, though, remember that the process writers of literature go through is not fundamentally different from your own writing process. Poets, playwrights, and authors of fiction make the same choices when creating their works of art as you should when you write papers for your classes or as we are as we write and rewrite these pages. Seeing through the author's choices may give you insight into the motives that fuel the poem, play, or story.

While all writers wrestle with many of the same choices, there is one important category of decision making where writers of imaginative literature have much more latitude than most others (including student writers and textbook authors): literary form. Creative writers probably know very early on whether their creation is going to be prose fiction, poetry, or drama—most master no more than one or two of these genres—but after that, choices about form abound. If the work is a play, will it be a one-act play or a five-hour epic? Will it be in prose or blank verse? If the work is fiction, will it be a short story, a novella, a novel, or the beginning of a trilogy? If the work is a poem, will it be free verse, blank verse, or in some other meter? A sonnet or a haiku? Whatever the choice, the attentive reader will notice and take it under consideration in his or her interpretation.

Writers of literature often presume that their readers will be acquainted with the characteristics of various literary forms. The poet who writes a **villanelle** signals readers to consider the poem in the context of other villanelles (of which Dylan Thomas's "Do Not Go Gentle into That Good Night" is a famous example). This is not to say, however, that the poet must adhere to the expectations that the chosen form raises; in fact, many poets (and writers in other genres as well) raise these expectations only to subvert them. If the reader is not aware of the form's specific traits, however, the writer's experimentalism will go unnoticed.

Thus while it is important to be sensitive to the expectations readers can reasonably bring to a literary work, it is even more important to remain receptive to what the work itself seems to be doing. Sometimes readers get so swept up in the emotion of a work of literature that they begin to pay more attention to their own emotion than to the work that evoked it in the first place. Other readers may bring such intense political, philosophical, or religious agendas to their reading that they cannot see the work except through the lens of their particular ideology.

Many flawed interpretations—interpretations that are unsupportable or only marginally supportable—have their origins in readings that are overpowered by misguided expectations; others, however, arise directly from the reader's overactive imagination, frequently as the direct result of the pressure the reader feels to come up with a novel interpretation. This can easily happen to students in college classes who are pressured to formulate "original" theses about their assignments. It also happens to literary critics (often untenured college professors caught in "publish or perish" employment situations) whose professional standing depends on the number of critical books and articles they publish.

Avoiding these errant readings is possible but difficult; it involves applying some tough, skeptical standards to one's own ideas. A good rule of thumb is **Occam's razor**, a principle that states that entities must not be complicated beyond what is necessary. Put another way, it suggests that the simplest theory that fits the facts of a problem is probably the best one. As seductive as convoluted, Byzantine interpretations can seem, they are usually not the simplest or most elegant solution; when you're trying to answer a question of interpretation, don't neglect the obvious. Readers have long debated the symbolic significance of the title creature in Elizabeth Bishop's poem "The Fish," and it certainly could represent many things; but the author's vivid description of the fish makes it clear that it is an actual fish. It is true that the sensitive reader must be receptive to multiple possibilities when it comes to interpreting symbols, but it's important to focus on the plausible and to pay attention to the literal meaning, even while exploring other possible nuances. To overlook the literal fish in favor of a purely symbolic interpretation of the poem is to miss the poem's point; it might not be *just* a fish, but it is a fish.

THINKING EXERCISES

1. Can you think of any interpretations of a literary work that you have heard or participated in that you thought were wrong? If so, why were they wrong?
2. Can you think of works that seem to be very open and obvious to understanding and interpretation that might still benefit from more analytical readings? Cite an example, and show how a more analytical reading might benefit the work.
3. As we've noted before, some recent trends in criticism and critical theory change the focus on how readers approach a text critically. Rather than searching the text for an accumulation of details that indicate subtextual themes that the writer may or may not have intended, the reader instead discusses how certain aspects of the literature's culture are revealed by the text. Do you deem this a valid approach? Why or why not?

4.3   AUTHORIAL INTENTION

As noted earlier, an ongoing issue in contemporary critical theory is **authorial intention**. Is it our goal as readers to identify and understand what the author of a story was "trying to say"? Is it even possible to discern beyond reasonable doubt what a poet means by a given poem? Does our appreciation of Joyce's "Araby" depend on our knowing what Joyce meant by the story, and—assuming that we could know his intention—would that be the only valid interpretation of it?

The practice of evaluating a work of literature based on the artist's explicit or perceived intention in creating it has been called the **intentional fallacy** (see section 2.2) by critics who maintained that attempts to recover an artist's intention are doomed to failure. If the work in question is older, and if there is no known commentary on it by its author, this proposition is not too hard to accept. All we can tell of *Beowulf*'s author's intention is the poem itself. But consider a novel by Stephen King, for instance, with an afterword that describes the composition of the novel and his intention behind it. Surely the author's own commentary would be relevant to the reader's understanding of the novel. What about his discussion of the novel with a talk show host? Conceivably, we could write or call Stephen King and just ask him what the novel means. Does that mean that his explanation necessarily supersedes all other interpretations of the novel?

These are issues worth bearing in mind when you approach the interpretation of literature. The role of authorial intention in the interpretation falls somewhere on a continuum between two points of view that, taken to their extremes, are equally absurd. At one extreme would be the belief that the author's intention is entirely unknowable and irrelevant to any reader's understanding of a given text. Such an assumption would mean that (in the case of the afterword to a Stephen King novel), King's commentary about his own work is utterly irrelevant to the reader's appreciation of it. Few critics would subscribe to this belief in its extreme form. On a certain practical level, authorial intention is not unknowable. It would be hard to maintain that Harriet Beecher Stowe did not intend *Uncle Tom's Cabin* to be a commentary on the inhumanity of slavery, for instance. And as we discussed earlier, our belief that an artist did intend *something* with a work of art (whether we believe we can reliably recover that intention or not) is a necessary precursor to interpreting it.

At the other extreme would be the point of view to which some beginning readers subscribe: the belief that the author's commentary on his or her work is supreme. Whereas many authors are unwilling to comment publicly on the meanings and motivations behind their writing, some don't hesitate to do so. Unfortunately, an author's commentary on his or her work is, by definition, authoritative. We say "unfortunately" because while most literary texts are open to a variety of possible interpretations, and indeed much of the pleasure in revisiting these works lies in the exploration of other possibilities, the authorial interpretation, when it is known, can obscure the other possibilities. Although it would be foolish to ignore what an author says about his or her work, it would be a shame to restrict one's own understanding of the work to what the author has identified as significant. Maybe the text contains possibilities that even the author may not have noticed.

The issue of authorial intention ultimately comes down to common sense. Extratextual authorial commentary about a literary text cannot safely be ignored. At the same time, it cannot be considered the final word on a given work. The author's authority over the text ends to a degree with its completion. After publication, the text's meaning comes from the interaction between the text and the reader. As readers, it is our responsibility to read the text carefully and thoroughly, using whatever means are at our disposal to arrive at a valid interpretation of the text. If the author has provided further information about the work in question, whether through footnotes, an introduction, or an interview, we must certainly take this information into account; however, we should keep in mind that these alternative sources of information are themselves texts and are also therefore subject to interpretation.

THINKING EXERCISES

1. If we consider authors who are no longer alive and who never offered explicit commentary on their own works, do you think we can assume that we know exactly what the authors' intentions were? Can you think of any creative texts for which you believe you know exactly what the author intended? What about texts for which you feel multiple readings and interpretations are supportable by evidence from the works themselves?

2. Do you perceive any dangers in placing too much emphasis on the idea that we'll never know what was actually intended by an author? What would those dangers be? How might they affect your readings of various works?

4.4   TIPS FOR THE PHYSICAL ACT OF READING

In addition to all the mental preparations for critical reading, such as examining metaphors, forms, and your own expectations, what physical considerations should we make? Some readers' ability to read difficult texts successfully might be more connected to the world external from their books than they suspect.

- Read literature with a pencil or highlighter in hand; you can mark passages that don't make sense or that seem to contain key points of information.
- Circle or underline words you don't know.
- Jot down notes about characters, setting, and themes.
- Don't read especially challenging texts when you're overly tired.
- Find a place to read that makes it easier for you to concentrate (library, coffee, shop, study nook).

৯ 5 ৫

Reading Fiction Actively

When reading fiction, one of the easiest ways to start is to break the story down to its basic components: plot, setting, tone, character, and theme. The last of those, **theme**, is often difficult to discern initially, but considering the other elements may help you come to understand the **subtext** of the story and its various themes. We'll discuss these elements in much more detail in the next chapter, but for now let's note that paying particular attention to these fundamental building blocks of fiction will help us better understand and appreciate the moves the writer makes. Furthermore, let's ask ourselves what steps the authors take to plant clues for our examination. In what ways do they work to meet our expectations? Or work against them?

Earlier, we discussed "Hills Like White Elephants" and "Araby," both included in Part Six. In reading those two stories (please do so now), pay attention to the rudimentary features of the stories (plot, setting, tone, and character), and ask yourself, what stands out or interests you? What doesn't fit in? How are your expectations met? How are they denied?

Each of these stories is notorious among students as well as scholars and professors for being obscure and even somewhat minimalist. Readers often feel that they're left hanging by the end of "Hills Like White Elephants" or "Araby"; however, such readers are often paying attention more to the plot than to the subtext and theme. To be an active, critical reader, you have to pay attention to each of the layers that make up a given story.

For example, much of our understanding of each story is based on the **setting**. If we examine Joyce's "Araby," we notice immediately that the young narrator lives on a "blind" street, which is to say a dead-end street. Joyce could easily have used the term "dead-end," but he chose *blind* instead. Later the boy watches the object of his crush through the *blind* on the door. Again, Joyce could have the boy watching through a curtain, a sash, or a keyhole, but he uses the word *blind*. References to light and dark and sight abound throughout the story, and at some level we realize that our narrator is in the dark and is blind to the realities of the situation. The story is about the boy's inability (initially) to comprehend the status of his relationship with his friend's sister. The fact that a blind street is a dead-end street helps us further understand that the boy's chances to win the young lady's heart are quite slim. Furthermore, although the story is too short to provide excessive **characterization**, we should note that the boy always refers to his romantic interest as "Mangan's sister" and not by her name. Perhaps this indicates that he is too self-involved in his drama (like most adolescents) to consider who she really is as a person.

Paying attention to author introductions and publication dates may also help in this regard. Knowing that the story was published in 1914 and is set in Dublin (presumably within a decade or two previous to the story) helps explain the heavy Catholic influence in the children's lives and also indicates to the observant reader that the boy is quite probably somewhat less sophisticated and wise in the way of the world than a young man of our current time would be. Perhaps his eyes "burn" in "anguish and anger" at the end of the story because he can clearly perceive his situation for the first time.

If we make a more detailed analysis of Hemingway's "Hills Like White Elephants," we realize that once again, an examination of the setting is a good place to start. Consider the opening lines of the story:

> The hills across the valley of the Ebro were long and white. On this side there was no shade and no trees and the station was between two lines of rails in the sun. Close against the side of the station there was the warm shadow of the building and a curtain, made of strings of bamboo beads, hung across the open door into the bar, to keep out flies. The American and the girl with him sat at a table in the shade, outside the building. It was very hot and the express from Barcelona would come in forty minutes. It stopped at this junction for two minutes and went on to Madrid.

Much of what we need to know about the themes and subtext of this story is incorporated in this opening paragraph. We don't recognize them immediately, of course; it is only through the accumulation of symbolic evidence that we'll come to understand the story's themes. We'll return to the first paragraph shortly; first, let's consider what else is taking place in the story.

The man and his companion (called either "the girl" or "Jig") are waiting at this train station, which we realize is in Spain (due to the author's mentioning of Madrid, Barcelona, and less obviously, the Ebro River). We know that the couple is unhappy about something; the **tone** of the story and the tone of their conversation clearly indicate tension between them. When Jig states that the hills "look like white elephants," the man replies, "I've never seen one." Later, upon trying absinthe (a liquor outlawed in the United States due to its degenerative effects on the liver), the woman notes, "It tastes like licorice," and the man says, "That's the way with everything." He is obviously distracted and not paying attention to her actual statements.

Jig, having finally had enough, fights back with sarcasm: "Yes. . . . Everything tastes of licorice. Especially all the things you've waited so long for, like absinthe." The anger and tension between the couple are made even more palpable when the man believes he is alleviating Jig's nerves by stating, almost out of context, "It's really an awfully simple operation, Jig. . . . It's not really an operation at all." Their mood seems to go from bad to worse; when he states again, later, that he "know[s] it's perfectly simple," Jig replies (italics ours), "Yes, *you* know it's perfectly simple." If we haven't realized it before, we know by this point that Jig is very reluctant to undergo whatever operation the man thinks she should have.

Most of us are worldly enough to realize by this point that the operation they're discussing is an abortion. There are several more symbolic points that add to our understanding, however. First, the story's title—derived from the woman's offhand comparison—highlights the expression "white elephants." The once common idiomatic phrase "white elephant," according to *Webster's New World Dictionary*, refers to "something from which little profit or use is derived; especially such a possession maintained at much expense" or "any object no longer desired by its owner but of possible value to others." The white elephant here is the fetus carried by the woman.

Now let's return to that first paragraph and our examination of the setting. The title and the protagonist's comparison, taken with the tension and discussion of the "simple" operation, invoke the idea of abortion. So what purpose might be served by setting the station between two sets of rails? One pair of rails leads in one direction, and the other pair leads in the other direction (as you would expect). The rails represent the choice the woman must make. Should she abort the child or not? Which way should she go?

The opening paragraph does even more than this for the reader when combined with later sequences in the story. At one point, the woman walks to the end of the station, and we see that on the "other side" of the valley are "fields of grain and trees along the banks of the Ebro." As she watches, however, the "shadow of a cloud move[s] across the field of grain." The train station is in the part of the valley where there is "no shade" and "no trees." Everything is dry, hot, arid, and lifeless. The setting not only implies choice but also establishes a dichotomy between life (the trees, fields, and river) and death (the hot, treeless plain of the station).

Furthermore, the couple are sitting in the shadow of the building; combined with the shadow of the cloud moving over the fields of grain, it's not too much of a stretch to wonder if this use of "shade" and "shadow" in the story is supposed to recall the "shadow of death" most famously evoked in the Twenty-Third Psalm.[1]

In terms of characterization, we know that the man, stressed and worried as he may be, is also trying to manipulate the woman. He tells her, "I don't want you to do it if you don't want to," but then says, "I'm perfectly willing to go through with it if it means anything to you." And he keeps telling her over and over again that the operation is "perfectly simple." Jig, on the other hand, must decide whether she's going to do what she thinks is right or what the American thinks is right.

What else should stand out to you as a reader? How about the use of the number *two* in the story? Every time he orders drinks, the American states "two," although he and Jig are the only people at their table. There are two lines of rails and two bags, and she pulls on two beads of the curtain. Does this signify that he wants to keep their family at "two," or does it signify that she is not one person now but two—or possibly both? Why does she pull on the beads of the curtain when she is uncomfortable? Are they supposed to symbolize prayer beads? As we'll state over and over again in this book, remember that the job of literature is not always to provide you with answers so much as with questions.[2]

One thing we know for sure is that Jig is not only uneasy with the idea of an abortion but feels it would be wrong in their circumstance. (As an aside, one should probably initially refrain from referring to this story as either "pro-life" or "pro-choice" in a modern political context, although a good argument could be made for either stance. The debate was quite different and even largely nonexistent in 1927, when this story was published.) When she stands and walks away and gazes on the mountains and "fields of grain and trees" on the other side of the valley, she says, "And we could have all this. . . . And we could have everything and every day we make it more impossible."

The American replies by saying, "We can have everything," and insisting that they can "go everywhere" and can "have the whole world," but Jig responds each time by saying, "No, we can't." Jig feels that they've lost focus on what is important in life and have instead lived lives of careless indulgence, focusing more on "look[ing] at things and try[ing] new drinks" and accumulating stickers of exotic locales on their baggage.

Even in this static story, it is also important to consider the **plot** and actions of the characters. At the end of the story, the American man "pick[s] up the two heavy bags and carrie[s] them around the station to the other tracks." When he returns to the table, the woman smiles at him; when he

---

[1] "Yea, though I walk through the valley of the shadow of death, I will fear no evil; for thou art with me; thy rod and thy staff they comfort me" (Psalms 23:4).
[2] Our reading of "Hills Like White Elephants" follows the standard line established by a number of critics; for bibliographical information or a more in-depth study of the story, please refer to Stanley Renner's article in Chapter 21. Our understanding of the end of the story is particularly influenced by Renner's reading.

asks if she feels better, she says, "I feel fine. . . . There's nothing wrong with me. I feel fine." Is she saying this ironically, because she's going to have an abortion although she is clearly uncomfortable with the idea? Or does the man's taking the suitcases to the *other* tracks indicate that he has had a change of heart and now she's actually truly happy? Students and critics argue both points of view. If we attach significance to his action in the plot, we do lend credit to the suggestion that he changes his position.

THINKING EXERCISES

1. What did you think of "Araby" and "Hills Like White Elephants" the first time you read them? Has your opinion of the stories changed after reading this chapter? Why or why not?
2. These stories were chosen as examples because they appear in a great many anthologies. Why do you think they are anthologized so often?
3. Do you think either story would benefit from a more active plotline? Are there any scenes you would like to see added to either story? Write one out—but try to stay true to the actual tone and theme of the story.

❧ 6 ❧

Engaging with Poetry

Just like drama and fiction, poems can often make use of setting, plot, character, and tone. In addition to considering those more narrative elements of verse, however, the reader of poetry should also pay even closer attention to the use of **figurative language**. Figurative language is writing or speech that makes use of imagery as well as metaphors and similes to broaden, deepen, and enrich our understanding of a description, place, person, or turn of phrase. Figurative language, metaphors, imagery, and the like are not unique to poetry—fiction and drama both make ample use of figurative language, as we've shown—but they are all essential to poetry because most modern poetry must practice, to some degree, economy. As short as "Araby" is, it still contains far more words than "Desert Places." Although poets will still occasionally write epics or long poems (like *The Waste Land*), most modern poems tend to be short, rarely taking more than a couple of pages. Use of figurative language, however, helps a poem get the most mileage out of its words.

At an even more microscopic level, part of a poem's meaning may be indicated by its verse style. The choice of **formal verse**, using a consistent rhyme scheme and a consistent meter, or **blank verse**, which has meter but doesn't rhyme, may simply reflect the stylistic dictates of the poet's day or mood; such facets as rhyme, line length, and stanza breaks can also help make a point of symbolic significance. The lines to Allen Ginsberg's poem "Howl" are exceptionally long, with few periods or other stops; the lines are meant to suggest an actual howl of anger and frustration. Lawrence Ferlinghetti's "Constantly Risking Absurdity" is a poem that compares poetry to the work of a high-wire acrobat; the words stretch back and forth across the page, reminiscent of the high-wire artist's transit, stepping softly along a thin cable.

A poem may use alliteration to call attention to a word or phrase; it may use sentence fragments to suggest a loss of coherence. It may use repetition

34

to make its point, as when Sylvia Plath's narrator in "Daddy" lapses into a German stutter, crying "Ich, ich, ich, ich, / I could hardly speak," describing the narrator's inability to clearly communicate her feelings about her deceased father while at the same time repeating the poem's central motif of comparing him to a Nazi and herself to a Jewish concentration camp victim.

6.1   EXAMPLE: ROBERT FROST

For an example of a poem in which the writer consciously works against the reader's assumptions and expectations in a way that demands deeper and more active reading, consider the following selection by Robert Frost.

Desert Places
(1936)

Snow falling and night falling fast, oh, fast
In a field I looked into going past,
And the ground almost covered smooth in snow,
But a few weeds and stubble showing last.

The woods around it have it—it is theirs.   5
All animals are smothered in their lairs.
I am too absent-spirited to count;
The loneliness includes me unawares.

And lonely as it is that loneliness
Will be more lonely ere it will be less—   10
A blanker whiteness of benighted snow
With no expression, nothing to express.

They cannot scare me with their empty spaces
Between stars—on stars where no human race is.
I have it in me so much nearer home   15
To scare myself with my own desert places.

What is it about this poem that asks for active reading? Examine the first two lines of the poem in conjunction with the title. Obviously, when most people think of "desert," they think of blinding heat, sand dunes, thirst, empty canteens, camels, and mirages. The mind conjures up place names like Sahara, Gobi, and Mojave. But "Desert Places" is about a snowy field near the woods at twilight. The use of snow, cold, and winter rather than heat and sand lets us know that the desert places do not exist within what we conventionally think of as the desert. A careful reading of the rest of the poem makes it clear that the true barren, lonely, and deserted place is within the narrator's own heart and soul. Not even the cold vacuum of outer space compares to his inner desolation.

The setting alone doesn't convey this, of course. It doesn't really have to—by the end of the poem, the narrator is telling the readers directly how he feels. Even prior to that point, however, we are told that he is too "absent-spirited" (line 7) to dispel the loneliness in the woods; use of strong descriptive words like *smothered* (as opposed to, say, *comfortable* or *snug*) (line 6) indicate to us that the narrator isn't in a particularly happy state of mind. He even goes so far as to say that the snow is a "blanker whiteness" with "no expression, nothing to express" (lines 11–12). What exactly are woods *supposed* to reflect to the casual observer? One could speculate that nature never "expresses" something to a person unless that person is particularly receptive; in fact, it may be that all nature ever does is reflect what is already inside someone. In the case of the narrator of this poem, he is empty and "absent-spirited"; consequently, the woods reflect nothing back to him.

As noted, the opening lines and title make it clear that this poem is asking for a deeper consideration than a casual skimming of the text will allow. But "Desert Places" provides us with a relatively obvious use of symbolic language, making the choice to spend time and effort on the poem easy for a reader.

However, as we've discussed before, there is an intrinsic danger in recognizing that there are layers and depths to a work of literature for which the reader may be compelled to dig. What if readers make certain assumptions about figurative or symbolic language and develop a reading of a work of literature that isn't justified by the text? Put bluntly, what if a reader's understanding of a given story, play, or poem is just wrong?

There is always a democratic impulse when reading literature, of course. We love to say that all of us have the right to our own opinions and that all readings are valid readings. As we have stressed and will stress repeatedly throughout this book, we thoroughly believe that most literature is sophisticated and multileveled enough to give rise to many legitimate and valid readings. This philosophy is one of the central tenets of postmodernist theory, as a matter of fact: since readers usually have no way of knowing *exactly* what is intended by the author of a given text, they must approach it with the understanding that it is open to various and contradictory interpretations.

Nevertheless, most literature is not written in a vacuum; it has been written in an effort to get something across to readers. Although we must acknowledge that often we cannot presume to know exactly what an author intended, we still owe it to that author to do our best to ascertain (through careful consideration and evaluation) what, to the best of our understanding, the writer has achieved or attempted to achieve.

By way of example, let's consider another Robert Frost poem, one that is widely quoted but often misunderstood.

The Road Not Taken
(1915)

Two roads diverged in a yellow wood,
And sorry I could not travel both

And be one traveler, long I stood
And looked down one as far as I could
To where it bent in the undergrowth;   5

Then took the other, as just as fair,
And having perhaps the better claim,
Because it was grassy and wanted wear;
Though as for that the passing there
Had worn them really about the same,   10

And both that morning equally lay
In leaves no step had trodden black.
Oh, I kept the first for another day!
Yet knowing how way leads on to way,
I doubted if I should ever come back.   15

I shall be telling this with a sigh
Somewhere ages and ages hence:
Two roads diverged in a wood, and I—
I took the one less traveled by,
And that has made all the difference.   20

Not only is this one of Frost's most beloved poems, but it is probably also his most misrepresented. "The Road Not Taken" is referred to constantly as a poem about nonconformity. Graduation speakers and football coaches quote the poem as an homage to individuality. M. Scott Peck's famous best-selling self-help book about choosing your own path in life, *The Road Less Traveled*, certainly refers to Frost's poem.

Our traveler does indeed find "two roads" that diverge "in a yellow wood"; his first response is to be "sorry" that he "could not travel both" (lines 1–2). He decides on one of the trails, stating initially that the one he chooses has "perhaps the better claim / Because it was grassy and wanted wear" (lines 7–8). Reflecting on the choice, however, he admits that in actuality, the "passing there / Had worn them really about the same" (lines 9–10). He goes on to say that the trails "both that morning equally lay / In leaves no step had trodden black" (lines 11–12). Although the poem does end with the lines "I took the one less traveled by, / And that has made all the difference" (lines 19–20), we now know that the road really wasn't any less traveled than the other.

But if the poem isn't about nonconformity and being an individual, what is it about? Why does he say that in the years to come he will be "telling this with a sigh" (line 16)? And why has the road he traveled "made all the difference" (line 20)?

To answer these questions, we should reconsider the poem, applying Occam's razor (discussed in section 4.2). Starting at the beginning, what are the initial things we notice about the first stanza? What are the first points made clear to the readers?

The first thing that readers must take into account is the title of the poem. Unlike the title of the famous self-help book by Peck, *The Road Less Traveled*, which indicates nonconformity, the title of the poem alludes to the road that wasn't taken. The poem is therefore at least partly about regret. Reading the text of the poem, we quickly realize that the traveler regrets the fact that he must irrevocably choose which of the two roads he will follow. He is "sorry" he "could not travel both," and he looks as far as possible down the path he does not take (line 4). In the second stanza, as we noted, he first states that the one he chooses has "perhaps the better claim" (line 7) due to its lack of wear, yet he immediately admits that the other is equally unworn.

Perhaps the speaker's sigh in the last stanza is because, although he has saved "the first for another day," in "knowing how way leads on to way," he doubts that he "should ever come back" (lines 13–15). A decision, once made, is made forever; we cannot undo our actions and reverse time. No matter where the first day of your college life is spent, you decided to spend it in one place and not another. If you marry, only one person can be your best man or maid of honor. Your entire life has come about as a result of a series of decisions by yourself and other people. The decisions you have made are what make you who you are in the place that you are; they have made "all the difference." These third-stanza lines imply the poem is not so much about nonconformity as it is about the necessity of having to make decisions in life. Should we extrapolate from the traveler's regret a reading that assumes he is often paralyzed by indecision and that he has a hard time living with the decisions he has made? You could possibly make a case for such an interpretation, but it would be an explication that relies heavily on presumption and guesswork—and one that seems to come too close to the edge of Occam's razor.

THINKING EXERCISES

1. Do you think all interpretations and explications of a work of literature are equally valid? Does a particular reading or interpretation of a work need to be justified through reasoned explanations?
2. Can you think of advertisements, articles, television shows, or films that have made out-of-context references to quotations from poems, plays, songs, stories, or films that misrepresent the work in question?
3. Have you ever disagreed with a teacher over the interpretation or analysis of a literary work? Or have you ever known another student who disagreed with a teacher's reading? How do you resolve such a conflict? Do you think such a debate adds to your understanding of a work or detracts from it?

6.2   EXAMPLE: SHAKESPEARE'S SONNETS

Often the effect a work of literature has on its audience depends on the interplay between the reader's expectations and the interpretation derived from careful, thorough readings. Many factors can shape the assumptions a reader brings to a text; although some of these are outside the writer's control, writers frequently use the conventions of genre to manipulate, and frequently to defy, the reader's expectations. Consider the following well-known sonnet by William Shakespeare.

Sonnet 18
(1609)

Shall I compare thee to a summer's day?
Thou art more lovely and more temperate:
Rough winds do shake the darling buds of May,
And summer's lease hath all too short a date:
Sometime too hot the eye of heaven shines,   *5*
And often is his gold complexion dimm'd;
And every fair from fair sometime declines,
By chance or nature's changing course untrimm'd;
But thy eternal summer shall not fade,
Nor lose possession of that fair thou ow'st;   *10*
Nor shall Death brag thou wander'st in his shade,
When in eternal lines to time thou grow'st:
So long as men can breathe or eyes can see,
So long lives this, and this gives life to thee.

As an English or Elizabethan **sonnet**,[1] the poem exhibits a structure that sends certain specific signals to the informed reader. Elizabethan sonnets are fourteen-line poems frequently dealing with the subject of love. While each poem is a discrete entity, the sonnet is often part of a larger group of sonnets on the same theme. Collectively, this group is known as a *sonnet cycle* (Edmund Spenser and Sir Philip Sidney also wrote well-known sonnet cycles). This sonnet, eighteenth in Shakespeare's sequence of 154 sonnets, stands on its own merits but also plays a role in the context of the collection as a whole. The sonnet form raises expectations about the poem's subject and method of development, yet rather than merely meeting these expectations, Shakespeare uses them to create a much more challenging statement about the power of poetry.

In addition to providing clues about the poem's theme, the sonnet form also assists the reader in sorting out the poem's syntax. Notice that the

---

[1]Sometimes Elizabethan sonnets are referred to as "Shakespearean sonnets," although other writers before and after Shakespeare wrote in the same form.

rhyme scheme of the Elizabethan sonnet (*abab cdcd efef gg*) encourages the reader to engage with the poem four lines at a time, with the concluding couplet connecting the rest of the sonnet to a more general theme, frequently one it shares with others in the same sequence or cycle. Readers new to Shakespeare's sonnets will find them much more accessible if they pay attention to these auditory signals.

Sonnet 18 opens by questioning the appropriateness of comparing the subject to a summer's day, though the person addressed is both "more lovely and more temperate" (line 2). "More lovely" than a summer's day smacks of **hyperbole**, but hyperbole is a common characteristic of the sonnet cycle. The second part of the line suggests that the subject's relatively even temperament is more appealing than the extreme temperatures of summer. The speaker continues by exploring the negative aspects of the summer season: its weather is sometimes severe, and summer itself is over all too soon. The phrase "darling buds of May" (line 3) suggests youth and beauty, conditions that the speaker laments as being all too temporary. The next passage expands on the negative characteristics of summer: excessive heat and sudden storms. When he states in line 7 that "every fair from fair sometimes declines," the speaker is observing that summer's supposed beauty is frequently less than beautiful, robbed of its attractiveness by chance or nature.

Although the reader may reasonably have expected the comparison of the subject to a summer's day to be both desirable and flattering, the speaker instead explores its inadequacy. In contrast to summer's severity and brevity, the subject's "eternal summer shall not fade" (line 9), nor shall it ever lose the beauty ("fair") that it possesses ("ow'st") in line 10. The subject's immortality is asserted in lines 11 and 12, and the metaphor of summer vegetation introduced earlier with "the darling buds of May" is sustained. Buds become flowers that bloom, wilt, and die. The subject, whose youth and beauty are described in terms of eternal summer, will not be found languishing in Death's shade but rather—in a continuation of the vegetation metaphor—grafted to time itself "in eternal lines" (line 12) and therefore thriving in eternal summer.

The concluding couplet sums up the poem by defining its overall theme, which happens to be similar to those of the poems surrounding it in the sonnet cycle. The "lines" of line 12 could be seen as referring to the growth of a plant or flower or to the subject's genealogy (bloodlines) or progeny; in fact, several of the preceding sonnets in the cycle urge the subject to strive for immortality by begetting children. However, lines 13 and 14 clearly assert that the poem itself will help grant the subject immortality. The word *this* in line 14 refers to the poem itself; thus the "lines" are most appropriately understood as the lines of the poem, along with the relevant gardening connotations of growth and heredity.

Ultimately, then, this love poem emphasizes the preservative power of poetry much more effectively than it describes the person to whom it is addressed. Not even the subject's gender is evident from the sonnet alone, though the context of the cycle indicates that the poem may be addressed to a young man whom the speaker admires. Rather than exploiting the power of poetry to praise the subject's beauty, the speaker uses the subject's beauty to extol the supremacy of his own verse. A careful reading of the poem reveals a much more complicated sentiment than its surface might suggest.

Shakespeare's Sonnet 130 plays a similar game with expectations, but much more dangerously. The poem is written in praise of his "mistress," but it is hard to imagine anyone initially being flattered by its rhetoric.

Sonnet 130
(1609)

My mistress' eyes are nothing like the sun;
Coral is far more red than her lips' red:
If snow be white, why then her breasts are dun;
If hairs be wires, black wires grow on her head.
I have seen roses damask'd, red and white,   5
But no such roses see I in her cheeks;
And in some perfumes is there more delight
Than in the breath that from my mistress reeks.
I love to hear her speak, yet well I know
That music hath a far more pleasing sound;   10
I grant I never saw a goddess go;
My mistress, when she walks, treads on the ground:
And yet by heaven, I think my love as rare
As any she belied with false compare.

The poem sets out to defy the poetic convention of hyperbolic praise. Rather than declare that his mistress's eyes are brighter or more beautiful than the sun, the speaker denies the possibility of comparison: they are "nothing like the sun" (line 1). This woman is in no way the fair, blonde Renaissance ideal other authors praise in their poems; her skin is not white as snow but rather "dun," a dull, dingy shade of brown (line 3). Her hair is black and apparently like wires; her complexion is in no way rosy. Her breath bears no resemblance to perfume, and her voice isn't as pleasingly sweet as music (though significantly, in line 9, the speaker "love[s] to hear her speak"). In lines 11 and 12, the speaker states directly that his mistress is no goddess, dispelling whatever doubt might remain for the reader about the mistress's divinity. Only the final couplet makes a substantially positive statement about the mistress.

As greeting card verse, this poem would be woefully inadequate. On the surface, the faint praise that concludes the sonnet seems to be too little, too late. Yet a clue from those last lines, coupled with a careful second trip through the poem focusing on what the poem actually says rather than what it seems to say, yields a much more positive interpretation. Just as Sonnet 18 turns out to assert the power of poetry as much as the immortality of the person being praised, Sonnet 130 is as much about the use of metaphor and simile as it is about the speaker's mistress. When the speaker says that she is as "rare / As any she belied with false compare" (lines 13–14), the speaker means that she is as valuable and as precious as any woman who has been represented falsely by hyperbolic, exaggerated similes.

Shakespeare is thus able to use the readers' expectations about sonnet conventions to call those very conventions into question. When the speaker says his "mistress' eyes are nothing like the sun" (line 1), he is not disparaging the brightness of her eyes but criticizing the absurd exaggeration of poems that compare eyes to suns. Likewise, even the whitest skin is not as white as snow, and—as the speaker may be suggesting—one can be beautiful without necessarily conforming to society's narrow definition of physical beauty.

Line 4 is similarly tricky; a casual reading suggests that the woman's hair is wiry, but literally, the speaker is merely saying that it is black. Furthermore, as the *Oxford English Dictionary* suggests, it was not unusual to compare hair to gold (or silver, copper, or even brass) wires; in Shakespeare's time, the word *wire* would have likened her hair to jewelry, not to electrical wire, wire fences, or wire brushes, as it would today. More to the point, the line implies and the end of the poem emphasizes that such comparisons (hair to wires) are of little value.

The speaker's assertion that there are no roses in his mistress's cheeks follows the pattern that has already been established. He may seem to be implying that her face lacks lively color, but in fact he is merely saying something that is quite literally true: there are no actual roses in her cheeks. Playfully, the speaker flirts with insult here just as he does in the next pair of lines, where he implies that the woman's breath is bad. Given the poem's preoccupation with the fallibility of metaphor, this can't be taken for granted. To modern readers, the word *reek* has only negative connotations, but in Shakespeare's time it was more neutral—though it's certain that a smell must be pretty strong in order to "reek," and when speaking of breath, a strong odor is usually a bad one. Still, all the speaker is literally saying is that some perfume smells better than his mistress's breath; the rest is subtext, and the poem has already warned its readers that the subtext is not to be trusted.

The poem concludes with a defiant assertion of the superiority of the speaker's mistress even in the face of her earthliness. Without being a goddess whose voice is more beautiful than music, she is as rare, as precious, as any other woman—specifically, she is as rare as any woman who has ever been "belied" by foolishly exaggerated similes.

The impact of Sonnet 130 lies largely in the poet's willingness to subvert the expectations of his readers. We expect hyperbolic comparisons, but the speaker disdains them. On first reading, we see insults directed at the mistress, but a more careful reading shows that the poet playfully avoids direct statements of his mistress's human failings even as he refuses to lie about them in the manner of conventional sonnets. Ultimately, the subject of the poem is not the mistress but the metaphor; readers who are too committed to their preconceived expectations will be caught by these poems. Careful readers bring expectations to what they read, but they remain sensitive to the clues of the text.

THINKING EXERCISES

1. We point out in the cases of both Robert Frost and William Shakespeare how these poets at times challenge expectations or convention. Can you think of other literary works that seem to defy established formulas or conventions?

2. Can you think of contemporary media that overuse hyperbole? Particularly examine songs, advertisements, news reports of dramatic events, and the like. Do you think that using too much hyperbole can eventually deaden the audience's respect for the subject of the exaggeration? Or do you think hyperbole is a useful technique?

❧ 7 ❧

Experiencing Drama

Drama is, of course, a form of prose or poetry (or some combination of the two), but drama is generally meant to be acted out and observed by an audience rather than read on the page (although one could argue that some playwrights, like Tennessee Williams, fully expect to be read as well as watched). Students rarely have the opportunities in literature classes to see plays, though, and are more often called on to read them. Plays are often difficult to understand or enjoy on the written page because they are meant to be acted out on the stage.

If you're having trouble reading a play, try approaching it more actively. Taking cues from the author's description (either from the dialogue or from stage directions), spend some preliminary effort on visualizing the stage. In a play like Samuel Beckett's *Endgame*, where the stage resembles the interior of a giant skull, such visualization may be vital to a full understanding of the play, and though the dialogue is minimal, Beckett's stage directions provide readers of the play with the ability to visualize both **setting** and action. In the case of Shakespeare, whose plays were performed with minimal stage sets, identify the setting and imagine it the way the contemporary audience of the Elizabethan period would have. Is it a tavern or a country garden? A bedroom or a battleground? Provide the play with a context.

When the stage is set, cast the play by visualizing the characters. When we read fiction, of course, much of this work is done for us, since writers often provide physical descriptions of their characters. Many playwrights do not, since they frequently have no idea who will be cast to play a given role. When reading a play, then, you are in charge of casting. You might find it useful to envision actors you know playing certain roles, again taking your cues from the text as the author presented it. John Goodman as Shakespeare's Falstaff is a reasonable choice; Harrison Ford as Falstaff is probably not.

Finally, when your virtual actors are at their places, remember that to perceive drama as it was intended, you must hear their words, not merely read them. This means reading actively and listening to what you read. Try reading the **dialogue** out loud, or at least with your lips moving. Delivery lies largely in the appropriate placement of emphasis, so try out different ways of reading the lines until you find the most appropriate inflection. Meanwhile, what are the characters doing while they're talking? Some playwrights provide meticulous descriptions of character actions in stage directions, while others, like Shakespeare, provide none, allowing the dialogue itself to guide the actor's interpretation of the character. Generally, the difference between amateur and professional productions of plays can be measured by whether the actors move and speak at the same time. Amateur actors make speeches and then move to the site of the next speech; better actors speak and move naturally. If you're going to the trouble to produce the play for yourself, why not make it a professional production?

Just as in poetry and fiction, we must pay attention to interesting choices in terms of setting and character names. Again, we should ask ourselves, what elements stand out as clues that may help our understanding? Young Prince Hal's enemy in Shakespeare's *Henry IV, Part I* is aptly named Hotspur. He is quick to anger and to action, just as you'd expect from his name. In Williams's play *The Glass Menagerie*, one of the main characters, Tom, is obsessed with escaping his monotonous life with its crowded store of responsibilities. When he returns home after having seen a magician's show and expresses wonder that the magician would free himself from a coffin that has been nailed shut without breaking a single board, we know that he, too, wishes for a quick, painless, magical escape. Our understanding of Susan Glaspell's *Trifles* (included in Part Six) is deepened when we realize that the play was first produced in 1916, before women were even allowed to vote.

As we've stated and restated, the best way to experience drama is to see it performed on the stage. Nevertheless, students will often be called on to read dramatic works for their literature classes. The rules of critical reading and thinking apply to understanding drama (whether one is seeing it performed or reading it on the page) just as they do to understanding fiction and poetry. Both Susan Glaspell's *Trifles* and Alice Childress's *Florence* (in Part Six) are short plays that reward critical reading. Please read them now before we proceed.

Each play is a short, one-act, one-scene dramatic work. Because there are no changes of scenery and no changes of acts, the stage is set only one way throughout each play. All the props are in place to help you understand the entire play. As always, consideration of the setting is a useful way to start your examination of the works. We're not told exactly when *Trifles* is set except that the weather outside is very cold. Given the lack of evidence to the contrary, readers will generally assume that a work is set around the time it is written or published, in this case, 1916. We can't state with certainty that the play is set exactly in 1916, but it is safe to assume that it is set within a few years of that date. Childress's *Florence* was first produced in 1949; we're also told in the stage directions that the play is set in the late 1940s in a "very small town in the South." This is particularly relevant in a play about civil rights and race relations, since it is written and set before the advances in civil rights that we associate with the 1950s and 1960s.

Trifles is a play about women's lives, the hardships women endure, and the inability of some men to understand women; it is set entirely in a kitchen. It's not too much of a generalization to say that at the time, cooking was widely thought in American society to be a domestic duty of wives and women, one of the "trifles" that Hale says women are "used to worrying over" (line 30). *Florence*, on the other hand, is set on a segregated train platform that is divided by a railing into a "white" side and a "colored" side. This division of the stage is in part realism; throughout the South, and in some other parts of the country at this time, whites and blacks were segregated at almost every level. They attended different schools, rode in different areas on buses and on trains, used different bathroom facilities, attended different theaters (or were seated in separate sections), frequented segregated restaurants, and attended segregated churches. Almost always, the segregation was to the detriment of African Americans. The railing on the stage in *Florence*, however, is doing more than just adding to the realism of the play. It clearly represents a greater, more deeply seated racial divide.

Consider the use of names in both plays. In *Trifles*, both the County Attorney and the Sheriff are referred to by their job titles. These men are allowed by society to define themselves by their occupations. The women in the play, however, are referred to by their married names. They are always called "Mrs. Hale," "Mrs. Peters," and "Mrs. Wright." The women are forced to define their sense of themselves through their married lives and their positions as wives. This becomes particularly important when Mrs. Hale starts drawing a distinction between the young single girl, Minnie Foster, and the married woman she becomes, Mrs. Wright.

In *Florence*, the African American characters are either referred to by their given names (Florence, who isn't actually in the play, and Marge, her sister), by familial names (Mama), or by job title (Porter). The white woman is referred to as "Mrs. Carter." In this case, the use of "Mrs." doesn't so much indicate her lack of autonomy as it does the fact that society automatically affords her a modicum of respect merely because she's white.

Both plays make use of literary **symbols** as well. In *Trifles*, the County Attorney finds that the preserves Mrs. Wright has canned (cooked and then stored in Mason jars with screw-down lids) have frozen and burst during the cold night. As a result, the glass is shattered and the jam has made a sticky mess on the shelves. Does this in some way represent Mrs. Wright's life? Has she too been bottled up in a freezing environment until she exploded? Later, Mrs. Hale and Mrs. Peters examine part of a quilt that has been poorly stitched. On the literal level, this is an indication that Mrs. Wright wasn't thinking levelly when she sewed that portion of the quilt. On a more figurative level, we should consider the **connotative meaning** implied by unstitching part of the quilt and then restitching it. Not only are the women covering up evidence of a crime, but in a sense they're "unraveling" a mystery and "putting it together." Furthermore, when we consider how quilts are made by sewing together separate pieces of cloth, does the act of sewing by Mrs. Hale reveal that she is, on some level, connecting with Mrs. Wright?

And of course, what the dead bird and cage represent in the play is fairly obvious; we're told that Minnie Foster was "kind of like a bird herself" (line 107). One can argue that she has in a sense led a caged life. Figuratively, her husband has strangled her emotionally just as he appears to have literally strangled the bird.

Generally speaking, *Florence* is subtler than *Trifles*, but the stage setting of the railing and the divided sides of the platform operates on a symbolic level. One of the only times we see someone crossing the line is when the porter crosses to sweep the other side of the platform. Mama isn't even allowed to cross over to use the women's bathroom. Whites accept the porter on their side because he is operating as a servant, just as the representative of the New York white upper class, Mrs. Carter, assumes that Mama wants Florence to gain employment as domestic help. Mrs. Carter is as much trapped on one side of the platform as Mama is. Mama is trapped by a discriminating and unjust society, and Mrs. Carter is trapped by the prejudices of her upbringing.

Characterization is important to each play, but particularly to *Florence*. We see in Mama an optimistic character who refuses to accept the status quo of racist society just as her daughter Florence (who never appears in the play) strives for success as an actress. Ironically, Mrs. Carter is a woman who obviously considers herself fair and kind-hearted and sympathetic to African Americans as she shows when she describes the **protagonist** of her brother's novel, Zelma. Mrs. Carter says of Zelma, "She can't face it! Living in a world where she almost belongs but not quite. . . . Oh it's so . . . tragic" (line 149). At the same time, however, she is so biased that she cannot comprehend why Mama resents the implication that a black woman would rather be white and is surprised when Mama says, "That ain't so! Not one bit it ain't" (line 150).

Students who read either play must be careful about their focus when writing or discussing the work. The point of *Trifles* is not whether Mrs. Wright actually murdered her husband (everyone in the play, including the two women who become sympathetic to her, has already assumed she is guilty of killing him). A paper arguing that Minnie Foster Wright actually killed John Wright or didn't kill him is beside the point; the question to be answered is why Mrs. Hale and Mrs. Peters don't offer to the County Attorney the circumstantial evidence they've discovered. When writing about *Florence*, students shouldn't just point out how unjust segregation was or how evil racism is (this is a given assumption in the play, or what Henry

James would call a **donnée**); instead, they'd be better off focusing on the use of the railing, and how Mrs. Carter's presumptions power her actions and beliefs. As we explain in Chapter 14, a thesis has to do more for the reader than point out the obvious.

THINKING EXERCISES

1. Susan Glaspell later rewrote *Trifles* as a short story titled "A Jury of Her Peers." Does that title affect your understanding of the play? If so, how?

2. Do you think Mrs. Hale and Mrs. Peters are justified in not showing the County Attorney what they have found? Why or why not?

3. Although Childress's play is titled *Florence*, the title character never appears in the play. Does she instead operate as a literary symbol? How so?

4. If Childress were going to convert *Florence* into a work of prose fiction (as Glaspell did *Trifles*), what would you suggest she title the story? Can you think of a title other than "Florence" that might indicate the theme to us like "A Jury of Her Peers" does?

᧝ 8 ᧞

Analytical Reading

Throughout Part Two, we've tried to give you some advice about analytical reading, since careful, thoughtful reading is an essential prerequisite to writing well about literature. Regardless of the poem, play, or story that is presented to you, try to remember these few basic points:

- Pay attention to the author's choices—character names, setting, manner of speech or clothing.
- Apply the rule of Occam's razor, the philosophical principle that the best explanation is usually the simplest one.
- Never assume that you completely know the author's intent or that the text only has one valid interpretation.

❧ 9 ❧

The Elements of Narrative

The primary thing that most students are asked to do when or after reading works of literature is to *analyze* them. We've gone into great detail in Parts One and Two on how to engage the text through critical reading; going a step further with literature through analysis is a natural progression. In Part Three, we're going to introduce you to (or remind you of) many terms and concepts associated with literary analysis. Although they're not absolutely essential to the appreciation of literature, you'll find that they make discussing it a lot easier. When you write about literature, you will want to incorporate these terms where they're appropriate, but you should avoid using them for their own sake. Nothing is worse than jargon-laden literary analysis that hides its ideas behind fancy terminology.

In its most basic and general sense, to *analyze* something means that you break it down into its component parts and try to comprehend how it all works together. This is true in engineering, in chemistry, and in literary studies. However, to understand how the various parts work together to form a cohesive whole, you must first come to understand the basic components or elements that you are asked to consider.

Although Chapter 9 is titled "The Elements of Narrative," bear in mind that many of the points we consider in it also apply to literary forms that aren't particularly narrative. Furthermore, we must be careful not to be too restrictive in our definition of narrative; it doesn't necessarily mean a story told in prose form. A dramatic work will almost always present a narrative, and many poems are narratives. Too frequently, when we hear "plot," we think of fiction or some other kind of prose narrative. When we hear "symbolism," we may think of poetry, and when we hear "dialogue," we think of drama. Yet many poems are narratives that contain plots; literary fiction often uses just as much symbolic, figurative language as many poems do; and dialogue can be an essential element in poetry or fiction as well as drama.

Considering the nature of literary fundamentals and how they transcend form boundaries and conventions, let's examine these essential elements in terms of how they apply to narrative in its various forms (and even in terms of how they apply to nonnarrative forms).

9.1   PLOT

Plot is most often considered the basic building block of fiction and drama, although it can play an important role in poetry as well. Reduced to its lowest and most simplistic terms, *plot* is the basic action of a narrative or the series of events that occur. Boy meets girl, boy loses girl, boy gets her back, and they kill themselves. Leave off the last clause and you have the plot to not only *Romeo and Juliet* but to almost every romantic comedy ever written, acted, or filmed. Plot is the basic skeleton beneath the body of the story (used here in the generic sense—we could be discussing the story from a narrative poem or a dramatic work) before the veins, arteries, muscles, capillaries, skin, and hair all make it into a complete organism.

Although we've noted that certain types of genre writing, such as suspense or mystery fiction, focus primarily on plot, every narrative has one, even if it's a minor component of the work (as in the case of "Hills Like White Elephants"). Similarly, every narrative also has a **structure**. *Structure* is closely connected to plot. When examining a work's structure, ask, how is the narrative arranged? Chronologically? Or does it start at one point and then tell most of the story through flashbacks? How does one point lead to the next? How is it organized, and how does everything tie together? Is it coherent, cohesive?

One of the most convenient ways of discussing plot is through consideration of **Freytag's pyramid**. Freytag used the geometric shape of a triangle (or pyramid) to visualize a typical plot structure. The left-hand rising slope of the pyramid (the opening of the plot) begins with an introduction to a general scenario or situation. Next comes what Freytag called the "rising action," meaning that the reader comes to understand the full implications and possible repercussions of the characters' actions; the narrative is usually made more complex through introduction of a *conflict* that stymies the characters' designs. The action eventually reaches a **climax**, a point where the various lines of the plot intersect and are in some way resolved; the climax is then followed by a "falling action" or **denouement** that provides overall resolution in the narrative: What does the future hold for these characters? How have they changed due to this occurrence in their lives?

Sometimes Freytag's pyramid is represented more as shown on page 52 than as a true pyramid, reflecting the fact that the resolution is usually much shorter than the rising action.

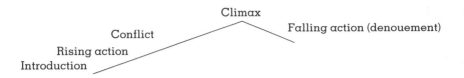

Let's consider Kate Chopin's short story "The Storm" (included in Part Six) in terms of this construction. The introduction lets us know that Bobinôt and his son Bibi are away from the house and Bobinôt's wife, Calixta; then we learn that she is going to be visited by Alcée and that she and he have some kind of past together. A storm is building, and he must wait it out in her company. What episode of *The Young and the Restless* could ask for anything more?

The rising action is indicated by the slow build of sexual tension between Calixta and Alcée; the conflict is both internal and external. Externally, Alcée is trying to seduce Calixta; internally, her conscience and fear of getting caught are at odds with her desire. The climax of the story (a more appropriate term in this case than usual) is obvious (paragraphs 25–28):

> The generous abundance of her passion, without guile or trickery, was like a white flame which penetrated and found response in depths of his own sensuous nature that had never yet been reached.
>
> When he touched her breasts they gave themselves up in quivering ecstasy, inviting his lips. Her mouth was a fountain of delight. And when he possessed her, they seemed to swoon together at the very borderland of life's mystery.
>
> He stayed cushioned upon her, breathless, dazed, enervated, with his heart beating like a hammer upon her. With one hand she clasped his head, her lips lightly touching his forehead. The other hand stroked with a soothing rhythm his muscular shoulders.
>
> The growl of the thunder was distant and passing away. The rain beat softly upon the shingles, inviting them to drowsiness and sleep. But they dared not yield.

The denouement or resolution in this story is interesting, given the context and time of its first publication (1898). Although a reader might expect a moral condemnation or a fall from grace for the lovers, no such thing occurs. Instead, Calixta is not discovered by Bobinôt, and neither she nor Alcée shows any particular remorse at their infidelity. She and Alcée both continue in their separate, happy marriages, happier due to their having succumbed to long-suppressed desires.

Often a plot is helped along through **exposition**. *Exposition* is information provided about the plot, setting, or characters in the text of the story.

Some exposition is always necessary; we won't be able to understand that a novel is about World War I if we aren't told when or where the fighting is taking place. Handled poorly, though, exposition is clunky and intrusive. Think of a television sitcom where the characters are trying to fill you in on their pasts. A friend of Calixta's has just happened over from next door, and states, "What! Alcée is coming over? Good gosh, I remember how you told me he kissed you!" Perhaps we're not being quite fair to the sitcom writers here; since the audience rarely has access to characters' thoughts in dramatic presentations (there are exceptions—the chorus in Greek tragedies, the soliloquy in Elizabethan drama, and the voice-over in modern films as well as in sitcoms), they can only grasp what is happening through things characters say or do. Subtlety is harder in dramatic writing.

Writers analyzing literature have to be careful about how much attention they pay to plot; we all have a tendency to want to recount everything occurring in a given narrative, but we must remember that our readers have read—but not necessarily understood—the text. Focus only on the actions in the plot that directly relate to your argument or main point in your writing, and even then, assume that the reader knows very well the scene or circumstance you're describing.

THINKING EXERCISES

1. Consider a play you have read or seen in terms of Freytag's pyramid. How does the action of the play conform to or vary from the basic pyramid structure? What events precede or follow the play's main climax? How useful is the pyramid in guiding your understanding of the play's plot?
2. Think about a story (short story, novel, play, film, or narrative poem) with which you are familiar, and imagine discussing that plot first with someone who is thoroughly unfamiliar with the story and then with someone who is intimately acquainted with it. How might the focus of these two discussions differ?

9.2   SETTING

The **setting** in a given work of literature is, like the plot, one of most essential and elemental components. Reduced to its most simplistic level, the *setting* is when and where a narrative (whether it's fiction, narrative poetry, or drama) takes place. Genres like westerns and science fiction are categorized as such in large part due to their settings (one is set in the American West during the nineteenth century, and the other is usually set in the future, often in space or on other planets). Sometimes the political or cultural **milieu** (background and circumstances) of a work is essential to our understanding as well.

The setting often has a lot to do with determining the flavor or **tone** of a work. Edgar Allan Poe's gothic masterpiece "The Fall of the House of Usher" begins:

> During the whole of a dull, dark and soundless day in the autumn of the year, when the clouds hung oppressively low in the heavens, I had been passing alone, on horseback, through a singularly dreary tract of country, and at length found myself, as the shades of the evening drew on, within view of the melancholy House of Usher.

The dark and mordant mood of the story is clearly indicated by the description of the setting in this opening passage; the reader knows at an almost instinctual level that what is to follow most likely won't be happy. Similarly, in Robert Hayden's poem "Those Winter Sundays" (included in Part Six), the speaker's description of the early morning cold "splintering, breaking" as the fire warms the house suggests the brittleness and fragility of the relationship between the speaker and his father.

Often the setting does far more than indicate the genre or the tone of a given work. In Chapter 5, we discussed how the **themes** of Hemingway's "Hills Like White Elephants" and Joyce's "Araby" are first revealed through the symbolic use of setting (the one story taking place at a railroad station between two lines of tracks and the other beginning on a "blind" street). Robert Frost's "Desert Places" (in section 6.1) works in part because it counters our expectations with its setting; indeed, many narrative poems depend greatly on setting for both their symbolic value and their worth in creating mood. Langston Hughes's poem "Theme for English B" (included in Part Six) assumes that most of its readers will understand the race- and class-oriented cultural dichotomies between the Ivy League institution Columbia University in New York and the borough of Harlem, which is adjacent to the university. The setting is key to establishing Hughes's theme of crossing racial boundaries.

Charlotte Perkins Gilman's story "The Yellow Wallpaper" (included in Part Six) makes much use of setting. The narrator has been prescribed a "rest cure" in a country estate she and her husband have rented for the summer. Although the narrator is presumably there to better her state of mental health, readers can't help but note that the windows to her room are barred, the bed is nailed down, and there is a "gate at the head of the stairs" (paragraph 53). Whether the narrator understands it or not at the beginning of the story (she presumes that the windows have been barred to keep children from falling out of the room, which she surmises might once have been a nursery), readers realize that at some level the setting is implying that the narrator is trapped or at least impeded by the surroundings and her situation.

Our appreciation of the story is developed further when we consider the cultural setting as well. "The Yellow Wallpaper" was published in 1892, and given the lack of contradictory evidence, the reader may assume that the story is set in the time period shortly before the year of publication. We would probably be safe in making the generalization that many women were forced by the gender biases and discriminatory practices of the day to lead lives that may have been unfulfilling to them; the circumstances of their lives must have kept many of them behind the figurative bars of a sexist society.

We may occasionally have to perform a little research (as well as pay close attention) when casual comments in a text refer us to people or events that would be recognizable in the author's cultural context but not in ours. A good example is when the narrator worries that her husband will send her "to Weir Mitchell in the fall" (paragraph 86). Although the name is not familiar to us now, it would have been quite familiar to the audience of 1892 (reacting much as modern audiences would if a contemporary character mused about being "sent to Betty Ford"). A convenient footnote in this case helps us understand just a bit more about the "rest cure" and the social context and setting.

While plays may use setting in the same ways that fiction and poetry do (to establish tone or mood or for symbolic effect), playwrights are also confronted with the challenge of using a limited number of set designs on a stage. In this case, the various objects and props that make up the set stage can be of great importance. The visual composition of materials and props on the stage is sometimes referred to by the French term *mise en scène* (literally, "placed on the stage"). Consider this excerpt from the scene description at the beginning of act 1, scene 1 of Lorraine Hansberry's play *A Raisin in the Sun*. The play is about a working-class African American family, the Youngers, who are saving enough money to move to a better neighborhood.

> [F]urnishings are typical and undistinguished and their primary feature now is that they have clearly had to accommodate the living of too many people for too many years—and they are tired. Still, we can see that at some time, a time probably no longer remembered by the family . . . [they] were actually selected with care and love and even hope—and brought to this apartment and arranged with taste and pride.
>
> That was a long time ago. Now the once loved pattern of the couch upholstery has to fight to show itself from under acres of crocheted doilies and couch covers which have themselves finally come to be more important than the upholstery. And here a table or a chair has been moved to disguise the worn places in the carpet. . . . Weariness has, in fact, won in this room. Everything has been polished, washed, sat on, used, scrubbed too often.

This may all seem a little too obvious to the reader of the play; clearly, the family is worn out. The family's lives in this place have beaten them down. But remember that a play is ordinarily intended not to be read but to be performed; audience members have to view the stage with a critical eye to realize what the set pieces say about the mood, tone, and themes of the play, since presumably they wouldn't have easy access to the description in the script.

Verisimilitude is another element of setting that also applies to character, plot, and other components of literature. A work can be said to possess *verisimilitude* when it tries to give a "true semblance" of life—that is, when a narrative attempts to be as realistic as possible. Characters speak the way they should speak, they live where and as they should live, and their actions are the actions of real people. For example, *A Raisin in the Sun* wouldn't be entirely realistic if Hansberry had her lower-working-class, African American characters speaking with British accents and discussing water polo. Instead, she has them speak with the kind of diction and syntax that would be appropriate to her characters.

The weight placed on verisimilitude naturally varies greatly from work to work. Over the course of its many years on television, the action show *Walker, Texas Ranger* has seen an absurd number of gunfights, hand-to-hand battles, and car wrecks. In one sense, the show lacks verisimilitude; it isn't really true to life. It's probably not much of a leap to assume that Walker has shot more than a hundred felons over the course of the series; in real life, any peace officers who found it necessary to discharge their firearms that routinely would at least be under investigation and would quite probably be in jail. Yet even within this nonrealistic television series, there is a kind of verisimilitude. Walker can't fly like Superman or block bullets like Wonder Woman. Rules of the physical universe apply. Even science fiction and fantasy writing can develop a kind of verisimilitude to which individual works must adhere.

Finally, before you begin writing about the setting in a given work of literature, make sure that you have a good reason for discussing the setting in your paper. Setting might sometimes be automatic. New York writers might naturally set their stories in Manhattan, for example, without necessarily attaching the specific meaning to that setting that a filmmaker like Woody Allen does. There's usually no need to discuss setting just for the sake of discussing it; again, your reader has read the same text you have. Rather, focus on the setting only when a consideration of it will particularly add to your overall argument or point. Our understandings of "Hills Like White Elephants," "Desert Places," and "Araby" are all greatly enriched by our consideration of setting; our appreciation of Gary Soto's "Oranges" (included in Part Six) depends less on the setting than it does characterization.

THINKING EXERCISES

1. In a narrative with a clearly identifiable setting, examine the author's *method* of communicating setting. What connotations about the narrative are implied by the setting? What role, if any, does setting play in your understanding of the work as a whole?

2. Consider a narrative in which the setting is unspecified or unclear. What external evidence (author's biography, story's publication date) might be useful to theorize a setting for the narrative? What internal evidence can you identify to support or contradict these conjectures?

3. We commonly use clothing styles, hairstyles, and modes of transportation to identify when films and television shows are set. But frequently, the trends depicted on the screen are polluted to some degree by the fashions in vogue during the production of the film or show. Can you think of a non-contemporary film or TV show where the styles of clothes and hair relate more to the era in which the narrative was filmed than to the time being depicted?

9.3   CHARACTER

Characters, of course, are the persons created by an author in a given work to people the narrative and to perform the actions of a given narrative. Many of a character's basic characteristics may be a function of setting and plot; if a work is about an English constable in 1870, the character will most likely be a physically capable white English male. The characters' feelings about money, sexism, race, or the government may be a function of their class, ethnicity, nationality, or gender, particularly if the author is paying attention to **verisimilitude** and is trying hard to create realistic characters. Insofar as understanding characters is concerned, however, their actions are more important than basic physical traits like hair, weight, and height, just as in real life.

F. Scott Fitzgerald died in 1940 before he completed his final novel, *The Last Tycoon*. However, the end of the original edition of the book contains various notes and fragments that Fitzgerald was using to complete the novel; one of these reads, "Character is action." What Fitzgerald may have meant by that notation is that we determine who a character *is* by what that character *does*. The primary rule of writing, that one should "show and not tell," is always important to bear in mind when considering a character.

Characters can be hard to grasp sometimes. Perhaps one states aloud, over and over, that she is mean and vicious, yet again and again we see her perform acts of kindness. As readers, we realize that this character may be modest or have issues with self-esteem, but in fact she is a kind and caring individual. Mark Twain's Huckleberry Finn is just such a character; as the narrator in *The Adventures of Huckleberry Finn* (published in 1885), he is sure that he will be damned by both society and God for helping the slave Jim escape from bondage. He feels that he is an awful person, not for the racism that has been conditioned into him by the slave-owning society of the 1840s (and for which modern audiences may judge him harshly) but because he is working against that same society. As readers, we realize that helping Jim escape is his chance for at least partial redemption.

Huck will also help us consider characters in another way. At the beginning of Twain's novel, Huck is just as casually racist as anyone else. By the end, however, Huck knows that Jim is one of his best friends. It would be wrong to think that Huck will become a crusader for race equality after the events that have transpired in the novel, but he has certainly learned. He has grown and developed and is therefore a *round character*. Round characters are dynamic. They reflect on their actions, and they undergo changes and progress. *Flat characters*, by contrast, are characters who stay the same no matter what they have encountered. It's easy for flat characters to devolve into **stereotypes**: the dumb jock, the brave sheriff, the wisecracking detective, the sultry femme fatale.

The central character in a narrative is often referred to as the **protagonist**. Note that it's not always accurate to call the protagonist the "hero" of the story, since in many narratives the main character is not at all heroic. Generally speaking, the plot of most narratives works to introduce a protagonist and the challenges besetting that character and shows how the protagonist will resolve those various problems. A character who works against the protagonist is called the **antagonist**. Frequently, literary narratives lack a clearly defined antagonist; their protagonists are often working against their own foibles.

When writing about character, it's tempting to spend time merely describing the character as depicted in the narrative; yet this is seldom useful to a reader who is familiar with the work in question, and it's perilously easy to descend from there into pure subjectivity, talking about which characters are engaging and which are despicable. Literary analysis doesn't really come into play until you consider what strategies the author has used to depict the characters and guide readers' perceptions and attitudes toward them. These strategies are known as **characterization**, and if you want to discuss characters in narratives, you will find that you have a lot more to say if you focus on how each character is revealed—through description, dialogue, and actions—rather than what kind of "virtual person" the literary character is.

THINKING EXERCISES

1. When you meet a flesh-and-blood person, what elements contribute to your first impression of his or her personality? In what order do you take in these elements? How is this similar to or different from the way characters are introduced in your favorite narrative?

2. Identify a protagonist from fiction, drama, or film who cannot be considered a hero. Does the characterization encourage you to identify with the character in spite of his or her flaws, or are you intended to stand in judgment of the character? What clues in the narrative control your allegiance to this flawed character?

9.4   DIALOGUE

Dialogue literally means a conversation between two people; however, in terms of literature, we can apply it to any conversation between characters. Most important, dialogue provides a way for authors to convey information about characters or plot to the readers, not directly but through the mouths of their characters.

As discussed previously, dialogue is one of the main tools authors have to accomplish **characterization**. In addition to whatever facts are baldly presented in a character's dialogue itself, readers learn things about the character's mood, social class, education, and background from how the person speaks. This indirect method of characterization is especially effective if an author is aiming for **verisimilitude** and plausible characters. Is the character young and hip or old and exceedingly formal? Is it a young character who speaks in the manner of an older, formally educated person? Just as we formulate impressions about real people we meet based on how they speak, we can also tell a lot about literary characters from their style of speech.

Similarly, authors may present **exposition** through dialogue; however, they must be careful not to have the speakers recite mountains of useful information in a totally unrealistic way. Imagine a conversation between Sue and Jack in which Jack says, "Oh, remember that debilitating spinal condition I have that we rarely speak of? Well, I'm still saving up for an operation someday!" Presumably, Sue knows Jack well enough that his mentioning his condition and the operation in such a way is absurd. If the characters are intended to be seen as realistic, the author would be better off presenting this background information more subtly. Drama, in particular, is required to make use of dialogue to establish themes, introduce background information, and set the tone.

Sometimes speakers will reveal their entire personalities, even confess to crimes, through dialogue, possibly without realizing they're doing so. Consider the following poem by the English poet Robert Browning.

My Last Duchess
(1842)

Ferrara:

That's my last Duchess painted on the wall,
Looking as if she were alive. I call
That piece a wonder, now: Frà Pandolf's hands
Worked busily a day, and there she stands.
Will't please you sit and look at her? I said   5
"Frà Pandolf" by design, for never read
Strangers like you that pictured countenance,
The depth and passion of its earnest glance,

But to myself they turned (since none puts by
The curtain I have drawn for you, but I)   *10*
And seemed as they would ask me, if they durst,
How such a glance came there; so, not the first
Are you to turn and ask thus. Sir, 'twas not
Her husband's presence only, called that spot
Of joy into the Duchess' cheek: perhaps   *15*
Frà Pandolf chanced to say, "Her mantle laps
Over my Lady's wrist too much," or "Paint
Must never hope to reproduce the faint
Half-flush that dies along her throat"; such stuff
Was courtesy, she thought, and cause enough   *20*
For calling up that spot of joy. She had
A heart . . . how shall I say? . . . too soon made glad,
Too easily impressed; she liked whate'er
She looked on, and her looks went everywhere.
Sir, 'twas all one! My favour at her breast,   *25*
The dropping of the daylight in the West,
The bough of cherries some officious fool
Broke in the orchard for her, the white mule
She rode with round the terrace—all and each
Would draw from her alike the approving speech,   *30*
Or blush, at least. She thanked men,—good; but thanked
Somehow . . . I know not how . . . as if she ranked
My gift of a nine-hundred-years-old name
With anybody's gift. Who'd stoop to blame
This sort of trifling? Even had you skill   *35*
In speech—(which I have not)—to make your will
Quite clear to such an one, and say, "Just this
Or that in you disgusts me; here you miss,
Or there exceed the mark"—and if she let
Herself be lessoned so, nor plainly set   *40*
Her wits to yours, forsooth, and made excuse,
—E'en then would be some stooping; and I choose
Never to stoop. Oh, sir, she smiled, no doubt,
Whene'er I passed her; but who passed without
Much the same smile? This grew; I gave commands;   *45*
Then all smiles stopped together. There she stands
As if alive. Will't please you rise? We'll meet
The company below, then. I repeat,
The Count your Master's known munificence
Is ample warrant that no just pretence   *50*
Of mine for dowry will be disallowed;
Though his fair daughter's self, as I avowed
At starting, is my object. Nay, we'll go
Together down, sir! Notice Neptune, though,
Taming a sea-horse, thought a rarity,   *55*
Which Claus of Innsbruck cast in bronze for me.

"My Last Duchess" is a **dramatic monologue**, meaning the poem is intended as a speech by an individual to a listener or an audience (as opposed to an internal rumination, as we find in most first-person-narrated poems, such as Frost's "Desert Places"). The character's speech in this poem is made to serve the dual purpose of establishing the setting and action of the poem and providing characterization of the speaker himself. Browning gives us clues about what's being depicted in the poem. The Duke of Ferrara speaks, providing subtle clues about the identity of his auditor, who is not explicitly identified as an emissary employed by a count until line 49. The duke's speech also suggests that he and his auditor have withdrawn from a larger group (lines 47–48) to arrange the terms of the coming wedding (lines 49–53). The auditor apparently offers to leave the duke alone to mourn for his "last duchess," judging from the duke's reaction in line 53. Thus the duke's speech hints at the existence of an entire narrative, as Browning subtly employs dialogue in the service of plot and setting exposition.

Even more significant are the duke's apparently unwitting (or uncaring) revelations about his own character. Ironically, his catalog of his late wife's shortcomings tells more about him than about his deceased wife. His character flaws come to the reader from the most unimpeachable of sources: his own mouth. Even without the helpful use of **symbols** (particularly the bronze sculpture of Neptune "taming a sea-horse"), readers easily realize that the speaker is a cold and controlling man. Such lines as "She had / A heart . . . how shall I say? . . . too soon made glad" (lines 21–22) and "I choose / Never to stoop" (lines 42–43) combine with "This grew; I gave commands; / Then all smiles stopped together" (lines 45–46) to chill the reader. Although the duke may wish to present himself to the emissary as a perfectly reasonable suitor, his manner and speech give him away as an arrogant, self-centered, and possibly abusive, even murderous, man.

THINKING EXERCISES

1. Browning characterizes the Duke of Ferrara entirely through dialogue. In addition to the passages identified in the text, what parts of the poem suggest the duke's controlling nature? What examples of particularly noteworthy dialogue have you read recently? How does the dialogue reveal setting, plot, or characterization?

2. Eavesdrop (subtly!) on a conversation in a public place. How much or how little can you learn about the speakers based on your brief observations?

9.5 THEME

We've already discussed **theme** at some length in the previous chapters. At its simplest level, *theme* is an idea or point being put forward by a work. The

major theme of a work would be the one that it is most focused on discussing, whether implicitly, through a subtextual use of symbolism and
figurative language, or explicitly. At the same time, a work may have several concurrent themes. James Joyce's "Araby" (in Part Six) simultaneously
conveys the themes of disillusionment, young love, and initiation into adulthood, among possible others.

Certain themes appear so often in literature that they seem to be universal. The canon is replete with works about our human struggle with the
inevitability of our mortality, from Dante's *The Divine Comedy* to Dylan
Thomas's "Do Not Go Gentle into That Good Night," from Jean Toomer's
"Reapers" to Robert Pinsky's "Dying." Another very familiar theme is *carpe
diem*, or "seize the day." The main sentiment of this theme might be
expressed as "Live life to its fullest now, because you don't live forever."
This theme appears in Marvell's "To His Coy Mistress," Longfellow's
"A Psalm of Life," Eliot's "The Love Song of J. Alfred Prufrock," Whitman's
Song of Myself, and any number of other works. Even subjects as dark and
seemingly individualistic as parental abuse show up often (Plath's "Daddy,"
Roethke's "My Papa's Waltz," Allison's *Bastard out of Carolina*).

If figurative language is used in a consistent or repetitive way to indicate
the theme, that usage constitutes a **motif**. Consider this excerpt from
"Araby" (paragraph 3); we have underlined words for emphasis.

> The space of sky above us was the colour of ever-changing violet and
> towards it the lamps of the street lifted their feeble lanterns. The cold air
> stung us and we played till our bodies glowed. Our shouts echoed in the
> silent street. The career of our play brought us through the <u>dark</u> muddy
> lanes behind the houses where we ran the gauntlet of the rough tribes from
> the cottages, to the back doors of the <u>dark</u> dripping gardens where odours
> arose from the ashpits, to the <u>dark</u> odorous stables where a coachman
> smoothed and combed the horse or shook music from the buckled harness.
> When we returned to the street <u>light</u> from the kitchen windows had filled
> the areas. . . . [I]f Mangan's sister came out on the doorstep to call her
> brother in to his tea we watched her from our <u>shadow</u> peer up and down the
> street. We waited to see whether she would remain or go in and, if she
> remained, we left our <u>shadow</u> and walked up to Mangan's steps resignedly.

The use of light, dark, and shadow in "Araby" is a motif that helps convey
thematic meaning. In this case, the narrator in "Araby" is literally in the dark
when it comes to understanding young women (or Mangan's sister, at least)
and his own feelings. This motif coincides with the story's use of "blindness"
and the narrator's return to darkness at the end of the story.

We've used Joyce's "Araby" as an example in this section partly because
Joyce appropriated the religious term **epiphany** in describing his fiction. An
epiphany occurs when a character has developed over the course of a work to
the point of gaining a sudden insight into her or his situation or circumstances.

The narrator's realization that he's made a fool of himself at the end of "Araby" is his epiphany as well as an essential part of growing up.

As we've indicated throughout this book, *theme*, in its various representations, will often be your primary focus when writing analyses. Many writing assignments may ask you to consider or explore a particular theme or motif in a given work as a way of involving you further with the text. Remember (as we'll examine in more detail later on) that pointing out the existence of a theme in a given piece is rarely enough; you have to prove why your recognition of the theme is essential to your understanding of the work.

THINKING EXERCISES

1. Because themes describe very general issues, it's possible that very different works might have themes in common. In your experience as a reader, what themes have you encountered most frequently? Are there certain themes that appeal to you more than others?

2. An image or reference must be repeated in order to be identified as a motif. In a work you've read recently or are currently reading that contains an identifiable motif, when did you recognize that the repetition had special significance?

9.6   POINT OF VIEW

Point of view refers to the standpoint of the speaker who is telling a given narrative or through whose mind the narrative is being filtered. There are several points of view, each with its own strengths and weaknesses. Point of view is one of the most essential components for authors to consider in constructing their narratives.

First-Person Point of View

A narrative in the **first person** is told by a narrator who is actually a participant in the events of the particular story, either as a **protagonist** or as a side character observing the action from a distance. The first-person point of view is generally characterized by a narrator who refers to himself or herself as "I." Huck Finn tells his own story in *The Adventures of Huckleberry Finn,* so the point of view is first-person. The Duke of Ferrara discusses his former wife with the emissary of the count in "My Last Duchess," so that work too is narrated in the first person. Joyce's "Araby" is another example, in which the apparently adult narrator recounts his experiences as a child.

Occasionally, we don't know the identity of the first-person narrator of a piece. As in "Araby," the narrator of "The Purloined Letter" by Poe is never named; similarly, we're never told the name of the traveler in Frost's "Desert Places" or "The Road Not Taken." Students often make the mistake of referring to the narrator by the author's name, especially when referring to what seems to be an intensely personal poem like "Desert Places." Such assumptions are dangerous, however. Poets create characters to speak for them as often as fiction writers do, although the narrator's identity is often less obvious than Ferrara's in "My Last Duchess." When writing about a poem like "Desert Places," don't refer to the speaker as "Frost"; instead, use the term *speaker* or *narrator*.

Third-Person Omniscient Point of View

A narrative in the *third-person omniscient* point of view is told by a narrator who is not part of the action of the story and who most often has no character at all; the narrative will dip into the thoughts of any number of characters in the story. Older escapist fiction often worked this way: "Cowboy Bob looked at Calamity Kate and thought he'd like to ask her to the Hootenanny. Looking back across the saloon at Cowboy Bob, Calamity Kate thought she wouldn't go to the dance with him if he were the last cowpoke on the prairie. Meanwhile, forty miles away, Dangerous Dalton and his desperate band of desperados rode toward Deadwood." Readers know what is going on in Bob's mind, in Kate's mind, and on the prairie forty miles away. Kate Chopin's story "The Storm" leaps from Bibi's and Bobinôt's points of view to Calixta's and at times to Alcée's. By breaking her story up into sections, however, Chopin keeps her use of varying perspectives from being as clumsy as our Cowboy Bob and Calamity Kate example.

Third-Person Limited Point of View

A narrative told through use of the *third-person limited* point of view is told by a detached narrator who is not a character in the story, but the story itself is focused through the consciousness of a single character. The reader is presented with only that character's perspective on what's happening. If we were to rework our example about Cowboy Bob into the *third-person limited*, the reader would know only what Cowboy Bob thinks and knows: "Cowboy Bob looked at Calamity Kate and thought he'd like to ask her to the Hootenanny. He ambled up to her and asked, 'Would you like to go to the dance with me on Friday?'"

When Bob approaches Calamity Kate to ask her to the dance, we are in suspense—will she say yes or no? The omniscient narrative leaves little mystery; readers already know that she'll turn him down and that shortly Dangerous Dalton and his gang will invade Deadwood. In the third-person limited version, by contrast, both Kate's refusal and the arrival of the group of marauders will come as a surprise. In modern fiction, third-person narratives more typically use limited rather than omniscient narrators. Henry James's *Daisy Miller* is told in the third-person limited, for example; the events of the story are filtered through Winterbourne's consciousness. Some writers like to have it both ways; in long, suspenseful, plot-driven novels (like those written by Tom Clancy), the narration will often leap from character to character in different sections, but not within a given scene.

Third-Person Objective Point of View

Occasionally, the third-person limited point of view is taken to such an extreme that readers have no idea what the characters are thinking at all; everything we know about the characters is derived from the dialogue and actions. This is called the *third-person objective* because readers are never given an insight into the characters' subjective points of view; rather, we must judge, evaluate, or analyze them from a more distant and more objective standpoint. Almost all drama works this way, with the occasional exception of characters who speak directly to the audience about their thoughts (many of Shakespeare's plays contain such passages, known as **soliloquies**). The third-person objective point of view is sometimes referred to as the *dramatic* point of view.

"Hills Like White Elephants" is written in the third-person objective. Consider how different the story would be if we saw everything through the man's eyes or if we had deeper access to Jig's thoughts. Certainly, the ending of the story would be less ambiguous, and there wouldn't be any confusion about the subject of their discussion—but the story's impact would be diminished.

Style and Experimentation in Point of View

Some characters represented through first-person narration in fiction seem so idiosyncratic and real to the reader that their voices take on a legitimacy of their own; by the end of *The Adventures of Huckleberry Finn*, the reader almost feels that Huck is a real person. Many of literature's most beloved characters are distinguished by the tone and voice of the first-person narration of their stories, from Pip in Charles Dickens's *Great Expectations* to the title character in Charlotte Brontë's *Jane Eyre* to Holden Caulfield in J. D. Salinger's *The Catcher in the Rye*.

To capture this feel of an interior voice, writers will sometimes have their third-person narration become so immersed in the character's consciousness that the result incorporates elements of first-person narration. For example, consider this sequence from Toni Morrison's *Sula* when Nel is forced by the latest of a string of calamities to face an uncertain future:

> Sweating with fear, she stepped to the kitchen door and onto the back porch. The lilac bushes preened at the railing, but there were no lilacs yet. Wasn't it

time? Surely it was time. She looked over the fence to Mrs. Rayford's yard. Hers were not in bloom either. Was it too late? (109)

Although the first two sentences are told from the third-person limited point of view, the query "Wasn't it time?" and the affirmation "Surely it was time" both come from Nel's perspective. The shift from third-person to first-person discourse is even more apparent in this excerpt from Hemingway's novel *For Whom the Bell Tolls*:

> The night was clear and his head felt as clear and cold as the air. He smelled the odor of the pine boughs under him, the piney smell of the crushed needles and the sharper odor of the resinous sap from the cut limbs. . . . This is the smell I love. This and fresh cut clover, the crushed sage as you ride after cattle, wood-smoke and burning leaves of autumn. That must be the odor of nostalgia, the smell of the smoke from the piles of rake leaves burning in the streets in the fall in Missoula. Which would you rather smell? Sweet grass the Indians used in their baskets? Smoked leather? The odor of the ground in the spring after rain? (260)

At times, first-person narration or third-person narration that approaches the first person in this manner will attempt to reflect the flow and free association of human thought; this technique is called **stream of consciousness**. One of the greatest (and earliest) examples of stream of consciousness comes from James Joyce's 1922 novel *Ulysses*. Leopold Bloom is leaving his house to attend a funeral:

> He crossed to the bright side, avoiding the loose cellarflap of number seventy-five. The sun was nearing the steeple of George's church. Be a warm day I fancy. Specially in these black clothes feel it more. Black conducts, reflects (refracts is it?) the heat. But I couldn't go in that light suit. Make a picnic of it. His eyelids sank quietly often as he walked in happy warmth. (57)

In this excerpt, we move from the third-person limited viewpoint to Leopold's consciousness; then we follow his chain of thoughts: black clothes will make the day even warmer, because the color either conducts, reflects—or perhaps the right word is refracts—the heat, but it would not be appropriate to wear a light and cooler suit to a funeral.

THINKING EXERCISES

1. Identify the point of view of whatever literary works you're reading currently, and try to imagine how they could be presented from different points of view. To what degree does their effect depend on point of view?

2. Do you have a favorite point of view? If so, which point of view is your favorite? Why do you think this is so?

3. If you were writing a story, what point of view would you be likely to use? Why?

9.7 TONE

Expressed at its simplest level, **tone** is the implicit or explicit attitude of the writer (or the **implied author**) toward the subject matter of a given work. Usually, readers are able to understand tone in terms of the emotions expressed by or within the piece. Is it humorous? Sad? Does it use sarcasm to be both funny and sad at the same time? Clearly, the tone throughout "Hills Like White Elephants" is one of tension and worry. Without the tone, the use of symbolic setting and the discursive rambling dialogue, with its mentions of an "operation," wouldn't cohere for the reader. However, the terse dialogue does indicate the tone for us, as shown in a few of the couple's remarks and rejoinders. Consider this exchange in the early part of the story (paragraphs 9–12):

> "They look like white elephants," she said.
> "I've never seen one," the man drank his beer.
> "No, you wouldn't have."
> "I might have," the man said. "Just because you say I wouldn't have doesn't prove anything."

His minimal, distracted reply to her first statement about the hills shows that he is worried; on the other hand, Jig's response shows the tension she feels, and he replies in kind. Things heat up when he says that what they're considering is "really an awfully simple operation" (paragraph 42) and that the need for the operation (her pregnancy) is the "only thing that's made us unhappy" (paragraph 50). Finally he says, "I've known lots of people that have done it." The sarcasm in her reply is palpable: "So have I. . . . And afterward they were all so happy" (paragraphs 53–54).

Similarly, a significant part of Shakespeare's meaning in Sonnet 130 (see section 6.2) is determined by the narrator's tone during the poem. Sonnet 130 has a playful tone throughout most of the poem (as shown by the rather comic comparisons to more goddesslike mistresses and choices of words like *reeks*). The playful tone is, on the one hand, appropriate to Shakespeare's toying with the rather inflated tone of love poems in the **sonnet** genre. On the other hand, it makes the declaration of love in the shift at the end of the sonnet when the speaker states, "And yet by heaven, I think my love as rare / As any she belied with false compare" (lines 13–14), all the more striking.

The tone of "My Last Duchess" is rather pompous, like the duke himself. Even if the reader hasn't identified the Duke of Ferrara's arrogance when he complains that his late wife's heart was "too soon made glad" (line 22), his scornful "and I choose / Never to stoop" makes his personality clear (lines 42–43).

Tone is often tied to the voice of a particular work. Readers tend to consider voice a function of first-person narration (consider the examples of Twain, Salinger, and Dickens cited earlier), but more stylized third-person narrations also show their own idiosyncratic voices, as exemplified by writers like James Joyce, Virginia Woolf, and Gabriel García Márquez.

Generally, most analytical papers won't focus too heavily on tone (unless your instructor assigns a particular topic on it), but tone can often point you in the right direction during your reading. At some level, we know that things won't work out in the end for the boy in "Araby" and Mangan's sister because of the melancholy tone of the story. We know that the woman and man in "Hills Like White Elephants" are angry and tense about something momentous in their lives because of that piece's tone. We realize that Chopin's short story "The Storm" is not going to be a diatribe against adultery because of its tone. Occasionally, tone is understated and carefully nuanced by the writer; the reader must be careful to catch the subtle shadings.

THINKING EXERCISES

1. Although the literary use of the word *tone* is in part a metaphorical reference to the world of music, and we use our "tone of voice" to assist listeners in understanding our speech, writers must control tone with only words and punctuation on the page. In a poem or story that you have read recently, try to identify exactly which words, phrases, and sentences establish the tone.

2. Do you find yourself drawn to works of a certain tone? Do you enjoy comedic stories more, or somber, sad ones? Bittersweet or silly? Consider your favorite books, movies, poems, plays, or songs; do they share similar moods and tone?

✦ 10 ✦

Figurative Language

Although we use **figures of speech** every day in conversation and in the most mundane writing tasks, it is probably true that **figurative language** occurs much more frequently in literary writing than in other kinds of communication. Interpreting figures of speech can be very difficult, because one of the defining characteristics of a figure of speech is that, depending on the type of figure, it either means something other than what it literally says (which we define as a **trope**) or it says what it means in an interesting or surprising way for artistic effect (a **rhetorical device**). These categories are provisional; many instances of figurative language are difficult to classify according to any preconceived system. Clearly, the use of figurative language opens up the danger of misinterpretation, which is why it is more suited to literature than to medicine, for instance, or architecture. But for writers, the risk of misinterpretation is more than outweighed by the possibility of communicating ideas in new and different ways. An architect designing a skyscraper might describe its height in feet and inches; a poet might say it reaches toward heaven or even compare it to the Tower of Babel. Each art speaks its own language.

The relationship between words and what they refer to is always a slippery issue. Think about it for a moment: what is it about the sound of the word *dog*, for instance, that means what we think of as a dog? Nothing—at least nothing inherent. The word *dog* refers to the animal we all know simply because we know it does; language relies on tradition and consensus, not on any intrinsic relationship between words and ideas. Figurative language takes this shaky relationship and stretches its limits even further. Metaphors, similes, symbols, intentional ambiguities, and other kinds of figurative language intentionally widen the gap between what is said and what is meant, forcing the reader to examine connections that are usually taken for granted.

Those ambiguous spaces are where literary art happens; as we have been suggesting all along, the most interesting literary texts are those that encourage and reward readers who are willing to work to cross those gaps.

10.1   TROPES

Many tropes suggest comparisons. One of the most easily identified of these is the **simile**, an explicitly stated comparison often signaled by the word *like* or *as*. Consider these lines (81–86) from Christina Rossetti's poem "Goblin Market" (included in Part Six):

> Laura stretch'd her gleaming neck
> Like a rush-imbedded swan,
> Like a lily from the beck,
> Like a moonlit poplar branch,
> Like a vessel at the launch
> When its last restraint is gone.

Notice the series of "Like . . ." lines that compare Laura's gesture to various images. These images are appropriate to both the setting and the tone. At first, the simile comparing her stretching forth her neck to a swan doing the same thing is very straightforward. The swan is a graceful bird whose neck appears vulnerable. The comparison to the lily in the next line underscores both the character's beauty and her fragility even further. The final simile in the passage, comparing her gesture to a vessel's being launched from its mooring, is visually more distant from the actual scene being described, but the idea of her having slipped her last restraint is apt in other ways. Though all similes do indeed compare things or ideas that are fundamentally different, the distance between the compared concepts can vary.

While similes, due to their signaling words *like* and *as*, are usually easy to recognize, metaphors are a little trickier, even though the metaphor is one of the most common tropes. On the simplest level, a **metaphor** is a comparison in which a word is applied to an idea that is not the literal meaning of that word. John Donne's *Meditation 17* is a virtual compendium of metaphors (the highly elaborate and sustained metaphors favored by Donne and other poets are, incidentally, known as **conceits**). Donne writes, "No man is an island, entire of itself; every man is a piece of the continent, a part of the main." This often-quoted metaphor exemplifies the function of metaphor. We know that no person is literally an island, but what is it about islands that Donne is saying does not apply to humanity? Islands are detached landmasses, so Donne seems to be saying that people are fundamentally attached to other people, as suggested by his comparison of a man to a piece of a continent. Donne knows that people are not islands, and we know that he's not trying to say that people are geological or geographical features; as mature readers, we are used to metaphor. But Donne, with his use of the metaphysical conceit, makes his metaphors surprising and explicit, forcing the reader to sort out the various possible relationships between the actual subject of his metaphor (often called the *tenor*) and the metaphorical term applied to it (often called the *vehicle*). In some metaphors, the relationship between tenor and vehicle is readily apparent, but in others, it is much more open to ambiguity or multiple interpretations.

Metaphors contribute to the pattern of imagery in a given literary work. **Imagery** is a rather slippery term used to refer to a given work's collection of images: an *image* is a vivid, concrete representation of some kind of sensory perception or perceptible object. Imagery can play a major role in the impression a literary work has on its readers, and careful attention to the imagery in a work can reveal subtle clues about its meaning.

Closely related to both imagery and the image, a **symbol**, simply put, is something that stands for something else. Unlike the vehicle component of a metaphor, the symbol is something that exists in the world of the text, like the bronze statue in "My Last Duchess," presented in section 9.4; unlike the image, the symbol suggests a specific meaning beyond or outside of its literal meaning. Some symbols are cultural (the cross, for instance, or the Union Jack), while others are specific to a particular author or work. It's important to remember that a symbol's meaning can be fluid and open to interpretation. Writing effectively about symbolism requires more than tallying symbols; it also requires analyzing their meaning and effect on the work as a whole.

Just as words and phrases can work locally as symbols or metaphors, whole works can also function in these ways. An **allegory**, for instance, is a narrative work that makes sense on the literal level but also suggests a reasonably coherent system of meaning on another level. Some allegories, like the medieval play *Everyman* or John Bunyan's epic, *The Pilgrim's Progress*, make their allegorical nature obvious through the use of naming conventions. The protagonist of Bunyan's narrative, for instance, is a man named Christian who embarks on a journey of self-discovery, guided at the outset by a character named Evangelist; later he meets characters named Pliant and Obstinate and gets bogged down in the Slough of Despond. Obviously, character names offer clues, and the reader's understanding of the story depends on the relationships between and among the abstract ideas and the characters and settings that represent them.

Other allegories are less obvious. Take Nathaniel Hawthorne's short story "Young Goodman Brown." Set in the Puritan town of Salem, Massachusetts, at roughly the same time as the infamous witch trials of the 1690s, "Young Goodman Brown" is about a young man who sets out into the woods on a dark night and encounters the devil. They journey together, and eventually the devil tries to convert Brown to his cause. The story can be interpreted allegorically, and there are certainly clues that invite such a read-ing, including a nod to the convention of significant character names in the case of his wife, Faith. But in Hawthorne's story, the allegorical interpreta-tion of Brown's night in the forest is by no means the only reasonable read-ing of the story; in fact, the story's conclusion actually emphasizes the choice the reader must make between the literal and metaphorical or dream inter-pretations of the tale. Most of the time, allegory will resemble what we see in "Young Goodman Brown" more than the directly stated allegory of *The Pilgrim's Progress*. Allegory is seldom a given when it comes to literary inter-pretation; it's a reading that we can try out on a work. Works that respond coherently to such readings can be said to be allegorical.

Other, more specialized kinds of tropes also bear mention here. **Personification**, the endowment of animals, objects, or abstract ideas with human qualities, is another specific figure closely related to metaphor. Similarly, **metonymy** refers to the practice of referring to an object or idea using a term for something closely associated with it. When a newscaster cites "the White House" as the source of information, it is clearly not the building itself that provided the information but the president or other rep-resentative of the executive branch of the government. For a literary exam-ple, consider this stanza from William Blake's poem "London":

How the Chimney-sweeper's cry
Every blackning Church appalls,
And the hapless Soldier's sigh
Runs in blood down Palace walls.

The poem talks about the suffering of the working poor and the institutions that profit directly or indirectly from it; "Church" and "Palace" are build-ings, but Blake uses the terms metonymically to refer to the institutions they house: the Church (the metonymy is inseparable from our complex under-standing of the term) and the government. A closely related trope is **synec-doche**, in which an object or concept is referred to by the name of one of its parts (as in "one hundred head of cattle" or "a village of three hundred souls"). The spaces between these figures of speech and the concepts to which they refer are one of the defining characteristics of literary language, and much of the pleasure of reading literature comes from successfully negotiating these spaces.

THINKING EXERCISES

1. Often we somewhat carelessly discuss "symbolism" in a literary work when we're actually talking about imagery. Consider some symbols you have encountered in literature, and identify what makes them symbolic. In other words, how do we know to interpret a symbol as a symbol?

2. Most of the examples in this chapter were drawn from poetry. Why do you suppose such tropes as imagery, symbolism, and metaphor seem to be much more prevalent in verse than in prose or drama?

10.2 RHETORICAL DEVICES

So far we have been discussing tropes, figures of speech in which words are used to signify ideas other than their literal meanings. The other major type of figurative language is the **rhetorical device** or **figure of speech** (as opposed to tropes, which can be called "figures of thought"—though as we have already pointed out, these categories are fluid, and the real significance of all of these figures is their effect on readers' understanding of the text). Many of the concepts from the study of rhetoric are just as useful in literary criticism, in part because the arts are related and in part because many writers studied classical rhetoric as a part of their education. One important and common rhetorical device is **apostrophe**, in which a speaker addresses somebody or something that isn't present for rhetorical effect, as in *Paradise Lost*, when Satan says in Book 4 (lines 108–10),

> So farewell, Hope, and with Hope farewell Fear,
> Farewell Remorse: all Good to me is lost;
> Evil, be thou my Good. . . .

Satan is speaking only to himself in a kind of **soliloquy**, so his direct address to these personified concepts is purely for rhetorical or poetic effect. The similarity to the other tropes we have discussed should be apparent: what is being said is not intended literally.

Many rhetorical figures are as common in conversation as they are in literature; one of them is the *rhetorical question*. This figure, a question to which no answer is expected, is beloved of educators everywhere. It is not asked to solicit opinion or information but rather to offer an assertion in an interesting way. Frequently, such questions are posed to suggest that they are in fact unanswerable or that there can be only one conceivable answer. In either case, they present the illusion of involving the person being addressed. For example, when an instructor asks, "What is art?" he or she knows that the students won't have a simple answer. Instead, the question sparks debate.

Hyperbole, or exaggeration, is another rhetorical device frequently found in everyday conversation. We have already seen how Shakespeare pokes fun at the hyperbolic conventions of the sonnet sequence in his Sonnet 130, which begins "My mistress' eyes are nothing like the sun." In "Goblin Market," Christina Rossetti makes use of hyperbole in this passage (lines 127–31):

> She dropp'd a tear more rare than pearl,
> Then suck'd their fruit globes fair or red:

Sweeter than honey from the rock,
Stronger than man-rejoicing wine,
Clearer than water flow'd that juice. . . .

Although the juice of the goblin fruit could conceivably be sweeter than honey, it's unlikely that Laura's tear is literally more rare than a pearl and impossible that the juice of any fruit could be clearer than water; yet the hyperbole is effective here, particularly given the supernatural nature of the goblins.

The similes in the Rossetti passage compare various objects that exist in the realm of the narrative—tears and juice—to other items that exist in the reader's experience but not as parts of the girls' encounter with the goblins: pearl, honey, wine, and water. Another kind of comparison, the **allusion**, draws a brief connection between the writer's subject and some other literary or historical person, object, or event. Generally, the allusion is not identified explicitly; part of the pleasure for the reader is in recognizing the allusion and understanding the likeness the writer is suggesting. In popular culture, the comedian Dennis Miller is known for his use of allusion; critics have observed that most people would need footnotes to fully appreciate his monologues. The more of Miller's allusions one recognizes, however, the more likely one is to enjoy his brand of humor. Of course, allusions are more common in literary works, and some make generous use of the device; the difficulty of T. S. Eliot's long poem *The Waste Land* lies largely in his liberal use of allusion. Allusions rely, obviously, on the audience's ability to connect with the cultural background of the writer.

Of all of the rhetorical devices, the most difficult to nail down is **irony**. Nearly everyone has tried and failed to communicate ironically at one time or another. *Irony* refers to language that communicates something other than its literal meaning for artistic or rhetorical effect. Irony is usually considered in several senses; many critics have offered classifications for categorizing different types of irony, a few of which we'll look at here. *Verbal irony* refers to a spoken statement that implies its opposite either through tone or through situation; *sarcasm* is a harsh, biting version of verbal irony. *Structural irony* is a more involved form of irony in which the whole work is designed to convey two parallel meanings; successful interpretation of such works depends on the reader's ability to see past what is being literally said by the narrative persona to what seems to be intended. Jonathan Swift's "Modest Proposal" is an example of this kind of irony; the speaker suggests that the Irish should export their babies as meat to generate revenue, but the astute reader understands that Swift is suggesting other more sensible and less monstrous methods of salvaging the Irish economy.

Dramatic irony is found in narratives (most frequently in plays, as the name suggests) when the audience knows something that a character does not. In *Oedipus Rex*, the audience knows the reason for the curse on Thebes, but the lead character does not. Oedipus, the play's protagonist, spends most of the play searching for the murderer of Laius, the king whom he has replaced; the audience knows that Oedipus himself is the culprit and moreover that Laius was his father and his wife, Jocasta, his mother. Further irony can be found in the fact that the whole tragic chain of events took place as a result of the characters' efforts to avoid them. Laius had tried to dispose of his son many years earlier because he believed the boy would grow up to kill him and not aware that the boy had grown up ignorant of his origin. Likewise, Oedipus returned to Thebes because it had been prophesied that he would kill his father and marry his mother. Since he believed his foster parents to be his only parents, he left home to avoid his fate, arriving by accident at the place where the horrible prophecy could come true. The whole play depends for its effect on this pattern of dramatic irony.

THINKING EXERCISES

1. In speech, we frequently use vocal inflection to signal the use of hyperbole, irony, and other rhetorical devices. In writing, we don't have these tools (hence the use of such "emoticons" as the sideways smiley faces used in e-mail to avoid misunderstandings). How do literary writers manage to signal their use of irony? Have you ever been confused by a writer's use of irony?

2. Christina Rossetti's "Goblin Market" is full of rhetorical figures. Choose a passage from it, identify the rhetorical figures, and consider their role in creating the poem's meaning. What would the poem be without them?

❧ 11 ❧

Prose Genres

As discussed in Chapter 1, the term **genre** in literature means "category" or "type" or "classification." We are constantly called on in life to place things and events into certain classifications so that we may communicate about them more effectively. For example, when you take your car to the repair shop, you'll usually be asked to tell them the make, model, and year of the car so that the shop can have the proper parts on hand and so that the proper mechanic is assigned to the car.

For the purposes of literary study, the most common genres or categories of literature are *fiction* and *nonfiction prose, poetry*, and *drama*. Each of these genres has its own characteristics and distinct traits, just as each genre may in turn be divided into a variety of *subgenres*. The following chapters will examine some of these categories so that you can use them in your own writing and discussions and so that when you encounter these terms in your reading, you'll know what the critics are talking about.

11.1 FICTION GENRES BY LENGTH

The term *genre* is rather ambiguous when referring to fiction. As we discussed in Part One, it might mean various categories of fiction in terms of the basic setting and plot. That is, is a given story in the genre (or subgenre) of mystery, science fiction, romance, fantasy, western? In fact, these categories of fiction are often called *genre fiction*. Since we discussed these earlier and it's usually not difficult to define a science fiction or mystery story, let's examine the other ways fiction might be categorized into different genres.

First, types of fiction may be defined by their lengths. It goes without saying that certain kinds of stories demand certain lengths appropriate to their style and subject matter. A book-length piece of prose fiction is a **novel**.

Although there is no exact length requirement for a work of fiction to be considered a novel, editors generally want one to be at least fifty or sixty thousand words long. On a more technical level, however, novels are more than just long stories; lengthy narratives may be told in epic poems or long plays (a faithful adaptation of *Hamlet*, for example, will last over three hours). A novel must be prose fiction, should ordinarily employ a narrative structure, and should show a character develop over time.

The term *novel* for a work of fiction came into being in English because the creation of a lengthy prose fiction was new—literally, *novel*—to the readers of the early eighteenth century. Writers on the European continent had been working in longer forms for some time, often using **stock characters** or flat characters in a series of adventures and episodes; such stories, cobbled together into a long narrative, form **picaresque** novels. Literary scholars disagree whether picaresque works (primarily books like Cervantes's *Don Quixote*, 1605) are truly the first novels or whether that distinction belongs to the English form, which focused more on **realism** and **verisimilitude** and the development of *round characters*, as demonstrated by novels like Daniel Defoe's *Robinson Crusoe* (1719) and *Moll Flanders* (1722).

A **novelette** is a lengthy story that is shorter than a novel. The term is used less these days, and quite often the term **novella** (which was once considered the work of fiction longer than a short story but shorter than a novelette) is used to refer to any work of prose fiction longer than a **short story** (for argument's sake, we'll say a work of fiction consisting of more than eighteen thousand words; remember that these numbers are arbitrary and differ from editor to editor) and shorter than a novel.[1] Stories of this middling length include Henry James's *The Turn of the Screw* and Joseph Conrad's *Heart of Darkness*. A short story is the shortest increment of fictional prose; a short story may be anywhere from a few hundred words (these one- to two-page stories are often referred to as *short-short stories*) to, again, around eighteen to twenty thousand words. Early short stories were often tales meant to excite or instruct, in the forms of parables or fables or ghost stories; during the middle of the nineteenth century, however, both Edgar Allan Poe and Nathaniel Hawthorne solidified the structure of short stories to make them a more literary form.

The differences in length between novels and shorter forms make for many other differences as well. Short stories must necessarily practice more economy than novels and often are more rigidly structured. Even so-called slice-of-life stories (as produced by Anton Chekhov) or minimalist stories (like those of Raymond Carver or Bobbie Ann Mason) are more sculpted than shapeless. Short stories generally aim at a unity of effect, building toward a single climax.

---

[1]*Benét's Reader's Encyclopedia* says a novel has at least sixty thousand words and a novella thirty to forty thousand; it has no entry for *novelette*.

THINKING EXERCISES

1. Consider your favorite works of fiction. In which fiction genre are they written?
2. On a more general level, do you prefer short stories, novels, or novellas? Why do you think you prefer this particular genre?

11.2   TYPES OF FICTION

There are many ways to categorize literary fiction other than by length, of course. Following is a list of genres in literary fiction that is by no means inclusive.

Romance

Many of the earliest novels were called **romances**. To modern readers, this is an ambiguous term, because to us it signifies either a story of romantic love or possibly a novel written by writers associated with literary Romanticism. In the early days of structured fiction (the late seventeenth and early eighteenth centuries), however, novels that were unrealistic, melodramatic tales of adventure and love were referred to (often in a pejorative sense) as *romances*. *Novels*, by contrast, were supposed to be serious books that dealt with realistic subjects. However, many writers (especially those associated with literary Romanticism like Mary Shelley, Nathaniel Hawthorne, and Herman Melville) wrote novels that could be considered "romances" that nevertheless dealt with serious themes without sacrificing literary merit.

Gothic Fiction

A work of **gothic** fiction is meant primarily to scare the reader. Ghosts, vampires, and other horrors present themselves; the protagonist is often vulnerable and exposed. Many critics consider Horace Walpole's *The Castle of Otranto* (1764) the first gothic novel; the form was further popularized by books like *The Mysteries of Udolpho* by Ann Radcliffe (1794) and *The Monk* by M. G. Lewis (1796). The word *gothic* came to be used for what today's audience might term horror novels because of their common settings: scary, medieval castles, monasteries, and ruins featuring Gothic architecture. Gothic fiction further distinguished itself because of its use of place and brooding atmospheres. Edgar Allan Poe elevated the form in short fiction in the mid-nineteenth century. Gothic fiction has not only survived to the present but has also tremendously influenced any number of writers, including Charlotte and Emily Brontë (in *Jane Eyre* and *Wuthering Heights*), Nathaniel Hawthorne (in *The Scarlet Letter*), and William Faulkner (in *Absalom, Absalom!*).

Bildungsroman

A **bildungsroman** is a story of apprenticeship and initiation in which a young character sets out on a road of trials and is initiated into adulthood with the help of one or more mentor figures. *Great Expectations* by Dickens and *The Adventures of Huckleberry Finn* by Twain are considered bildungsromans; so, for that matter, are George Lucas's *Star Wars* movies. Although bildungsromans were once considered stories of male initiation into manhood, many novels with female protagonists—like Jane Austen's *Mansfield Park* or Carson McCullers's *The Heart Is a Lonely Hunter*—also fit the category.

Novel of Manners

A book can be considered a **novel of manners** when the plot and setting comment on the society, customs, and culture of a given place and time. Often the characters in a novel of manners may be controlled by or in conflict with the conventions of the surrounding culture. Most of Jane Austen's novels fall into this category, as do works by Henry James (for example, *The American*) and Edith Wharton (*The Age of Innocence*).

Roman à Clef

A **roman à clef**, or, literally, a "novel with a key," is a narrative in which the character and plot scenarios actually refer to real people, living or dead, and "true" situations (as defined by the author). For example, the novel *Primary Colors*, published anonymously in 1998, told the story of a southern politician whose character was obviously closely based on that of the sitting president, Bill Clinton. Such novels will often gain early notoriety due to their presentation of a particular group or social set. *The Sun Also Rises* by Hemingway was initially a roman à clef (although its origins have become obscure enough that most current readers don't read it as such); other examples include Nathaniel Hawthorne's *The Blithedale Romance* and Jack Kerouac's *On the Road*.

Frame Story

At its simplest level, a **frame story** involves a story within a story. Generally, the *frame* or outer story provides a setup through which a secondary story might be told. At its more sophisticated levels, the interior narrative's themes might have some bearing on characters in the frame. One of the most famous frame stories, told in verse, would be Chaucer's *Canterbury Tales*, wherein a group of pilgrims traveling to Canterbury spin yarns to entertain and edify each other. Other prominent examples would be Emily Brontë's *Wuthering Heights*, Conrad's *Heart of Darkness*, and James's *The Turn of the Screw*.

Magical Realism

Although elements of **magical realism** have existed since the age of Elizabethan theater and even appeared in the work of early-twentieth-century writers such as William Faulkner, the term has largely been applied to the work of Latin American writers of the second half of the twentieth century like Gabriel García Márquez and Jorge Luis Borges. In magical realism, surreal, supernatural, or magical events occur during the course of a narrative. However, these magical events are not in themselves alarming or cause for great excitement; they are an organic part of an otherwise realistic setting and plot. Although this movement is, as stated earlier, most often ascribed to Central and South American authors, writers from many other cultures around the world produce fiction that could be considered magical realism, including writers like the African American novelist Toni Morrison and the Italian writers Italo Calvino and Umberto Eco.

THINKING EXERCISES

1. Consider works you've read either for literature courses or on your own. Can you place any of them in any of the categories discussed in this section? Or in multiple categories at once? Can you think of movies or television shows you've seen that also fit any of these categories?

2. If you were setting out to write a novel or short story, do you think your work would fall into one of the categories described in this section? If so, which one? If not, why wouldn't it?

11.3   NONFICTION

Nonfiction is, as you might suppose, prose writing that does not try to construct a fictional narrative. Traditionally, nonfiction has been given less attention than the other literary genres; nonfiction prose that did earn notice tended to be either extraordinarily well written or of premier historical importance, or both (for example, Frederick Douglass's *Narrative of the Life of an American Slave* or the Declaration of Independence). The increasing popularity of the memoir, however, has led in recent years to the distinction between *creative nonfiction* and *expository nonfiction*.

Any work of prose written to explain something—whether it's the owner's manual to a Ford Taurus, a guide to creating computer games, or a literary essay analyzing "Araby"—is a work of expository writing. **Exposition** is the setting forth of facts or ideas or a detailed explanation of something. A biography of a celebrity or politician is expository writing in that the biography is telling the story of that person's life and trying to explain how life events have brought the person to his or her current position.

A book-length analysis of Christina Rossetti's poetry is also a work of expository nonfiction.

Nonfiction has long seemed too broad a term for the various works to which it applies. Memoirs, in particular, seem to push the limit of genre categorization: although an autobiography or memoir may purport to be nonfiction, it may be constructed similarly to a novel, incorporating dialogue, characterization, figurative language, and so on. Isak Dinesen's *Out of Africa* is a notable example. Furthermore, these novelistic elements could be applied to the reporting of factual events so that the story is as gripping and profound as a novel, as exemplified by Truman Capote's 1965 book *In Cold Blood*, which the author called a "nonfiction novel."

In the latter half of the 1960s, a number of writers (most notably Tom Wolfe and Hunter S. Thompson) continued to write nonfiction accounts in highly stylized prose that was, again, reminiscent of fiction; this style of writing was usually referred to as the **New Journalism**. Finally, both memoirs and nonfiction narratives surged in popularity in the 1990s. Books like Frank McCourt's *Angela's Ashes*, John Berendt's *Midnight in the Garden of Good and Evil*, Jon Krakauer's *Into Thin Air,* and Sebastian Junger's *The Perfect Storm* captured the imagination of the reading public. To describe the creative style of these books, the genre term **creative nonfiction** came into vogue, although the term had long been a part of the lexicon, albeit rarely used.

~12~

Poetry Forms and Genres

As in prose, certain distinctions between genres of poetry can be made simply on the basis of length. For a poem to be considered an **epic**, for instance, it must exhibit certain qualities, one of which is substantial length. There is no firm rule for length in the case of an epic, any more than there is a strict word count cutoff for the short story; yet substantial length is part of what makes a poem an epic. Epics also have many other characteristics in common. The epic is a narrative poem with a hero of great social stature, and the action of the poem is frequently national or international in scope and setting, even to the point of involving supernatural forces. Many epics begin *in medias res* (Latin for "in the middle of things") and feature long lists (called "catalogs") of ships or warriors. *Paradise Lost*, for instance, begins *after* the expulsion of Satan and his minions from heaven and provides, in book 1, a lengthy catalog of said minions and the confusion they cause the human race later in history. Like many of the epics Milton was emulating, *Paradise Lost* also begins by invoking the Muse, a divine mythological patroness of the arts.

As you can see, although length is an important issue when categorizing poems, other considerations are just as important. Genre is usually suggested by form, but the relationship between form and content is much more organic and integral in poetry than it is in drama and narrative prose. As noted in the discussion of Shakespeare's sonnets in section 6.2, the shape of the poem is often enough to suggest the genre into which the poem falls, but with that categorization also come certain expectations regarding subject and theme. Rhyme, meter, and stanza forms are defined and discussed in much greater detail later in this chapter, but they are relevant to our goal of defining the various types of poems.

12.1   TYPES OF POEMS

We have already hinted at some of the broadest distinctions to be made between different types of poems. *Narrative poetry* is, as you would imagine, poetry that tells a story much in the manner of fiction (or creative non-fiction). The epic is just one example of the narrative poem. *Lyric poetry*, in contrast, does not tell a story. Rather, the **lyric poem** is comparatively brief and generally nonnarrative, giving the impression of being the subjective utterance of a single speaker. Clearly, this encompasses a lot of poetry, and if the definition seems nebulous, it's due to the nearly infinite variety of the genre. Somewhere between these two distinctions lies *dramatic poetry*, which is poetry that employs dramatic form, devices, or techniques. In some cases, the line between dramatic poem and poetic drama can become blurred, as in T. S. Eliot's *Murder in the Cathedral*; in general, though, a verse drama (like those of Shakespeare, Marlowe, and many others) is quite distinct from the dramatic poem, of which Browning's "My Last Duchess" (in section 9.4) is an excellent example.

Within these three broad classes of poetry are numerous subcategories. Some of the more common ones you're likely to run into are described next.

Ballad

A **ballad** is a narrative poem that is written to be sung. Like most songs, the ballad is generally marked by a regular meter and rhyme. In fact, many English folk ballads share the same stanza form, known as the *ballad stanza*. The original ballads were transmitted orally; many featured formulaic repetition that would have aided memorization. These folk ballads have often been imitated by later singer-songwriters such as Bob Dylan as well as by poets in the form of literary ballads, narrative poems written in the form of the earlier songs. Dudley Randall's "Ballad of Birmingham" is a notable example of the literary ballad.

Romance

The **romance** is another kind of narrative poem. More self-consciously literary than the ballad, the form became popular during the Middle Ages, and most of the verse romances you are likely to encounter hail from that period. Like the epic, the romance features the exploits of prominent persons: knights, princes, kings, and ladies of noble birth. Many romances deal with the adventures of King Arthur and his knights, and often the narrative revolves around a quest. *Sir Gawain and the Green Knight* is a good example of the Arthurian romance. Romances differ from epics in their subject matter (courtly love as opposed to heroic battle) and gravity; romances generally avoid matters of cosmic import in favor of lighter concerns.

Sonnet

The **sonnet** is one of the most rigid forms of lyric poetry. There are two main kinds of sonnet: the English (Elizabethan or Shakespearean) and the Italian (Petrarchan). Both types generally have fourteen lines of iambic pentameter and follow one of several rhyme schemes. The difference between them is the grouping of lines. The English sonnet usually consists of three *quatrains* (groups of four lines) and a *couplet* (a group of two lines). The rhyme scheme is often *abab, cdcd, efef, gg*. The Italian sonnet, by contrast, is divided into an *octave* (a group of eight lines) and a *sestet* (a group of six lines). These groupings cannot properly be called stanzas, since they are generally not separated by extra white space; however, the rhyme scheme and the sense of the poem will usually conform to these groupings. Typically, the Italian sonnet's rhyme scheme uses only five rhymes: *abba, abba, cdecde*. Although each sonnet is a complete poem unto itself, it is often also part of a *sonnet cycle* or *sequence*, a group of sonnets on a similar theme.

Villanelle

Another highly formal and demanding type of lyric poem is the **villanelle**, of which Dylan Thomas's "Do Not Go Gentle into That Good Night" is probably the best-known example in English. The form itself is, however, French in origin. The villanelle is a poem of nineteen lines—five three-line stanzas and a concluding four-line stanza—with a complicated system of repeated lines. Because lines 1 and 3 are repeated verbatim throughout the poem, narrative progress is nearly impossible to convey; the villanelle's effect originates largely in that repetition.

Haiku

The **haiku** originated in Japan, and the rules that govern its form—three lines of five, seven, and five syllables—are so language-dependent that haiku written in English can only approximate the effect of Japanese haiku. The haiku paints an exceptionally brief verbal image that is intended to evoke a specific emotion in its audience.

Ode

As a form or genre of lyrical poem, the **ode** is defined less by its similarity to other odes in terms of meter and rhyme than by the seriousness of its subject matter and an internal consistency of stanza form. The *Pindaric ode* is characterized by the alternation of three different stanza types. The *Horatian ode* consists of one stanza type that can take almost any form as long as it is consistent throughout the poem. The stanzas of the *irregular ode* can vary in length, rhyme, and meter. The ode is usually presented in an elevated style, and its theme is public rather than personal.

Elegy

Although the term originally applied to any poem that used the elegiac meter, including love poems, most readers today understand an **elegy** to be a comparatively long lyrical meditation on a serious theme such as death or loss. The tone of the elegy is mournful. Gray's "Elegy Written in a Country Churchyard" and Tennyson's *In Memoriam* are two well-known examples of the form. It's not uncommon for people to confuse the words *elegy* and *eulogy*; the latter refers to a speech of praise, often for someone who has died. Marc Antony's speech on the death of the emperor in Shakespeare's *Julius Caesar* is a famous eulogy.

Dramatic Monologue

As the name suggests, the **dramatic monologue** is a poem that reveals the thoughts of a single speaker (a character who is not the poet) in an identifiable dramatic context. In other words, the reader is able to determine who is speaking, as well as the setting and situation of the speech. The goal of the poem is to reveal the inner thoughts and character of the speaker through the speech alone. Obviously, the form is related to the **soliloquy** in drama; in prose, **interior monologue** serves a similar function. Often the dramatic monologue is used to give the reader insight into a remarkable character who might be quite different from both the poet and the majority of the audience, as in Browning's "Porphyria's Lover," in which the speaker has just strangled his lover with her own hair, and Tennyson's "Ulysses," in which the title character, having returned from his epic journeys, expresses dissatisfaction with the quiet life that he can look forward to in Ithaca and so sets out westward on a final adventure. Browning's "My Last Duchess" (in section 9.4) is a dramatic monologue. In each of these poems and most other representatives of the genre, the audience is left to construe the poem's situation—and sometimes its speaker—from clues scattered through the text of the poem.

THINKING EXERCISES

1. Consider your favorite poems. In which poetic genres are they written?
2. Do you prefer formal verse, with rhyme and meter, or free verse? Why?

12.2   PROSODY AND POETIC DICTION

As we have noted, most of the elements of literary language we've been discussing can be found in more than one type of literary work. Dialogue, for instance, is almost essential to drama and is common in prose fiction and poetry as well. In contrast, **prosody**—the study of *versification*, or the structure of poetry or verse—applies almost exclusively to poetry. We have pointed out, however, that the lines between the genres of literature are not always firm; many plays are written in verse, some prose fiction resembles poetry and uses poetic devices, and some contemporary poetry looks and reads very much like prose. Thus the principles we are about to examine will to varying degrees be relevant not only to poetry but to other kinds of literary writing as well.

Prosody is frequently referred to as the "science of poetry," and it is true that as an approach to the art form, it focuses more on sound and quantifiable characteristics of verse than on emotion, feeling, or any of the other more nebulous issues generally associated with poetry. As we shall see, though, how a poem makes us feel frequently has a great deal to do with how it sounds; this kind of analysis is therefore an important part of studying poetry. Prosody analyzes three different qualities of poetry: **meter**, the recurrence of a pattern of **rhythm** (the "beat" of stressed and unstressed syllables) in verse; **rhyme**, the repetition of ending sounds in two or more words which usually—though not always—appear at the end of lines in rhymed poetry; and **stanzas**, sequences of lines in a poem that are set off typographically and sometimes distinguished by recurring patterns of rhyme. Each stanza of a poem often contains the same number of lines and rhyme patterns as the other stanzas in the poem.

Many readers of poetry are daunted by prosody. Even college students who—as we did—gravitated to English classes in part due to a distaste for math and science may find the subject dangerously reminiscent of their worst experiences in the classroom. Sometimes it seems that the process of **scansion**—a method of describing rhythms that involves grouping, counting, and marking accented and unaccented syllables—is akin to cutting open the goose that lays the golden eggs: after the vivisection, the magic is gone. It could be argued, however, that true appreciation of poetry depends on a thorough understanding of it and that focusing on prosody is a necessary means to achieving the fullest possible comprehension of a poem and the way it works.

Whole books have been written on the subject of prosody, so we cannot hope to do justice to the subject here. Instead, we'll introduce some general principles and their applicability to reading, understanding, and writing about poetry. More detail can be found in books devoted only to poetry or in dictionaries of literary terminology.

Meter

Until the modern period, **meter** (in one form or another) was one of the most important defining characteristics of English-language poetry. Meter refers to the overall pattern of rhythm a poem exhibits, though the rhythm of individual lines in the poem will probably vary. Meter is described in terms of the type and number of feet present in a line of poetry. A **foot** is the fundamental repeating unit of rhythm, comparable to the measure in music; most of these units consist of two or three syllables and are distinguished by the number and placement of stressed syllables within them. Some of the most common feet are listed in the table below. Incidentally, the following marks are commonly used in scansion: ˘ indicates an unstressed syllable, and ´ indicates an accented one. Thus the syllables of the first line of Shakespeare's Sonnet 18 would be marked as follows:

Shăll Í cŏmpáre thĕe tó ă súmmĕr's dáy?

The repeating unit here is the **iamb**, a two-syllable foot consisting of an unstressed syllable followed by a stressed syllable: ˘ ´. Once the overall rhythm has been identified, it's possible to go through the line and mark the divisions between the feet:

Shăll Í | cŏmpáre | thĕe tó | ă súm | mĕr's dáy?

Note that it's not uncommon for the words in a line to ignore the boundaries of the feet; given that most feet are only two or three syllables in length, longer words will simply span several feet. Furthermore, different readers will impose different inflections on the line; many readers would read the line with *thee* accented and *to* unaccented or with the two words given roughly the same degree of emphasis. Although these may seem like insignificant issues, the whole meaning of a poem can hinge on the placement of stress within a given line.

SOME COMMON METRICAL FEET

NAME	PATTERN	EXAMPLE
Iamb	˘ ´	dĕspáir
Trochee	´ ˘	hórsemăn
Spondee	´ ´	wínegláss
Anapest	˘ ˘ ´	ăftĕrnóon
Dactyl	´ ˘ ˘	ápplĕ-cărt

Identifying the repeating unit of rhythm in a line is the first part of determining the meter; the second is identifying the usual number of feet per line in the poem. In the case of Shakespeare's Sonnet 18, as with most sonnets in English, the meter is *iambic pentameter*, meaning that the unit of repeated rhythm is the iamb and that there are five of them per line. Other meters encountered in English poetry include *monometer* (one foot), *dimeter* (two feet), *trimeter* (three feet), *tetrameter* (four feet), *hexameter* (six feet), and *heptameter* (seven feet).

As we noted, it is important to remember that iambic pentameter is not a Procrustean bed into which each and every line of every sonnet must be forced; a poem's meter is an overall description of the rhythm of its lines, but individual lines will vary and must be read according to the cadences of natural English speech. Consider, for instance, the second line of Shakespeare's Sonnet 130:

> Córăl | ĭs fár | mŏre réd | thăn hĕr | líps' réd:

Reading this line strictly according to the rhythm of iambic pentameter would change its meaning entirely, since *Coral* must be pronounced with the first syllable accented, or else it becomes *Corral* and the sense of the line is lost. This metrical variation should not be considered a flaw in the poem; in fact, it has been argued that the most important thing about rules in poetry is the interesting ways great poets find to break them. Strict adherence to the rules of meter often results in lackluster poetry at best and doggerel at worst; a certain amount of variation, whether through the inclusion of different kinds of feet or the addition or subtraction of them in various lines of a poem, allows the poet to control the poem's pace as well as the placement of emphasis. Thus while many poems can be described in terms of their meter, the rhythm of individual lines within the poem can be expected to vary, and readers should let the syntax of the lines determine their rhythm rather than try to impose a predefined meter on them.

It has been said that iambic pentameter is the meter best suited to verse in the English language, since it corresponds most closely to the natural rhythms of speech. It makes sense, then, that one of the most common forms of poetry in English since the early 1500s is **blank verse**, which has meter (usually iambic pentameter) but does not rhyme. Not long after its introduction into the language, Marlowe, Shakespeare, and other dramatists used blank verse in their plays, and in *Paradise Lost*, Milton established it as the meter of serious poetry in English.

Once a poem's meter has been identified, what does it have to do with the poem's meaning? Meter affects meaning in a variety of ways. First of all, patterns give pleasure. It must be acknowledged that meter does not just happen in a poem by accident. The presence of meter assures the reader that the poem's language is unusual, that it deserves to be read as poetry and not as prose or some accidental utterance. There are other ways of communicating the same information, of course, but historically, meter has been one of a poet's chief means of making poetic language special.

Sound Effects: Rhyme and Repetition

Even though many poems do not rhyme, rhyme is the quality of language that most clearly distinguishes a piece of writing as a poem. From early childhood, the poems future readers are exposed to generally feature rhyme and meter. The fact that nursery rhymes and most songs feature rhyme as one of their chief poetic strategies is not a coincidence; both genres are composed primarily for oral recitation, and rhyme is a useful mnemonic device. Most people even learn the alphabet by singing it to the tune of "Twinkle, Twinkle Little Star" and emphasizing the rhyming letter names at the end of phrases. It has been suggested that rhyming became a poetic device as a result of its effectiveness as an aid to memorization and that priests in the Catholic church introduced rhyme to help worshipers memorize songs and responses.

Rhyme has persisted into the era of widespread literacy as a poetic device for several reasons, the first of which, as with meter, is visceral, perhaps even prelinguistic: readers and listeners take pleasure in rhymes. The gratification a mature reader might take in reading Christina Rossetti's "Goblin Market" has largely to do with its theme, symbolism, and narrative, but—even though we don't recommend it—even a small child would enjoy hearing it read aloud simply because of its pleasant sound. The rhyme is not regular (as befits a poem about two sisters' encounter with the temptations tendered by the wild goblins), but it is nonetheless pervasive and captivating. Consider the following passage (lines 105–114):

Laura stared but did not stir,	*a*
Long'd but had no money:	*b*
The whisk-tail'd merchant bade her taste	*c*
In tones as smooth as honey,	*b*
The cat-faced purr'd,	*a*
The rat-faced spoke a word	*a*
Of welcome, and the snail-paced even was heard;	*a*
One parrot-voiced and jolly	*d*
Cried "Pretty Goblin" still for "Pretty Polly";	*d*
One whistled like a bird.	*a*

The letters to the right of the poem represent the conventional way of designating rhyme. The ending sound of the first line in the passage is assigned the letter *a*, and all lines that end with words rhyming with that sound will be marked with the same letter. Each new ending sound is assigned a new letter, and thus it becomes possible to describe the *rhyme scheme*, the overall pattern in which rhyming sounds occur in a stanza or poem. The use of rhyme patterns to delineate stanzas will be discussed shortly (note that we have already made use of this convention in our discussion of the sonnet form in section 12.1).

There are many variations of rhyme in addition to the *end rhymes* identified by the letters; note, for instance, the *internal rhyme* consisting of the correspondence of *cat-faced*, *rat-faced*, and *snail-paced* in the Rossetti passage. In addition to distinguishing types of rhyme by the placement of the rhyming sounds in the line, readers sometimes classify rhymes as *masculine* (when the rhyme takes place on the last, accented syllable, as in *purr'd* and *word*) or *feminine* (when the accented rhyming syllables are followed by unaccented syllables that match exactly, as in *money* and *honey*).

Rhymes are also described in terms of the degree of correspondence between the sounds. So far we have been talking mostly about *perfect* or *true rhymes*, where the ending sounds of the rhyming syllables correspond exactly. But poets frequently make use of rhymes that are more tenuous; *imperfect* or *slant rhymes* are commonly found in poetry, as in the following passage from "Goblin Market" (lines 116–22):

> "Good folk, I have no coin;
> To take were to purloin:
> I have no copper in my purse,
> I have no silver either,
> And all my gold is on the furze
> That shakes in windy weather
> Above the rusty heather."

Purse and *furze* are not exact rhymes; though the vowel sounds are the same, the ending consonants are only similar (this repetition of similar vowel sounds in the stressed syllables of words that end differently is known as **assonance**). Likewise, the rhyme of *either* with *weather* and *heather* is only partial. This is not a reflection on the poet's skill; imperfect rhymes are a useful part of a poet's repertoire.

At the other end of the spectrum from the imperfect rhyme is the *forced rhyme*, a rhyme that seems to subordinate the sense of the poem to the demands of the rhyme scheme; forced rhymes usually have a humorous effect, as in Byron's *Don Juan*: (canto 1, stanza 5)

> Brave men were living before Agamemnon
> And since, exceeding valorous and sage,
> A good deal like him too, though quite the same none;
> But then they shone not on the poet's page,
> And so have been forgotten:—I condemn none,
> But can't find any in the present age
> Fit for my poem (that is, for my new one);
> So, as I said, I'll take my friend Don Juan.

Accomplished wordsmiths like Byron often make skillful use of forced rhyme; the difference between forced rhyme and bad poetry lies in the correspondence between the rhyme and the desired effect. Note that Byron intends for the reader to intentionally anglicize the name *Juan* so that it is pronounced "joo-un" to rhyme with "new one."

Other types of sound repetition are also common in poetry. **Alliteration,** the repetition of initial consonant sounds (usually in accented syllables, whether or not they are the first syllables in a word), is one such device, very common in Old English and Middle English poetry. This pair of lines from "Goblin Market" exhibits alliteration (lines 91–92):

> When they reach'd where Laura was
> They stood stock still upon the moss. . . .

In the first line, the initial sounds of *when* and *was* alliterate; the correspondence with the unaccented *where* is almost incidental. In the second line, the phrase "stood stock still," with its strongly alliterated series of accented syllables, is a very effective use of the device.

It is easy, when analyzing a poem in terms of rhyme, assonance, and alliteration, to get so wrapped up in identifying instances of sound repetition that their significance is ignored. Remember, though, that these linguistic devices can contribute to our perception or understanding of the poem. The question worth pursuing is not merely whether or not a poem rhymes, but rather, why does it rhyme, if indeed it does? What is the effect of rhyme (or assonance or alliteration) in the poem?

As we have noted, one of the common effects of these correspondences is the aesthetic pleasure many people take in patterns, be they musical, linguistic, or visual. Beyond that, however, sound repetition can be used to control the reader's attention; words that rhyme or alliterate tend to be emphasized. Furthermore, a correspondence of rhyme often suggests a connection in meaning between the words. During the first O. J. Simpson trial, defense attorney Johnnie Cochran's famous assertion about the bloody glove—"If it doesn't fit, you must acquit"—depended largely on rhyme for its effectiveness. Finally, repeated sound elements like rhyme, assonance, and alliteration frequently communicate in the manner of **onomatopoeia**: strictly defined as referring to words that mean what they sound like (*fizz*, for instance, or *bang*), in the broader sense the term can also apply to verses or prose passages that somehow suggest, via auditory means, what they describe. Consider these sentences from the conclusion of James Joyce's story "The Dead," in which the protagonist, Gabriel Conroy, stares out the window of a hotel room at the falling snow and meditates on the inevitability of death:

> It was falling on every part of the dark central plain, on the treeless hills, falling softly upon the Bog of Allen and, farther westward, softly falling into the dark mutinous Shannon waves. . . . His soul swooned slowly as he heard the snow falling faintly through the universe and faintly falling, like the descent of their last end, upon all the living and the dead.

The rhythm of the sentences evokes a feeling that is appropriate to the mood of the story. A **rhetorical device** called **chiasmus** (literally "crossover," a reversal of word order in similar phrases) is evident in both sentences: "falling softly . . . softly falling" and "falling faintly . . . faintly falling," lending the lines a poetic feel that is almost hypnotic. Furthermore, the alliterated *s* and *f* sounds use onomatopoeia to echo the sensation of the snow falling in the quiet hours before dawn. As in the best poems, the tone and sound of the passage are utterly appropriate to its meaning.

Stanzas

A **stanza** is a group of lines in a poem, often but not always set apart from other stanzas by a line space. Often—but again, not always—stanzas are also defined by a recurring pattern of rhyme. Stanzas are generally thought of as being uniform in length, but they need not be. The Middle English romance *Sir Gawain and the Green Knight,* for instance, is divided into stanzas of varying length; the ending of each is marked by a kind of refrain, a rhyming figure known as the *bob and wheel,* but the length is determined by the subject matter, much like a paragraph in prose. Indeed, in blank verse, the passages set apart by line breaks are called *verse paragraphs.* With few exceptions, though, the stanza is a group of lines defined by rhyme and designated typographically by extra line spacing.

Stanzas come in all shapes and sizes. Some recurring patterns—the **couplet** (two rhymed lines of equal length), the **tercet** (a group of three lines, usually with one rhyme), and the **quatrain** (a group of four lines that often rhymes *abab* or *abba*)—are usually not called stanzas unless they are set apart from the rest of the poem typographically; they are, however, common and readily identifiable. Many other stanza forms are common enough to have earned names of their own, including **terza rima** (a system of tercets with interlocking rhyme) and **ottava rima** (an eight-line stanza that rhymes *abababcc,* as in Byron's *Don Juan,* a stanza of which we have already examined). The *ballad stanza,* common to many English ballads (and contemporary poems and popular songs modeled on those ballads) is a stanza of four lines (alternating four and three accents per line) with an *abab* or *abcb* rhyme scheme.

Regardless of the form stanzas take, they are traditionally determined by structural repetition, whether that repetition is a particular rhyme scheme, a system of meter, or some combination of these. In much modern and contemporary poetry, though, and specifically in **free verse**, the stanza can often be determined by more arbitrary means: simply by the shape of words on the page and the relationship between the groups of words and the white space that surrounds them. As we shall see when we examine free verse in detail, stanzas as structuring elements take on an even greater role in the absence of regular rhyme and meter.

Stanza patterns serve several important functions in poetry. As noted earlier, they often help the reader determine what genre the poet has in mind; for instance, no poet will ever use the very complicated nine-line *Spenserian stanza* without intending that the work be read with a specific literary context in mind. But the stanza also determines to a great degree the pace of the poem and thus the way it is performed and perceived by the careful reader. And as we saw earlier, attention to line groupings in a poem (such as the quatrains in a Shakespearean sonnet) can actually be a great help in trying to understand the poem's syntax and overall meaning.

Free Verse

After this discussion of the significance of traditional structuring elements in verse, it might seem strange to turn our attention to **free verse**, which is verse without regular metrical form or a uniform overall rhyme scheme. If, as we have been suggesting, form is essential to the function of poetry, what are the structuring elements that make free verse work?

The answer to that question lies in the description of free verse in the preceding paragraph. Free verse is not necessarily poetry without rhythm, though it does not sustain a regular meter. Sometimes a poet can flirt with a traditional meter or use a series of evolving but identifiable meters; at other times, it might seem that the poet is working consciously to avoid using a specific meter. A poet writing in free verse can also make use of rhyme, though there will not be an overall rhyme scheme that directs the course of the poem. It's important to remember that the freedom implied by the phrase "free verse" is not an absolute freedom from structure or convention: the very nature of language requires that except in the case of particularly experimental works, certain rules (such as those governing syntax) are generally recognized and adhered to.

Free verse, then, does not mean formless verse; it means freedom from the obligation to impose a rigid, regular structure on the expression of one's ideas. Consider the following analogy: for many students, going to college means moving away from home for the first time and moving away also from the externally imposed structure of parental rules. First-year college students are suddenly able to go where they want to go whenever they want to. Some students drown in all of this free, unstructured time; the distractions from studying lead their college career to a speedy end. Successful students, however, generally find it possible to structure their time according to their own priorities. Their self-imposed rules might not be the same rules their parents would have imposed, but they provide enough structure for academic success.

Free verse works the same way. Instead of more traditional structuring elements like meter, regular rhyme, and strict stanza patterns, free verse can be structured by elements like line breaks, stanza groupings, and typography— the visual layout of words and lines on the page. The line break is used to direct emphasis to the words that end one line and begin another. Often the line break, used in conjunction with nonstandard punctuation, can be used to separate words momentarily from their syntactic role in the sentence, forcing the reader to decide consciously how the words work in relation to each other. Eloquent ambiguities present themselves in the spaces between lines.

The grouping of lines into stanzas can have a similar effect. Remember as you read free verse that the placement of line breaks and stanza breaks—and the arrangement of left and right margins throughout the poem—are the result of conscious decisions on the part of the poet, so it's appropriate and even necessary to examine the possible effects those choices have on readers' understanding of the poems. These tools are among the most important formal elements the poet can use. Remember, though, that the generalizations we offer here about free verse may apply in different ways to different poems; each poem makes its own rules, just as the successful students in our analogy will determine schedules that best suit their needs and temperaments.

THINKING EXERCISES

1. In a poem that uses regular meter or rhyme (or both), identify the structuring elements at work, and consider how these elements function in support of the poem's theme and overall effect.

2. Consider the form of a free-verse poem of your choice. Where do you see evidence of the poet's structuring choices? How would different line breaks and line groupings change the poem's effect?

3. Compose a sonnet on a subject of your choosing, paying attention not only to rhyme and meter but also to the groupings of quatrains and couplet (for an English sonnet) or octet and sestet (for an Italian sonnet).

✣13✣

Drama

As we have noted, many of the considerations that apply to fiction and poetry apply to drama as well. Since drama almost always involves some element of narrative, many of the issues relevant to fiction also pertain, to drama, and since so many plays are written in verse, they can also be analyzed in terms of versification. We therefore suggest that to study drama, you should also familiarize yourself with the sections on narrative and, if necessary, poetry. Drama does, however, have its own specific set of concerns.

13.1   DRAMATIC CONVENTIONS

One issue in all narrative literature that becomes extremely important in drama is the "willing suspension of disbelief." This phrase signifies the audience's willingness to pretend that the actors on the stage or screen are not actors but the characters they are playing. The audience also agrees to pretend that the stage on which the action takes place is not merely a stage but a public forum in Thebes or a garden apartment in New Orleans.

Willing suspension of disbelief is a slippery idea. We can remember being utterly astonished by the special effects in the original *Star Wars* movie (later retitled *Star Wars Episode IV: A New Hope*) when it was released back in 1977. Today, looking at an unremastered copy of that original film, some of the special effects seem clumsy. Luke's landspeeder doesn't hover quite as magically as it did nearly three decades ago. It has become harder to suspend our disbelief and simply enjoy the archetypal story of good and evil.

If the story is good enough, though, audiences are willing to make such allowances. When you think about it, it seems pretty silly that Lois Lane can't see that Clark Kent is Superman in eyeglasses. But if the story can make you want to believe it, it's a successful story. Play audiences in Renaissance

England had an even more difficult time of it, as they had to be willing to overlook the fact that the roles of women were played by young men, since women were not permitted to act. Yet the popularity of the theater in that period attests to the audience's success in looking past the subterfuge.

Of course, reading fiction also involves the suspension of disbelief. If we are wholly immersed in a story, we may be able to forget, temporarily, that it is fiction; thus we can laugh or cry at the fates of people who never existed. As a play audience, though, we are asked to believe a lot more. Consider, for instance, the **aside**, a brief speech by a character in a play directly to the audience, usually to reveal the character's inner thoughts; though the audience can clearly hear the character speaking, we are supposed to accept that the other characters on the stage cannot. The **soliloquy** is an even more artificial convention because it is an even more extended speech delivered while the character is alone on the stage (or being ignored by the other characters). A real person behaving this way would merit psychiatric attention. Such challenges to realism are necessary evils on the stage, however, and the best dramatists use them to great effect. The best-known passages from Shakespeare are in fact soliloquies.

The very layout of the stage, and the audience's relationship to it, is another convention special to the genre of drama. The **fourth wall** is the term for the invisible wall through which the audience supposedly watches the action of the play. The actors pretend that the wall exists, and the audience pretends to believe that for the characters the wall *does* exist. In the twentieth century, it became popular to challenge this convention; actors would break the plane of the fourth wall for comedic or dramatic effect, occasionally climbing or leaping into the audience or rising from the audience to join the action onstage.

As our examples illustrate, the concept of **verisimilitude**—the appearance of reality—has evolved greatly over the course of history. Greek drama, with its masks and chorus, no doubt seemed natural enough to the audience of the day, but today it seems highly stylized and formal. Later in the history of drama, some critics posited the *three unities* as requirements for verisimilitude. The *unity of action* suggests that a successful play will depict an action that is whole; it has a beginning, middle, and end, and the parts are clearly related. The *unity of place* required that the action of the play be limited to a single location. The *unity of time* required that the time represented by the play be limited to the play's actual real-time duration or at the most the events of a single day.

While unity of action is a quality that most conventional plays adhere to, unity of place and unity of time have never been seriously considered as requirements, especially in English drama. Plays like Shakespeare's *Richard III* and Marlowe's *Doctor Faustus* span much longer periods of time than a single day: months in the former, decades in the latter. Shakespeare's *Henry V* takes place on both sides of the English Channel. In experimental theater, even the unity of action is open to challenge.

THINKING EXERCISES

1. Have you ever seen a play? Which dramatic style best describes the play you've seen?
2. It's easy to think of the advantages film has over the stage. However, can you think of advantages that staged drama has over film?

13.2   SUBGENRES OF DRAMA

The traditional distinctions of genre historically applied to drama are tragedy and comedy. As a form of drama, a **tragedy** has, since Aristotle, traditionally been understood to chronicle the fall of a person from a position of honor or privilege for the purpose of evoking fear and pity that lead to **catharsis**—emotional renewal through vicarious participation in the events depicted. Often the tragic hero's very virtues lead him or her to a disastrous decision, technically known as **hamartia**, which is loosely translated as "tragic flaw." In any case, the play describes in a serious or solemn manner a series of connected events that lead up to the catastrophic climax.

Comedy is defined in dramatic terms as drama that is intended to amuse. While tragedies show the fall of their protagonists from a high place to a low one, comedies depict the opposite: complications are resolved, and the boy and the girl get married and seem ready to live happily ever after. Even when disasters happen in comedies, the audience is usually safe in assuming that no irreversible tragedy will take place. On the whole, the action is lighter and the presentation less solemn and weighty.

Several subgenres of tragedy and comedy can be identified, along with some other genres of drama that do not fit neatly into either broad category.

Classical Tragedy

Since the time of Aristotle, *Oedipus Rex* has been considered the prime example of the tragedy. *Classical tragedy* refers to plays that conform most strictly to the rules set forth by Aristotle. Most of these plays are classical in origin, but more modern plays written in imitation of the earlier ones also fall into this category.

Romantic Tragedy

Most of Shakespeare's tragedies fall into the classification of *romantic tragedy*. The goals, methods, and tone of the romantic tragedy are more varied, and there is frequently greater concentration on character than on plot.

Domestic Tragedy

Domestic tragedy differs from other forms of tragedy by concentrating not on a highborn or noble protagonist but on a person of common birth. Though the form is several centuries old, economic factors made it a very popular genre in the twentieth century. Arthur Miller's *Death of a Salesman* is a well-known domestic tragedy.

Revenge Tragedy

The *revenge tragedy* takes the quest for revenge as its subject. Often, as in *Hamlet*, the protagonist is guided toward revenge by the ghost of the slain party but is plagued by hesitation and other obstacles.

Romantic Comedy

In the case of *romantic comedy*, literary usage and common usage coincide. The romantic comedy is a play in which romantic love is the main subject. The play's complications are usually construed as obstacles to love between the hero and heroine (who frequently don't like each other at the outset of the action, though the audience and the other characters may be able to see that they make a good match). A happy ending, often in the form of a wedding, is the almost inevitable result.

Farce

Farce describes a play that tries to evoke laughter less through wit than through gags. Improbable situations, cross-dressing, mistaken identities, crude humor, sight gags, and slapstick are the stock-in-trade of farce. Well-known plays with farcical elements—though they cannot properly be called farces—include many of Shakespeare's comedies as well as Oscar Wilde's play *The Importance of Being Earnest*.

Comedy of Manners

Comparable to the novel of manners, the *comedy of manners* is a play that represents, often satirically, the social mores of the upper class. The goal is generally to highlight the superficiality and artificiality of that group. Most English comedy of the Restoration and eighteenth century can be placed into this category, as can Wilde's *The Importance of Being Earnest*.

Mystery and Morality Plays

Both of these genres were popular in the Middle Ages. The **mystery play** was based on a biblical event such as the construction of Noah's Ark or the shepherds' visit to the infant Jesus. A **morality play** was an allegorical drama in which the protagonist is beset by abstract concepts in human form. *The Second Shepherd's Play* of the Wakefield Cycle is an example of the first type, and *Everyman* is an example of the second.

Chronicle or History Plays

The English **chronicle play** or **history play** used historical chronicles as its source and represented the reign of a single monarch. Many featured elements of the romantic comedy (as in Act 5 of Shakespeare's *Henry V*), and others featured elements of tragedy (as in Shakespeare's *Richard III*).

Theater of the Absurd

In the **theater of the absurd**, the drama abandons realism to underscore the essential emptiness and meaninglessness of the human condition. Isolation and disconnectedness are common themes; unity of action, based as it is on an assumption of the validity of cause and effect, is not required.

THINKING EXERCISES

1. Think of plays that you have seen (or films, bearing in mind that a lot of movies start as plays). Into which categories do you think the plays you've seen would fall?
2. Can you think of ways in which entirely modern plays and films you have seen are descended from more traditional genres? Can you think of any television shows that you enjoy that could be classified in one of the categories discussed in this chapter?

✌14 ✌

From Reading to Writing

We've devoted a lot of time so far to discussing ways of reading and thinking about literature, which we believe to be worthy activities in their own right. Now, though, we move on to ways of recording and communicating ideas about literature. From a pragmatic standpoint, analytical writing skills are essential; in an academic setting, your ideas can't be evaluated until they've been communicated, and the written word is usually the medium of choice. So if you want to make the grade, you have to be able to write well. The same principle of making the grade holds true, though more metaphorically, in the world outside the classroom: the value of knowledge is quite limited unless it can be communicated effectively, and communication skills are among those most valued by customers, employers, and voters.

By this point in your academic career, you will no doubt have witnessed the importance of writing skills in college. In the next few chapters, we're going to discuss some of the principles of good academic writing as they specifically relate to writing about literature. Ideally, you will come to see that developing and communicating ideas about literature are the logical next steps in the process of active understanding that began with reading. Consider this: why is it more fun to see a movie with a friend than it is to see the same movie alone? After all, with friends there is more danger of distraction or interruption. The answer is that part of our enjoyment comes from sharing the experience. We can exchange observations during the movie, and if the movie warrants it, we can discuss it afterward. Often we revise our opinion of the movie based on our friends' reactions and opinions. We can exchange quotations from it and relive scenes from it. Writing about literature (or film, for that matter) can give us some of the same enjoyment.

But, it can be argued, writing is more difficult than conversation, and the pleasures it offers may not balance the effort good writing requires. It is undeniable that good writing requires effort. It forces us to develop our ideas more fully and to organize them more systematically than we otherwise would. It compels us to defend our opinions with evidence rather than with mere vehemence. It may even force us to change those opinions in the face of compelling counterarguments. These are all good things.

By now you've learned about the principles of composition in high school or college English courses. The good news is that what you learned there will continue to serve you well as you devote yourself to writing about literature. Your literary essay or research paper will, for instance, feature adequate support for a clearly stated thesis, just as any other college paper would. Correspondingly, it might prove worthwhile for us to revisit some of these principles in the specific context of literary analysis.

14.1   "RULES" FOR GOOD WRITING

Many books about writing try to make it sound easy. They seem to imply that if writing doesn't come easily to you, you must not be doing it right. We don't agree. We believe that learning how to write well is important, and like most important things, it's not always easy. Let's face it: you've been learning about writing for most of your life as a student, and you already know that it can be frustrating. The instructor's expectations do not always seem clear, and worse, they are not always consistent with the expectations of your past teachers and professors. It would be a lot easier if there were just one right way of doing things.

Unfortunately, that's not the case. Many textbooks present a collection of "rules for good writing," but to suggest that those rules are universal would be misleading, since different writing situations will necessarily require different strategies. Even the so-called rules of grammar are open to debate and are subject to evolution according to changes in the world at large. A generation ago, for instance, the masculine singular pronoun was used when the gender of the antecedent was not specified. A sentence like *Everyone should bring his book to class* would have been considered perfectly acceptable. Today, though, the masculine singular pronoun is no longer used in these situations, since words like *everyone* refer to both males and females. Consequently, we see what was once an egregious grammar "error" being accepted in all but the most formal of situations: *Everyone should bring their books to class*. In most informal settings, speakers today consider the disagreement in number between the plural pronoun *their* and its grammatically singular antecedent *everyone* preferable to the sexist use of the masculine pronoun.[1]

---

[1]There are, of course, ways of reconciling the apparently contradictory needs of traditional grammar and gender-neutral language. One option is to use *his or her* instead of *his*, though this can quickly become awkward: *Everyone must bring his or her book*. The other is to change the antecedent into something plural: *All students must bring their books*. In formal writing situations, one of these alternatives is preferable to sexist language or pronoun-antecedent disagreement.

Many of the rules of good writing aren't technically "rules" at all. Every semester, we meet students who have been taught not to use the word *you* in an essay, or the word *I* (we prefer the use of *I* to the awkward and often affected constructions like *the present writer* that students devise to circumvent it). Other students have been told that paragraphs must have no fewer than three sentences, or five, or even seven. Some students spend more time agonizing over the width of their margins than they do proofreading their essays, though presumably the words of the essay are more important than the white space that surrounds them.

Most of these "rules" have their origins in sound principles. In most academic writing situations, there is no call to address the reader directly; thus the use of *you* is discouraged. Use of the second-person pronoun can make your composition sound more like a letter to the professor than an analytical essay. In situations such as this textbook, where informal or semiformal advice is being offered, however, the use of *you* may be warranted, if only because it would be wordy and awkward to avoid. Similarly, first-person discourse is often discouraged in academic writing because it feels less formal and because phrases like "I think" and "it seems to me" sound apologetic if not redundant (since the assertions and observations in an essay are assumed to be those of the author unless they are specifically attributed to somebody else). And paragraph development is an important quality of academic writing, though there is no universally agreed minimum number of sentences per paragraph, and short paragraphs have their place even in formal writing. Thus many of these rules can be useful as guidelines if not prerequisites.

The important thing about any writing "rule"—including the ones we'll suggest later as "practical advice"—is to understand the underlying motivation. If you understand the rules, you can decide whether they apply to your project and what the consequences of breaking them would be. Writing an essay means making decisions. Writing is, simply put, deciding what to say and how to say it. Good writing means good decision making based on what is appropriate to the requirements of the writing situation. Generally, if the "rule" comes from your current instructor, it's a safe bet that it's relevant, and you violate it at your peril. Likewise, some standards of grammar will certainly apply in any college writing situation. And of course it should go without saying that it is unwise and inappropriate to use racist, sexist, vulgar, or profane language in an academic essay (except perhaps in the context of quotation). The rule of thumb is to use language that's appropriate to the writing situation; knowing what's appropriate is the key.

THINKING EXERCISES

1. Think about some of the writing rules you have learned during your academic career. Can you identify the reasons behind some of these rules?

Which rules seem "written in stone," and which seem variable depending on the situation?

2.   Although the rule of thumb that you should use language appropriate to the situation seems vague, we all make unconscious decisions about appropriate language choices every time we speak. For the rest of the day, think about how you communicate with family, professors, coworkers, and fellow students—especially in instances where you communicate the same information to different people. What differences, if any, do you detect in word choice, sentence length, accent, and volume? How are these choices similar to the ones you might make as a writer?

14.2   WRITING AS A PROCESS

The feeling of having completed a major assignment is one of the great pleasures of the academic life, so it's no surprise that students are frequently in a hurry to experience it. Like any complex process, however, writing cannot be rushed without sacrificing quality. Writing would be a lot easier if it were a thoroughly linear process: we could merely start at the beginning of our paper, type out an effective introduction that leads into an intriguing thesis, follow it up with convincing supporting evidence, tie it all up with a thought-provoking conclusion, and print it out—all at a sitting! Most of the time writers spend "writing" is actually spent thinking; if the pauses for thought could be eliminated, the average paper could be written in a couple of hours, and this book could have been written in a matter of days.

Of course, those pauses are the essence of the writing process. Without thought, writing is merely typing. Certainly it's possible to rush a writing project, and anyone who has been a student for long has done it—even writing instructors (and textbook authors). It's safe to say, however, that few good essays are the result of rush jobs or one-sitting marathon typing sessions. It simply takes time for the process to run its course.

Procrastination, therefore, is the number one enemy of good writing. Procrastinators often allow themselves to be backed into a corner and wind up receiving a lower grade than they should have received or even failing the assignment; many cases of plagiarism are the result of students' waiting too long to begin their papers and then panicking and seeking a way out. The best way to avoid this trap is to begin the writing process well in advance of the due date. We know how hard this can be, since you undoubtedly have many other tasks due before the assigned paper. However, good writing doesn't just happen, and it doesn't happen all at once. You have to make it happen—on many successive occasions.

After you have read the work or works to be addressed in the essay you are going to write, one excellent way to get the writing process rolling is simply to sit down and write something: make some notes on your topic, write an e-mail to your instructor (or yourself) detailing your plans for the paper, or rewrite the assignment you have been given in your own words. The purpose is to start thinking actively about the assignment you need to fulfill. Even if you have days or weeks to complete the paper, and even if you intend to begin the paper days or weeks from the time the assignment is made, a little active work on it early on will get your mind working on the issues. If the essay you need to write is "on your mind," you may find that ideas come to you when you're driving, cooking, or exercising. This may not save you any time when you actually sit down to write, but it's likely that your writing will be more thoughtful and insightful. Give the process time to work, and the product you produce will reflect it.

In this chapter, we discuss the idea of writing as discovery; later chapters cover the process of further developing and organizing your ideas and presenting them in an appropriate format. We realize that by this point in your career as a college writer, you have probably already found out what works for you, so the intent is not to force you to conform to any sort of "right" way of doing things. Rather, we want to offer some suggestions for writing papers that will help you use your time to the best possible effect while ensuring that the paper you produce is as good as it can possibly be.

When inspiration strikes, the discovery stage of the writing process can seem almost instantaneous—you suddenly *know* what you want to write about, as if by magic or by chance. In writing, however, chance favors the prepared mind, and writers prepare for "inspiration" by reading carefully and giving themselves time to ruminate on what they have taken in. We challenge you to prepare yourself for inspiration before it strikes. Give the writing process the chance and time to work.

THINKING EXERCISES

1. Do you ever procrastinate when writing a paper? If so, what are some of the ways you waste time? How can you avoid procrastinating?
2. One way to start off writing is to engage in freewriting. Just let your mind wander and write down everything you can think of on your topic. Do you think this exercise can help you get started on your paper more easily?

14.3   TOPICS AND ASSIGNMENTS

Many students are surprised to learn that the content of their writing—what their essay actually says—is its most important quality. It is true that mechanical errors can cause a paper to receive a failing grade, but no essay ever earned an A by virtue of grammar and punctuation alone. There is no substitute for having something worthwhile to say. No amount of eloquence can effectively mask the absence of substance in an essay or research paper.

In order for effective communication to take place, something has to be communicated.

The good news is that you don't need to know exactly what you want to say before you set pen to paper (or fingers to keyboard). As you develop your ideas into a draft, you'll find that they change and evolve; at this stage, such evolution is desirable. After you've discovered exactly what you want your essay to say (by letting it say it in rough form), you can develop and refine the support and presentation so that the resulting essay is not an undigested record of your discovery but an assertion of your argument.

The logical place to start with any writing task is with the assignment itself. By now you will have realized that not all assignments are alike; some writing prompts are so detailed that they nearly answer themselves, while others are so nebulous that you're left with little or no idea what direction you're expected to follow. In the case of the highly specific assignment, the intended audience of the essay is usually clear, and often the purpose of the essay is spelled out explicitly as well. Though these assignments may at first appear to obstruct student creativity, many students prefer them because they leave fewer variables for the writer to resolve to the grader's satisfaction. The most difficult part of getting started with such an assignment is making sure that you understand the assignment fully and clearly. Consider the following essay prompt:

> Much of the challenge to understanding Joyce's *Dubliners* lies in relating the events and descriptions of the stories to their climaxes. In an essay of at least 750 words addressed to other members of the class, identify the events, conversations, and descriptions in "Araby" that might seem random to the first-time reader of Joyce, and show how they relate to the story's overall theme. In other words, show how the story constitutes a unified whole with specific references to its various parts.

The prompt gives the student a lot to start with. The minimum length of the assignment—a legitimate concern for students—is clearly defined, as is the subject of the essay. The audience of class members suggests that the essay should be addressed to readers who are at least somewhat familiar with the essay's subject matter; thus the writer can refer to characters and plot incidents without having to provide extensive background information.

This is not to suggest, however, that it's an easy question to answer. A careful reading of the prompt reveals the central question it raises: what is the "overall theme" of the story to which all of the component details somehow relate? Since the prompt does not specify a theme, the essay will need to identify one, and the details it identifies and discusses will need to support the argument that this theme is central to the story.

Another challenging element to this particular prompt is that it seems to be encouraging a listing of story elements without necessarily pointing toward a particular **thesis**. As you know, an essay's thesis is its main point expressed as a sentence. The thesis may or may not be an actual sentence in the essay, but every essay must obviously have a main point expressible in sentence form. What will be the main point of an essay based on this prompt? The prompt itself doesn't suggest it, but it will probably have to do with identifying the main theme of "Araby" and proving its importance to the work. Arriving at the essay's thesis is not necessarily the first step toward writing the essay, however; as we have already pointed out, the first phase of the writing process is discovery. By collecting the information the prompt asks for, the writer will no doubt begin to identify one or more themes that can be advanced as the story's main theme. The writer may even consider and reject a succession of such themes before choosing the emphasis of the essay, the theme to which most of the details can be related; this is all an essential part of the discovery process, and it takes time.

If some prompts are very specific in their requirements, others specify little more than the minimum length and the general subject matter. Some instructors may make assignments like "write a research paper of eight to ten pages on one or more of the works we have read this semester," making the choice of topics part of the writing process. This approach leaves the writer with many more choices, though these choices will eventually lead to the same destination: a provisional thesis. In this case, the writer is responsible not only for providing the answer but also for providing a viable question.

THINKING EXERCISES

1. Examine the writing prompts and essay questions that follow selections in whatever literature anthologies and writing textbooks are available to you. What elements do they have in common? Given the choice, what kinds of questions do you prefer to answer? Can yes-or-no questions lead to good essays?
2. Make a list of several "universal" essay prompts—ones that can be adapted to nearly any work of literature. What kinds of changes would be necessary to apply the "Araby" prompt to another short story? To a play? To a poem?

14.4   ASKING THE RIGHT QUESTION

As we observed in the preceding section, and as you have no doubt experienced at first hand, understanding the assignment is the key to success. Clearly, a careful reading of a detailed essay prompt will often lead directly to an effective thesis statement. But when the assignment is nebulous, stating only the required length, the general subject matter, and perhaps the number of sources, it's up to the writer to determine the audience, scope, and direction of the essay.

What makes a good topic for an essay about literature? A simple but unhelpful answer is that good papers are about interesting topics. But good writing can make nearly any topic interesting. Originality is considered a plus, but at the college level, a paper does not need to discover something entirely new in order to be effective. It's usually enough to present and support a coherent argument effectively.

So let's assume you've been given a fairly open writing assignment. If you've been given your choice of works to write about, here are some suggested guidelines:

- **CHOOSE A WORK YOU UNDERSTAND.**   There's nothing worse than writing an essay based on a flawed understanding of the literary work. A beautiful house constructed on a faulty foundation is worthless. Discussing the work with others who have read it will often let you know if you're off base or if there are variant interpretations you need to deal with in your essay.

- **MAKE IT A CHALLENGE.**   Although it's important to choose a work that's accessible, writing a paper about a work that is too transparent can be very difficult. In our discussion of the literary canon earlier in the book, we suggested that literary writing is writing that rewards active, analytical reading. You may be tempted to pick something easy as the topic of your essay. You should ask yourself, though, whether it seems easy because there are levels of subtext that you're not catching. Also, if the meaning of the work is obvious, what are you going to say about it in your essay that won't be obvious to readers who are also familiar with the work?

- **CHOOSE SOMETHING SUBSTANTIAL.**   If the assignment calls for a ten-page essay, you might want to consider choosing a subject of appropriate substance. It is certainly possible to write a paper of that length on a single sonnet, but if the assignment allows, you might find that following a theme or motif through two or three sonnets gives you a lot more to talk about.

- **DON'T BITE OFF MORE THAN YOU CAN CHEW.**   Effective papers give appropriate treatment to their topics. If you've been assigned a thousand-word essay, don't try to write it on "tragedy in Shakespeare's plays." You'll certainly have plenty to say, but there's no way to avoid superficiality if your budget is only a thousand words. It's more challenging, but ultimately much more effective, to choose a narrower topic and analyze it more thoroughly.

When you've chosen the work or works you want to write about, you're ready to start looking for a topic, assuming that your instructor did not specify a topic when making the assignment. A good place to start is with what interests you; if you're interested in a particular story element, literary device, or dramatic **trope**, you have a much better chance of presenting it to your readers in an interesting way. What stands out as surprising or unusual? What don't you understand about the story, novel, poem, or play? Any of these questions can be a good place to start your investigations. Remember that you're addressing an audience familiar with the work in question; you don't necessarily need to summarize it or assert its aesthetic merit. The goal, at this stage in the writing process, is to formulate a question about your subject that your essay will eventually answer. The answer to that question will be your thesis, but for the thesis to be effective, you have to ask the right question.

What kind of question leads to an effective paper? First of all, you'll want to avoid questions with easy, obvious answers or answers that don't require further elaboration. Yes-or-no questions are out. "How" and "why" questions are generally more fruitful than fact-based questions, though this is not always true. A paper addressing a factual question that does not have a generally accepted answer can be very interesting. "When was *Beowulf* written?" is a valid starting point for an analytical essay, since the dating of the poem is still a subject of scholarly debate. The dating of Christina Rossetti's "Goblin Market" is not, however, so if you're interested in talking about it, you'd be better off asking a more detailed question, such as, "In what way is 'Goblin Market' a product of the era in which it was written?" Some writers distinguish between *literary scholarship*, which involves establishing or debating particular biographical, historical, or textual facts, and *literary interpretation*, which advances a particular explanation of a text. The distinction is useful, though obviously each kind of analysis involves elements of the other. In either case, of course, the paper will move from the facts, if known, to the whys and hows. These questions are the essence of analysis.

Selecting these questions is easier than it might first appear. As you reread the text you intend to write about (and this step is essential!), pay close attention to the elements—thematic, structural, or other—that stand out to you. Why do you notice them? What issues do they raise? Mark the passages in your text, make notes, and look for connections. Sometimes the question presents itself immediately, and sometimes it is more elusive. Consider the following list of generic essay prompts. Some of them will work better than others on particular works, and all of them will need to be refined and modified to fit the works you have chosen to write about, but they may help you get started.

- In a literary work that is intended to be a discrete, coherent whole, identify a passage, chapter, or scene that does not immediately seem to connect to the work's main idea, and discuss the relationship of the part to the whole.
- Consider the work in relationship to the rest of the author's **oeuvre** (body of work) or selections from it. How does this work resemble the author's other writing, and how does it differ? When you consider these works chronologically, is it possible to identify a progression of ideas?
- Consider the role of the work in the literary **canon**. If it is canonical, how has it earned its place? If it is not canonical, why not? Should it be?
- In the case of noncontemporary literature, what does the work suggest about its time, and about the values of its author and first audience?

- Does the work suggest the influence of earlier writers or philosophers you have studied? Discuss the effects of such influences on the work in question.
- In the case of narrative, what strategies of **characterization** does the author use to control the readers' sympathies with regard to the protagonist and other central characters?
- Does **setting** play a significant role in the work in question? This can be an opportunity to incorporate, judiciously, any special knowledge you might have about various regions or occupations.
- Do any objects, items, or characters in the work seem to have value as **symbols** of something beyond their literal meaning? What clues in the text suggest that they are to be interpreted symbolically? What do they mean as symbols, and how does the symbolic meaning relate to the literal one?
- If you have read two or more works on the same topic, contrast them, identifying important differences between them and accounting for those differences.
- Identify language or situations that are ambiguous and explore the ambiguities, with an aim toward either resolving them or explaining how the ambiguous nature of the passage affects your interpretation of the work as a whole.
- Meaningful repetitions of significant words or phrases may signal a **motif** that is important to the work. Trace the motif through the work and discuss its role in creating meaning. Remember that the first step may be to demonstrate that the motif *is* a motif.

This list is a collection of suggestions, and it's not intended to limit any more creative possibilities that might occur to you as you read. Rather, it should show you the kind of question that might lead to an effective essay on a literary topic. Chances are that most of these questions can be addressed with minimal secondary research; in a later chapter, we'll address ways of incorporating literary research into every stage of the writing process.

THINKING EXERCISES

1. Do you think considering a text in the various ways we suggest in this chapter could be helpful in writing a paper? Why or why not?
2. Make a list of the elements in a given literary text that seem to help convey its basic theme. Will any of the features you've noticed be helpful in writing a paper about the text?

14.5   FROM QUESTION TO THESIS

Once you have selected a question, the next step, predictably, is to attempt to answer it. That answer, in sentence form, will be your provisional **thesis**. As we noted earlier, the thesis is a sentence that contains the main idea of your essay. Though there is no set rule (unless your instructor tells you otherwise), it's a good idea to put that sentence somewhere in your introduction, since there's usually no reason to hide the main point of your essay. It's possible to write an essay in which the thesis sentence is never explicitly stated, but in doing so, you run a greater risk of being misinterpreted. Furthermore, a clear statement of your thesis in the introduction can help you stay on track as you craft your first draft.

Remember, though, that unless you're responding to a very specific essay prompt, the question that you've formulated is at this stage a provisional one, and therefore your thesis will also be subject to change. Give yourself time (and permission!) to revise your goals as you begin to write. Specifically, you may need to revise your goals in terms of scope. If you've taken on a topic that's too broad for the space and time you've been allotted, find a way to narrow it down. If—and this is much less likely—you've chosen a topic about which there's just not enough to say, you'll need to find another topic or broaden the one you've started with. In any case, it's best to make these decisions as early in the process as possible.

When you're working on the first draft, a good place to start is with the question you've asked (or been asked) and the provisional thesis you intend to test and prove during the course of your paper. Do not spend too much time on the introduction at this point, because things are still fluid; in the course of working through your paper, you may refine your question or even change your mind about the answer. If that happens, the time you've spent agonizing over the exact wording of your introduction will have been wasted—or worse, you'll avoid changing the content of your paper for the better because you're so taken with your introduction. In any case, though the question is an important part of the writing process, it need not be explicitly asked in the final draft, though the answer—your clearly stated thesis—should be evident.

As you begin arranging evidence to support your thesis, remember that the significance of the thesis itself matters. If you're talking about the way the narrator represents himself in a James Joyce short story, your readers need to know why that's significant. Subject your thesis to the "So what?" test. Why is the question you're asking important, and why is your thesis the best answer to the question? Why should someone who is interested in this work of literature care about the assertions you're making? It's frequently a good idea to address the "So what?" test directly in your essay. Obviously, your topic is important to you, since you've chosen to write about it and you're probably going to be graded on the essay. Similarly, it's important to the instructor, who must read the essay regardless of his or her personal interest in the topic. Of course, nobody wants to spend a lot of time writing about something insignificant, and nobody wants to waste time reading it, so spend a little time in your paper showing your readers why they should care about the topic you've chosen. Don't be intimidated by this—your topic and thesis are significant, but you have to make that significance as clear to your audience as it is to you.

THINKING EXERCISES

1. Compare the list of "universal" essay prompts you compiled earlier to the list in section 14.4 and to literary essay topics you've dealt with in the past. How do the questions suggest the structure an effective answer might take? What kinds of words and syntax make it easier to formulate provisional answers?

2. Choose a literary work with which you are familiar, and formulate theses in response to several of the prompts in section 14.4 (as well as to the "universal" questions you created earlier). Then subject these theses to the "So what?" test. Which ones would make the best essays? How would you go about supporting these theses in the body of your paper?

᠉15᠉

Formulating an Argument

So far, we've discussed how you can create a **thesis** or argument based on questions implicit in the text. Remember that a thesis should be reasonably assertive and to the point, but it doesn't necessarily have to follow all those rules your eleventh-grade teacher required of you. Most college instructors don't want your thesis underlined; it should be clear without that extra effort. Nor, for that matter, does it have to be the first sentence of your paper any more than it has to be the last sentence of the first paragraph.

Basically, your main argument should be made reasonably clear somewhere in the introductory section of your paper. A particularly long and complex paper might require a particularly long and complex introduction (not to mention an involved presentation of the thesis). Readers should not have to wonder what your main point is as they progress toward the initial arguments supporting your position. And as we've stated several times already, your thesis should not be absurdly simple or obvious. For example, you wouldn't develop a whole paper to the effect that Romeo and Juliet fall in love with each other or one that claims as its central point that Toni Morrison is interested in African American themes. Each of these observations is so patently obvious as to be a given; there is no need to present an argument proving what is already an established fact.

Remember that your goal is to edify or enlighten a reader who has read the text in question but has not necessarily understood it in the way that you have. You don't have to repeat obvious parts of the plot or storyline because the reader is already familiar with them. Rather, you have to explain, explicate, or analyze sections of the text so that the reader can grasp your point of view regarding them.

Bear in mind, however, that you *are* arguing a point. Although there are many valid literary analyses that strive to provide both sides of an issue, such fence-straddling essays are very difficult to write. Unless an assignment requires you to consider contradictory arguments, you'll usually be better off sticking to one side of an argument or the other.

This doesn't mean that student writers should utterly disregard opinions that contradict their own; a useful rhetorical strategy is to bring up opposing ideas in order to refute them. If, for example, you write that the duchess in Robert Browning's "My Last Duchess" escapes her husband through death, whereas another writer you've researched believes that the duchess is forever trapped by him because she is represented in the portrait under his control, you could strengthen your case by pointing out any flaws you perceive in the opposing argument.

Another wise choice when selecting a thesis is to avoid proving negatives. For example, if your class has reached a consensus that Robert Frost's "Stopping by Woods on a Snowy Evening" is about a man considering death, writing a paper proving that the poem *doesn't* have the deeper meaning or subtextual references to death can be very difficult. It's usually easier to show that a particular theme, motif, or reading of the text is valid than it is to prove it isn't valid.

One final point: remember that your main goal is to write successful papers. Sometimes this means not just doing a good job but doing the job the instructor has asked you to do. Throughout Part Four, we offer advice on how to write analytical, critical essays from a very general perspective; often, however, instructors will give students very explicit instructions on the kind of paper they are to write. For example, we suggest that a student should *generally* stay away from using too much biography in explication of texts. Sometimes, though—particularly in the case of highly autobiographical writers like Sylvia Plath or when dealing with memoirs by writers like Frederick Douglass or Frank McCourt—teachers might ask that you consider the biography of the author in your explication. Or perhaps you will be called on to compare a story or poem to events in your own life. When in doubt, ask your teacher for further details about the assignment at hand.

THINKING EXERCISES

1. Can you think of a work of literature you've studied that has contradictory interpretations? Do you believe that one interpretation of the text is more valid than the other? Why?

2. Considering the same text, can you develop a convincing argument supporting the other interpretation? Can you see how such an exercise might be useful in establishing your own argument?

15.1   DEVELOPING PROOF AND EVIDENCE

In many ways, a student writer is similar to an attorney bringing evidence to bear. Rather than having to convince a jury of an alleged felon's innocence or guilt, scholarly writers must convince their audience (classmates, instructors, or readers who have read but possibly not understood or appreciated the text on all levels) of the validity of their analytical arguments.

Sometimes students have a tendency to discuss each aspect of a given work during their analysis of the work. They will break a story down the way we broke stories down for discussion in Part Three and carefully discuss **characterization, setting, tone, dialogue, point of view**, and so on. This kind of organization can result in a paper that is too fragmented. Also, not every element of a given work of literature will always help convey theme, and correspondingly, not every element of a given work necessarily needs discussion in great detail. If your critical analysis is a thesis-driven paper, each point you make must support the position put forward by the thesis or central argument. For example, if understanding the rhyme scheme of Frost's "Desert Places" doesn't contribute to our overall understanding of the poem, don't dedicate space in a short paper to discussing the rhyme scheme. On the other hand, our discussion of Shakespeare's sonnets in section 6.2 showed how understanding the rhyme scheme of the English sonnet can help contribute to our understanding and appreciation of the poems; discussion of this particular element is therefore warranted. Each item you bring up in a paper should contribute to proving the point at hand.

Students often get sidetracked when they read (as they should) the introductions to various authors and works in anthologies. Or students will peruse handouts from their instructors or take copious notes and look up texts or writers on the Internet. As a result, students will often find out many interesting things about the authors, the characters, the setting, or some other aspect of the work they are researching. Generally, teachers are pleased that students take this extra interest.

However, a problem arises when students want to incorporate all the various interesting things they have learned into their papers. For example, let's assume that you're writing a short paper on Childress's one-act play *Florence* (in Part Six), and your argument is focused on the railing in the middle of the train platform stage set; you intend to prove that it is being used as a metaphor for segregation and racial inequity. Perhaps in doing a bit of research you learned that Childress also wrote a novel in 1973 titled *A Hero Ain't Nothin' but a Sandwich* that was later adapted on film. Although this fact may be very interesting, does it really belong in a short analytical paper that is trying to explain the central metaphor of a play written in 1949? Most likely not.

Nor, for that matter, is a short paper on *Florence* probably the right place for students to express their outrage over the injustice of a segregated society. Alice Childress has already done a better job of expressing that outrage through the creative outlet of the play. The job of the student in a literature course is not to offer a social commentary on the pre–Civil Rights era South but to help readers understand and appreciate the work that Childress has done. At certain times and places, students may and should weigh in with their own opinions on matters and offer up more than just an interpretation of the text, but often this tendency has the effect of cluttering a paper and distracting readers from the central analysis. As we stated earlier, the obvious exception to this advice is when your instructor specifically asks that you consider other texts, biography, social context, moral issues, and so on.

Even if the point you're making is quite relevant to your overall analysis, the relevance of each section of your argument should be clearly explained. Use transitions and statements that indicate the significance of a particular section. All too often, students will remember some explanation of a metaphor or symbol from class discussion but then fail to prove adequately the explanation to a reader's satisfaction in a paper. In essence, they jump from point A to point D, bypassing B and C. It's as if a prosecutor said to a jury, "Since Sam likes pepperoni pizza, he is guilty of stealing from Joey" without also proving that Sam stole a blank check from Joey and used it to pay for a pizza. Saying that Sam stole from Joey because he likes pizza doesn't make sense; saying that Sam likes pizza and took Joey's check to pay for a pizza does.

For example, when writing about Chopin's story "The Storm," a student recalls that the class discussed how the actual storm in the story served as a metaphor for the storm of passion between Alcée and Calixta. The student writes, "The storm shows that Calixta and Alcée are interested in each other." Although this statement may be somewhat true, the assertion doesn't stand on its own here. The writer has to explain the point through developing this section of the analysis or argument in clear, logical order.

In the next section of this chapter, we'll discuss the importance of organizing your paper. For now, consider this example. In outline form, the development of your argument about symbolism in "The Storm" might look something like this:

THESIS: THE ACTUAL STORM REPRESENTS THE LOVERS' PASSION.
1. Calixta's husband is away when Alcée drops by her house.
2. A storm is building, just as the two are suddenly together.
3. Calixta and Alcée have a history of sexual tension.
4. Perhaps the building storm symbolizes the building sexual tension between Calixta and Alcée.
5. The rainstorm begins, and Calixta and Alcée give in to their mutual attraction for each other, thus reinforcing the interpretation that the storm represents their passion.

Notice that stripped down, the outline looks a lot like a summary; in composing your argument, however, you should only bring up issues of plot or characterization if they help support your interpretation. This example clearly builds its case and takes care not to assume that symbolic interpretations are a given. Rather, they must be asserted and then supported through reference to relevant sections of the text and explanations as to the relevance of those sections. In this case, the analytical assertion is that "the building storm symbolizes the building sexual tension between Calixta and Alcée." The writer first provides the context: Alcée and Calixta are alone together. Then the assertion is developed through reference to the flashbacks that indicate Calixta and Alcée's history; finally, the analysis is rounded off by showing that the culmination of the storm mirrors the culmination of their love affair.

When writing about a particularly short story like "The Storm," it's easy to stay on track and ensure that everything you write contributes to the central analysis or thesis of the paper. As we stated earlier, however, always make sure that your point is relevant and that its relevance is clear to the reader.

For example, a student might also note in the paper that Calixta is doing laundry for her family when Alcée arrives. Taken by itself, this observation doesn't seem particularly significant. But the student may go on to say that Calixta's washing the clothes shows her performing the duties of a wife and mother by restrictive nineteenth-century standards and that her temporary desertion of her laundry and sewing chores for Alcée shows that she is temporarily relinquishing her role as wife and mother. Suddenly, this brief observation about Calixta's chores adds to the overall understanding of the story. Furthermore, this point contributes to the earlier argument that the storm itself represents their passion for each other in that the storm interrupts her duties as much as Alcée does.

When students or writers are chiefly concerned with developing their analysis or interpretation only from the text itself and don't use outside source materials—articles, Web sites, forewords, and documentaries—they are proving their point by using only the *primary source* or *primary text* or, as we stated, the literary work itself. A paper could very possibly refer to more than one primary text. An essay analyzing "Desert Places" by Frost could refer to his poem "The Road Not Taken" as a way of proving part of its argument. Or perhaps students are called on to discuss the influences of one writer on another (say, Henry James on Edith Wharton); in this case, a student might compare James's *The Portrait of a Lady* to Wharton's *The Age of Innocence*, referring in each case to a primary source.

The term *secondary source* is a bit more complicated. If a paper assignment for a literature course asks that students use secondary sources to support their various thesis arguments, the instructor usually intends for the students to research literary journals and books of literary criticism in order to find out what various published critics and scholars have said about the work or works in question. So, for example, if a student writing a paper on "Hills Like White Elephants" quotes an article by Joseph R. Urgo from the journal *The Explicator,* Urgo's article is a secondary source.

In some cases, however, students may be called on to write nontraditional assignments. For example, a teacher might ask that students read racist, proslavery tracts taken from slave states in the 1830s in order to gain perspective on Frederick Douglass's *Narrative of the Life of an American Slave*. Here those proslavery political tracts are a historical secondary source. Or possibly students could be asked to read parts of writers' biographies and to argue in their papers how writers' lives influenced their work; although this technique is sometimes referred to as **biographical criticism**, the biography itself is nevertheless a kind of secondary source.

The main thing to remember when referring to a secondary source is that you should quote it only if the quotation contributes to your analysis. As we'll discuss further in later chapters, never include a quotation from an article just because you can or because you're required to use a certain number of sources; the included quotation from a secondary source must have value in your analysis.

THINKING EXERCISES

1. Choose a favorite hobby or sport you enjoy. Using short phrases, make a quick list of things you know about the sport. (For example, a racquetball player might write things like "four-wall racquetball is more fun than three-wall," "need goggles," and "use the wrist, not the arm.")

2. On a new piece of paper, develop an argument about the hobby or sport. Is it better than others, should it receive more attention, is it dangerous? Now check your first list again. How many of your observations about the hobby or sport are actually relevant or helpful in proving your argument?

3. Choose a lengthy literary work you've studied at some point—a novel, play, memoir, or long poem—and perform the same exercises. Make a list of everything you know about the text, and then develop an outline of an argument that helps a reader better understand or appreciate the text. How many of your initial observations are pertinent?

4. Have you ever done research for a project of any sort and realized that some of the material discovered through research wasn't useful to your project? How did you come to realize that not all the research discoveries were helpful?

15.2   ORGANIZATION AND STRUCTURE

Although there are any number of ways that a writer can organize an essay, one thing that almost everyone can agree on is that a good analytical essay must be organized and not randomly thrown together. Too often, students write thoughts down as ideas come to them and then fail to revise their thoughts to make them more cohesive, thus turning in papers that are only a step or two removed from journal-style freewriting.

As we have stated, the student writer has to make a lot of choices and answer a number of questions when confronted with organizing a paper. One of the first questions is, *When* should a writer organize an essay? Some writers elaborately plan out their papers in outline form before they write their first sentences; thus before they finish the first paragraph, they know how the paper will end. Others lay their notes out around them, blaze through a rough draft off the tops of their heads, and then sit back and plan a carefully organized second draft. This method is made easier in these days of writing on computers and cutting and pasting in word processing programs.

Since organization is such a big part of the prewriting stage, let's examine other possible steps you might want to take before writing your essay.

- **REREADING THE PRIMARY TEXT.**   You need to know what you're writing about forward and backward. If you've followed our earlier advice and marked up your book and your notes as you've read and noticed points of interest, these markings will help you in rereading all of shorter texts and parts or all of longer texts.

- **TAKING AND REVIEWING NOTES.**   If you are an extensive note taker during class discussion and lectures, go back and review those notes; try to ascertain which notes will help you write your paper. Even if you don't take many during class, write new notes as you think your project through. Don't worry about being organized during the note-taking stage; just be sure to get everything down on paper, on note cards, or in your computer.

- **DOING REQUIRED RESEARCH.**   If research is required, start to do it after rereading the text and reviewing your notes. Remember that it's OK to start your research without having a clear idea of a thesis; in fact, literary research is usually more rewarding if you approach it with an open mind. Remember, however, that not everything you find in research will necessarily be useful to you. Much that you may think is interesting may not prove helpful to the paper at hand.

Having completed these stages, you can choose what comes next: either an outline or a "zero" draft that will come before the outlining stage. For most people, outlining before starting a first draft is helpful; for people who suffer from writer's block and are willing to drastically rewrite early drafts, however, writing a free draft (or zero draft) before outlining may help unlock the floodgates.

Your outline doesn't have to follow any standard format—it doesn't necessarily have to make use of roman numerals, capital letters, lowercase letters, or anything else. It doesn't necessarily have to be written on note cards, nor does it necessarily have to conform to the automatic outlining feature in your word processing program. But you must have an outline, and the outline should clearly reflect the scheme or plan that you will use to organize your paper.

Some of the problems that you will encounter when planning an outline for a paper are similar to the ones you encounter when developing a thesis.

One thing you will have to consider in each case is the matter of *scope*. The complexity and detail of your thesis and outline should conform to the length of the assignment as presented to you by the instructor. If a professor is asking you for a five-page paper on *Florence* by Alice Childress, you probably don't have room to develop a long, thoroughly detailed, well-researched argument that examines the complexity of segregation codes. Quite probably you should mostly stick to explicating the text in support of your thesis.

This consideration of scope, detail, and length is somewhat illustrated by two of the terms instructors will often use when requiring a paper. Sometimes they ask for an **explication**, and sometimes they ask for an **analysis**. In common usage, these words would seem to be practically synonymous. Strictly speaking, however, they have slightly different connotations. *Explication*, according to the dictionary, involves "intensive scrutiny and interpretation of the interrelated details of a written work, especially a literary one." Often instructors use this term when they want you to consider almost every aspect of a given work in your goal to ascertain, establish, and discuss the theme and your own interpretation of the work's meaning. A particularly thorough explication might begin with a summary and continue by considering every nuance of a given work.

Analysis, by contrast, is defined as "the separation or breaking up of a whole into its parts and the examination of these parts to reveal their nature, function, or interrelationship." Implicit in the word *analysis* is the concept that one isn't necessarily required to understand every complex facet of a given text; rather, the writer teases out a single, significant thread that helps contribute to the audience's understanding of the whole cloth of the text.

Let's say your professor is asking for a four- to five-page paper on something you've read before your midterm. You could possibly write a fairly complete explication of a short work like "Araby," "Desert Places," or *Florence* in your short paper. On the other hand, what if you're required to write on Shakespeare's *Hamlet*? Thousands of books and articles have been written on *Hamlet*; how can you possibly detail, explain, explicate, and interpret everything going on in this wondrously complex play in only four or five pages? You can't. However, you may be able to choose a single element of the play you'd like to concentrate on that will still accomplish the primary goal of the analytical paper: to enlighten a reader who has read the text in question but not necessarily understood it in the way that you have. So a paper on fatherhood in *Hamlet* focusing on King Hamlet (the Ghost), Polonius, and Claudius (Prince Hamlet's stepfather and uncle), could be fruitful and enlightening yet not woefully underdeveloped. In short, make sure your idea for a paper is matched by the scope of the assignment. Don't bite off too much or too little.

Once you've developed a pretty good idea for a thesis that matches the paper assignment and you're comfortable with the text in question and feel that you understand it pretty well, you're ready to create your outline and then get to work. Upon reaching this stage, you must decide how to organize your essay. There are several ways to organize a paper, and each has its advantages and disadvantages.

One technique is to argue your points in *order of importance*, progressing from the most important to the least. This may work well because you spend the most time (and words) on the biggest issues in the essay, and you cut right to the chase; however, the last part of your paper might inadvertently include a few "these are also important" points that you feel are necessary but don't require as much development. The resulting paper may be somewhat lopsided. Sometimes a writer may counterbalance the paper by saving up a very important point for the final argument in the paper.

You can also organize your paper in *text order*, which is to say in the same order as the text, but the problem here is that your paper may tend to lack focus. If we learn a lot about a character in the first chapter of a novel and again in the tenth chapter of the novel, are you going to desert your discussion of this character for half your essay and then return to it?

Perhaps the most useful technique is a combination of the two. Following this technique, writers would tackle each new issue when they arrive at it in the text, but as soon as they introduce the argument or assertion, they can leapfrog to other places in the poem, play, story, or essay that help them prove their point. Then, upon finishing this part of the argument, they move on to the next important item in the text. In the case of a student essay for a literature course, an "important item" is any item that directly relates to the thesis the student is trying to prove.

Here is an example of an essay outline of this sort:

THESIS: The women in Susan Glaspell's *Trifles* are united through their empathy for Mrs. Wright and in response to the casual sexism of the men.

INTRODUCTORY SECTION: Thesis, Mrs. Wright's situation—no children, lives in a hollow, attitude of the men.

DISCUSS SETTING FURTHER: Play published in 1916, before women could vote or serve on juries in most places (consult research?). What the "hollow" might mean, the cold of winter, the scene being set in a kitchen, which would have been considered "domestic" or "women's" space. What might the exploded preserves mean?

DISCUSS NAMES: The women having to use their husbands' names, the different names for Minnie Foster and Mrs. Wright.

DISCUSS THE QUILT: May represent two things—the women unraveling the mystery and piecing it back together, and the women symbolically uniting with Minnie Foster Wright. And of course, they're covering up the murder.

DISCUSS THE BIRD AND BIRDCAGE: How the bird in a sense represents Minnie; the cage represents her life; Mr. Wright killing bird equates to how her life has been; strangling him with rope is poetic justice.

DISCUSS MRS. HALE AND MRS. PETERS'S DECISION AND CONCLUSION: Why the women decide not to submit the proof to the County Attorney; does "knot it" = "not guilty"?

Note that this essay seems initially to approach the play in the chronological order of the plot, following the text order, but very quickly it moves around from point to point. Remember that the primary goal for your plan of organization is that your argument be clearly and logically developed. Use transition sentences and phrases to set up the next point; don't tackle points of the argument at random, but instead make sure each element should appear where it does. And always make sure your argument is clearly relevant to the overall point of the paper.

Among professors' biggest complaints about poor student papers are lack of *coherence* and *cohesiveness*. *Coherence* in a paper means that each point is clearly stated; its relevance is manifest, its importance undeniable. *Cohesiveness* in a paper means that the paper should, as a whole, hang together. Each point should naturally and logically lead to the next; no section of the paper should seem tangential, digressive, or out of place.

Let's examine these concepts through use of examples from another profession. If you were an architect, you couldn't just sketch plans for a major building project—say, a fifteen-story office building—on notebook paper, drawing freehand and just guessing at scale and distances. Instead, you would have to draw up your plans meticulously on blueprint paper, making proper use of architectural symbols and measuring each line to scale. As an architect, your plans would have to demonstrate *coherence*; they would have to speak clearly to the engineers and construction experts who will take the plans and make them into reality.

Second, an architect must work closely with construction engineers and take great pains to work out how the weight of walls and floors will be distributed; you'd have to pay very careful attention to air conditioning and ventilation, placement of elevator shafts, safety codes, and the like. Each little part of your master blueprint relates to some other part; the blueprints must demonstrate remarkable *cohesiveness*. If you fail to take any small factor into account, the building could collapse before it is even completed. Similarly, a paper that doesn't argue each point coherently and tie the various elements of an argument together cohesively will fall apart before reaching its conclusion.

THINKING EXERCISES

1. Think of a favorite movie or novel or story you know. Briefly jot down its plot outline, also noting use of symbolic or figurative elements. Does outlining it increase your understanding of the work? Or rather, do you better appreciate the efforts of the screenwriter and the director?
2. If you have any old literature papers from previous semesters or classes, examine them and then try to make an outline for what you wrote (if you still have the outline, disregard it and try to create one from reading the text

of your essay itself). Do you see ways you could improve the coherence of various points? Is the paper cohesive?

15.3   INTRODUCTIONS AND CONCLUSIONS

By now we've discussed coming up with a general topic and sharpening that topic into a thesis; we've discussed ways to get your mind ready to write, and we've talked about rereading the text, taking and reviewing notes, deciding whether you need to do research, developing a strong outline for the paper, and making sure that you stay clearly and firmly on track.

For many students, outlining isn't too difficult; they already have an innate sense of how to develop their analysis. Unfortunately, however, many students get stumped writing their introductions and their conclusions. Often students dwell on these two small components of their papers far longer than on other more complex and perhaps more involved sections of their paper.

Perhaps the main problem students have with introductions isn't actually a problem with the introductions per se; rather, it's a problem getting started on the paper in the first place. For some students, however, the problem really is that they're not sure how to begin a paper that they're quite ready to write. For these students, a useful technique might be to bypass the introduction altogether at first and leap right into the paper. Then, once they've finished the remainder of the draft, they can return to the beginning and write the introduction. In fact, it is often easier to concentrate on an introductory section of a paper *after* you've focused your thoughts through outlining and drafting.

Notice that in the preceding paragraph we referred to an "introductory section" rather than an "introductory paragraph." It may be that your introduction is longer than just the first paragraph, and perhaps even your first paragraph won't explicitly deal with the analysis you're working on. Many students have been taught to have an introduction that clearly states the (often underlined) thesis and then to enumerate the points (three of them, according to the time-honored formula) that will be made to help prove the thesis. In college writing, however, you can feel free to be a little more adventurous with your introduction.

Often the goal of middle and secondary school teachers is to help students realize that they need to organize their papers; having introductions openly state the actual scheme of organization helps students stick to their plans or outlines. The problem with these outline-style introductory paragraphs, however, is that they tend to make the essay redundant and possibly awkward. In fact, many of the methods students have been taught to employ automatically in the opening paragraphs of essays become so familiar to instructors reading these papers as to constitute monumental clichés. For example, the introduction that begins with the definition of some slightly obscure word that will presumably connect to the thesis has become a cliché. Similarly, the analytical essay that tells a few lines about the student writer's life as a way of informing the reader that the essay's author can identify with the literary work at hand, or a series of questions asking readers if they've ever worried or wondered about certain relevant points, or a statement about how the world used to be during the author's time—all have become stultifyingly familiar.

The main goal of a paper's introduction is to give readers a clear idea of your overall point. Although we've stated that you don't necessarily have to immediately foist your thesis upon readers, they should still have a solid understanding of the essay's goal by the end of the first page or so. Obviously, more complicated essays written about more complicated topics may require more than a page or two; a 350-page dissertation might well require a twenty-page introduction. For most shorter student papers, however, the first full page of print should be enough to get the point across.

As always in writing, your goal is to be lucid and interesting. If you've done your job with the thesis, then you don't have to worry about positing an argument that is absurdly obvious or not worth arguing ("'Desert Places' takes place during winter" or something equally obvious). Also, literary analysis is not written for the kind of audience that a general humor article for a popular magazine would be written for. Although having an introduction that engages your audience is a good thing, you don't have to "hook" your readers to drag them unwillingly to the second page. There's more to a good introduction than simply capturing the readers' attention.

Finally, one of the principal errors that students make in their essays is writing a lengthy preamble tying the essay or literary work being discussed to some vast external generality. Students wax on about life in these modern times and how rough it is or how people in the world have now learned lessons or how all women were treated once upon a time or how everyone now knows better than to make the mistakes people used to make. Usually, you should avoid making sweeping generalizations about culture, history, the nature of youth, the state of the nation, or anything else; just stick to the text and your analysis of it. Although you may often see published articles that start by placing a work of literature in the context of an author's career or discussing the author's life or discussing the general cultural context of a piece, you must recognize that published authors and scholars are usually more qualified to make such generalizations (and even in those cases, they're not always a good idea).

Conclusions, unfortunately, are even more difficult to write than introductions. Often students have been taught to merely restate the objectives that were posited in the introduction; instead of writing "In this paper, I will prove points A, B, and C," the student writes, "In conclusion, we have considered points A, B, and C." Such a conclusion reads awkwardly, is repetitive, and comes across as amateurish.

In fact, you should avoid generic tag openings to conclusions like "To sum up" and "In conclusion," and you should avoid presuming that you've converted your reader as implied by statements like "You can see that I have proved these points." The main goal of a conclusion is to let readers know that they've reached the end of your argument. It may be that you should restate whatever objective you established at the beginning of the paper, but not if it makes the paper redundant. Another thing you can possibly do in your conclusion is to restate the relevance of your point or points to a reader's understanding of the text. Again, avoid this if it makes the paper repetitious or redundant. Longer papers may be able to get away with a brief recapitulation of the argument; shorter ones usually don't need one. The main goal is to end your analysis with all loose threads tied up. If you realize that you've asked questions that you never answered, more revision is in order. Never let questions you've raised go unanswered.

THINKING EXERCISES

1. Examine a critical article in a textbook, in this book, or in a research source. Do you find the introduction to be effective? If so, how it is effective? What techniques does the article's author employ?

2. Perform the same exercise with a conclusion. Again, is it effective? If so, what makes it effective?

15.4 REVISING YOUR PAPER

Completing the first draft of your essay is an accomplishment, but there is still plenty of work to do. Too often, due to procrastination, students are forced to submit their first drafts as final drafts, depriving themselves of the opportunity to craft their essays into highly effective pieces of verbal communication. Try to have your draft written several days in advance of the due date so that you can take the steps necessary to devise the best essay possible.

Student writers tend to equate *revision* and *editing* with *proofreading*, but each of these processes has a different goal and a different focus. In practice, of course, you might revise and edit, or edit and proofread, or do all three, all at the same time. In fact, you've probably been doing a little of all three as you've been writing your first draft. When the draft is done, though, we encourage you to approach each step separately so that you can focus on the different kinds of improvements you can make in your essay.

The process of turning a first draft into a final draft can be considered in several different ways, but however you look at it, you should plan on moving from the general to the specific, as the tapering triangles in the diagram suggest. When you *revise*, you're looking at the essay as a whole and

reconsidering s content. When you *edit*, you're focusing on the effectiveness
of paragra and sentences, concentrating on organization and style.
During the *ofreading* stage, the emphasis is on mechanics at the level of
sentence rds, and punctuation. Don't waste time proofreading before
you rev d edit; don't worry about spelling until you've made sure your
parag are doing what you want them to do.

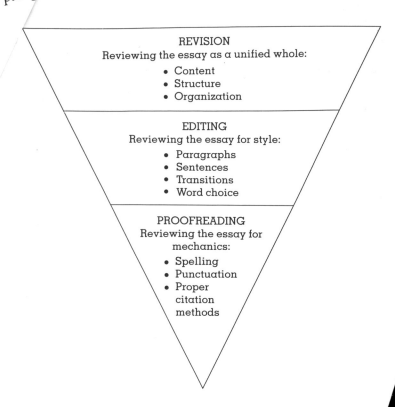

REVISION
Reviewing the essay as a unified whole:
- Content
- Structure
- Organization

EDITING
Reviewing the essay for style:
- Paragraphs
- Sentences
- Transitions
- Word choice

PROOFREADING
Reviewing the essay for
mechanics:
- Spelling
- Punctuation
- Proper
  citation
  methods

Revision

The word *revise* literally means "look again," and as the first st
process of turning a first draft into a final draft, this "looking aga
be understood as broadly as possible. At this point, you're ree
your entire essay. To do this properly, you need to approach the
outside, as if you were not its author. Ideally, after completing t
you should have time to set it aside and think about somethin
eral hours or even days. When you look back at the paper,
reading it the way any other reader would: critically, with
works and what doesn't work.

At this point, your attention should be on content and l... issues. *You* already know what you want your paper to say, bu... structural stranger (with the appropriate background knowledge) be able... ould a total the argument your paper is setting forth? Since the goal of your pa...nderstand municate your ideas about your subject to your readers, you need t... to com- that the paper is meaningful not just to you personally but to a wider... sure as well. Some composition theorists talk about the difference between ...nce based" and "reader-based" prose. Chances are that your first draft ... writer-based—meaningful to you but perhaps not to others. During the pr... of revision, you'll want to make sure that your prose communicates your me... ing on its own terms, regardless of what the reader may (or may not) bring ... the subject; in other words, revision involves, in part, moving from the writer-based mode of composition to the reader-based prose of the finished essay.

Along with deciding what should and should not be included in your essay, you should also ensure that the organization of your essay is appropriate to the subject matter and that your thesis and main supporting points are arranged and explained in the most effective way possible. What's missing from the essay? How much weight should each of your supporting para-graphs be granted in the paper? Where will your thesis be stated in the essay? ...is is the stage in which these questions need to be consciously addressed. ...ember that it is seldom desirable in expository writing to obscure your ...or supporting points, so make sure careful readers will be able to iden-...n. Though you may or may not have written your essay from an actual ...is stage of the writing process demands that you consider the formal ...t of elements in your essay. Make an outline of your essay's main ...e it to make sure that the movement from point to point makes ...on't be afraid to make major changes to your essay at this ...rd *revision* suggests, as we have noted, large-scale rewriting.

...paring the draft for final submission involves taking ...ays what you want it to say and making sure that it ...s effectively as possible. Obviously, most of your ...mpleted by now, since otherwise you'll be mak-...phs and sentences that may not survive the

...t the level of the paragraph, editing con-...o without saying that you need to make ...mmatically correct. But there's much ...ng errors. Fundamentally, editing is ...s clear and as smooth as it can be. ...le, mechanics, and word choice.

...argument are organized appropriately ...s, it's time to give your introduction and conclusion more consideration. The introduction should communicate, not obscure, the essay's topic and thesis. Make sure that the scope and subject of your argument are clearly articulated. As we noted earlier, the introduction of a college-level essay must do more than simply "get the readers' attention," since presumably the readers of such an essay will have attention spans equal to the challenge. Rather, the essay's subject matter should be presented in a manner that makes it appealing to readers, perhaps by identifying the essay's importance to the understanding of the author or work it discusses. Generally speaking, the introduction should also leave no doubt as to the essay's topic, if not its thesis.

The conclusion to an essay of literary analysis should, similarly, function just as in any expository essay. Use the conclusion to underscore your main points, but do not raise new points or questions in the concluding paragraphs. When your essay is over, it should be clear to your readers why it has concluded, and all the questions raised in your essay should have been answered. Avoid simply restating the points you offered in your introduction, but don't hesitate to refer to it; this is an effective way of achieving closure.

Transitions are another important element of good writing that should be fine-tuned during the editing process. Effective transitions are a significant attribute of reader-based prose. You've created an argument, and now you must make sure that you lead your readers through it safely. Make sure that the relationship between ideas is evident, and don't worry that you might be making your argument too obvious; you already know what you're saying, but the reader does not. Underscoring the connections among related thoughts will only make your argument clearer and more accessible to your readers.

The editing stage is also the appropriate time to take on one of the most important, and yet most slippery, elements of writing: style. Good style is, essentially, the right words in the right places. The goal is not simply to use words correctly but to choose the best words and phrases for a particular situation. How do you judge whether a word or phrase is the best one possible? If you choose language that is concrete and specific, you'll be on the right track. Always avoid wordiness for its own sake; if words or phrases aren't contributing to the goals of the paper, delete them and replace them with more effective alternatives. The best test for style is to read your paper aloud to yourself or, better yet, to have someone read it to you. If something sounds awkward or unnatural, make the necessary changes. Listen to your paper as if you were not its author, and be hard on it. Every improvement you make to your paper is one that your instructor won't have to suggest to you when he or she is grading it. One warning about seeking help bears mentioning, however: in most cases, it's considered acceptable to get somebody else's opinion of your essay and for others to offer general suggestions for improvement, but if you allow someone else to rewrite your paper for you, you are almost certainly violating your institution's academic integrity policy. Make sure you know what the rules are for your institution, and make sure you stay within them.

Proofreading

Proofreading is the process of finding and correcting grammatical and mechanical errors in your writing. At this stage, having passed through the revision and editing stages, you'll be making few, if any, large-scale changes to your essay. This final stage of manuscript preparation is, unfortunately, the only one many students think matters, and although it is certainly true that a poorly proofread essay will usually receive a low grade, it's equally true that most instructors focus more on content and presentation than on cosmetic errors. Good proofreading means catching and fixing every little problem in your paper: every spelling error, every grammar problem, every misplaced piece of punctuation. Let's face it: these little errors can quickly erode a writer's credibility. At worst, too many errors can suggest that you don't know any better; indeed, the best they can communicate is that you're sloppy and careless. Neither is the message you want to convey.

Proofreading somebody else's writing is much easier than proofreading one's own, as we have been reminded repeatedly during the preparation of this book. Therefore, you may choose to seek the help of another reader to point out your oversights; as suggested earlier, there's generally nothing wrong with this, but make sure that all of the work you submit for a grade is your own and not the work of an outside editor or proofreader.

Whether or not you have somebody else look over a draft of your paper before you hand it in, here are a few suggestions for successful proofreading.

- **DO NOT RELY ON YOUR COMPUTER TO PROOFREAD FOR YOU.** Spell checkers are certainly useful, but they're far from perfect. They may not catch misused words (*who's* for *whose*, for instance). Grammar and style checkers are less benign; they frequently identify as wrong sentences that are grammatically correct, offering alternatives that are incorrect or stylistically inept. Remember that computers cannot read as humans read. Though these devices can help in manuscript preparation and the identification of simple errors, there is no substitute for the human eyes and the human mind when it comes to critical evaluation of writing.

- **READ YOUR PAPER BACKWARD—SENTENCE BY SENTENCE, WORD BY WORD.** One of the hardest parts of proofreading is the temptation to build up momentum as you go through your paper. Consequently, the first page winds up perfect, but the last page is essentially untouched rough draft. The problem here is the persistence of memory. We end up reading not the essay on paper (or on screen) but the essay in our brain from which the written essay is derived. Needless to say, the imaginary essay is perfect, and if we only proofread that virtual, perfect piece of writing, we're in for a nasty surprise later on, since that's not the one that receives the grade. One great way to focus on the real essay is to read it in reverse, one sentence at a time, starting at the end. This way, you're considering each sentence on its own terms, and there's no way you can build up momentum and rush through the job. Don't worry that you're missing out on the continuity and logic of your essay; those are issues you've already worked on during the revision and editing stages.

- **KNOW YOUR WEAKNESSES, AND WORK TO CORRECT THEM.** Each of us has our own strengths and weaknesses. Some of us may never spell a word wrong, while others may never write a sentence fragment or a comma splice. What aspects of academic writing have given you trouble in the past? These are the issues you'll want to pay the most attention to at this point. Do not think that writing just comes more easily to others than it does to you. This is probably true in some cases, but in general, better writers are simply those who spend more time improving their drafts.

- **FINISH UP WITH A FORMAT CHECK.** Each instructor has a specific set of expectations about paper format, so you might as well make sure you follow them, since in some cases failure to do so may result in a lower grade. Make sure that your pages are numbered correctly and that you've observed appropriate documentation and manuscript preparation rules. If the instructor has not given you specific guidelines, follow those of the Modern Language Association (see Chapter 24).

FINAL DRAFT CHECKLIST

REVISION: REVIEWING FOR CONTENT AND ORGANIZATION

- Is the thesis stated clearly and effectively?
- Are the ideas developed sufficiently?
- Is there sufficient and relevant support for my argument?
- Are counterarguments rebutted successfully?
- Is the overall pattern of organization logical?
- Is the paper interesting?

EDITING: REVIEWING FOR STYLE

- Have awkward spots been smoothed over?
- Have wordy and redundant passages been pared down?
- Are the transitions between ideas clear and helpful?

PROOFREADING: REVIEWING FOR MECHANICS

- Are verb tenses appropriate and consistent throughout the essay?
- Do the subjects and verbs of each sentence agree in number?
- Do pronouns agree with their antecedents in number?
- Have spelling errors and punctuation mistakes been corrected?
- Are all citations properly punctuated?

$\backsim 16 \backsim$

Citing Primary Texts and Formatting Your Paper

Throughout this text, we've stated that a critical analysis essay is quite often an argumentative or persuasive essay. All argumentative essays are built on the same basic blocks: the writer asserts a **thesis** and then puts forth evidence to support that thesis. In a literary analysis, evidence will quite often take the form of a brief quotation from the text being analyzed, followed by the essay writer's interpretations or analysis. However, you shouldn't just throw any given quoted line into the paper, and when you do use quotations in your paper, you must follow the proper procedures. Please remember that this chapter is mostly concerned with how you cite quotations from primary texts; secondary texts offer a different array of problems, and we deal with those in Part Five.

16.1 CITING PRIMARY TEXTS

Use Quotations Appropriately

As we discuss throughout this book, you don't use quotations merely to prove you've read the text. You use quotations that help prove your point in a clear and succinct fashion or that are particularly interesting or dramatic. For whatever reason you use them, your quotations must prove useful to your paper. Deciding when to use quotations in papers is difficult; if you use too few, you're "telling" in your analysis rather than "showing," and your paper may tend to be vague; if you use too many, each quotation loses its importance, and it may seem to the instructor as if you're not so much building an analysis as stringing together a series of passages. Note the difference in the following "right" and "wrong" quotations. The quotations that are incorrect include phrases and passages that don't further the analysis.

WRONG: The boy in "Araby" tells how his house is "detached from its neighbours in a square ground" and that the other houses "gazed at one another with brown imperturbable faces" (52). More important, the narrator lives on a "blind" street, which foreshadows his own figurative blindness (52).

RIGHT: The narrator in "Araby" lives on a "blind" street, which foreshadows his own figurative blindness (52).

WRONG: The speaker, the Duke of Ferrara, says to the count's man, "Will't please you rise?" when they become ready to meet the rest of the company (47).

RIGHT: The duke brags that "none puts by / The curtain" he has drawn but himself, again showing his need to control the late duchess (9-10).

Be Accurate in Your Quotations

You must be completely accurate in your quotations. Any changes you make to a quoted text must be indicated by enclosing the changes in brackets. For that matter, such indicated changes are warranted only if you are trying to integrate the quotations into the syntax of your sentence. Usually it is better to rearrange your sentence so that you don't have to resort to this tactic. On the other hand, sometimes pronouns or similar words are vague because they have been excerpted from the text, in which case the essay writer may wish to substitute the proper noun for clarification. The one exception to this need for complete and utter accuracy is that you may substitute your own sentence's punctuation for the closing punctuation of a quotation. Take, for example, this passage from James Joyce's "Araby":

> Every morning I lay on the floor in the front parlour watching her door. The blind was pulled down to within an inch of the sash so that I could not be seen. When she came out on the doorstep my heart leaped. I ran to the hall, seized my books and followed her.

CHANGING THE END PUNCTUATION: The narrator tells us that "the blind was pulled down." In a sense, his own ability to judge his situation is also closed; he too is "blind" (52).

CHANGING WORDS WITHIN A QUOTATION: The narrator tells us that "the blind [is] pulled down." In a sense, his own ability to judge his situation is also closed; he too is "blind" (52).

CHANGING WORDS FOR CLARITY: The narrator states that "[w]hen [Mangan's sister] came out on the doorstep [his] heart leaped" (52).

Again, note that the change of verb tense in the second quotation is to make the quoted line from the text parallel to the usage of the **literary present tense** throughout the rest of the quotation. You should also observe that a quotation with lots of brackets (like the third example) is difficult to read;

try to break up passages and integrate them into your own sentences in such a way as to minimize the use of brackets.

If you delete words from a quotation, use an *ellipsis* to indicate where the words have been deleted. An ellipsis is three periods with spaces between them. If the section you delete is the last part of a sentence, insert a period first and then the ellipsis, for a total of four periods, with a space after each.

> **ELLIPSIS TO INDICATE DELETED WORDS:** The narrator tells us, "Every morning [he] lay on the floor in the front parlour watching her door. The blind was pulled down to within an inch of the sash. . . . When she came out on the doorstep [his] heart leaped" (52).

Never begin a quotation with an ellipsis; the case of the first letter and the context of your sentence should make it clear whether you're quoting from the beginning of a sentence or the middle.

Cite the Page Numbers of Prose Quotations

As noted earlier in the text, any writing that is not some form of verse is a form of prose. Any time you quote from a prose text of any sort—an article or essay, a story, or a novel, among other things—you must indicate which page the quotation is taken from. You should also make sure to cite the text on the Works Cited page at the end of your paper. Not all teachers demand that you prepare a Works Cited page when using only primary texts, but unless you are told otherwise, you should always provide information on any text you refer to in your paper. Note that in the following examples, the writer doesn't have to write "page" in the parentheses; the number is obviously the page number. Also note that the order at the end of a quotation proceeds as follows: ending quotation mark, space, open parenthesis, number, close parenthesis, period. Furthermore, the parenthetical citation should usually come at the end of the sentence where a quotation is used. If a paragraph is particularly short or if a series of quotations are used in a paragraph that all come from the same page, you can place your citation at the end of the paragraph. If you are writing a particularly complicated sentence that refers to lines from various parts of the text, it may be better to place the corresponding parenthetical citation directly after each quotation rather than at the end of the sentence or paragraph. This may be a more common problem when discussing poetry; in prose analysis, it's probably better just to rearrange your sentence.

EXAMPLES

> The narrator notes that Mangan's sister turns "a silver bracelet round and round her wrist" (53).
>
> We are told that Calixta has "not seen [Alcée] very often since her marriage, and never alone" (221).

When the American absent-mindedly states that he has "never seen" any white elephants and later says, "That's the way with everything," when the girl compares absinthe to licorice, we realize how distracted and bothered he actually is (150-51).

The opening setting of the story indicates that the man and woman have choices to make as they sit "between two lines of rails in the sun" (150), but it is only later that Jig understands that they could have "everything," and that "every day [they] make it more impossible" (152).

Cite the Line Numbers of Verse Quotations

As the next few examples should make clear, citing a quotation from a poem differs significantly from citing a quotation from a work of prose. First, when quoting words or lines from a poem, you indicate the line number rather than the page number. You do this because, often, a poem's entirety may exist on only one or very few pages; noting the page number doesn't really help the reader zero in on the part of the poem you're referring to.

The narrator states that he is "sorry [he] could not travel both" (2).

The "blanker whiteness of benighted snow" that has "nothing to express" to the narrator of "Desert Places" shows how emotionally void the speaker truly is (11-12).

Show Line Breaks in Shorter Verse Quotations

When quoting more than one line of a poem or other forms of verse or when quoting sections of multiple lines that include line breaks, you must indicate the line breaks in the verse through use of a forward slash (preceded and followed by a space) to indicate where the line break is.

We first grasp the Duke of Ferrara's controlling nature when he states, "Sir, 'twas not / Her husband's presence only, called that spot / Of joy into the Duchess' cheek" (13-15).

The true nature of the narrator's appreciation for his love is explained when the narrator tells his mistress that "in eternal lines to time thou [will] grow'st: / So long as men can breathe or eyes can see, / So long lives this, and this gives life to thee" (12-14).

Indent Any Quotation of More than Three Lines

Regardless of the genre, indent any quotation that is more than three lines long one inch from the left margin. The rules change when you indent a quotation. Since the indentation shows where the quoted material begins, you do not use quotation marks. However, since we now don't know exactly where the quoted material ends, you do leave in the original punctuation and follow it with the parenthetical notation of the page number. If quoting more than three lines of verse, make sure that your line breaks are the same as the original line breaks in the poem or dramatic verse. MLA style (see Chapter 24) states that the quoted material should be double-spaced, but some instructors prefer single-spaced quotations; be sure to ascertain your instructor's preference. If quoting a text that contains paragraph breaks, indent the first line of the second and subsequent paragraphs an extra half inch from the indented margin.

PROSE EXAMPLE

> The setting in "Hills Like White Elephants" is richly symbolic; the description of the setting in the opening paragraph contains almost everything the reader needs to know to understand the story:
>
>> The hills across the valley of the Ebro were long and white. On this side there was no shade and no trees and the station was between two lines of rails in the sun. Close against the side of the station there was the warm shadow of the building and a curtain, made of strings of bamboo beads, hung across the open door into the bar, to keep out flies. The American and the girl with him sat at a table in the shade, outside the building. It was very hot and the express from Barcelona would come
>> in forty minutes. It stopped at this junction for two minutes and went on to Madrid. (150)
>
> The two rails represent choice, and the two sides of the river seem to indicate the division between life and death. The use of "shadow" and "shade" prefigure the significance of the woman's choice.

VERSE EXAMPLE

> The narrator does make it clear that he is not truly choosing the other path when he states that he
>
>> Then took the other, as just as fair,
>> And having perhaps the better claim,
>> Because it was grassy and wanted wear;
>> Though as for that the passing there
>> Had worn them really about the same. . . . (6-10)
>
> In truth, the only difference between the paths is that he chooses one and leaves the other for later.

Quote Drama Precisely

For our purposes here, remember that the genre of **drama** straddles two categories: prose (most modern plays) and verse (classic Greek tragedy, Renaissance drama, Restoration era drama). The rules for quoting a prose play (like *Trifles, Florence,* or *Cat on a Hot Tin Roof*) are the same as for quoting any other work of prose; simply give the page number from the text and then give full information on the Works Cited page. Some instructors do want quotations from plays with act or scene divisions (*The Glass Menagerie*, for example, is split into five scenes) to indicate the act or scene number in addition to the page number (similar to how works of dramatic verse are cited). For drama written in verse, the rules are more or less the same as those for verse, except that you should also indicate the act and scene numbers as well as the line numbers. Traditionally, these were indicated by uppercase roman numeral (act), lowercase roman numeral (scene), and the line number. The more current method is to use standard arabic numeration. In either case, separate act, scene, and lines with periods (but no spaces). Remember that as with poetry, when quoting from a play written in verse, you must show the line breaks, either using slashes in quotations shorter than three lines or breaking the lines in the appropriate places if using a longer indented quotation.

QUOTING DRAMA IN BLANK VERSE, TRADITIONAL NOTATION: Brabantio tells Othello, "Look to her, Moor, if thou hast eyes to see; / She has deceived her father and may thee" (I.iii.291-92).

QUOTING DRAMA IN BLANK VERSE, MODERN NOTATION: Brabantio tells Othello, "Look to her, Moor, if thou hast eyes to see; / She has deceived her father and may thee" (1.3.291-92).

QUOTING PROSE DRAMA: Mrs. Hale mentions to Mrs. Peters that she remembers when Mrs. Wright was "Minnie Foster, one of the town girls singing in the choir" (215).

QUOTING MORE THAN THREE LINES OF DRAMA IN BLANK VERSE: Iago subverts Brabantio's remark to Othello and waters the seed of doubt planted by the father-in-law when he says:

> She that, so young, could give out such a seeming,
> To seel her father's eyes up close as oak--
> He thought 'twas witchcraft--but I am much to blame;
> I humbly do beseech you of your pardon
> For too much loving you. (3.3.209–12)

Again, Iago shows his guile through his use of doubts that Othello already possesses.

Integrate Quotations into the Syntax of Your Sentence

One of the biggest problems many students have with using quotations isn't so much how many quotations to use or which quotations to use but rather how to insert the quotations into the body of their text properly. The quotation should be integrated into the text in such a way that the sentence or paragraph containing the inserted quotation still reads smoothly and coherently. The syntax should be seamless; the quotation should not seem forced into a passage, nor should it make the rest of the passage awkward. If you scan back over each of the examples used in this chapter, you'll see that the quotations have been led up to in the preceding sentences so that they fit smoothly into the rhythm of the sentences in which they are used. Quotations can be efficiently integrated into your papers in a variety of ways.

One of the most important techniques to remember is that you should lead up to the quotation with an introductory or transitional sentence. The quotation should not have to stand by itself. This may create other problems, of course. Your paper is in the present tense, but the quote may be in the past tense, so how can you use the quotation as part of your sentence? As we showed earlier, small changes to the quotation to make the passage flow more articulately are allowed, as long as you show the changes made by placing them in brackets. It is often preferable that you rearrange your sentence so that the quotation and the sentence around it still read coherently without a lot of bracketing.

WRONG: The narrator is sorry he can't travel both paths: "And sorry I could not travel both / And be one traveler" (2).

RIGHT: The narrator states that he is "sorry [he] could not travel both" (2).

WRONG: Calixta has been very lonely. Chopin writes, "She had not seen him very often since her marriage, and never alone" (221).

RIGHT: We are told that Calixta has "not seen [Alcée] very often since her marriage, and never alone" (221).

Do Not Identify the Primary Text in Your Citation

If you are using quotations from more than one source, each quotation is credited by author and page number (see Chapter 24). However, if all your quotations are from the primary text on which your paper is based, it is unnecessary to indicate anything more than the page number for each quote.

WRONG: The narrator notes that Mangan's sister turns "a silver bracelet round and round her wrist" (Joyce 53).

RIGHT: The narrator notes that Mangan's sister turns "a silver bracelet round and round her wrist" (53).

Use Single Quotation Marks inside Doubles

Quotations are enclosed in double quotation marks. But when the quoted material includes the title of a short work (perhaps a character refers to "The Road Not Taken") or another quotation, all such interior quotations must be enclosed in *single* quotation marks. (This is standard American usage; in the United Kingdom, the approach is the reverse: single quotation marks go around the outer quotation and double quotation around the inner one.)

Sam says to Joe, "Yeah, I read 'The Road Not Taken.' It changed my life" (451).

The narrator replies to his adversary, "I do not care to hear your 'opinion,' sir; I know what I think of you" (99).

16.2   FORMATTING YOUR PAPER

One point that we've made throughout this text is the importance of following your instructor's guidelines. All of us have tastes, preferences, and pet peeves. As always, do your best to find out exactly how your instructor wants you to format papers and how they should be submitted.

Many instructors in English simplify this process a good bit for students by simply following MLA style (see Chapter 24). Put simply, in an MLA-formatted paper, you don't use a cover sheet or a report binder unless the instructor requests one. Rather, you begin with a heading at the upper left that indicates, on separate lines, your name, your teacher's name, the class number, and the date. Each page should have one-inch margins; each page should have a header with the writer's last name, followed by the page number, at the upper right, one-half inch from the top. The entire paper should be double-spaced. You would obviously follow MLA style in citing all quoted materials. Most instructors require that you use a standard 12-point font such as Times New Roman, Courier, or Arial; it's always a good idea to ask which font your professor requires.

The following pages present an example of an MLA-formatted paper.

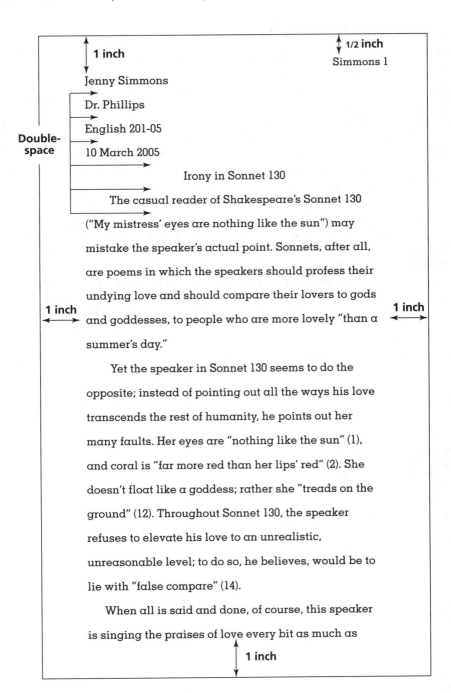

1 inch

1/2 inch

Simmons 1

Double-space

Jenny Simmons

Dr. Phillips

English 201-05

10 March 2005

Irony in Sonnet 130

The casual reader of Shakespeare's Sonnet 130 ("My mistress' eyes are nothing like the sun") may mistake the speaker's actual point. Sonnets, after all, are poems in which the speakers should profess their undying love and should compare their lovers to gods and goddesses, to people who are more lovely "than a summer's day."

1 inch

1 inch

Yet the speaker in Sonnet 130 seems to do the opposite; instead of pointing out all the ways his love transcends the rest of humanity, he points out her many faults. Her eyes are "nothing like the sun" (1), and coral is "far more red than her lips' red" (2). She doesn't float like a goddess; rather she "treads on the ground" (12). Throughout Sonnet 130, the speaker refuses to elevate his love to an unrealistic, unreasonable level; to do so, he believes, would be to lie with "false compare" (14).

When all is said and done, of course, this speaker is singing the praises of love every bit as much as

1 inch

1 inch

1/2 inch

Simmons 2

those people who feel their lovers are celestial

beings. What seem to be insults--stating that his

mistress's breath "reeks," for example (8)--are actually

indications of the speaker's great love; this is the

essential irony of the sonnet.

Anyone, the poet implies, can love a goddess or a

god; what does it say about a love if one or both of the

participants are perfect and wonderful? Yet despite all

1 inch   the deficiencies of the speaker's mistress, his love for   1 inch

her is "as rare" as any poet's love for any so-called

perfect lover. One could even argue that his love is

greater, for he loves her for who she is, despite the fact

that she is a mere mortal--or perhaps because of it.

～17～

Practical Advice

Below we've made a brief and by no means inclusive list of recommendations to bear in mind when writing papers for your literature courses. Some of this advice may seem familiar, because we've discussed many of these various tips throughout this book. The main thing you should bear in mind before reading these recommendations or starting your paper is to *follow the assignment*. Although the great majority of writers in the academy favor the literary present tense, for instance, if your teacher expressly states that you are to use the past tense, then use the past tense. By and large, though, most instructors were taught in the same way and have quite similar ideas about what constitutes good writing. Observing these conventions won't automatically make your paper great, but failing to observe them might affect your grade.

Literary Present Tense

Always write about literature in the **literary present tense**. Although the work may have been written many years ago, it still exists today. Note these examples:

WRONG: Charlotte Perkins Gilman <u>showed</u> the oppression of the artistry of women in turn-of-the-century America.

RIGHT: Charlotte Perkins Gilman <u>shows</u> the oppression of the artistry of women in turn-of-the-century America.

RIGHT: The narrator in Frost's poem <u>is</u> not a nonconformist; rather, he <u>laments</u> the necessity of making a choice.

RIGHT: Hughes's narrator <u>describes</u> various kinds of music in order to show that an individual <u>may cross</u> cultural boundaries.

Avoid Obvious or Irrelevant Biography

Unless you are especially assigned to discuss an author's biography in the development of your argument, disregard long discussions of the author's life *unless it directly relates to your analysis.*

WRONG: Robert Frost grew up in New England, and in this poem about making choices, he describes how it feels to leave one path for another.

RIGHT: Frost's poem "The Road Not Taken" is about making choices and how it feels to leave one path for another.

WRONG: James Joyce was Irish, and as an Irishman he decided to write about growing up as a boy in Ireland.

RIGHT: Gilman herself underwent a rest treatment similar to the one that is prescribed the narrator of "The Yellow Wallpaper"; surely the narrator's desire to write despite the warnings of her husband and doctor reflects Gilman's own struggles.

Avoid Excessive Summarizing

Unless you are told otherwise, assume that your audience has also read the text in question. You do not need to retell the plot of a story or play or the narrative arc of a poem; your reader knows those elements as well as you do. Instead, you must concentrate on the subtler aspects of the work that readers may have missed. For example, if you attended a movie like *Titanic* with a friend, you wouldn't tell your friend on the way home that the movie was about a love story on a giant boat that hit an iceberg and sank. If, however, you remark on the recurring scenes of the ship's designer winding a clock and then argue that this may relate symbolically to the fact that the young lovers will have only a short time together, your friend's understanding of the movie will be enriched. Make sure that whatever summary you provide obviously serves the goal of illustrating a specific analytical point, and do not allow the summary to take control of your essay.

WRONG: A woman is sent to a rest home by her husband. He is named John. She is locked in a room that has yellow wallpaper in it. There are bars on the windows and the bed is nailed down. They don't let her write, and she doesn't like the wallpaper.

RIGHT: Although the narrator believes that the room is a nursery, the bars on the window and the gate on the stairs tell a different story: she is imprisoned.

Avoid Aesthetic Evaluations

Remember that an analytical paper is not the same as a review. Your job is to consider some aspect of the text, to develop a reading of it, or to explicate all or part of it, not to state whether the text is good, bad, worth reading, or a waste of time. A piece of writing can be very well crafted yet yield very little to analysis; correspondingly, a badly written work can prove quite interesting.

WRONG: This excellent poem by Langston Hughes really causes you to think.

RIGHT: Langston Hughes's poem challenges our preconceptions about race.

WRONG: Susan Glaspell is a wonderful writer who makes some interesting points about gender politics.

RIGHT: *Trifles* makes interesting points about gender politics.

Avoid Personal Asides and Responses

Students in literature courses are often required to keep journals or to submit responses to works of literature that state how they enjoyed a particular assignment or what they found worth noting in a given text. In more formal analytical writings, however, personal asides and responses tend to be digressive and to distract the reader from the actual point the writer is trying to make. They should generally be avoided if not specifically required by an assignment. Again, an analysis has different objectives than a review.

WRONG: I thought Alice Childress's *Florence* was good because I could relate to it and because it tells us about society.

RIGHT: Alice Childress's *Florence* discusses the inherent racism of segregated society.

WRONG: Even though I think *Trifles* was kind of boring and old-fashioned, the use of symbolism to develop feminist issues interests me.

RIGHT: *Trifles* develops feminist issues through symbolism.

Avoid Value Judgments

Although some authors may write stories, plays, or poems that are straightforward morality tales, they are also quite often interested in painting complex portraits of complex individuals. Your goal when reading a literary work that contains characters you consider moral or immoral is not to judge the characters as if they were human beings of your acquaintance—after all, as characters, they're fictional creations of the author, intended to serve a function—but rather to strive to understand the meaning of their actions or the nature of their character, whether good or bad.

WRONG: Holden Caulfield curses too much in *The Catcher in the Rye* and as a result is not a good person.

RIGHT: Perhaps Holden's cursing is just another act of camouflage; he is attempting to disguise his vulnerability from the cold world around him.

WRONG: The man in "Hills Like White Elephants" is clearly a jerk for trying to get the girl to have an abortion.

RIGHT: We can see from the American's attempts to manipulate Jig that he is not ready to be the parent of a child.

Avoid References to the Composition of the Essay

Students often refer to the actual writing process itself in their papers. Introductions state, "In this paper, I will prove so-and-so," or conclusions state, "In conclusion, I have therefore proved so-and-so," or they will use self-referencing phrases as awkward transitions: "Now let us look at so-and-so." The first problem with this rhetorical method is that it is often quite awkward. Second, it is presumptive—how can you be sure you will prove or have proved a point to the reader's satisfaction? Finally, it is redundant. Your point should be made clearly through whatever argument is being put forth; you don't need to say "I will prove" something if your paper is actually setting out to prove it.

WRONG: In my paper, I will show that the goblin market in Rossetti's poem represents the wildness of youth.

WRONG: When I was asked to write an analysis of "Goblin Market," I thought, "How will I ever do this?"

RIGHT: The goblin market in Rossetti's poem represents the wildness of youth.

Refer to Authors by Their Last Names

Students will often assume a certain familiarity with favorite texts and favorite writers that is out of place in a formal essay. Furthermore, using a writer's first name is usually imprecise and confusing. Don't refer to writers like Shakespeare and Faulkner as "Will and Bill" or to Emily Dickinson and Alice Childress as "Emily and Alice."

WRONG: Robert uses nature as a way of examining the human spirit.

RIGHT: Frost uses nature as a way of examining the human spirit.

Always Have a Title

Although this is not a hard and fast rule with some teachers, most instructors want papers to have titles. A good title can both provide a clear indication of your purpose and possibly generate interest in the paper. Professors and scholars are given to using titles with colons in them, so that part of the title can be a clever or interesting play on words while the other half clearly states what the paper will be about. Although this practice has become so routine that some academics now refer to the vast majority of scholarly titles as suffering from "colonitis," it can be useful. Some writers like to use a quotation from the text for part of their title. Here are some sample titles:

And Baby Makes Three: Decisions and Choices in "Hills Like White Elephants"
Blinded by the Light: The Narrator's Blindness in "Araby"

Avoid Language That Is Too Informal

Most students were taught in grammar school to avoid personal, informal language in formal academic papers. They were told that one should never use the first person, contractions, or colloquial expressions. These rules are often not held in such high esteem in college classrooms; many professors don't mind if you use contractions or the first person (although, as always, it's best to ask to make sure). However, there is a sound principle behind this seemingly old-fashioned and rigid rule. Generally speaking, the more informal a paper or section of an essay is, the less clear it is. Use of the first person tends to make sentences awkward or to clutter up the language, weaken a statement, or obscure the point. Use of the first person also makes it easy to digress.

Similarly, many teachers don't appreciate the use of the second person (*you*) in formal papers. We use it throughout this book, along with the first person *we*, because we are trying to create a dialogue between teachers (the authors) and students (the readers). We consciously decided to take an informal approach to facilitate effective communication. However, does the use of the second person actually help in the formation of a literary analysis? Most likely not. As we've stated before, don't be scared of using informal styles, but be aware that your goal is always clarity.

WRONG: In my opinion, the narrator in "Desert Places" is melancholy and sad.

RIGHT: The narrator in "Desert Places" is melancholy and sad.

WRONG: Like, what is with this chick in "Goblin Market"? She is totally out of bounds.

RIGHT: Laura in "Goblin Market" refuses to abide by conventional rules.

RIGHT: I disagree with Simpson's statement that Mangan's sister is manipulating the narrator of "Araby"; rather, he manipulates himself.

WRONG: You would think that Laura in "Goblin Market" is completely scared by what she encounters, but you'd be wrong.

RIGHT: Laura in "Goblin Market" reacts to her experiences in contradictory ways.

Avoid Language That Is Too Formal or Too Wordy

Far from being too informal in their essays, some students have the opposite problem: they try to write in superformal, professorial, academic language. Unfortunately, most undergraduates haven't been trained to use such language properly, and again, clarity is sacrificed. Students use the passive voice too much (see the next section) when trying to write too formally, and they often make obscure word choices in order to sound more academic. Similarly, instead of saying something clearly in a few words, they arrange it into a complicated series of phrases that obscure the point being made.

WRONG: In "Araby," the image of blindness is depicted by the boy's actions.

RIGHT: The boy in "Araby" is figuratively blind.

WRONG: It may be seen that the narrator in "Desert Places" is portrayed by Frost as empty inside.

RIGHT: The narrator in "Desert Places" is empty inside.

Avoid the Passive Voice

In the *passive voice*, the subject of the sentence is acted on (possibly by an object) rather than performing an action (possibly on an object). To put it another way, a passive sentence is constructed in inverted order. For example, *The boy hit the ball* is active; *The ball was hit by the boy* is passive. The fact that the sentence is in the past tense or that a helping or linking verb (*was*) and the main predicate are used together (*hit*) is not what makes it passive (although such complex verb constructions are usually a by-product of the passive construction); the fact that the grammatical subject of the second sentence (*ball*) is the *receiver* rather than the *performer* of the action (*hit*) is what makes it passive. Although there are times when the passive construction is appropriate, you should approach it warily. If the same information can be conveyed in both active and passive fashion—as in our "Boy hit ball" example—the active is generally to be preferred for its directness and clarity.

WRONG: The fact that this is her last chance for sexual freedom is known very well by Calixta.

RIGHT: Calixta knows very well that this is her last chance at sexual freedom.

WRONG: The choice that is made by the speaker of "The Road Not Taken" is immaterial.

RIGHT: The speaker's choice in "The Road Not Taken" is immaterial.

Use Only Useful Quotations

We discuss how to use quotations from primary, secondary, and other sources at great length in this book. However, you must remember that any quotation you choose from a given text, whether it's the primary source (the work you're writing about) or a secondary one (a book or an article on the work you're writing about), isn't there just to prove you've read the text. It must serve a purpose.

WRONG: The snow in "Desert Places" is falling "fast, oh, fast" as the narrator walks past woods where he sees the snow-covered brush (1).

RIGHT: When the speaker notes that "all animals are smothered in their lairs," we should pay attention to his choice of the verb *smothered* (6).

WRONG: This "important Dublin story" by Joyce is about a boy growing up on a dead-end street (O'Hare 42).

RIGHT: We're told from the very beginning of "Araby" that the boy lives on a "blind" street; one critic notes that the "colloquial reference to a dead-end street reflects the narrator's figurative blindness" (O'Hare 42).

Indicate Titles Correctly

The rules of academic writing require that you consistently and correctly indicate what genre a work falls into through appropriate title-indicative punctuation. This is a very simple thing to get right, but it proves a constant problem for students. Put simply, if a work is long (book-length or close to it), underline or italicize the title (but be consistent with how you choose to indicate the titles of all such works). Underlining is preferred in MLA style, but check with your instructor. If the piece is short, place the title in quotation marks.

EXAMPLES

NOVEL OR NOVELLA: *The Sound and the Fury* or <u>The Turn of the Screw</u>

BOOK-LENGTH MEMOIR: <u>Narrative of the Life of an American Slave</u> or *'Tis*

SHORT STORY: "Araby"

A SINGLE POEM: "Goblin Market"

A BOOK OF POETRY OR A BOOK-LENGTH POEM: <u>Ariel</u> or *A Boy's Will*

A PLAY: *Hamlet* or <u>A Raisin in the Sun</u>

A SHORT ESSAY: "Shooting an Elephant"

A FILM: <u>Titanic</u> or *O Brother, Where Art Thou?*

A CRITICAL BOOK: *The Yoknapatawpha Country* or <u>Joyce and Feminism</u>

A CRITICAL ARTICLE: "Blindness as Symbol in 'Araby'"

You should also note that song titles are placed in quotation marks, while the titles of albums or CDs are underlined or italicized. Likewise, the names of ships and the titles of paintings are underlined or italicized.

Know the Difference between Hyphens and Dashes

This last tip may fall more into the category of pet peeves you should avoid, but many instructors do share this pet peeve. To insert a dash—the punctuation mark meant to break up the flow of a sentence while you insert a parenthetical comment—type *two* hyphens, not one. One hyphen works to pull words together or to separate syllables in words at the end of lines; a dash works to push words apart. There should be no spacing on either side of a dash. Many word processing programs automatically convert two hyphens into a dash.

WRONG: Emily Dickinson-the poet-loved dashes.

RIGHT: Emily Dickinson--the poet--loved dashes.

✌18✌

Jane Shortfall
Dr. Tuffman
English 101 Section 07
18 January 2005

The Heart in "Desert Places"

The excellent poem by the important poet Robert Frost, "Desert   **A.**
Places," is about a man who is walking or riding past a field in the
woods one day. He stops and stares into the snow and wonders where
the animals are, and then he thinks about how lonely the woods are; he
then says that he's not scared of the empty space between stars."I have   **B.**
it in me so much nearer home To scare myself with my own desert
places" (15-16). To me, I think this is a poem about how the natural   **C. D.**
landscape reflects the interior landscape of Robert Frost's heart.   **E.**

We start with the man riding or walking past the woods and
looking into them for animals, as when he states in this beautiful   **F. G.**
line, "Snow falling and night falling fast, oh, fast In a field I looked   **H.**
into going past" (1-2). If it's snowing, it's winter, and winter is very
cold. Temperatures have been known to become so cold in winter that
car radiators freeze and deep lakes freeze over so that people can
skate on them. As he walks past, he looks for animals but can't find   **I. J.**
any because they're "smothered in their lairs" (6). It's interesting to   **K.**
me that he uses a word like *smothered* instead of *safe* or *comfortable*.   **L.**
It shows his mental state.

He says the loneliness of the woods will get worse before it
gets better. And "[a] blanker whiteness of benighted snow With no   **M. N.**
expression, nothing to express" (11-12). The surrounding woods have
no expression because he has nothing inside him; they're reflecting
the speaker's own state. I feel he is too lonely, too depressed, and he
probably shouldn't be out in the woods in the first place. Why is he
there? We'll never know, but one thing is for sure: he's depressed.   **O.**

Then he says:

> "They cannot scare me with their empty spaces
> Between stars--on stars where no human race is.
> I have it in me so much nearer home
> To scare myself with my own desert places" (13-16).   **P.**

This is where we realize how depressed he is and that the woods and
snow seem cold and lonely because, really, that's how he feels. He
doesn't know human warmth, and nothing will ever save him; "I have
it in me so much nearer home To scare myself with my own desert
places" (15-16).   **Q.**

Sample Student Essay

(Proportions shown in this paper have been adjusted to fit the space limitations of this book. Follow the actual dimensions shown in the margins and the guidelines discussed in the commentary, along with your instructor's directions.)

COMMENTARY

A. There are two problems here: first, the statement "poem by . . . poet" is redundant. Second, avoid evaluative comments like "excellent poem" and "important poet." The assignment is not to review the worthiness of the poem but to analyze it.

B. Too much retelling and summary. Remember that the reader has read the poem!

C. As it is, this quotation is placed awkwardly into the introduction. It should be integrated so that it flows with the syntax of the sentence. Also, the student has failed to use a slash to indicate the break between the lines of poetry. They should read, "I have it in me so much nearer home / To scare myself with my own desert places" (15-16).

D. One should avoid colloquial, informal statements like "to me, I think" or "in my opinion." "To me, I think" is not only awkward, it also weakens the statement by implying that the writer is not quite sure and worries that others might disagree.

E. The writer must not assume that the narrator is Frost. Refer to him as the "speaker" or the "narrator" or even the "poet" but not as Frost.

F. Again, don't summarize the action of the poem unless it directly relates to an analytical point; assume that the reader has read the poem.

G. Avoid evaluations like "this beautiful line."

H. The writer has again failed to show the line break.

I. This is too much of a digression and statement of the obvious. How does this truly contribute to the analysis?

J. This is another case of too much summary, and the text presumes too much when it argues that the speaker is looking for animals. We can't be sure that's his purpose.

K. This quotation is nicely integrated into the line.

L. Again, although the point may be valid, we don't need the qualifying comment that the word choice is "interesting" to the writer.

M. Again, there's too much summary here.

N. The writer has again failed to insert the slash to indicate the line break. Furthermore, this line feels forced into this part of the paper. Make sure the quotation flows naturally with the surrounding syntax. As used here, it does not even form a complete sentence.

O. In this paragraph, the writer remembers to use the term *speaker* instead of saying *Frost*. However, the writer does assume too much by digressing with the comments about the narrator's mental condition and the writer's belief that the narrator "shouldn't be out in the woods in the first place."

P. A paper this short probably doesn't need a quotation this long, and there should also be more of a transition before it. The writer did correctly indent this quotation due to its being longer than three lines and properly used the poem's actual line breaks. However, there shouldn't be any quotation marks on indented quotations (the indentation indicates the beginning of the quotation), and the period in indented quotations precedes the parenthetical page notation.

Q. The writer has again presumed too much and has again failed to show the line break or to integrate the quotation into the syntax.

≈19≈

Alan Average
Professor Grady
English 101 Section 08
16 June 2005

Thou Shalt Not Commit Adultery: Symbolism and Sin
in Kate Chopin's Short Story "The Storm"   A.

Kate Chopin was born Catherine O'Flaherty on July 12, 1850, to
Thomas O'Flaherty and Eliza Faris (Motley 10). Kate was the youngest   B. C.
of three children; when she was five, her father died. In 1868, she
graduated from the St. Louis Academy of the Sacred Heart and
became a debutante. Two years later, she married Oscar Chopin and
moved to New Orleans, where she gave birth to six children. In 1882,
her husband died, and Kate had to take over the family business,
eventually moving her family back to St. Louis to be closer to her
living relatives. Kate began writing fiction in 1889, and her most
famous novel, *The Awakening*, was published in 1899.   D.

"The Storm" was written by Kate Chopin in 1898. It is a sequel to   E.
an earlier story, "At the 'Cadian Ball." "The Storm" is the story of Bibi   F.
and Bobinôt, a four-year-old child and his father, who are trapped   G.
away from home during a spell of inclement weather. While they are
away, Calixta, their wife and mother, engages in carnal relations   H.
with Alcée, a man whom she made out with "five years" ago (Chopin).   I. J.
An exegesis of the story with focus on its utilization of symbolism will   K.
reveal Kate Chopin's attitude toward adultery.

The storm itself is the story's dominant symbol:

> "The rain beat upon the low, shingled roof with a force and
> clatter that threatened to break an entrance and deluge
> them there. They were in the dining room--the sitting
> room--the general utility room. Adjoining was her bed room,
> with Bibi's couch along side her own. The door stood open,
> and the room with its white, monumental bed, its closed
> shutters, looked dim and mysterious." (Chopin)   L.

The storm itself is a symbol of the passion between the two lustful
lovers, and the description of the bedroom is also symbolic. White   M.
represents purity, innocence, and virginity, just as Calixta did the first
time Alcée kissed her at Assumption, and the bedroom, with its open
door, suggests a mystery to be explored. While the storm rages,
Calixta laughs, "a revelation in that dim, mysterious chamber; as
white as the couch she lay upon. Her firm, elastic flesh that was
knowing for the first time its birthright, was like a creamy lily that the

Sample Student Essay
(Proportions shown in this paper have been adjusted to fit the space limitations of this book.
Follow the actual dimensions shown in the margins and the guidelines discussed in the com-
mentary, along with your instructor's directions.)

COMMENTARY

A. This is quite a bit of title for one relatively short paper. Also, while the title attempts to link the literary device of symbolism to the writer's moral judgment about adultery, the connection is not adequately borne out by the essay.

B. There is usually no need to document information that can be found in any general encyclopedia.

C. Avoid referring to authors by their first names. "Chopin" or "Kate Chopin" would be appropriate forms.

D. How is all of this information relevant to the paper's purpose? The biographical details contained in this paragraph may in fact be relevant to the essay's overall theme, but the writer is not showing how they are connected, and at the end of the first paragraph of the paper, the reader has no idea of its topic or theme outside of what hints the title provides. The paper is flying off on a tangent almost before it's started.

E. This sentence is in the passive voice. It is also a piece of information that is being wasted, since it's unconnected to the argument being advanced.

F. This is potentially useful information; how does it relate to the purpose of this paper? How does knowing this help readers understand the story more effectively? The point needs to be developed.

G. Although these are the first characters introduced, the story really focuses on Calixta and Alcée, making this sentence somewhat misleading.

H. Avoiding vulgarity is admirable, but avoid stilted or archaic language as well.

I. Inconsistent tone; slang expression.

J. There is no need to quote and document this brief phrase; when you quote from the story, however, you must include the page number, since your source is a printed book.

K. Use direct language whenever possible. For example, the choice of the word *utilization* rather than *use* may imply that the writer seeks more to impress than to communicate clearly.

L. Indented quotations have quotation marks only where they appear in the original text; therefore, the marks at the start and at the end of the passage are unnecessary. Also, the page number is required here, and MLA style calls for the parenthetical citation to come *after* the end punctuation in an indented quotation.

M. This clause deflects the paragraph somewhat; the paragraph should by all indications focus on the storm, but the second half of it dwells much more on the bedroom and the whiteness of Calixta's flesh.

Average 2

sun invites to contribute to its breath and perfume to the undying life
of the world" (Chopin).   **N.**

Adultery is a serious problem in our society today, yet Kate Chopin's
story "The Storm" suggests that as long as the wronged
parties (Bibi, Bobinôt, and Alcée's wife, Clarisse) never find out about
it, no harm has been done. In writing a story that condones infidelity as
a means of reinvigorating married couples, Chopin is saying that if
you don't get caught, no crime or sin has been committed. If everyone
thought this way, the American family would be a thing of the past,
since all it takes is a big storm, and then "every one [would be] happy."   **O.**

N. The author's name is unnecessary here, since there's little or no chance for confusion; the page number, however, is required. Also, it is often an effective tactic to avoid ending a paragraph with a quotation; take the opportunity to underscore the point the quotation is intended to make: the repetition of the words *dim* and *mysterious* from the earlier descriptions, along with this "creamy lily" simile and several other references to the whiteness of Calixta's skin.

O. This conclusion represents another digression, since it takes the reader away from symbolism and toward a minisermon on the evils of adultery. In doing so, moreover, the essay may very well be overlooking the story's point. Since the child and husband are the first characters we meet, and since they are described in positive terms, it's hard to argue that Calixta earns more of our sympathy than they do. It's likely that there is some level of irony present in the story's last words.

৵ 20 ৵

Research Methods
in the Digital Age

This section is not intended to be a primer on libraries or library science, of course, which is beyond the scope of this book, but instead will focus on helping you conduct research for a paper of literary analysis. Most college students have had at least some exposure to libraries and research methods in high school; at the same time, most high school libraries don't have the kinds of resources that even small college libraries have. Having so much material available online and through databases, of course, has done much to equalize libraries. You can connect to an important database like InfoTrac just as easily through a small liberal arts college library as you can through a major university's library.

As your instructors have probably told you repeatedly in your high school and college careers, conducting research for literary analysis has changed drastically over the last couple of decades. Not so long ago, a person researching a critical article would begin looking for relevant books by flipping through the library's card catalog, writing down all call numbers and notes. The card catalog's descriptions of books were sparse when they existed at all. For finding articles, you would have to turn to large print compendiums like the *Reader's Guide to Periodical Literature*. Even the research-friendly *MLA Bibliography* was published in gigantic yearly volumes with microscopic print. To find articles on, say, Kate Chopin, a researcher would pull down a year volume (say, 1975) and then look up Chopin, copy down the bibliographical entries, and repeat the task for each year's index. Then the researcher would have to look up the abbreviated journal and book titles in the title index of the *Bibliography* and write those down. At that point, the researcher would have to go to the card catalog to see whether the various journals and periodicals were available in the library and where they were located.

With its explosion of personal computers, the Internet and the World Wide Web, searchable databases, CD-ROM publications, e-zines and e-journals, the Information Age has revolutionized and greatly altered research in every field. The locations of books and articles—and often electronic versions of the books and articles themselves—are at your very fingertips. As you'd expect, however, the great benefits of research in the digital age are matched by the complexity of methods you must employ to make effective use of these resources. Different libraries will provide access to different resources, and we cannot hope to account for such diversity in these few pages, so we've chosen to focus on general principles. Remember that the research librarians on staff at your institution have been trained to assist you in your explorations and will be happy to do so, particularly if you demonstrate your willingness to take an active role in the process. These professionals may be the most important and most underused resources your library provides.

When researching a literary text, it's useful to remember that certain "rules of search" are fairly universal, as we discuss throughout the chapter. Also remember the advice we offered earlier: critical books and articles that focus on the works by the author will be more useful, most likely, than biographical studies (again, there are many exceptions to this point). Before beginning, you should know which text and author you're writing about, and you should be fairly confident in your basic understanding of the text in question. However, you should also keep an open mind about the articles and books you encounter. Some may challenge your preconceptions and the general critical consensus on certain works. Remember that you don't have to agree with every reading of every text, and for that matter, a reading that challenges preexisting notions of a text can enlighten, strengthen, or change your own understanding of that text.

Although we go into detail about reading criticism in Chapter 21, for now it may be useful to remember that from a greatly simplified vantage point, critical texts fall into two categories: either they're interpretive texts that require very little knowledge of critical theory to understand, or they're secondary readings making use of cultural and theoretical studies. Both approaches and the dozens of ways of mixing the two together or focusing them can be very useful to students and readers. Ultimately, it comes down to the paper you want to write. The one danger with texts drawing heavily on critical theory is that they are often jargon-laden and filled with dense prose; most often they're written for other scholars and professors (who are presumed to have a working knowledge of the theoretical background in question) rather than lay readers or undergraduate students. Still, even complicated and jargon-rich critical articles can be very rewarding and can greatly aid in your research, if you read with patience and persistence.

20.1   DATABASE SEARCHES

A useful way to start your research paper may be to search any electronic databases available to you. There are a number of helpful search banks, but by far the most helpful is still the *MLA Bibliography*. As we've noted before, the MLA is the Modern Language Association, a large consortium of academic departments and scholars (mostly professors) concerned with studies in modern languages. The MLA provides two especially valuable resources to the student researching a paper in literature: the *MLA Bibliography* and the *MLA Handbook for Writers of Research Papers* (detailed in Chapter 24), which sets out the rules of bibliographical citation.

The *MLA Bibliography* is an extensive bibliography of the articles and books published in language and literature studies. Almost every legitimate or refereed scholarly journal (*refereed* means that a panel of independent professors and scholars reviews articles before recommending them for publication) that publishes articles of literary interest is indexed in the *MLA Bibliography*. The electronic version of the *Bibliography* provides citations back to 1963, and the print version began in 1921.[1]

The *MLA Bibliography* is published electronically in a number of different ways. Several Internet database providers (like the Gale Group's InfoTrac, OCLC, Ovid, and EBSCO) also provide access to the *Bibliography* (as long as the library subscribes to the appropriate database). Furthermore, the *Bibliography* is published on CD-ROM periodically and made available through services like SilverPlatter; consumers can also buy the *Bibliography* CD directly from the MLA.

Because the *Bibliography* is available in a variety of formats from a variety of electronic publishers, we can't tell you precisely how to conduct a search, but there are certain basic rules to searching databases that are practically universal and are sure to come in handy.

In most cases, you can search a database in four ways: by *author*, by *title*, by *subject*, and by *keyword*. One mistake students make is assuming that an author search will find everything written *about* a particular author when in reality it will look for everything in the database *by* that author. Even though the writer you're researching—say, Langston Hughes—may have had hundreds of articles written about him, since he hasn't written any articles for literary journals in the last forty years, his name might not appear. The same problem is true for a title search. Entering "Langston Hughes" in a title search will lead only to books or articles published with the exact title "Langston Hughes" or titles containing those words.

By far the best way to begin research on a database is to use the subject search and the keyword search. If these two choices are not available on the first search screen, see if they're available on the advanced search screen (as is

---

[1]The MLA Web site, <http://www.mla.org>, provides helpful information about both versions of the *Bibliography*.

the case when using "keyword" on InfoTrac's edition of the *MLA Bibliography*). InfoTrac's search engine presupposes that this is the right choice to make and offers you a toggle you can click so that your author search can actually be conducted as "author as subject."

When using the keyword search, it is often useful to combine terms. For example, if you enter "Faulkner" in the author as subject search, more than five thousand critical books and articles turn up. The keyword search allows you to tailor and trim the responses. You don't want *every* book and article on *every* writer named Faulkner; instead, if you're researching William Faulkner's story "A Rose for Emily," you use extra search words joined by a capitalized AND to indicate that all given terms should be present. If you enter "Faulkner AND Emily AND Rose" in a keyword search, you're presented with a much more manageable eighty-seven citations. There are other ways to trim this down to size as well. First, you can make sure to specify that all the critical works must be published in English (useful if you're less than fluent in secondary languages); you can also decide to examine only articles published in refereed journals (although this may have the unwanted side effect of excluding books and several undergraduate-friendly journals from your citation list) or to show only items added since the last update or to show only items published after a certain date; and if your search engine has full-text capabilities (that is, the database contains full online text copies of some of the articles), you can ask it to return only citations with full text. Our eighty-seven-item "Rose for Emily" search dropped to thirty items when we clicked on "Limit the current search to refereed journals." However, it is most likely that you would want to browse the whole list of eighty-seven items published. Remember that not all of them will be useful, not all of them will be available, and not all of them will be intelligible.

The next stage after conducting what seems to be a fruitful database search is to construct a *mark list*. Think of a mark list as a menu at a sushi bar. In such a restaurant, you're often handed a paper menu with all the various kinds of sushi and other foods you can order; you check off with a pencil each item you wish to order. On your database's mark list, you carefully scroll through each title provided by your search. Many titles alone will instantly reveal whether the text is of interest to you; if the title by itself doesn't automatically include or exclude the article or book, click on the title itself. This will sometimes provide you with a brief description (called an *abstract*) of what the text is about (and in some databases may actually include the whole text of the article, as mentioned earlier).

For each title or description that seems relevant to your search, click the mark box to the side of each title brought up by the bibliography search. After you have scrolled through and reviewed all eighty-seven items returned on your "Faulkner AND Rose AND Emily" search, you can then choose "View the mark list" to review the titles that you found interesting. With most search engines you can either print this page of citations or e-mail it to yourself.

Either way, you've made a great start. From here, you need to access your library catalog to see which of the books and journals on your mark list are available either in your library or possibly at other local libraries.

Be creative in your searches. Don't assume that a story or poem or play must be indexed in a certain way; use several synonyms and alternative search terms when searching for articles, and be aware that articles not directly related to your paper might also be helpful. If your focus in the "Rose for Emily" paper is on Emily Grierson's need to hold onto time, then searches on "Faulkner AND time" (150 citations) might be useful as well (a modified search of "Faulkner AND Emily AND time" returns only six citations).

Also, remember that literary research is not an exact science. You should always approach a research project with the assumption that you will discard far more of your research than you use. If your assignment requires a minimum of five sources, then you should first procure far more than five, because it is very doubtful that all five of the first sources you locate will actually prove of value in your paper.

We have focused on the *MLA Bibliography* database, but remember that the methods we have described—using subject and keyword searches, limiting your searches, constructing a mark list, and printing or e-mailing the mark list—apply to most databases that you can search. Although the *MLA Bibliography* should usually be your first source, it doesn't necessarily have to be your only one.

As we noted, some databases can retrieve full digital text files. This can be very useful; instead of trying to track down an elusive journal or finding that the one issue you need is missing from the stacks, you can have the entire article e-mailed to you, ready to print. However, one of the problems with full-text retrieval is that you can very quickly become spoiled by it. Students love having access to the entire article in the luxury of their own homes or dorm rooms. They can cut and paste important, relevant passages right into the text of their papers (properly citing them, of course) and save on the cost of copies or print fees if the article is retained on their own computers.

You should always bear in mind, however, that there are many important books and articles that are not available in digital form, and the full-text retrieval option won't allow you to access those. Furthermore, for the most part, only articles published since the mid-1990s are available for full-text retrieval; older articles are preserved in print or on microfilm but not always digitally. Take advantage of digitally available texts when you can, but don't limit yourself to them.

20.2 USING THE LIBRARY

Most university libraries are far more than book repositories. They are information centers where students and scholars can use the Internet, access multiple databases, watch educational and other videos and DVDs, listen to compact discs, examine journals and periodicals of every type, and follow news from around the world (and from decades back, as well, usually preserved on microfilm or microfiche). And of course you can still find books at the library too.

Searching for Books

Traditionally, most students begin researching papers by checking the library catalog and shelves to see what books are available on their topics. Searching for books first can often be very fruitful, but it can also be frustrating. Not every author or every topic, of course, warrants an entire book. The more widely studied and taught a writer is, the more likely that books will have been written about that writer. Shakespeare's works are taught in every English-speaking college in the world, so anyone researching Shakespeare can count on finding many books and articles about him and his writing. Authors who are less represented in the canon, however, may not have many scholarly books published about them, and even if a few have been published, your library may not have immediate access to them.

The first thing to remember about college libraries is that for the most part, they organize their books by the Library of Congress filing system. This is a system that groups books by subject (rather than placing them in alphabetical order or using some other system), which makes literary research much easier.

At a typical bookstore, books are divided first into genres and then arranged alphabetically. One aisle contains mystery fiction, another computer books, another literary fiction, another essays and creative nonfiction, and so on. If you wanted to find books by William Faulkner and about William Faulkner, you might have to visit several separate aisles in the store. By contrast, in a college library, you would enter "William Faulkner" into the electronic catalog's search bank, and a number of books by or about William Faulkner would be listed on your screen. By each will be a *call number* (which in Faulkner's case will always begin with PS3511.A86, no matter which college you're using, because that's the Library of Congress designation) that is specific to each book in the Faulkner section. So after finding out what the call number is, you can go to the right part of the library and find the right aisle of shelves (the PS3511 section in this case), and you'll find that all the books written by Faulkner, about Faulkner's work, and on Faulkner himself are shelved together in the library. Your research gets off to a great start when you begin browsing the various critical titles and works that are all located on the same shelves.

You can't assume that every book that has relevance to your research is listed here, however. Let's take for example a search for Alice Childress. You could plug her into the catalog search engine and find the right call number; then you'd look in the "stacks" or bookshelves to find the books listed for her. But what if a great article on her is in an anthology on African American women writers? Since the entire book isn't dedicated to Childress, it wouldn't be in her section of the stacks. However, if you've also used the *MLA*

Bibliography or another database to locate articles on Childress (as described in section 20.1), you should have the proper title for the anthology to look up in the catalog. Also remember that most library catalogs, now that they're generally electronic, use similar search engines to the ones we discussed for databases. Many of the same principles apply. Use keyword and subject searches rather than just author and title searches.

Once you make it to the shelves where the information on the author you're researching is stored, you'll have to sort through the various books on hand and decide which seem to be useful to your project. Obviously, the most useful books at first glance are critical studies or anthologies of critical essays. These books are usually focused squarely on an author's various works and are meant to add to the ongoing discussion of them. Many of the books on the shelves will be works by the author; although you may not need another copy of the primary text you're writing about, flipping through some of these other books might reveal interesting forewords, introductions, notes, and afterwords that will serve you in your paper.

It goes without saying that all works of literature are not equally represented in terms of critical works devoted to them. Generally, the more obscure the work you're writing about, the less chance it has that an entire book will be dedicated to it. By the same token, it is very rare that even universally beloved and studied poems (like Robert Frost's "After Apple Picking," Robert Lowell's "For the Union Dead," or Elizabeth Bishop's "The Fish") will have entire books dedicated to them. Instead, small sections of books or brief passages might be devoted to the work you're writing about.

In each case, the work you have to do might at first seem overwhelming. How can you possibly take the time to read several books in their entirety? The answer for most undergraduates is that you can't. However, what you can do is make use of the table of contents and the index. Look up the work you're researching and the characters you're discussing, and see if any chapter titles relate to various themes or motifs you plan to touch on. Although you won't find an entire book dedicated to "After Apple Picking," you may well find several books dedicated to Frost's poetry in general.

As we noted in an earlier chapter, beware of biographies; by definition, they focus on an author's life and are not meant to be works of criticism. Some life studies are called "critical biographies," however, implying that the book not only traces the life of the author in question but also offers critical commentary on the author's works.

Here's a tip: whenever you can, make copies of the pages that are of interest to you rather than checking out the whole book. This technique is useful for many reasons. First, if you're part of a large class that has a limited number of research topics, you're being kind to the students who come after you who may need to access the information in the book you've checked out. Second, you don't have to worry about lugging the book around and remembering to return it by a deadline (especially if all the information you need is located on two pages of the foreword); you can also freely mark up your copied pages without damaging the book itself. You will be subjected to the copying charges, of course, but often these charges are minimal compared to fees for overdue or lost books. *Always copy the copyright page* and any other information you will need for your Works Cited list. You'll save yourself a lot of frantic last-minute scrambling for publication information. Make sure the page numbers are clearly legible on the pages you've copied as well.

Journals

Scholarly journals that focus on literary studies are often the best bets for students researching critical papers. As we stated, it's very rare for an entire book to be dedicated to a single poem, short story, or play (other than perhaps particularly momentous ones by writers of great stature, like Shakespeare), but articles are continuously being published that focus on such works. As we noted earlier, journals are more available to researchers than ever because so many of them also distribute electronic versions of their articles to various databases. The types of journals that may be useful to students run the gamut from straightforward journals written with the student audience in mind (like *The Explicator*) to jargon-laden professional journals intended to be read by professors or graduate students (like *Publications of the Modern Language Association*, usually called *PMLA* for short). Most research papers are more effective if they draw from a variety of sources, from straightforward critical studies and older collections of essays about an author's works to new theoretical approaches and recent journal articles.

Different classes and different papers require different levels of research. Very few professors would ask that their first- and second-year students read several critical books in their entirety while working on a short research paper, but at the same time, professors would expect their graduate students preparing twenty-five-page seminar papers to have conducted such research. Some instructors may not mind students in first-year classes using *The Explicator* or databases like MagillOnLiterature and its Masterplots essays, but they would expect their upper-division students to draw research from more sophisticated sources. The best way to be sure, of course, is to ask your instructor whether certain sources are acceptable or not. Particularly beware of compendiums like *Contemporary Literary Criticism* and the *Dictionary of Literary Biography*. Although these sources are often very useful, they are sometimes condensed amalgamations excerpted from other sources. Such sources can be a good way to find out more in general about a writer and the writer's work, but for actual sources for your paper, you need to turn to full, focused articles on the work in question.

Journals will be made available to you in a number of ways in the library. The most recent editions of each will be in the stacks or on the shelves where all new journals are housed. Older editions will generally be shelved in a different part of the library, and often they will be bound together. It is not uncommon to find four separate issues of a quarterly literary journal bound together under the year they were published. Space is always at a premium in libraries, and some facilities conserve space by converting journals to microfilm and microfiche (just as they do newspapers). The newest trend, as you might expect, is for libraries to scan older journals and to preserve the pages digitally. Some no longer subscribe to print journals when electronic versions are available. What this means for the student researcher is that you have to be patient and persistent; a source is just as helpful if printed from the computer or microfilm as it is from the original print source, although it may be documented differently.

Remember that journal articles published prior to 1963 will not be listed in the electronic version of the *MLA Bibliography*. To find older articles, you can fall back on tried-and-true sources like the *Reader's Guide to Periodical Literature* or earlier print versions of the *MLA Bibliography*, or refer to a journal's own published index.

Interlibrary Loan

Students have more resources at hand than they realize. First, many college libraries are members of consortiums, and a student ID from one library will often allow you to check out materials from other college libraries in your region. Your best source for this (and for much of the research process) is, of course, the reference librarian. Remember, though, that librarians know about your project only what you decide to tell; the more informative you are, the more they can help you.

One of the primary ways they can help you is through interlibrary loan. If you find a great book via the *MLA Bibliography* but your library doesn't have a copy, you can request one through interlibrary loan. The library staff will work to find a copy in a nearby library and then have the book shipped to your home library for pickup. Although there may be a nominal charge, this service is often provided free (although the late fines are usually a bit stiffer). Similarly, if you find an article from a journal that the library doesn't subscribe to and that is not available digitally, the library can have a copy sent to you. As you would expect, there is often a delay of several days before the library can receive a copy of the book or article requested. To take advantage of interlibrary loan, you really need to start your research early.

20.3   EVALUATING INTERNET SOURCES: CAN YOU TRUST THIS WEB SITE?

Students are often confused by what they see as contradictory attitudes on the part of their professors where research sources are concerned. Why is it that information from InfoTrac is acceptable but material from a particular Web site is not? Aren't they both electronic sources, and aren't those allowed? Although these questions are valid, professors have good reasons for bias against some Internet sources.

First, bear in mind the huge distinction between a *database* source and an *Internet* source. A database is, in a sense, an immense electronic filing cabinet. Articles housed in larger databases like InfoTrac and Lexis-Nexis have been previously published in journals (in print or electronic form or both). As such, they have been subjected to an editorial and review process. Such articles are usually written by well-informed scholars, academics, and professionals; their works are scrutinized by editors and often also by a panel of other scholars and experts before being accepted for publication. Thus a number of informed readers have already accepted such articles as worthy and have to a degree passed judgment on several aspects of them. Does the material being published present new or reconsidered information, rather than rehashing old arguments? Is the reasoning sound? Has the writer done enough research? Should the writer make use of a particular kind of cultural or critical theory to help prove the argument at hand? Even databases that solicit short essays for undergraduate and non-academic audiences, like the MagillOnLiterature Masterplots series, ensure that their writers have credentials and carefully review the submitted essays.

Most refereed journals are fairly exclusive; scholars and educators have to put an awful lot of work into the articles they wish to publish in such journals. On the other hand, the various literary sites available on the World Wide Web through the Internet are about as exclusive as the phone book. This comparison is actually quite accurate: all you have to do to have your number published in the White Pages is pay a fee to the telephone company to keep your local service running. Similarly, to have a Web site, you merely have to pay a provider for server space.

Anyone who is familiar with the Web knows that there are hundreds of thousands of horrible, useless, and even harmful sites, advocating everything from plagiarism to child pornography to neo-Nazism. However, the Web has a multitude of incredibly useful sites as well. So how is a researcher supposed to draw distinctions?

For example, a student writer may be conducting research on "The Negro Speaks of Rivers" by Langston Hughes. Through a lot of diligent trimming, the student eventually narrows the search down to fifteen or twenty sites that are actually focused on Hughes's poetry. However, the researcher is still presented with a problem. Some of these sites, for example, may be personal Web sites where other college students have posted their own essays from their literature classes. If so, have these students actually conducted research, or do the papers merely reflect class discussion and professors' lectures? In such cases, the students may well be using information originally derived from other sources without citing the sources used.

Or perhaps a site is one of the hundreds on the Web that are intended to "help" the student writer but are in essence plagiarism promotion sites.

Students from all over the country post papers on these sites and download papers as well. Again, are you sure this is a site you want to quote as a reliable source in your research paper? Probably not.

But there are some sites on the Internet that can be quite useful. There are literary sites that strive to provide the kind of service that databases provide. Such sites are necessary, for not all readers are students and educators, and hence they may not have access to the databases that people in the academic world have. Although professors may often decry sites such as the free-of-charge Sparknotes.com or the pay site of the old mainstay Cliffs Notes (<http://www.cliffsnotes.com>), largely because they summarize the plots of novels and plays and thereby allow lazier students to read the summaries rather than the actual work, such sites do provide useful services and can be valuable research aids. Again, many instructors would not consider these legitimate sources for literary research.

Your best bets for trustworthy Internet sources are professional sites associated with literary societies and journals and sites associated with universities that specialize in various literary studies. One example of the latter would be Southeast Missouri State's Center for Faulkner Studies (at <http://www6. semo.edu/cfs>). Such sites may provide valuable resources. Or search for sites maintained by a bona fide association dedicated to the study and appreciation of an author's life and works, like the Kate Chopin Society (at <http://members.tripod.com/kchopin_society>). The Web address (URL) suffix can sometimes be a useful indicator of the site's legitimacy: ".edu" sites are hosted by colleges and universities (you should remember, of course, that just because a fellow college student or even a professor maintains a Web site, that doesn't necessarily make it useful), and ".gov" sites are sponsored by various government agencies.

Because of the need to distinguish between good and bad sites, never turn to the Internet as your first step in research. Investigate articles available to you in journals and through databases, and examine the books in the library first. Educate yourself in the area you're investigating so that you will recognize questionable assertions and papers that don't properly list sources. Consider Internet research as a supplement to your other research rather than the main thrust of your studies.

20.4   QUICK TIPS FOR LITERARY RESEARCH

- **START EARLY.**   The earlier you begin, the more thorough you can be. You can take advantage of interlibrary loans and the resources of other libraries. Perhaps books that are checked out when you begin your research will be returned (and your name will be first on the waiting list). You can also possibly finish drafts early enough to present them to your professor or tutors for help in revision.

- **CHOOSE A TOPIC AND PLAN YOUR WORK, BUT BE FLEXIBLE.**   You obviously have to have *some* idea of what you're researching when you begin your research.

However, it's okay not to have a firmly fixed **thesis** in place (assuming that your instructor has not assigned one to you) so that you're open to the sources you read. Your thesis should evolve with your research.

- **START WITH A DATABASE SEARCH.**   The best place to start is the *MLA Bibliography*; then move on to other useful databases. Remember to use keyword and subject searches. Mark all interesting citations, and then either print them or e-mail them to yourself.

- **CHECK FOR FULL-TEXT RETRIEVAL.**   Also remember to check the citations you found during your database search to see if you can retrieve the full text of any articles electronically.

- **CHECK YOUR MARKED CITATION LIST AGAINST THE LIBRARY CATALOG.**   If you have e-mailed the list to yourself or printed it at the library, the next step is to cross-check your list of possible sources against the library's computer to see what books and journals are available in your library. Always bear in mind that not everything you find will be immediately available.

- **LOOK FOR BOOKS, AND CHECK THE SHELVES.**   Electronic indexing is a funny thing; you never know when a valuable source may have been missed for some inexplicable reason. You should look up books on your subject in the library catalog and then physically look through the shelves in the corresponding section. Remember to check indexes and tables of contents to help ascertain whether a book is useful to you or not. Biographies are generally not as helpful as critical studies.

- **MAKE COPIES.**   By copying the pages you need from books, you don't have to worry about returning the books, you can mark up the copied pages, and you don't have to carry as much weight around in your bookbag or backpack. Always reproduce copyright pages for citation purposes. Most journals can't be checked out anyway, so you often have no choice but to copy articles from journals.

- **LOOK FOR JOURNAL ARTICLES IN VARIOUS MEDIA.**   It's great if you can make copies of journals that the library keeps in the stacks. However, also be prepared to look for articles that are available only in electronic format or that have been microfilmed or placed on microfiche. Most libraries' microfilm or microfiche viewers will print pages from the film or fiche.

- **EXAMINE THE WORKS CITED AND BIBLIOGRAPHY PAGES OF YOUR SOURCES FOR LEADS TO OTHER SOURCES.**   Remember that the articles you're reading and books you're using for your research paper are for the most part research papers themselves; examine their bibliographies for additional sources you may find useful.

- **ARRANGE FOR INTERLIBRARY LOANS IF NECESSARY.**   Your library may not have the books or journals you need, but another one might, and if you act early enough, your library may be able to acquire the sources you need.

- **TAKE NOTES AS YOU GO.**   You should probably have a folder or section of a notebook dedicated to your research paper. Ideas for further research may come to you as you search a database or book or journal, but if you don't write them down, they can be forgotten all too easily. Also, as you read articles and books and commentaries, be sure to write notes on each particular piece. Indicate where the work fits in your overall plan, write what you think the most important aspects of the article or book are, and describe why you think it will be useful to you. Taking notes like this will prove of great benefit when you develop a working outline.

- **EVALUATE YOUR SOURCES THROUGHOUT.**   Approach this process with an open mind as you begin researching your paper. However, as you proceed, you should eventually begin deciding on a thesis. As you do so, ask yourself which sources you've found will and will not be useful to you in writing your essay. Remember, you don't have to agree with a source for it to prove useful; one effective rhetorical strategy is to introduce ideas you dispute and to strengthen your own case by refuting the opposition's. However, some sources may not contribute anything to your argument. Never use a source or quote material that is superfluous or digressive.

- **USE YOUR WORD PROCESSING SKILLS WHEN DRAFTING.**   As you prepare an outline for your paper, consider where secondary sources may come in handy. You might type them directly into an outline or a separate file so that they can be cut and pasted directly into your paper and then properly cited in the MLA style (see Chapter 24).

♪ 2 1 ♫

Reading Literary Criticism

The following article by Stanley Renner on Ernest Hemingway's "Hills Like White Elephants" is a good example of the kind of literary criticism you might encounter as you study and prepare to write about literature. Reading literary criticism is usually not easy, but it can be very rewarding. Just as when you read anything else, your goal is not simply to find what you want to find in a critical article; you must make your best effort to determine the article's meaning responsibly. We have provided comments throughout the article to highlight certain clues and signals that guide you through the critic's argument.

Moving to the Girl's Side of "Hills Like White Elephants"

Stanley Renner

Hemingway Review 15.1 (1995): 27–42

Although most of the features of "Hills Like White Elephants" have been well discussed and understood, so that Paul Smith, in his 1989 survey of opinion on the story, can wonder if there is anything left to say about it (209), what has not been satisfactorily resolved is the question of the **A.** ending. In view of the fact that Hemingway leaves virtually everything, even what is at issue between the girl and the American, for the reader to "figure" out, meanwhile unobtrusively

A. A critic who chooses to address a literary work about which much has been written must demonstrate the relevance of his or her interpretation by showing how it differs from other, more established interpretations. Renner is establishing a context for his thesis, and it may be worthwhile to examine Smith's book since, according to Renner, it contains a "survey of

supplying what is needed to understand the story's structure and conflict, it seems logical to assume that he also expected the reader to be able to answer the question left by the story's ending: What are the couple going to do about the girl's pregnancy? Yet the ending has seemed stubbornly indeterminate. A majority of commentators, by my count, assume that the girl will have the abortion in order to please and thus keep her lover. But a considerable minority find these arguments unconvincing and conclude that the story leaves the question open.

Giving a new twist to the majority opinion, Howard L. Hannum has recently argued that the girl will indeed have the abortion but then, the relationship irreparably ruptured, will leave her American companion.[1] Hannum is right, I believe, to argue that published commentary has not looked closely enough at the development of the female character through the story and "has underestimated Jig's character considerably" (53). But a study of Hemingway's characterization of the pregnant girl as she struggles with the American's wishes and her own feelings points, in my view, toward the conclusion that she decides not to have an abortion, and her companion, though not without strong misgivings, acquiesces in her decision.[2] Close analysis of the girl's utterances and movements in the context of the story's carefully constructed setting reveals that she first discovers and then decides to follow her own true feelings about not only what to do about the child she is carrying but also what will be the most fully rewarding direction to take in life.

To follow the girl's development in "Hills Like White Elephants," it is essential to have a clear sense of the setting in which her development takes place. As the story opens, the girl and her companion are sitting at a table outside a bar in a railroad station in Spain trying to decide what to do about her pregnancy. Although it is never stated, they are trying to agree on whether or not she should have an abortion; and it becomes clear that the girl is reluctant to accede to her companion's determined urging that an abortion would be an

B.

C.

D.

E.

---

opinion on the story." Remember that an article's list of Works Cited can be a very useful tool for the student writer.

B. Here Renner asserts that Hemingway's goal in the story was not to raise an unanswerable question but to provide clues that would allow the reader to understand the situation. This is significant, since it reveals an essential critical assumption about Hemingway's purpose and by extension the purpose of literary writing in general.

C. The opening paragraph tells us the article's subject: the conclusion of "Hills Like White Elephants." The author has implied that he does not agree with the majority that the woman intends to have the abortion—if he did, why write the article?

D. Here, in the space of a sentence, is the thrust of Renner's argument. The sentence that follows summarizes the supporting evidence Renner's article will explore in detail. Taken together, the two sentences function as an abstract for the entire article; as you read the rest of the article, pay attention to how each element or paragraph supports the assertions Renner makes in this passage.

E. The strategies a critic uses to develop an argument are—or should be—the same you have been taught to use to develop arguments in your own writing. You know that clear topic sentences are road signs you can use to guide your reader through your argument; pay attention to how the author uses them to build support for his interpretation of the story.

F. easy solution to their problem. The station where this drama takes place sits "between two lines of rails in the sun" (39). Here setting neatly reinforces conflict: the two lines of rails, presumably going in opposite directions, represent figuratively the decision point at which

G. the couple find themselves. They must choose which way to go, to have the abortion or the child. The rail lines run through a river valley with, naturally enough, a line of hills rising up on either side. The hills on one side of the valley are dry and barren; those on the other side are described with imagery of living, growing things. Thus in choosing whether to abort or to have the child, the couple are choosing between two ways of life. The choice of abortion is associated with the arid sterility of the hills on the barren side of the valley and by extension with the aimless, hedonistic life they have been leading. The choice of having the child is associated with the living, growing things on the other side of the valley, the "fields of grain and trees along the banks of the Ebro," the river as archetypal symbol of the stream of life.

H. typal symbol of the stream of life.

In this setting, then, Hemingway works out the story's conflict, which revolves around the development of his female character. Viewed analytically, the drama may be seen to

I. take place in four movements. In the first movement we are shown the stereotypical passive female, not even knowing her own mind, accustomed to following a masterful male for her direction in life. In movement two she comes to a dramatic realization of her own mind—her own welfare, dreams, and values. In movement three she asserts herself for the first time. And in the final movement we see the result of her development toward self-realization: the reluctant and still somewhat resentful capitulation of her male companion.

The first three-fifths of the story sketch in a classic portrait of the deferential female, without a strong identity, an accessory to the male, to whom she has been accustomed to look, although now with growing reluctance, for support and direction. Clearly the American is the leader in their relationship: he knows Spanish, the language of the country in which

F. We have warned you repeatedly against summarizing the literary work you are writing about, to the point where you may wonder what you *can* say about it. Notice, however, how Renner uses summary not to retell the story but to remind readers familiar with Hemingway's story of what they will need to remember to follow the development of his argument.

G. This sentence reveals something of the critic's approach to reading the story; the treatment of setting is not mere description but an assertion of the relevance of all the story's details to the effect Hemingway desires to produce.

H. Notice the critic's judicious use of literary terminology. His article is based on the assumption that setting functions symbolically in the story.

I. This structural analysis is significant not only as an aid to understanding Hemingway's story but also for perceiving the organization of the present article. Attention to clues like these can make reading articles a lot easier.

they are traveling, he is knowledgeable about drinks, and he is in charge of their luggage and thus, presumably, of the destination of their travels. There can be little doubt that the couple's life together as the story opens has been conducted along lines that suit the American's desires: their travels looking at things and trying new drinks revolve around "all the hotels where they had spent nights." This is a male's sexual playhouse, which, not surprisingly, the American is loath to give up. Ironically underscoring his assumption of leadership in the relationship, Hemingway makes him the expert even on abortion, a uniquely female issue. He knows what the operation consists of, how simple and "natural" it is, "lots of people that have done it," and that it will make them happy again, as they were before the girl got pregnant. By making the American so cavalier about a procedure he knows nothing about, one that would be an ordeal not for him but for the girl, fraught not only with physical trauma and danger but also with significant mental, moral, and perhaps religious conflict, Hemingway shows a sensitive understanding of what abortion means to the woman involved.

As in the opening movement the couple resume their discussion of what to do about the girl's pregnancy, the focus is on developing the conflicting viewpoints of the two parties involved. The American argues single-mindedly for the abortion. The girl's mind, however, appears to be divided. She is accustomed to following the lead of her male companion, but in this situation she finds herself uncomfortable with the direction he wants to take. Conditioned to be led by others, she does not know her own mind and therefore cannot articulate it to her male leader. The real drama of the opening movement of "Hills Like White Elephants," constructed with surprising insight by its still youthful male writer, shows the girl struggling to break out of her conditioned deference and assert her own feelings, although at this stage she doesn't even know what they are. After the opening paragraph, setting the scene, the first movement of "Hills Like White Elephants" settles into a dialogue between the

J.

J. This focus on the female's choice suggests a feminist perspective; however another critic, also arguing from a feminist perspective, might argue what is essentially the other point of view, that the woman accedes to her companion's wishes, subordinating her own. It's important to understand that no literary theory necessarily and automatically yields a particular interpretation of a given work; although different critics might consider the same evidence from similar perspectives, their conclusions may differ radically.

American, who wants to perpetuate the status quo of the couple's relationship, and the girl, who, in the habit of doing what he wants, has not yet developed the mechanism to know what she wants, much less to articulate it. Thus she cannot forthrightly contest her companion's urging, but neither, because of what is at stake in this case, can she stifle her own feelings, which express themselves involuntarily in the form of sarcasm and figurative language. Hemingway accomplishes a great deal through suggesting tone of voice, obviating the necessity of authorial commentary. He has obviously listened well to voices engaged in argument and has captured with remarkable

K. precision the games people play.

But readers must pay attention not only to what is said but also to where the characters are when they say it. In the first movement they are on one side of the station next to the bar sitting "at a table in the shade, outside the building" (39). This side of the station, facing out toward the hills on the same side of the valley, where "there was no shade and no trees," has been

L. widely associated with the barrenness and sterility both of the implications of going through with an abortion and of the current state of the couple's relationship. Understandably, it is when she looks "off at the line of hills" on this side of the station—hills "white in the sun" in

M. country that "was brown and dry"—that she utters her memorable simile: "They look like white elephants." Although various explanations have been offered of what this observation might mean, the telling point is, surely, that for the girl the child growing within her is a white elephant in the proverbial sense: something she cannot just throw away but for which, in her present circumstances, she has no use; some-

N. thing that is awkwardly, burdensomely in the way. Thus Hemingway finds a poignant way to suggest the girl's true feelings about her predicament, which she remains unable to communicate forthrightly to her companion. The simile also reveals at least some sensitivity on Hemingway's part to the dilemma of a girl pregnant and unmarried, which is more than can be said about the American in the story. His

K. This discussion of tone, like the earlier discussion of symbolism, is an effective example of how these elements of literature can be components of sophisticated analyses. These issues are not being explored in a vacuum but are being subordinated to the author's whole argument.

L. Here the author acknowledges that this part of his argument is based on widely accepted authority rather than original interpretation. The reference to general authority makes the argument more rather than less credible, since it clearly fits what others have been saying about Hemingway's story.

M. Notice the effective and economical use of short quotations in this sentence.

N. Here the critic addresses an essential piece of data: the definition of "white elephant." He does not offer the interpretation as original, but he acknowledges its significance in the context.

inability to put himself in her place is precisely the point behind his reply to her musing about white elephants—"I've never seen one"—and her sarcastic response, "No, you *wouldn't* have" (the emphasis I have added should be obvious). The American would have had no experience with white elephants like the ones troubling the girl because, obviously, he would never have been pregnant with a partner urging him to get an abortion.

Throughout the first movement of the story, while the girl cannot state her feelings directly, they nevertheless express themselves **O.** indirectly through sarcasm and also silence. When, for example, the American, the expert on abortion, describes the procedure—"It's just to let the air in" (41)—"The girl did not say anything." As a female she surely knows something about her own anatomy and about what happens in an abortion—a surgical procedure in which, in that time and place, dilation is followed by curettage. But in the first movement she does not dignify his self-serving ignorance with a response. If his may be called sarcasm through silence, she continues throughout this movement to employ vocal sarcasm, as in her rejoinder that she too has known lots of people who have had abortions "And afterward they were all *so* happy" (41, again obvious emphasis added). The first movement ends in a crescendo as the girl, her inner conflict becoming increasingly intense, throws the American's urgings back at him with a bitter sarcasm that exposes their self-serving hollowness. The movement climaxes in her exasperated outburst: "Then I'll do it. Because I don't care about me" (41).

It is curious that for some readers this is the end of the story. The girl repeats "And I'll do it and then everything will be fine" (42), and the **P.** decision is made. She will have the abortion because she wants to keep the American happy, placing his worry over the complications that her pregnancy will create for him above what the abortion will mean for her. But we are only three-fifths of the way through the story, and the remaining two-fifths are a good deal more than anticlimax. Even at this point the decision

O.   Again, this is another highly effective topic sentence. The article's impact is not compromised by clarity—quite the contrary.

P.   Renner's argument clearly relies heavily on accepting his reading of the tone of the girl's dialogue. It is not difficult to accept this interpretation, however, since Hemingway's carefully crafted dialogue conveys her tone very effectively. And as he soon points out, the man's response indicates his understanding of her tone, even if the reader is unable to hear it.

remains unsettled. If readers have misheard the girl's exasperation as acquiescence, the American has not. In fact, her statement that she will have the abortion because she does not care about herself is really an ironic attack on his own stubborn selfishness. This movement ends with a repetition of his acknowledgment that it is, after all, her decision: she should have the child if she really feels strongly about it. And at this point the American is beginning to realize that she does feel strongly about it, strongly enough to lash back at his selfish insistence that she abort the pregnancy. Thus when the girl seems to give in to the American's urging, "The literal sense of her remark," as Hannum points out, "is 'Since you force me to do this, you don't care about me'" (50). The heavy sarcasm of the statement shows how she really feels: that an abortion would be dangerous for her, that in having one she would have to give up herself, and that in insisting on the abortion the American cares only about himself. It is clear from his response that, unlike many readers, he hears what she is really saying: he says "I don't want you to do it if you feel *that* way" (42, emphasis added but clearly indicated in the dialogue). It is just at this point, with both the girl and the American beginning to realize not only what her feelings are but how strong they are, that the story takes a pivotal turn, in terms of both structure and character development:

> The girl stood up and walked to the end of the station. Across, on the other side, were fields of grain and trees along the banks of the Ebro. Far away, beyond the river, were mountains. The shadow of a cloud moved across the field of grain and she saw the river through the trees. (42)

Q.   Renner uses long quotations sparingly. This one is necessary because it establishes the symbolic function of the landscape.

For one thing, as has been widely recognized, these lines, beginning the second movement of the story, contain the definitive clue to the structural incorporation of theme into setting. The sentence "Across, on the other side, were fields of grain and trees along the banks of the

Ebro" stands in pointed contrast to the story's second sentence: "On this side there was no shade and no trees and the station was between two lines of rails in the sun." Thus are setting and conflict intertwined. "On this side" are all the values associated with abortion: sterility, aridity, the taste of licorice, and the pregnancy as a white elephant on the girl's hands. "Across, on the other side," are the val-

R.   ues associated with having the child: fertility, the water of life, fruitfulness—in short, pregnancy as a precious, even sacred, manifestation of the living power of nature.

R.   This is a succinct and useful statement of the symbolic role of setting in the story.

But more significantly, in terms of the dramatic conflict, the beginning of the second movement of "Hills Like White Elephants" represents a decisive turning point in the development of the female character. When "The girl stood up and walked to the end of the station," she effectively distances herself from the influence of her male companion and enables herself, evidently for the first time, to realize what is in her own mind. In choosing to write his story from the dramatic point of view, Hemingway set himself the problem of how to show, not tell, what is going on in the minds of his characters. Now he uses the physical movement of his character within a carefully defined setting to represent a pivotal movement of mind. Thus, figuratively speaking, the girl's movement to a point where she can look out to the other side of the station shows the freeing of her mind from the control of the American and her development toward discovering her own feelings, represented figuratively by the other side of the valley she now sees for the

S.   first time. The living things that now appear to her view—the trees, the "fields of grain" that suggest the cycle of life in nature, the river as the stream and water of life—all show that she is powerfully drawn to the full involvement in the life process that having a child signifies.

S.   This sentence asserts the most significant interpretive issue in the article; the symbolic significance of the landscape takes on a greater importance since it comments on her decision to move from one side of the station to the other.

T.   It has long been recognized that the two sides of the valley of the Ebro represent two ways of life, one a sterile perpetuation of the aimless hedonism the couple have been pursuing, the other a participation in life in its full natural sense. Hemingway signals this

T.   Again, Renner's acknowledgment of his argument's basis in earlier, widely accepted readings of the story adds to its persuasiveness, since it invokes other authority than his own.

opposition by the paired phrases that introduce the description of the two sides: "On this side" are all the values associated with abortion; "Across, on the other side," are all the values associated with having the child. Equally clearly, however, the two sides of the setting are identified with the two characters involved in the conflict. This side, the side of the abortion, is the American's side. The other side, with its imagery of life and fertility, is the girl's side. Throughout this movement of "Hills Like White Elephants" the girl keeps her distance from the American, remaining in a position to maintain her own viewpoint. Now she begins, although still obliquely, to express her own wishes. Her musing "And we could have all this" implies her sense that her side, her view of their future, would result in a fuller life than his. A debate over the point ensues, and as the first movement ended with the American's dawning awareness that she does indeed feel "that way," so the second movement ends as he tries to persuade her that she "mustn't feel that way" and, as Hannum notes, calls her "back in the shade" of his side of the issue and "struggles to regain control" of her (51).

U.   The third movement begins, as do all four movements of the story, with a descriptive paragraph that positions the characters pointedly within the highly symbolic setting. The girl rejoins the American at the table outside the bar on his side of the station where again what she faces is "the hills on the dry side of the valley," and he resumes his double talk, assuring her that he will go along with what she wants while stubbornly pressuring her to do what he wants.

V.   She is again physically on his side of the station and the decision, but her mind remains on her side, to which she tries to persuade him by implying that her pregnancy could mean something to him and allaying his fear that they would not be able to "get along" with the added burden of a child. But their dialogue in this movement lapses again into his hypocritical protestations of disinterest and her sarcastic rejoinders until, exasperated to the breaking point, the girl at last explodes with real feeling. Even though she still does not state in direct

U. Notice the author's use of transitional words and phrases to guide readers through the argument. He has introduced a four-movement outline of the story, and phrases like this one effectively remind us of where we are in the article's topography.

V. This sentence sounds a lot like summary, but notice how the next sentence adds analysis—there is no need for the reader to wonder why the critic is retelling the story.

terms her feeling that there can be more to life than their aimless hedonism, she nevertheless does, evidently for the first time, assert herself openly against the American. The point behind the seven repetitions of "please" with which

W. she tells him, though still indirectly, to shut up, is to show, not tell, the real intensity of her resistance both to what he wants for their relationship and to the hypocrisy of his efforts to per-

X. suade her. That hypocrisy is precisely what Hemingway underlines when, just at this point, the American looks at their suitcases and the "labels on them from all the hotels where they had spent nights" and then claims yet again that he has no selfish interest in the abortion decision—doesn't "care anything about it" (43). Readers surely know what a young man and woman do when, on a pleasure trip, they spend nights together in hotels and surely also recognize that it is the unencumbered sexual playhouse the American has been enjoying that he stubbornly tries to preserve throughout the

Y. struggle over the abortion decision. Presumably the girl too sees what the reader sees and draws a similar conclusion; thus when her companion claims, while looking at the labels on the luggage, that he has no selfish interest in the decision, the glaring hypocrisy pushes her to the limit of her self-control: "'I'll scream,' the girl said."

This is the climactic turning point in "Hills Like White Elephants." What the girl's outbursts have made clear to the American is just how strong her resistance to having an abortion is. She does not say, of course, when pressed to the breaking point, "I can't can't can't can't can't can't can't go through with an abortion." She says "Would you please please please please please please please stop talking." But it is clear from his response—"But I don't want you to"—that he understands what her words really mean: in the strongest terms of which she is capable she has told him that she does not want to have an abortion and will listen to no more of his self-serving pleading for her to do so. Six times throughout the episode he has declared that the decision is ultimately up to her. Now he knows unequivocally how she

W. Student use of such informal language would probably earn red ink; in the hands of the professional writer, though, it's both startling and effective. Use such strategies with care.

X. This distinction between showing and telling brings up an interesting point about the goal of explicatory literary criticism: the article attempts to tell what the literary work shows.

Y. This is possibly an overstatement of the significance of the trunk, and it may be that the American is trying to preserve something other than the "unencumbered sexual playhouse" of the relationship. However, given the general plausibility of the argument so far, we can mark the passage with a question mark and move on.

feels and can press her no further. Not quite the utter Hemingway cad he is sometimes taken to be, he accedes to the girl's overpowering reluctance, proposes to "take the bags over to the other side of the station"—her side—and gets an approving smile from the girl.

Of course, this analysis of the climax of "Hills Like White Elephants" puts heavy stress on the word *other*. Indeed, when several years ago Mary Dell Fletcher called attention to the possibly pivotal significance of the phrase "the other side," she could not bring herself to draw the logical conclusion from her own insight and

Z. left the question of the ending open (18). But the design of the story amply justifies putting decisive weight on the opposition between "this side" and "the other side." It is no overstatement to say that the whole story is structured around the two contrasting sides of the valley. Unmistakably, this division translates into an opposition between the American's values on this side and the girl's on the other. It seems pointless to worry, as Fletcher does, whether or not the actual facts of the setting will support such a reading. Perhaps, indeed, at the actual station in Spain, " 'this side' is a switch line (or siding) and 'the other side' a main line and boarding place for trains going either direction" (18). Equally irrelevant to an understanding of "Hills Like White Elephants" is the knowledge, reported by an observer of the actual landscape on which the story was apparently based, "that both the fertile fields and the dry hills are on the same side (northeast) of the tracks" (Hannum n. 7). Artists routinely rearrange the actual details on which their works are based.

In truth, the precise facts of the trains and tracks are left vague in the story, very likely because the real significance of these elements lies not in their literal but in their figurative implications. The train the girl and the American appear to be waiting for, the one that is coming "in five minutes" near the end of the story, is presumably "the express from Barcelona" that "stopped at this junction for two minutes and went on to Madrid" (39). If the story is read as ending with the girl, against her

Z. Notice the effective inclusion of paraphrase. Rhetorically, the critic's position with regard to Fletcher's argument is precarious; he at once agrees and disagrees with her.

own compelling reluctance, giving in to the American's urging, then the train is headed to Madrid for an abortion. Pamela Smiley, however, studies the couple's language "in the context of a train ride to the Barcelona abortion clinic" (290).[3] If the place of the abortion is Barcelona, then the train headed in that direction could not be the one they are about to board at the story's end; and if indeed the trains running on the two lines of rails do run in opposite directions, then the train to the abortion clinic would logically run on the American's side of the station, a logic that neatly supports my argument that they are headed in the direction of the girl's side of things. All that speculation about the literal facts of place and direction, however, enticing as it may be, yields place to the figurative use

AA. Hemingway makes of the setting: the station as the decision point for the couple, a "junction" (39) of their opposing viewpoints; the two lines of rails representing the opposite choices available to them; and the two sides of the valley representing two opposing directions in life, this side the way the American wants to go and the other side the way the girl wants to go. When the American carries their luggage to the other side, the whole weight of the story's figurative logic comes down on the conclusion that he is accepting her side of the issue.

The remaining details of the story, although they have been read quite comfortably from the viewpoint that the girl is going to have an abortion, work even better when it is understood that she has decided to have the child. Her surprising smile, for example, mentioned twice near the end of the third movement and again in the fourth and final movement, indicates a decisive change in mood that simply does not square with how she would feel if she were really facing an abortion. The girl, unable to bear any more of her companion's self-serving persuasive tactics, has just told him she will scream if he does not shut up. The waitress appears with the second round of beers and reports that the train—presumably, since it is the only one mentioned, the express from Barcelona to Madrid—"comes in five

AA.   Renner pays lip service to the earlier debate about the physical geography of the setting's real-world analogue, but even though it supports his reading, he is compelled to dismiss its relevance since it's not very convincing.

minutes"; and "the girl smile[s] brightly at the woman, to thank her" (43). It might be argued that the smile, mere politeness to the waitress, has nothing to do with her feelings about having an abortion. But in this story everything has to do with her feelings about having an abortion. Moreover, she has been unable throughout the story to keep her feelings about it out of anything she has said or done. How could she now, a moment later, smile "brightly" at the news that the train that will carry her to the dilation and curettage procedure is nearing the station? The significance of this point to the story's logic is underscored by the fact that the adverb *brightly*, telling the reader how the girl smiles, is the story's only authorial intrusion into the dramatic point of view of "Hills Like White Elephants," an understandable lapse, to be sure, because a smile does not have a tone of voice, Hemingway's usual method of showing how the girl is feeling in

BB. the story. It must have taken a compelling sense that telling the reader precisely how the girl is smiling at her decision point is crucial to his design to cause such a notorious taker-

CC. outer to put something in.

How, one might well ask, in view of the girl's near-hysterical aversion to the idea of abortion, would she be smiling if she were really about to board a train taking her to have the operation? If she were able to smile at all, would she not be smiling bitterly, ironically— out of the same sarcastic exasperation with which she has characteristically responded to the American's pleading? Nor does this logic change if she has decided to have the abortion only to leave her companion, except, perhaps, that in this case she might smile with something of a "you may think you've won but you'll see" attitude, hard to put in one adverb. The logic of the story's design enjoins the conclusion that she smiles brightly at the waitress's announcement of the train because she is no longer headed in the direction of having the abortion that she has contemplated only with intense distress. When, now, the American proposes to "take the bags over to the other side of the station," she smiles at him because, since

BB. Renner is asking a single word to carry a great deal of his argument's weight, and if he were writing about a different author, this argument might be less persuasive; however, since Hemingway's use of language is so Spartan and controlled, the argument is credible.

CC. This is another instance of informal language that might work better in the context of professional writing than in a student essay.

he has stopped pressing her and is going her way, she will not have to scream.

In the brief concluding movement, which again begins with a narrative passage noting position and movement, the American carries the couple's luggage to the other side of the station, stopping to have an Anis on the way back, a detail perhaps indicating that he is accepting the medicinal flavor of the prospect

DD. he is facing. As his attitude toward her pregnancy left a licorice taste in the girl's mouth, so the prospect of going her way, he fears, will lead to bad-tasting consequences for him. On the other hand, it occurs to him, other people survive the experience he is facing. He looks at the other people drinking around him and observes that "They were all waiting reasonably for the train" (44). These are people taking the same train as he and his pregnant companion: they are going in the girl's direction toward the fullness of life signified by its natural cycle—a direction, by the way, in this sense much more fittingly called "all perfectly natural" than the operation to abort the child that the American had described in those terms. If so many people go this way reasonably, he muses, maybe his fears are unreasonable. Although he still "could not see the train"—that is, cannot visualize the future that going in the girl's direction will bring—he uneasily accepts his fate.

But not without one last flare-up of his own

EE. feelings. Returning to the girl, still sitting at their table, he turns her sarcasm back on her. How tempting it is, after losing a contest, to get at least something back. Suppose that you have just given in in a dispute. Still not fully convinced by your opponent's side of the issue and smarting at being beaten down, what you say or imply, with self-justifying sarcasm, is something like "OK. You've got your way—I hope you're satisfied" or "I hope you feel better now" or, as the American says, "Do you feel better?"—getting in a final dig. But the girl is not having any of the recrimination he wants her to feel for getting her own way. In perhaps the only point at which the story's sympathy for the girl wavers, there may be just a hint of smug

DD. This is one of the less compelling pieces of support for the argument, but it does attempt to explain the author's choice of Anis over another beverage.

EE. You may have noticed that this is a sentence fragment. It is used here consciously, for dramatic effect. In student writing, it's best to avoid such gestures unless you know that your instructor's policy permits them and that you can use them masterfully.

FF. triumph in her reply "I feel fine. . . . There's nothing wrong with me. I feel fine" (44).

In "Hills Like White Elephants," it is instructive to note, Hemingway shows his female character undergoing essentially the same kind of struggle as Clara Middleton in

GG. George Meredith's novel *The Egoist*: first to discover her own mind in a contest with the male will and then to assert her own interests.[4] (The fact that *The Ordeal of Richard Feverel* turns up in "The Three-Day Blow" establishes that Hemingway knew something about Meredith and his preoccupation with female and male cross-purposes.) In *The Egoist* Clara Middleton, accustomed to following along in the tow of her patriarchal father, has drifted into an engagement with the imperious Willoughby Patterne, whom, when her own mind finally rouses itself and makes her true feelings known to her, she discovers she cannot stand. At length she is able to understand how she allowed herself to get into such a predicament: "I have learnt," she explains, "that the ideal of conduct for women is to subject their minds to the part of an accompaniment" (84). This is precisely the state in which we encounter the girl in "Hills Like White Elephants": accompanying her male companion here and there around Spain, in bed, and next to an abortion clinic in accordance with his desires. Suddenly, however, both Clara and Hemingway's girl find themselves in situations in which they can no longer drift along in mindless accompaniment. But both find themselves painfully unequipped to assert their own feelings. Clara Middleton, musing to Laetitia Dale over the predicament she is in, is struck by the realization "That very few women are able to be straight-forwardly sincere in their speech, however much they may desire to be" (132). Both the novel and the story generate suspense by making readers wonder whether the women will be able to assert themselves or will be overpowered by a male whom they will find intolerable: Clara to marry a monster of male egoism, the girl in Hemingway's story to abort an experience she implies she has waited so long for. The summation of Clara's plight by the narrative voice in *The Egoist* provides an apt commentary

FF. It is also possible that the girl is only now coming to the realization that she does in fact feel fine; this possibility doesn't affect Renner's argument either way.

GG. This facet of Renner's argument may interest you if you are familiar with George Meredith's work; if not, you should still read this section carefully to see what insights it might offer you as you prepare to write your essay. Renner provides sufficient summary for those who have not read the novel (whereas he can presume an audience familiar with one of Hemingway's most famous short stories, he cannot make the same presumption about Meredith work). If you are working on a term paper and have time to explore other primary works, such hints as these will certainly benefit you.

on what in the story is left to be inferred. While "not many men are trained to courage," the narrator allows,

> young women are trained to cowardice. For them to front an evil with plain speech is to be guilty of effrontery and forfeit the waxen polish of purity, and therewith their commanding place in the market. They are trained to please man's taste, for which purpose they soon learn to live out of themselves, and look on themselves as he looks, almost as little disturbed as he by the undiscovered. (204)

Neither Clara nor Hemingway's girl is able decisively to undo her conditioning in feminine deference, but both, energized by the arousal of the undiscovered—their true feelings—manage through indirect means to avoid the evil which they are unable to confront with plain speech. Clara is saved by the help of others and a *deus ex machina*, and the girl by the mere vehemence of her feelings, the import of which the American understands even though she never can say plainly what she means.

So firmly does the story's sympathy side with the girl and her values, so strong is her repugnance toward the idea of abortion, and so critical is the story of the male's self-serving **HH.** reluctance to shoulder the responsibility of the child he has begotten that the reading I have proposed seems the most logical resolution to its conflict. Hemingway's insistent exposure of the self-centered motives of his male character extends to the naming of the characters in the story. He names his male character "the American" apparently to generalize about an American male attitude toward the responsibility of parenthood, perhaps in contrast to the Europeans, presumably Spaniards, who are waiting "reasonably" for the train that symbolizes moving forward into reproductive life. In his naming of the female character it has not escaped notice that "The girl is called 'Jig' but only twice in the entire story, in successive

HH. This sentence serves to recap the thesis and major supporting elements of the gender conflict in the story. However, the following sentence is the paragraph's topic sentence.

addresses by the American" and that the sexual innuendo implied by the word " 'Jig' expresses all too well what the girl had meant to the American" (Hannum 46). With its denotations of a jerky up-and-down or to-and-fro motion and of any mechanical device operated in a jerky "jigging" motion, the term's long-standing connotation of sexual innuendo creates pointed implications of how the American thinks of the girl—as an apparatus for "the old in-out, in-out" (as Alex callously calls it in *A Clockwork Orange*) of sexual intercourse. What has not been justly credited, however, is that the girl is never called Jig by the authorial voice—only by the American. Hemingway scrupulously dissociates his narrative voice from the American's sexual instrumentalization of his female companion, setting an example not followed by many of the story's commentators.

If, however, the naming of his female companion represents Hemingway's way of exposing the demeaning way the American thinks of her, what are we to make of the fact that the authorial voice calls her, an adult female and pregnant, "the girl" throughout the story, a naming, to readers sensitive to gender-biased language, almost as belittling as "Jig"? In responding to this question one may not fall back on the explanation that Hemingway does

II. this unintentionally. As Nadine DeVost has demonstrated in impressive detail, he used the designations "girl," "woman," and "wife" with careful deliberation to suggest nuances of female sexual status and orientation in his fiction. It must be acknowledged, in view of current national concerns, that the mere fact that a female is pregnant does not assure that she is not still a girl. Hemingway's use of "girl" in "Hills Like White Elephants" follows a similar logic, one not utterly at odds with the principles of gender neutrality. DeVost notes that in stories like "Hills Like White Elephants" Hemingway often used the term "girl" to refer to "female characters whose sexual identity and/or maturity is not recognized or acknowledged by another important character" (51). But it is precisely the point of "Hills Like White Elephants," in the reading proposed in this essay, that the

II. In the preceding paragraph, the author emphasizes Hemingway's condemnation of the male character's attitude toward the woman; here, however, he notes that she is always referred to with apparent condescension as "the girl."

girl's maturity is not recognized through most of the story by the authorial persona as well. As has been argued, her achievement of mature self-knowledge and assertion is the main line of development in the story. Even though chronologically adult, as we assume, and pregnant, she has allowed herself to be guided as if she were still a child—thus, by definition, a "girl." Only when she discovers her own mind and takes charge of her own life does she become mature and a woman.

And, indeed, in the final movement of the story, which begins when the American carries their luggage to the other side of the station, she is no longer referred to as "the girl." It would have been too heavy-handed, surely, for the story now to call her "woman." But there is at least some evidence to suggest that Hemingway takes pains to avoid calling her a girl now that she is no longer being guided like a child. When it becomes necessary to refer to her in the final movement, it has been fully ten lines since she was last named by a noun. The remoteness of that referent would seem to dictate a repetition of the noun. The fact that Hemingway instead strains the reference, as nowhere else in the story, and uses the pronoun *she* may indicate his awareness that in the logic of his story "girl" is no longer an appropriate designation for his female character. (Although I have avoided calling her "Jig" and thus assuming the American's sexually demeaning perspective toward her, I have not scrupled against following the story's logic and calling her "girl" until her climactic transformation near the end.)

The girl's—now woman's—achievement of mature self-direction may be reflected also in the tone of the final movement. If, as I have proposed, she feels triumphant at the end, perhaps she deserves to feel good, not simply about getting the better of the American but about becoming her own person. Then the line "There's nothing wrong with *me*" (emphasis added), in keeping with the story's persistent reliance on suggesting irony or sarcasm in tone of voice, may well imply her realization that there is something wrong with her companion. Whether or not, as Hannum believes, such a

JJ.   This conclusion, though by itself rather tenuous, becomes much more plausible when considered in connection with the rest of the evidence the article offers, especially in light of the care Hemingway has taken with the subtleties of language.

realization, which has been clear to most readers all along, means she will dump the American, at least it does imply that she has become able to make a more clear-sighted estimation, and perhaps a better choice, of men.

In any case, although "Hills Like White Elephants" has generated a good deal of admiration through the years for its technical virtuosity, the story has not received all the credit it deserves. For one thing, for those who cannot completely shake the notion that the responsible writer should not leave readers hanging, left with crucial unanswered questions like "How does the story end? Is she going to get an abortion or not?" Hemingway has, I believe, provided the means by which they can reach the closure toward which the drama proceeds logically, movement by movement. For another thing, the story turns out to be even more right-minded, in terms of current sympathies, than has been generally perceived. Not only does it side with its female character's values, it also understands and sensitively dramatizes her struggle to take charge of her own arena, to have

KK. a say about the direction of her own life. Finally, it shows a Hemingway more perceptive about the underlying dynamics of female-male relationships than he has often been given credit for.

KK. Ultimately, Renner argues that Hemingway's sympathies are profeminist.

NOTES

[1]Although Hannum may be technically correct to assert that "the dynamic possibility of Jig's having the abortion and then leaving the American has not really been considered" (47), it has at least been mentioned by Brenner, for whom the story ends with "Jig's abortion and separation from her companion" (12).

[2]Smith's survey found that "No one has argued that [the girl] has decided to bear the child" (211), but J. F. Kobler states at the end of his brief discussion of the bead curtain that when in the last paragraph of the story the girl says, "I feel fine," "she means that she feels fine in her pregnancy and intends to remain in that condition for her normal term" (7).

[3]The story remains vague about which way is which, and Smiley provides no evidence to support her assumption that the abortion clinic is in Barcelona. Other critics—for example, Kenneth G. Johnston (127) and Fletcher (18)—assume that the place of the abortion is Madrid.

[4]Pamela Smiley, in her study of the dialogue in "Hills Like White Elephants" in the light of recent theorizing about the different ways women and men communicate, argues cogently that the girl's "language is traditionally feminine," but she fails to follow through to the logic of her own observations, as when she writes, "Unfortunately, Jig smiles at the American at a point when common sense indicates that she should have the most hostility toward him" (297). Overlooking the girl's decisive, though still indirect, assertion of her own wishes and the capitulation of the American, who has understood her real meaning, Smiley concludes that "The final conflict in the story leaves the issue of abortion unresolved."

WORKS CITED

Brenner, Gary. *Concealments in Hemingway's Works*. Columbus: Ohio State UP, 1983.

DeVost, Nadine. "Hemingway's Girls: Unnaming and Renaming Hemingway's Female Characters." *Hemingway Review* 14.1 (1994): 46–59.

Fletcher, Mary Dell. "Hemingway's 'Hills Like White Elephants.'" *Explicator* 38.4 (1980): 16–18.

Hannum, Howard L. "'Jig Jig to Dirty Ears': White Elephants to Let." *Hemingway Review* 11.1 (1991): 4, 6–54.

Hemingway, Ernest. *Men Without Women*. New York: Scribner's, 1927.

Johnston, Kenneth G. *The Tip of the Iceberg. Hemingway and the Short Story*. Greenwood, FL: Penkevill, 1987.

Kobler, J. F. "Hemingway's 'Hills Like White Elephants.'" *Explicator* 38.4 (1980): 6–7.

Meredith, George. *The Egoist*. 1879. Norton Critical Edition. Ed. Robert M. Adams. New York: Norton, 1979.

Smiley, Pamela. "Gender-Linked Miscommunication in 'Hills Like White Elephants.'" *New Critical Approaches to the Short Stories of Ernest Hemingway*. Ed. Jackson J. Benson. Durham: Duke UP, 1990. 288–99, 492–93.

Smith, Paul. *A Reader's Guide to the Short Stories of Ernest Hemingway*. Boston: Hall, 1989.

LL.

LL. *The Explicator* is a journal that specializes in brief articles focusing on very specific passages. These articles can be highly useful if they deal with issues you're addressing in your essay, but you may frequently find them to be of marginal relevance. If you access the articles electronically, use the abstracts to determine quickly whether the article will be useful to you.

⁓22⁓

Practical Advice for Reading and Evaluating Literary Criticism

- *You must understand the article.* When you are reading literary criticism as a part of the research process, with the goal of writing an essay of literary analysis, you are responsible for understanding any source you choose to incorporate in your essay. It may be tempting to quote random sentences from a source in order to pad your Works Cited page, but when you invoke a critic's name as an authority, you should make every attempt to understand that authority's point of view.

- *Look up words you don't understand.* This should go without saying. Make sure you understand the words as well as how they're being used in context. Focus on literary terminology, but include other kinds of words as well. You won't be able to understand the critical work if you don't understand the words with which it's written.

- *Try to understand the critic's approach.* Every reader brings certain assumptions to any given text: assumptions about the nature of reality, political and religious predispositions, and assumptions about the role of literary texts and the best methods of interpreting them. Many literary critics are famously associated with particular categories or schools of literary criticism (several of which are discussed in Chapter 25). Stephen Greenblatt, for instance, is associated with **New Historicism**, and Ernest Jones with **psychoanalytic criticism**. It is more common, though, for critics to reveal their assumptions and critical points of view more subtly and organically, as Stanley Renner does in the article presented in Chapter 21. His concern with gender issues in the article associates him with **feminist criticism**, and considering the article in terms of that school of thought is quite fruitful. Even his assumption that Hemingway intended for the careful reader to be able to identify the young woman's decision and her feelings toward it suggests a certain attitude toward the function of literature.

An interesting side note involves moral stances in general. As a reader and a writer, you should pay careful attention to your own beliefs and how they affect your attitudes toward what you read. You should also take note of whatever evidence suggests a particular moral stance on the part of a critic or author. For instance, the Renner article addresses a woman's decision to have (or not to have) an abortion. Abortion is a topic on which few people are neutral, and it's likely that your own attitude toward abortion affects your reading of Hemingway's story, just as your perception of Renner's attitude toward abortion might influence your understanding of his argument. Note that the critic judiciously avoids overt judgment of the young woman's decision to keep her child, though he clearly approves of her will to make that decision for herself. What is the critic's attitude toward abortion in general? Or Hemingway's? Neither the story nor the article can answer that question.

• *Identify the article's thesis and main supporting details.*   The best way to understand a critical article is methodically. Remember that as a piece of expository writing, the article will have a stated or implied **thesis**, and it will present arguments in support of that thesis. As you're working through the article, try to identify its thesis and main supporting details. Look for the topic sentences of paragraphs, and try to understand how each paragraph or section contributes to the author's stated purpose.

• *Keep track of transitional words and phrases.*   Transitional words and phrases are the bread crumbs writers drop to lead their readers through the forest of their ideas. As you read literary criticism, pay attention to transitions; they tell you where you are and how what you're reading fits into the big picture. We have pointed out how some of these transitions function in Chapter 21; don't ignore these useful clues.

• *Consider the piece of literary criticism as a work of expository writing.* Although the article or chapter might be longer and more detailed than the essay or term paper you're writing, remember that it's essentially the same kind of writing. You already know the strategies you use to get your points across, so look for those same strategies in the critic's work. You'll find the article to be more accessible, and you may find strategies you can implement in your own writing projects. Remember that critical works, like the literary works they discuss, are also texts to be analyzed, explored, and tested.

• *Make reading notes in the margins.*   If you own the copy of the article or book you're reading, don't hesitate to make notes in the margins. They'll be useful when you look back through the article in search of specific passages. Of course, it's also useful to keep notes in a separate notebook or word processing file.

• *Take notes verbatim.*   We find it useful, when reading literary criticism, to take notes in the form of quotations, with page breaks indicated if necessary. This is particularly a good idea if you're taking notes with a computer, since you can paste in notes as quotations or paraphrase them as you choose. If you try to paraphrase from paraphrased notes, however, you may find yourself unconsciously plagiarizing the source text. We have found that some of the notes we took in undergraduate courses come in handy long after the course is over.

• *Evaluate the worth of the argument.*   As a careful reader, you are qualified to assess the value of arguments you understand. Is the author's reasoning valid, or is it founded on a faulty understanding of the text? Do not assume that just because an article or book was published, it is reliable (needless to say, this goes double for Internet sources, which are frequently self-published). In his article on "Hills Like White Elephants," Renner examines several earlier readings of Hemingway's story, identifying points of agreement and disagreement. In your own writing, you will find it necessary to formulate your own response to each of the critical sources you consider; how much of that response you choose to incorporate in your own essay will depend on its usefulness to your purpose. Incidentally, a critic's commentary on earlier critical works can be a very good indicator of his or her critical stance.

• *Don't ignore the Works Cited page.*   A good Works Cited page can be your best friend. If you are searching for more sources for your essay, look at the sources of the critical works you've already used, and work your way back through them. Not only can that list tell you a lot about the background assumptions of the critic, but it can also provide you with a useful list of sources to consult as you proceed with your own inquiries. Some works, usually books, might provide an annotated bibliography that not only lists potentially useful sources but also describes and evaluates them, saving you the effort of wading through sources that turn out to be of limited use to your current project.

✿ 23 ✿

Plagiarism and Academic Honesty

What is plagiarism? On the face of it, that should be an easy question to answer: to plagiarize is to appropriate someone else's words or ideas and represent them as your own. For many, though, plagiarism is not a black-and-white issue but is rather various shades of gray. Students who would never dream of smuggling a cheat sheet into an exam, for instance, might find themselves making liberal use of unacknowledged Internet sources. It seems different somehow. It seems almost like research. But there are differences between honest research and plagiarism.

To hear most English professors talk, academic dishonesty is reaching epidemic proportions around the country. Is the problem worse now than it was a decade ago or a generation ago? And if so, why is it worse? Although some cynics might suggest that today's students are simply less scrupulous than their predecessors, there are other obvious and logical explanations for the phenomenon. Most of the problem can be attributed to the ease with which information can be exchanged electronically. When most of your professors were in school, they never had to be told to remove all electronic devices from their desks before an exam; some of us, in fact, would have been unsure of what constituted an electronic device. But mobile phones, text pagers, and the Internet have made cheating and plagiarism a lot easier.

A generation ago, it took a certain amount of effort to plagiarize an essay. Finding a source to plagiarize probably required a trip to the library to browse through books or journals. Students who wanted to buy term papers from "term paper mills" had first to locate these businesses (usually through classified ads in magazines like *Rolling Stone*) and then to send money via the U.S. Postal Service; delivery of the essay they purchased would take days or even weeks. Even "borrowing" papers from other students involved a tremendous amount of effort, since the papers would, at the very least, need to be retyped in their entirety—often on a manual typewriter (ask your grandparents about these exasperating devices). It was easier just to write the essay legitimately. Still, some students probably cheated.

In the twenty-first century, however, committing plagiarism is much less work. Journal articles and books are available online, so the student who is more resourceful than industrious need never darken the door of a library. "Paper mill" term papers are available for immediate purchase online—just enter the credit card number and download the "A" paper. Essays borrowed from fellow students can be shared by e-mail and reprinted in the blink of an eye (after correcting whatever errors their instructors might have marked).

And then there's the World Wide Web! Copy a paragraph from one site, paste a phrase from another, and the essay practically seems to write itself. What used to take hours or days now can be accomplished in minutes or even seconds. It seems like magic, but it's merely technology. Needless to say, however, the fact that cheating is easy doesn't make it right.

Generally, plagiarists fall into two categories: those who plagiarize on purpose and those who do so accidentally. The first group will probably always be with us, though perhaps the right combination of incentives to do right and penalties for doing wrong can persuade them to give it up. In the past, students who plagiarized did so on purpose. They knew they were doing something wrong because plagiarism required some effort and because it looked and felt substantially different from the legitimate research they had been trained to do. Now, though, the waters are a little muddier. High school students are often encouraged to treat "research projects" as Internet scavenger hunts, and if the resulting collection of quotations and media files is undocumented, it's not a big deal—just do a search for them on the Internet! Indeed, people use the Internet every day for legitimate research and collaborative writing, so what's the problem?

Of course, plagiarism is a very big deal. In recent years, even respected authors, academics, and journalists have been embarrassed or discredited by accusations of plagiarism. To most educators, the most disturbing thing about this process of patchwork plagiarism is that many students don't seem to understand that there's something wrong with it. They seem to think that what they're doing is research. By now, from working through this book, it should be obvious that the reading, research, and writing processes, when done correctly, require the dedication of a reasonable amount of time and effort. We hope you see that the rewards that come with full and honest engagement with these processes make the commitment of time worthwhile and that you won't get the same full, rich experience of working with a literary work if you "borrow" sentences or ideas about it for your writing. Often it's only when you sit down to write about a story, play, or poem that you come to understand its depth and complexity—the attributes that make it a significant part of the literary canon. Understanding is, after all, the point of reading, and it would be a shame to deprive yourself of the experience.

If that argument against plagiarism doesn't persuade you, there are always the penalties, which range from failure on the assignment to suspension or expulsion. Often the reason for failing the course also becomes a part of the student's permanent record. These penalties vary from one institution to another, of course, so you will want to familiarize yourself with your school's academic honesty policy, which will probably include specific definitions of plagiarism and cheating. You will no doubt be held accountable for the rules whether or not you're familiar with them; generally, ignorance is not considered an excuse.

So how does one avoid "accidental" plagiarism? The short answer, quite simply, is to use legitimate sources for your information and to document your sources appropriately. We discuss the legitimacy of sources and correct documentation style throughout Part Five of this book. Scrupulous documentation adds to the credibility of your argument because it sends a message to the reader that you have done your homework, you know what you're talking about, and you can be trusted.

Somewhere in the education process, every student has been told that people who cheat only cheat themselves, and there's truth in that saying. Every semester, we are surprised by the number of students who seem willing to pay for an education and then do everything they can to avoid actually getting that education. All along, we have tried to assert the real value of active engagement with literary texts, and the bottom line with regard to plagiarism is this: you might get caught or you might not get caught, but by passing up the opportunity for dynamic interaction with literary and critical texts, you're already paying the penalty. Look at your writing assignments as opportunities to participate in the great, ongoing conversation about the human condition, and don't let anybody else speak for you.

THINKING EXERCISES

1. Do an Internet search on "plagiarism" or "academic dishonesty." Look for news reports about journalists or scholars accused of plagiarism. How do their motivations and methods compare to those of people who plagiarize in college classes? What penalties are associated with these acts?

2. Research the academic honesty policies of various colleges and universities. How do they compare with the one in place at your institution?

❧ *24* ❧

MLA Documentation Style

We have mentioned the Modern Language Association (MLA) several times in earlier chapters. As we noted, one of the helpful services the MLA has performed for the academic community is providing a set of documentation and citation rules. Before the MLA style became the norm in the humanities, research papers made use of a jumble of more cumbersome styles. Students had to use footnotes or endnotes, which made for awkward reading. Also, although a particular book might be used over and over as a source, each use would demand its own separate footnote or endnote. Although a number of disciplines still require use of footnote and endnote methods of documentation in research papers (as exemplified by *The Chicago Manual of Style* and Kate Turabian's *Manual for Writers of Term Papers, Theses, and Dissertations*), the MLA style of documentation has become the standard for literary studies.

One of the reasons why MLA style is so easy to use is that a writer has to prepare only one bibliographical entry for each source used. In a paper using footnote documentation, the writer must place a bibliographical entry at the bottom of the page each time a source is used and then a secondary entry in the bibliography at the end of the paper.[1] MLA style requires only that the writer mention the author and page number when citing a particular source in the research paper; the reader can then refer to the Works Cited page at the end of the paper to find out more about the source the writer has used. Like other methods for citing research, the documentation style of the MLA can change (particularly where electronic sources are concerned), so it is important that students keep up with the latest MLA rules for documentation. The rules presented in this book reflect the sixth edition of the *MLA Handbook for Writers of Research Papers*, by Joseph Gibaldi, published in 2003.

[1]As this text demonstrates, MLA-style papers may make use of footnotes or endnotes too, but usually to address points or issues that digress from the development of the text's primary issues.

24.1   UNDERSTANDING MLA DOCUMENTATION

When Do You Cite a Source?

We discussed plagiarism at more length in Chapter 23, but this has become such an important issue in colleges lately that the point bears repeating. You *must* cite your source anytime you use any *exact words*, any *para-phrased thoughts*, or *any ideas, facts,* or *statistics whatsoever* from a secondary source.

How Do You Cite a Source?

There are two ways to cite a source. The better way is to integrate the quoted author's name into your sentence and then cite the page number (if using a print source) or possibly a paragraph number (preferred by some instructors if the source is electronic) in parentheses at the end of the sentence. The other method is to list both the author's name and the page or paragraph number in the parentheses. If your quotation stretches from one page of the source to another, simply indicate this in the parenthetical note by placing a hyphen between first and last page of the quotation. If the quotation appears in a magazine or newspaper and runs on nonconsecutive pages, indicate the page where the quoted material begins and then add a plus sign (+) after the number (for example, if your quotation begins at the end of page 77 and concludes on page 102, you would indicate the page number by typing "77+").

Note also that quotation marks end the quoted material; they are then followed by the parenthetical citation, which is followed by the ending punctuation. Generally speaking, the parenthetical citation should come at the end of the sentence where you've made use of the quotation; it's sometimes acceptable to delay the parenthetical notation until the end of the paragraph, as long as it's clear which quotation (or paraphrased idea) the citation refers to. It's usually awkward to use multiple quotations from different sections of books or articles in one sentence, but if you do so, include the specific parenthetical citation after each quotation.

EXAMPLES

As Romein notes, "Holden Caulfield is frightened of the adult world" (97).

One critic notes, "Holden Caulfield is frightened of the adult world" (Romein 97).

Holden is scared of adulthood (Romein 97-98).

What If the Source Doesn't Have an Attributed Author?

If the source you're using doesn't have an attributed author (not uncommon with Web site articles or newspaper stories), use the title. If the title is particularly long, use a shortened form of the title that includes a key word or two. Remember that the parenthetical citation must lead the reader clearly to the corresponding entry on the Works Cited page.

EXAMPLES

> Although Calixta may be "frustrated by her marriage," she has no plan to end it ("Chopin's 'Storm'" 4).
>
> At least one critic notes that the railing in the middle of the stage is "essential" to understanding the play ("Plays" 7).

What If I Have More than One Source by the Same Author?

When an author is represented by more than one source, you need to indicate which source is used when deriving a quotation or idea. Although normally you don't need to include the title in your text when using a quotation, you can do so in this situation, or you may refer to the title in the parenthetical notation.

EXAMPLES

> As Brooks notes in <u>The Yoknapatawpha Country</u>, Faulkner makes use of the same families over and over (91).
>
> Simmons argues that the boy in "Araby" knows "very well what he is getting into" ("Understanding 'Araby'" 42+).
>
> Drowota has pointed out that "the traveler is unsure of the future" ("Road" 7) and that the poem focuses not on "nonconformity but rather on the necessity of making decisions" ("Reading Frost" 31).

QUICK TIPS

- It's useful to write your Works Cited page as you begin drafting your paper; if you have multiple sources by a single author (which means you'll have to include more than the name and page or paragraph number), or if you are missing any Works Cited information, you'll know early rather than late in the composition process.
- Integrate quotations. As we point out at various places in this text and as most of our examples illustrate, your sentence structure should flow. Don't just shove a quotation into a line.
- Take advantage of your word processing skills. As you type your outline, decide where certain quotations and facts from your sources will support your argument. Type the quotations and ideas you are citing directly into your outline, and then cut and paste them from your outline document directly into your paper. Remember, though, you'll need to edit carefully to ensure that the syntax still flows properly. Furthermore, you can type your Works Cited information directly into the same text file.

24.2   WORKS CITED ENTRIES IN MLA STYLE

1. A Book by One Author
2. A Book by Two or More Authors

3. Two or More Works by the Same Author
4. A Translated Work
5. A Republished Book
6. A Work in an Anthology
7. A Multivolume Book
8. An Introduction, Preface, Foreword, or Afterword
9. The Published Proceedings of a Conference
10. A Dissertation (Unpublished or Published)
11. An Article in a Scholarly Journal with Continuous Pagination
12. An Article in a Scholarly Journal with Each Issue Paginated Separately
13. An Article in a Newspaper (Signed or Unsigned)
14. An Article in a Magazine
15. A Review
16. A Film or Video Recording
17. An Interview
18. A Lecture
19. A Work from an Information Database
20. A Professional or Personal Web Site
21. An Online Book
22. An Online Book That Is Part of a Series or Database
23. An Article in an Online Journal
24. An Article from an Online Newspaper or Wire Service
25. An Article from an Online Magazine
26. An Online Review
27. An E-Mail Communication
28. An Online Posting

PRINT SOURCES

1. A BOOK BY ONE AUTHOR

Almost always, your Works Cited entry for a book by a single author will follow this format:

> Author, Name Inverted. <u>Book Title</u>. City: Press, year. (Use a hanging indent for each line after the first for each citation).

When the press is a university press (as they often are in literary scholarship), you may abbreviate *university* as "U" and *press* as "P." The title of the book may be either underlined or italicized; either way, be consistent throughout your list. (We have generally italicized book titles throughout this text; for this section, we are underlining instead so that our examples will more closely conform to the examples in the *MLA Handbook*). If the city is ambiguous or unclear, indicate the state or nation of publication (use the two-letter postal abbreviation for U.S. states). If the publishing company includes more than one name, use only the first (see the second example in item 2).

Bell, Vereen. <u>The Achievement of Cormac McCarthy</u>. Baton Rouge: Louisiana State UP, 1988.

2. A BOOK BY TWO OR MORE AUTHORS

When citing sources with multiple authors, list the authors in the order in which they are presented on the title page of the book. Invert only the name of the first author. When there are more than three authors, name only the first and add *et al.* (a Latin abbreviation for "and others"), in regular type.

Two or Three Authors

Arnold, Edwin T., and Dawn Trouard. <u>Reading Faulkner</u>: Sanctuary. Oxford: UP of Mississippi, 1996.

More than Three Authors

Craig, Albert, et al. <u>The Heritage of World Civilizations</u>. Upper Saddle River: Prentice, 2002.

3. TWO OR MORE WORKS BY THE SAME AUTHOR

When citing two or more books by the same person or persons, only list the author for the first Works Cited entry. In the following entry, type three hyphens instead; this indicates that the same author wrote the work as the one in the preceding entry. Place the two entries in alphabetical order based on the first letter of the title (ignoring the articles *The, A,* and *An*).

Brooks, Cleanth. <u>William Faulkner: First Encounters</u>. New Haven: Yale UP, 1983.

---. <u>William Faulkner: The Yoknapatawpha Country</u>. New Haven: Yale UP, 1963.

4. A TRANSLATED WORK

Although the work is listed by author, your citation should indicate which translation you used.

Roth, Joseph. <u>The Radetzky March</u>. Trans. Joachim Neugroschel. 1932. New York: Overlook, 1992.

5. A REPUBLISHED BOOK

Often students using a novel in their literature courses will look at the publication date of the latest printing of their book and list that as the publication date; this seems to suggest that *Pride and Prejudice* was written in 1995 or *Moby-Dick* was first published in 1980. Be sure to list the original publication date just after the title and then to note the publication date of your edition at the end of the entry. Some presses are lax when it comes to providing the original publication dates of reprinted texts, but finding the original date shouldn't be too difficult.

Fitzgerald, F. Scott. <u>The Great Gatsby</u>. 1925. New York: Scribner's, 1995.

6. A WORK IN AN ANTHOLOGY

Students frequently make the mistake of citing an essay in an anthology of many essays or even citing the primary text (which they have access to in a large literary anthology) and then listing the editor of the anthology as the writer rather than the actual author of the text being cited. Many instructors share this pet peeve; you should take special care to make sure the person listed in your parenthetical notation and on the Works Cited page is actually the person whose words you're citing. Note that you will also include the page numbers of the work within the anthology at the end of the entry. Remember that this entry must reflect the edition being used; if using a book with multiple volumes, show which volume you're using.

A Single-Volume Anthology

Wright, Richard. "The Man Who Was Almost a Man." <u>Literature and the Writing Process</u>. 6th ed. Ed. Elizabeth McMahan, Susan Day, and Robert Funk. Upper Saddle River: Prentice, 2002. 275-83.

A Multivolume Anthology

Wright, Richard. "The Man Who Was Almost a Man." <u>Anthology of American Literature</u>. Ed. George McMichael et al. Vol. 2. Upper Saddle River: Prentice, 2000. 1426-34.

7. A MULTIVOLUME BOOK

As suggested in item 6, many books (including a lot of literary anthologies) are released in multiple volumes. Whether your citation is drawn from each volume or from one, your Works Cited entry should properly reflect your source.

McMichael, George, et al., eds. <u>The Prentice Hall Anthology of American Literature</u>. 7th ed. 2 vols. Upper Saddle River: Prentice, 2000.

8. AN INTRODUCTION, PREFACE, FOREWORD, OR AFTERWORD

The prefatory or closing materials in books are often quite useful when writing research papers. Remember, however, that you should cite these sections only if you're making use of them. Also remember that the foreword or afterword is often by a different author than the text.

Gordimer, Nadine. Introduction. <u>The Radetzky March</u>. By Joseph Roth. Trans. Joachim Neugroschel. 1932. New York: Overlook, 1992. iii-xx.

9. THE PUBLISHED PROCEEDINGS OF A CONFERENCE

Scholars, professors, and teachers of every level are expected to engage in various kinds of professional development. Attending professional conferences is one of the most common ways for them to be exposed to the work of other scholars and also to read their own work to an audience of peers. Occasionally, a sampling of the papers at a conference is published.

The Entire Publication

Barendse, Nancy, ed. <u>Approaches to the Literary Studies Workshop: Proceedings from the National Alliance of Teachers of Literature Conference, November 1994, Auburn University</u>. Charleston: Charleston Southern UP, 1995.

A Single Presentation from the Published Proceedings

Phillips, David. "Shakespeare and Responses." <u>Approaches to the Literary Studies Workshop: Proceedings from the National Alliance of Teachers of Literature Conference, November 1994, Auburn University</u>. Ed. Nancy Barendse. Charleston: Charleston Southern UP, 1995. 115-29.

10. A DISSERTATION (UNPUBLISHED OR PUBLISHED)

Most doctoral candidates in literary studies (as well as in most other disciplines) are required to write and defend a dissertation before their degree is conferred. Often their dissertations are published as scholarly works. These dissertations can be quite valuable in literary research. Notice that the title of an unpublished dissertation is not underlined. Under the citation for a published dissertation, the University Microfilms International (UMI) number may be listed as well.

An Unpublished Dissertation

Phillips, David. "Promoting the Nation: The Rise of Ethno-Nationalism and Renaissance Drama." Diss. U Nevada-Las Vegas, 1996.

A Published Dissertation

Kang, Hee. The Snopes Trilogy: Rereading Faulkner's Masculine and Feminine. Diss. U of Alabama, 1992. Ann Arbor: UMI, 1992. 092442.

11. AN ARTICLE IN A SCHOLARLY JOURNAL WITH CONTINUOUS PAGINATION

Many scholarly journals number pages consecutively throughout each volume (usually corresponding to the academic year of publication) rather than starting each separate issue with page 1. In these cases, you do not need to indicate the issue number or the month, because the pagination will run from issue to issue. If you're unsure of the pagination, cite the article as if each issue were paginated separately. If articles are unsigned (very rare in scholarly journals), cite the title first, alphabetized by the first word in the title (excluding articles).

Fuston-White, Jeanna. "'From the Seen to the Told': The Construction of Subjectivity in Toni Morrison's Beloved." African American Review 36 (2002): 461-74.

12. AN ARTICLE IN A SCHOLARLY JOURNAL WITH EACH ISSUE PAGINATED SEPARATELY

For journals that start each issue on page 1, you need to indicate the volume and issue number. Some journals also publish double issues. If so, see if the journal actually divides the content between the issues. If the journal does not distinguish between the issues in the contents, list both.

Baker, Christopher. "Chopin's 'The Storm.'" Explicator 52.4 (1994): 225-26.

Quintelli-Neary, Marguerite. "Retelling the Sorrows in Edna O'Brien's Country Girls Trilogy." Nua: Studies in Contemporary Irish Writing 4.1-2 (2003): 65-76.

13. AN ARTICLE IN A NEWSPAPER (SIGNED OR UNSIGNED)

Articles in newspapers are cited much like journal articles except that the exact date must be given. Notice that often newspaper stories do not appear on sequential pages (for example, a story may begin on page D13 and then be completed on page D17). In these cases, use of a plus sign (+) indicates that the pages are not sequential.

A Signed Article

Steinberg, Jacques. "A Rocker and a Revered Author Bond for a Cause." New York Times 20 Mar. 2003: E1+.

An Unsigned Article

"U.S. and Qatar Sign Pact to Update Bases." New York Times 12 Dec. 2002: A2.

14. AN ARTICLE IN A MAGAZINE

Magazine articles, whether signed or unsigned, follow more or less the same form as articles in newspapers. Even if a magazine provides volume and issue numbers, use only the date on the cover.

Corliss, Richard. "April 15, 1938: Birth of the Superhero." Time 31 Mar. 2003: 21.

15.   A REVIEW

Many magazines and most literary journals publish reviews; often reviewers may have some insight into the work being reviewed that may be of use to you in your research.

A Signed Review

Judd, Elizabeth. "The Plotless Wonder." Rev. of Making Things Better, by Anita
     Brookner. Atlantic Monthly Apr. 2003: 109.

An Unsigned Review

"Empire." Rev. of British Imperialism, 1688-2000, by J. Cain and A. G. Hopkins.
     Atlantic Monthly Apr. 2003: 91.

16.   A FILM OR VIDEO RECORDING

If you are citing a film in general, begin with the title. However, if you are specifically referring to an individual's contribution, begin with that person's name.

Miller's Crossing. Dir. Ethan Coen and Joel Coen. Perf. Gabriel Byrne, Albert Finney,
     and John Turturro. 20th Century Fox, 1990.

17.   AN INTERVIEW

There are a few varieties of interviews that might be cited in a scholarly paper. You may be making use of a broadcast television interview, or a published interview, or a personal interview conducted by yourself.

A Radio or Television Interview

Russo, Richard. Interview with Terry Gross. Fresh Air. Natl. Public Radio. WJWJ,
     Beaufort, SC. 19 Aug. 2002.

A Published Interview

Hollander, John. Interview with Ernest Suarez. Five Points 6.1 (2001): 48-68.

A Personal Interview

Pinker, Steven. Telephone interview. 4 Apr. 2004.

18.   A LECTURE

In most cases, your instructors and professors don't want you to attribute points in your text to their classroom lectures (although you should ask to make sure). If you attend a more formal lecture and make use of the information, however, you should cite the source properly.

Zimmerman, David. "My Ethiopian Experience." Charleston Southern Reading
     Series. Charleston, SC. 5 Apr. 2003.

ELECTRONIC SOURCES

Electronic citations can be challenging. Computer networks and communications have exploded in recent years, and the services, journals, and publications available online have evolved rapidly. Information databases are generally available in two varieties; either the information is published periodically on CD-ROM or it is available through an online connection (usually accessed by libraries). This can be particularly confusing because certain services, like InfoTrac, may be accessed through either method, depending on the school or library you're using to access them. You'll begin with the author's name, the article title, the original source (book or journal), and the issue and page range, as you would in citing any other source. Then you indicate the database used (the *Expanded Academic Index ASAP* database from InfoTrac in the example is one of the most popular), the place or site you used to access it, the online publication date if available, and the access date. If using a CD-ROM, instead use the date of publication. When in doubt as to which service your school uses, ask your librarian or your instructor. When listing the Web address, don't use the long, complex URL for the page; use the URL for the page from which you launched your search. (Long URLs can only be broken after a slash.)

19.   A WORK FROM AN INFORMATION DATABASE

An Article from an Online Database

Kearns, Katherine. "The Nullification of Edna Pontellier." American Literature 63.1 (1991): 62-89. Expanded Academic Index ASAP. InfoTrac. Charleston Southern U Lib., 3 Feb. 2004 <http://web7.infotrac.galegroup.com>.

An Article from a Publication in a CD-ROM Database

Kearns, Katherine. "The Nullification of Edna Pontellier." American Literature 63.1 (1991): 62-89. CD-ROM. SilverPlatter. May 2003.

20.   A PROFESSIONAL OR PERSONAL WEB SITE

As we have stated several times in the text, you should be very wary of using a Web site unless you are certain that it is trustworthy. Note that since there is no print publication date for Web sites, you should provide the online publication date (or date of last update) if it's available, placing this date before the date of access.

A Professional Web Site

William Faulkner Society Home Page. Ed. Anne Goodwyn Jones. 12 July 2004. 2 Aug. 2004 <http://www.english.ufl.edu/faulkner/>.

A Personal Web Site

Romein, Tunis. Home page. 25 Sept. 2004 <http://www.csuniv.edu/english/romeint>.

21.   AN ONLINE BOOK

Melville, Herman. Moby Dick. New York: Harper, 1851. 6 Feb. 2003 <http://www.textlibrary.com/TITLE/moby-dic/>.

22.   AN ONLINE BOOK THAT IS PART OF A SERIES OR DATABASE

Fitzgerald, F. Scott. This Side of Paradise. New York: Scribner's, 1920. Bartelby.com: Great Books Online. 1999. 5 Oct. 2004 <http://www.bartleby.com/115/>.

23.   AN ARTICLE IN AN ONLINE JOURNAL

Wiener, Gary. "Administrating Poetry." InPosse Review 15 (2003). 13 May 2003 <http://webdelsol.com/InPosse/weiner15.htm>.

24.   AN ARTICLE FROM AN ONLINE NEWSPAPER OR WIRE SERVICE

In this type of entry, the first date indicates when the article was first published by the newspaper or wire service, and the second date shows when you accessed it.

Eckholm, Eric. "China Threatens Execution in Intentional Spreading of SARS." New York Times on the Web 15 May 2003. 25 May 2003 <http://www.nytimes.com/2003/05/15/international/asia/15CND-CHINA.html>.

25. AN ARTICLE FROM AN ONLINE MAGAZINE

> Spiers, Elizabeth. "Don't Hate David Amsden Because He's Brilliant, Celebrated and 23." <u>Salon.com</u>. 12 May 2003. 21 May 2003 <http://www.salon.com/books/int/2003/05/12/amsden/index_np.htm*l*>.

26. AN ONLINE REVIEW

> Miles, Jonathan. Rev. of <u>The Fruit of Stone</u>, by Mark Spragg. <u>New York Times Book Review Online</u>. 18 Aug. 2002. 15 May 2003 <http://www.nytimes.com/2002/08/18/books/html>.

27. AN E-MAIL COMMUNICATION

When citing an individual's electronic mail message, list the name of the writer, the title or subject line of the message (indicated by quotation marks), and to whom the message was written.

> Brown, James S. "Re: Joyce Article." E-mail to Scott Yarbrough. 15 Aug. 1999.

28. AN ONLINE POSTING

> Stock, Scott. "The Insincere 80s." Online posting. 7 May 2003. Slate.com: Enter the Fray Discussion Forum. 22 May 2003 <http://bbs.slate.msn.com/?id=3936 &m=6800657>.

24.3   SAMPLE WORKS CITED PAGE

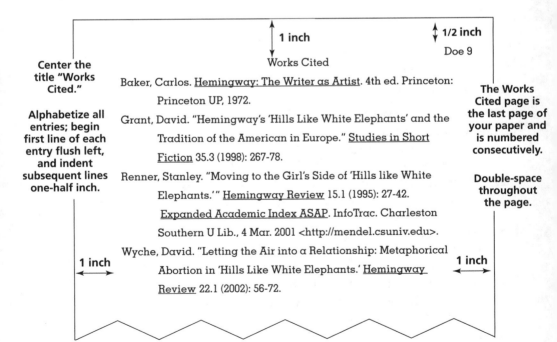

24.4 SAMPLE STUDENT RESEARCH PAPER

Faith Bafford

Dr. Yarbrough

English 112-14

3 April 2003

Life or Death

In "Hills Like White Elephants," Ernest Hemingway presents a subtle struggle between life and death that mirrors the struggle for empowerment that exists between the American and the girl Jig. Even as they have a choice over whether they will or will not abort their unborn child, Jig too must make a choice: is she going to allow herself to follow the American's lead, or is she going to stand her ground and make her own choices?

Stanley Renner notes that at the beginning of the story the American and the girl are apparently "trying to agree on whether or not she should have an abortion" (28). Before the girl's pregnancy, their focus as a couple has been entirely centered upon themselves; as Holladay puts it, "[t]heir life together up to this point seems to have been composed primarily of travel and aimless self-gratification" (7). Until now, they have both been free to do whatever they wish without having to worry about how their actions affect others. They have led carefree, meaningless lives, where all they do--as Jig says--is "look at new things and try new drinks" (Hemingway 249). The "labels on [their luggage] from all the hotels where they [have] spent nights" give further evidence to their lives of casual ease, their traveling wherever whim takes them, responsible only to themselves (250). Now, however, these carefree days are imperiled, and the couple is faced with a choice. The question remains as to whose choice it is.

Renner notes that a number of critics have pointed out that the use of the term <u>girl</u> rather than <u>woman</u> shows that the American thinks of her in a "demeaning way" and that, initially at least, she lacks power and is under the control of her male companion (39). Urgo writes that she "possesses none of the man's cultural resources" and that the train junction is also partially representative of the "clash of male and female sources of power and authority" (36). The American, notes Urgo, "controls the language, translating the girl's desires from English to Spanish. He controls the money, paying for their drinks. He has access to scientific information; specifically, how one lets in the air to have an abortion" (36).

The reader first realizes the girl's longing for another kind of lifestyle when she says that the hills "look like white elephants" (Hemingway 248). Stanley Kozikowski states that the girl sees the child inside her just as she sees the hills "like white elephants-- fearfully unwanted but precious" (107). While she knows from the start that she wishes to keep her baby, her dilemma is which choice is the best choice for herself and the baby and how the American (the father) will react if she has the baby.

It is imperative to recognize the significance of the setting where the American and the girl are discussing the possible abortion. They are on the train station bar's patio in "the warm shadow of the building," with the bar just beyond a bead curtain (Hemingway 248). The shadow of the building in a way symbolizes the shadow of death, and that death is ready to take the unborn and "unwanted" baby at any moment. It also appears to be a place where the couple are figuratively hiding from dealing with the situation they have created. Not only is the girl's pregnancy a problem in itself, but it brings up the question of the validity of the couple's relationship. If the girl has the baby, both the American's and the girl's lives will be vastly changed. Instead of continuing to enjoy the seemingly endless freedom they now have, they will both have to accept the responsibility that comes with having a child. It will mean that they both must sacrifice many of their own personal desires, such as continuing to travel and spending

Bafford 3

nights out drinking. For the girl, it will mean that she must take a step toward womanhood. She will have to leave her own childlike ways behind her, and the American will be forced to acknowledge that she is doing so--thus changing the unequal power dynamic that exists between them.

As Renner has pointed out, the significance of the two lines of rail tracks must not be overlooked. First, they are an example of the two outcomes that the girl must choose from regarding her baby. She can go one way and have the abortion, or she can go the exact opposite way and have her baby. However, the tracks also mean something deeper besides the obvious decision debated here. According to Renner, on one side there are "dry and barren" hills across a valley, and on the other side there are hills "described with living, growing things." Therefore, the tracks are an example of how "in choosing whether to abort or to have the child, the couple are choosing between two ways of life" (28).

The station itself is a crossroads for the couple. Their decision about which way to go evidently reflects their decision about the abortion. While they are free to choose either way, their conflicting wishes cause the long argument in the story. Throughout the story, the girl seems to be set on having the baby, though the man is trying to talk her into having an abortion. He repeatedly makes the claim that an abortion is a "perfectly simple operation," as if by his making light of the procedure he might make the entire situation go away (Hemingway 249). However, by the end of the story, as Renner argues, the American finally comes to admit that by his own actions he is responsible for the baby and that he is willing to abide by her choice.

What "Hills Like White Elephants" ultimately boils down to is "the critical necessity of taking responsibility for the quality of one's own life," as stated by Holladay (7). Until a person can accept responsibility for his or her life, the person will not be able to prove himself or herself

Bafford 4

responsible for anyone else. The "girl" must be willing to change the power dynamic she's trapped in and become a woman; when she finally steps forward and makes the choice herself, then she will be ready to accept the responsibility that perhaps can even mean life or death for another person, such as the unborn baby in this story.

Bafford 5

Works Cited

Hemingway, Ernest. "Hills Like White Elephants." *Literature and the Writing Process.* 6th ed. Ed. Elizabeth McMahan, Susan Day, and Robert Funk. Upper Saddle River: Prentice, 2002. 248-51.

Holladay, Hal. "Essay Review of 'Hills Like White Elephants.'" *Masterplots II: Short Story Series* (1986). EBSCO Host: MagillOnLiterature. Charleston Southern U Lib., 2 Apr. 2003 <http://www.csuniv.edu/library/databases.html>.

Kozikowski, Stanley. "Hemingway's 'Hills Like White Elephants.'" Explicator 52.2 (1994): 107-09.

Renner, Stanley. "Moving to the Girl's Side of 'Hills Like White Elephants.'" Hemingway Review 15.1 (1995): 27-42.

Urgo, Joseph. "Hemingway's 'Hills Like White Elephants.'" Explicator 46.3 (1988): 35-37.

🜲 25 🜲

A Brief Introduction
to Critical Theory

Literary criticism, it should be clear by now, is the attempt to analyze and comprehend works of literature. **Critical theory**, in turn, analyzes that process of interpretation. As casual readers, we may not pay much attention to *how* we interpret what we read. From our perspective, we simply read and understand. But the study of critical theory focuses attention on the process itself and on the assumptions on which any given act of interpretation is based.

Consciously or unconsciously, every work of literary criticism, whether it's an essay you're writing for a literature class or a scholarly article you're reading about a favorite text, accepts certain premises about the function of language, the role of structure and form, and the relationship of the text to its surrounding culture. Sometimes these assumptions are implied tacitly, and the emphasis remains focused on the text itself. Frequently, though, these assumptions and their validity become central subjects of the discussion, and the literary work being analyzed takes a back seat to a dialogue about the nature of interpretation. Critical works that foreground such discussions are said to be more theoretical in their orientation; often they read more like philosophy than literary analysis.

It would be impossible for a chapter in a textbook like this to provide you with a thorough and complete grounding in critical theory; indeed, a multitude of books have been dedicated to this very purpose. However, in your literary research as college students, you will often run across articles and books that are written with the basic premises and methodologies of these theories in mind. If nothing else, this brief introduction should help you recognize and understand the theoretical framework behind theory-based books and articles you encounter and perhaps help you begin to integrate these reading strategies into your own critical writing.

In this chapter, you'll probably notice a difference in our language and the level of our diction. We've tried to keep most of our book pretty conversational; however, many of the ideas you'll be exposed to in our discussion of literary theory are sophisticated and quite complicated. As you might expect, explaining these complex ideas requires more sophisticated and complicated language.

Although it seems as if critical theory has become a much more visible component of mainstream literary criticism in the past few decades, it has a history dating back thousands of years. In *The Mirror and the Lamp*, M. H. Abrams suggests that the history of literary criticism can be viewed in terms of four categories or theories of criticism: the *mimetic theory*, the *pragmatic theory*, the *expressive theory*, and the *objective theory*. Most surveys of critical theory begin with Aristotle's *Poetics*, in which he discusses mimesis (the poet's impulse toward imitation) as the appeal of a work of tragic or epic poetry. Before Aristotle, Plato likewise offered mimesis as the impulse that drives artistic creation, but unlike Plato—who maintained that the artist attempts to imitate natural objects that are in turn imitations of ideal types of divine origin—Aristotle argued that works of tragic and epic poetry attempt to imitate noble actions. Aristotle maintained that while tragedy evokes the emotions of pity and terror in its audience, these emotions are subsequently purged through a process he termed **catharsis**.

Eventually, Aristotle's mimetic theory of art was joined or complicated by the so-called pragmatic theory, which focused on the effect a work of art has on its audience and maintained that the proper purpose of art is to delight and instruct. Notice that the two theories seem to complement each other; the mimetic theory focuses on the relationship between the text and its subject, while the pragmatic theory focuses on the relationship between the text and its audience.

These two theories coexisted for centuries (and even today they haven't gone away), but during the Romantic period, writers and critics began to pay more attention to the relationship between the text and its creator. The author, and the text as a reflection of the author's attitudes and personality, became the critic's central concern, according to the expressive theory. William Wordsworth's preface to *Lyrical Ballads* contains an important description of this theory with respect to poetry.

In the twentieth century, this concentration on the text as the expression of the artist's emotions and impulses evolved, predictably, into a concentration on the text itself, more specifically on the forms, patterns, and structure each text contains. The work of art became supreme, and to varying degrees, critics attempted to consider it on its own terms, with minimal reference to author, audience, or the external reality to which the text might refer. The objective theory therefore suggests that the critic should aspire to a scientifically detached approach to literary text, downplaying the significance of mimesis, audience, and author.

Some readers are apprehensive about shifting their attention away from primary texts—the poems, stories, novels, and plays that entertain them—toward these theoretical issues, which are at times so esoteric that they seem to have nothing at all to do with literary reading. These readers maintain that theory-oriented critics are adding layers of confusion to texts rather than stripping them away to get at true meaning. There is more than a kernel of truth to this complaint. The system of tenure and promotion at many colleges and universities demands that scholars produce scholarship, and in literary studies, this necessarily means finding new things to say about literary texts. Since there is a finite number of literary texts that reward intense scrutiny (though this number is probably much larger than scholars imagine), it follows that one way of finding something new to say in a critical article or book is to apply a new approach to a familiar work of literature. This explains why, after more than six hundred years, dialogue is still going on about the "Wife of Bath's Tale" from Chaucer's *Canterbury Tales*. These new approaches are part of what keeps literature alive for succeeding generations.

Another objection some readers have to the focus on critical theory is that the literary text becomes less important than the critic's own text. In a theoretical article of **feminist criticism** dealing with Susan Glaspell's play *Trifles*, the focus might be not on Glaspell herself, or on the play for that matter, but on the critical theory in question. Sometimes, rather than using the theory to elucidate the nuances of the literary text, the literary text is instead used to demonstrate the workings of the theory, or to test its validity and applicability. Some readers will certainly find the subordination of the literary text to the critical text distasteful. Consider, though, that one of the functions of any argument you might construct, whether oral or written, formal or informal, is to demonstrate that you are reasonable, that you are capable of constructing a valid argument or interpretation of a given situation. The **thesis** of your essay may argue that **irony** in Glaspell's play *Trifles* hinges on the difference between masculine and feminine interpretations of the words *trifles* and *knot* in the play, but a significant subtext your paper communicates is that the approach you're bringing to the text is a valid one. In a sense, you are using the play to demonstrate the validity of your approach to it, even as you are using your analysis to explore the nuances of the play.

Most literary criticism works in much the same way. Theoretical works merely shift the emphasis a little more toward the act of interpretation itself. Just as psychology, history, economics, and **gender theory** are applied to literature to produce informative readings of texts, literature is simultaneously applied to these various fields of study to test and change them. In the discussion of **New Historicism** later in this chapter, for instance, you'll see that history is not treated as a fossilized, static entity alongside which literary texts can be measured. Instead, history is dynamic, and our understanding of it is subject to constant revision. Literary texts play a role in that revision; as we come to understand them differently, they reflect differently on their historical period. This new insight into their historical context, in turn, might complicate our understanding of the literary text. History, then, is another kind of text, and as we look at each text in light of the other, we learn that there is no universal, knowable version of history to apply to the text, nor is there a single definitive reading of a literary text that will tell us for sure what we want to know about history. Most theories concern themselves with the function of language in a given work, a work's cultural contexts, or its structure, and any application of that theory to a literary text is in some way a test of that theory's applicability.

This all seems very circular, as if it's part of an argument that will never be resolved. At times, it can indeed be very frustrating. However, it's also part of the joy of studying literature, because if the conversation about these texts were ever to be resolved, if there were nothing more to say or discover or learn about these texts, they would die in a sense. Rereading Robert Frost's poetry would give no pleasure; we could instead consult the definitive reading of the poems and get everything we needed to know from the authoritative **exegesis**. Happily, though, that's not how it works. Some people liken critical theory to the fairy tale about cutting open the goose that laid the golden eggs. Yes, it's possible to get so wrapped up in critical theory that interest in the literary text becomes secondary. But in the broad field of literary studies, there is plenty of room for different interests and emphases. However you read, there is a theory of language and culture that underlies your reading, and it pays to be aware of it. What role it plays in your analysis of a given literary text, though, is up to you.

In this chapter, we briefly describe several varieties of contemporary literary theory, which should encompass most of the approaches you will encounter in your exploration of literary criticism. This should make reading literary criticism easier; you'll be a lot more comfortable with the articles and analyses you're reading if you can identify the approach the critic is applying to the text in question. Be aware, though, that the overview we're providing barely scratches the surface of these critical approaches. In order to put these theories into practice, you'd need to familiarize yourself with the seminal critical texts that form the theoretical basis for each of the approaches. For now, though, we don't expect you to become practitioners of one of these kinds of reading on the basis of what we provide here, but it's important to be able to recognize them when you come across them in your reading.

RECOMMENDED READING ON THE HISTORY AND DEVELOPMENT OF CRITICAL THEORY

M. H. Abrams, *The Mirror and the Lamp: Romantic Theory and the Critical Tradition*
Hazard Adams and Leroy Searle, eds., *Critical Theory since 1965*
Peter Barry, *Beginning Theory: An Introduction to Literary and Cultural Theory*
Charles E. Bressler, *Literary Criticism: An Introduction to Theory and Practice*
Jonathan Culler, *Literary Theory: A Very Short Introduction*

Terry Eagleton, *Literary Theory: An Introduction*
David Kirby, *What Is a Book?*
J. Hillis Miller, *Theory Now and Then*

25.1   NEW CRITICISM

New Criticism is hardly the newest form of criticism being practiced. In fact, it's doubtful that you'll find it used as a working critical framework or school of critical theory in a strict sense at all these days. From the late 1930s through the 1960s, however, New Criticism was the dominant critical school for American and English literary scholars. Although some contemporary poststructuralist critics may profess scorn for New Criticism and its adherents, many of the school's conventions and methods have proved very influential in the development of later literary studies and critical theory.

Origins of New Criticism

The New Criticism school was initially formed as a reaction against the kind of nonanalytical criticism that focused heavily on plot, the perceived moral stance of a work or an author, or the enjoyment readers derived from characters, which at its best was called **New Humanism**. At one level, this kind of subjective criticism is reminiscent of a movie review that pans a particularly artful film because the reviewer couldn't identify with it or didn't like a character, regardless of the overall excellence of the script, the acting, or the technical mastery of the director or cinematographer. New Humanism was a slightly more sophisticated variety of this kind of criticism that focused on the moral standards and ethical virtues of texts.

Influenced on the one hand by I. A. Richards's *Practical Criticism* (1929), William Empson's *Seven Types of Ambiguity* (1930), and landmark T. S. Eliot essays like "Tradition and the Individual Talent" (1920) and "The Function of Criticism" (1933), and on the other hand by the work of **formalists** who believed that the study of the form of the literary work was far more important than the consideration of its content (especially because, in their view, in the best literary works, form influences content), New Criticism was espoused by critics also associated with the Southern Agrarian movement (whose views on culture and literature were put forth in the collection of essays *I'll Take My Stand* in 1930). The principles of New Criticism were first popularized by Cleanth Brooks and Robert Penn Warren's textbook, *Understanding Poetry* (1938). The school of New Criticism takes its name from a 1941 book by John Crowe Ransom.

New Criticism in Practice

Like the Formalism that influences it, New Criticism mostly centers on poetry as the preeminent literary art; many of its fundamental ideas are more suited to the study of poetry than they are to the study of fiction,

creative nonfiction, or **drama**. New Critics saw each work as an entirely self-contained art object, an artifact that may be understood entirely from its own words, form, and patterns. The cultural context, the author's intentions, or biographical allusions are all unimportant; rather, the reader must take the work (again, often a poem) at its own value and develop all explication and interpretation from the work itself as it stands alone.

Most scholars, readers, and critics automatically seek authorial intention when they read works of literature; we don't only want to know what the work says, we also want to try and decipher through deductive reasoning the goals and ambitions of the author. The New Critics referred to this as the **intentional fallacy**.[1] Although a reader should not disdain obvious clues for interpretation presented by the author, the author's wishes are ultimately inconsequential compared to the actual achievement of the work of literature. The goal of the scholar and critic is to discuss what is actually in the text, not whether the author intended for it to be there or not. Furthermore, most often when reading works of literature—particularly those by authors long since dead—the reader rarely has the luxury of consulting the author or being able to "know" truly the author's intention. As we noted earlier in this text, recognition of the intentional fallacy is still an important part of literary studies.

The other pitfall that New Critics thought waylaid readers is the **affective fallacy**. Too often, New Critics felt, readers focused too much on how a work of literature affected them—on how it made them feel, on their emotional responses, on their like or dislike of character or wordplay or whatever. Rather than focusing on such details, the goal of the reader, scholar, or critic must instead be to understand how a particular text works, not what effect it achieves.

For a New Critical approach to work, the reader must first be carefully trained in the methods and techniques of literary craft. If studying poems, readers must have a thorough understanding of **prosody** and be well schooled in poetic traditions and conventions. New Criticism emphasizes **close reading**, which means more or less what it seems to mean: readers carefully and analytically consider the text—and only the text—from a variety of angles, examining every component, and try to learn what is accomplished by the text. Great attention is paid by New Critics to the etymology of words, the origins of their meanings and the various ways that they have been defined over the course of time. Similarly, words should be considered for both their **denotative meaning**—their dictionary definition—and their **connotative meaning,** or implied meaning, including whatever associations the word might conjure up. Consider, for instance, the opening sentence of James Joyce's "Araby," where a street is described as being "blind," meaning

---

[1]The terms *intentional fallacy* and *affective fallacy* (discussed in the next paragraph) were coined by Monroe Beardsley and William Wimsatt in the 1940s in an essay later republished in *The Verbal Icon* (1954).

it's a dead-end street. The negative connotation of *blind* suits Joyce's purpose; a realtor, however, would probably prefer describing the street using the more positive French term *cul-de-sac.*

Like the formalists—and many classify the New Critics as formalists, although they considered themselves a separate movement—New Critics believe that comprehending the structure of a given text is essential to understanding its meaning. If we're reading a **sonnet**, why did the author choose the sonnet form? Why did he or she choose the Petrarchan or Italian style over the English sonnet form? If, in a different poem, the author employs a certain **rhyme** scheme, what poetic goal is achieved by that rhyme scheme? What does the **meter** accomplish? If a poem is **free verse**, what can we learn from the absence of meter or from the line breaks?

Accordingly, a New Critical reading pays a good bit of attention to the overall organic unity of a text. How does it all work together? How do the separate elements in some way cohere to develop a single, significant point? Similar emphasis is placed on comprehending the use of **metaphor**, **imagery**, and **symbol** in the text; the New Critic believes that all these disparate elements must join together to form a single, organic, coherent work of literary art.

New Criticism does make allowance for the contradiction that exists when various elements of a supposedly unified work seem to point in different directions and work against organic and artistic unity. A critic of a different school might see such separation as indicative of various stresses and influences on either the text or the writer and use a discussion of the text's lack of coherence to evaluate the influence of the author's life on the text or possibly to examine the cultural context or pervasive themes that occur throughout the author's **oeuvre**. However, a New Critical scholar would say that such "tension" between elements of the text results in what Cleanth Brooks refers to as "irony and paradox." Various kinds of **irony**—where (at its simplest and most basic level) the thing stated is other than the thing implied in order to achieve some purpose—may be used, as well as *paradox*—when two elements of a supposedly unified piece seem to contradict each other. Such tension, however, results in ambiguity, which in itself becomes a useful tool for achieving artistic unity in a given text.

As noted earlier, the New Criticism approach to literature isn't much practiced as a school of critical theory anymore; however, its techniques and methods have profoundly influenced the world of literary study. Work by New Critics directly contributed to the shaping of the **Chicago School** of critics, who applied formalist techniques to Aristotelian principles of rhetoric and the arts. The foremost critic of the Chicago School is Wayne C. Booth, who codified the beliefs of his school in *The Rhetoric of Fiction* (1961).

Later waves of critics and theorists have decried New Criticism for a variety of reasons. The New Critical approach implies that there is a single, learnable "correct" way to read a text, whereas poststructuralist thought teaches that there is never any single proper way to approach a literary work. Furthermore, many feel that the New Critical method of approaching a work as if it were written in a vacuum, ignoring the cultural context and political ideologies surrounding the text, is inherently flawed. No work is ever written in a vacuum; it is always an artifact of the culture that produced it.

Despite the disdain that later theorists have for New Criticism, however, its stress on close reading and part-by-part analysis of the text has proved significant to all critics. In fact, close reading in itself is the primary method of deconstructionist approaches to reading and analysis. Just as the New Critics demanded that critics and scholars be well versed in literature and literary traditions, poststructuralist critics demand that critics be knowledgeable about whatever school of theory they are using to discuss and analyze a given text. If nothing else, the proponents of New Criticism made it clear that critical studies of literature were worthwhile and rewarding.

RECOMMENDED READING ON NEW CRITICISM

Cleanth Brooks, *The Well Wrought Urn*

Cleanth Brooks and Robert Penn Warren, *Understanding Poetry*

Northrop Frye, *Anatomy of Criticism: Four Essays*

T. S. Eliot, *The Sacred Wood* (collected essays)

William Empson, *Seven Types of Ambiguity*

John Crowe Ransom, *The New Criticism*

I. A. Richards, *Practical Criticism: A Study of Literary Judgment*

René Wellek and Austin Warren, *Theory of Literature*

W. K. Wimsatt Jr., with Monroe Beardsley, *The Verbal Icon: Studies in the Meaning of Poetry*

25.2 PSYCHOANALYTIC CRITICISM

Psychoanalytic criticism, like many other modern and contemporary modes of literary criticism, is the application of a cultural phenomenon—in this case, modern psychology—to the interpretation of literary texts. To understand this particular mode of literary analysis, we should first make sure we understand exactly what psychoanalysis is and is not. Founded by the Viennese doctor and scholar Sigmund Freud (1856–1939), psychoanalysis is a set of theories concerning the relationship between conscious and unconscious thought processes, as well as a technical procedure for investigating unconscious mental processes and for treating mental illness.

If you've taken a psychology course recently, you may have noticed that Freud and his theories are not always presented in great detail; in some courses, in fact, they may be treated with very little respect at all. Certainly, contemporary explorations of the functions of the mind and the treatment of mental illness go far beyond Freud's discoveries and methods, and as

English professors, we would never argue that Freud should be considered the end of modern psychology, though many consider him to be the beginning of it. Freud's relevance to the contemporary theory and practice of psychology is still a subject of debate, a debate into which most literary scholars shouldn't enter. Regardless of Freud's usefulness to the practicing psychologist, however, the relationship between Freudian psychoanalysis and literary criticism is very significant.

Freud and his followers referred to psychoanalysis as the "talking cure." The role of the analyst was to elicit and interpret the patient's narratives. We're all familiar with the popular image of the analyst in the overstuffed chair, with the patient lying on the couch, free-associating or talking about childhood memories or recent dreams. The analyst might guide the patient with questions and encouragement but generally tries to lead the patient to the truth rather than impose an interpretation on the patient's narrative from a position of authority. The goal of the talking cure is the exploration of the unconscious, which in Freudian terms is the hidden part of the mind, the contents of which the **ego** or conscious mind—what we mean when we say "I"—is unaware. (Freud described the human mind as being composed of three impulses that are often in conflict: the **id**, which is the source of our primal instincts and libido; the **superego**, which functions like the conscience to temper the often antisocial impulses of the id; and the ego, the "I" part of the self that interacts with the outside world and mediates between the id and the superego). Ideally, the patient finds a healthy way to redirect the negative energy generated by unhealthy ways of coping with problems into more productive coping strategies. This process is called *sublimation*, and obviously, its effectiveness depends on the successful discovery of what is hidden in the unconscious. It's important to note that Freud didn't invent or discover the unconscious, nor did he claim to. He merely argued that the root of people's motivations and of their problems could frequently be found in the unconscious, and this is the assumption on which Freudian psychoanalysis is based.

So how do these ideas and impulses find their way into the unconscious in the first place? They are filed there by the ego through a process called *repression*, the process by which the ego hides away the things that it can't or doesn't want to include in its coherent worldview. We know that there are traumatic things we "put out of our mind" in order to get on with our lives; in the Freudian model, we're not putting them out of our minds at all but instead hiding them in the vast junk drawer of the unconscious. A healthier way of dealing with these ideas would involve making these experiences and impulses a part of our consciousness and finding an acceptable explanation, or interpretation if you will, that would allow for their integration. The analyst, therefore, asks many of the same questions that the literary critic might ask during the process of interpretation.

As we have seen, however, what's hidden in the unconscious mind is not normally available to the conscious mind. But according to Freud, what has been repressed will ultimately return, like the body in a Hitchcock film, the telltale heart in the Poe story, or the ghost in *Hamlet*, forcing itself to the surface, haunting us with little half-glimpses of what we've forgotten we ever knew and what we've tried to hide away from ourselves and others. These unwelcome, repressed thoughts and experiences can surface whenever we let our conscious guard down: in dreams, daydreams, fantasies, and slips of the tongue. Freudian psychoanalysis involves, among other things, the interpretation of these glimpses.

The parallels between the Freudian psychoanalyst and the literary critic should therefore be evident, as should the relationship between the patient's narrative and the text of a literary work. Narrative is, after all, one of the main ways we look at the world. We make up stories about "reality" and tell them to ourselves and to others. Anytime you ask why something happened or why someone is the way he or she is and answer with a cause-and-effect hypothesis about that person's childhood or other experience, you're using narrative as a way of understanding psychology. Freud viewed this kind of narrative— including memories and dream stories—as a window to the unconscious.

There are, of course, problems with this analogy, and some of the psychological criticism you encounter in your explorations may reflect these problems. Early critics in particular interpreted the literary work as if it were a symptom of its author's neurosis rather than a work of the imagination. Certainly, writing can be a kind of therapy, as anyone who has ever kept a journal or diary would probably attest, but it's reductive to suggest that all writing is therapy; and to assume that literary texts are essentially symptoms that reveal their authors' neuroses is dangerously so.

Popular culture frequently represents Sigmund Freud, and by association the stereotypical practitioner of psychoanalysis, as little more than a sex-obsessed Peeping Tom with diplomas on the wall. The most frequently vilified postulates of Freudian psychoanalytic theory are easy to mock, after all: the *Oedipus complex*, the child's desire to eliminate the parent of the same sex and replace him or her in the affections of the other parent, for instance, seems ridiculous and offensive on the surface. Most people, no matter how honestly they search their memories, will be unable to recall serious homicidal feelings toward their parents—much less sexual feelings.

This leads directly to the facet of Freudian theory that most people find the hardest to accept: infantile sexuality. The idea that infants and toddlers are capable of longing for sexual intimacy with their parents or anybody else seems, on the face of it, disgusting. However, neither the Oedipus complex nor the theory of infantile sexuality on which it is predicated is as scandalous, or for that matter as sexual, as we assume when the theories are introduced to us. Though Freud argued that infants feel sexual desire for their mothers (and in the case of female infants, in later stages of development, for their fathers), it has to be acknowledged that in general, small children don't know that much about sex as we generally intend the term. What they do know about, though, is physical pleasure—this should be evident to anyone who has seen a baby cry when placed in the crib. The mother is seen as the source of all pleasure (which is by definition physical pleasure at that age), and as soon as the father is identified as a rival for the mother's affection, the Oedipus complex comes into play, with a succession of results that correspond to various stages of development: the desire to eliminate the father to bask alone in the affections of the mother, fear of the father and the punishment that might arise for these patricidal impulses (commonly called *castration anxiety*), and eventually identification with the father and a desire to emulate and even venerate him, along with guilt over the earlier feelings of ill will. Ultimately, the "voice of the father" with which the healthy individual eventually reconciles becomes internalized as a part of the superego.

The most important thing to recognize, though, is that in life as in art, the Oedipus complex has more to do with the ambivalent relationship between father and son than it does with attraction between mother and son. You'll see this in *Hamlet,* the *Odyssey, Oedipus,* Lawrence's *Sons and Lovers,* and even films like *The Lion King.* Freud argued that the Oedipus complex, passing through these various stages, is a normal part of the process of maturation. Robert Hayden's poem "Those Winter Sundays" (included in Part Six) suggests the speaker's belated reconciliation with his father, whose nonverbal demonstrations of love he is only beginning to understand.

So you say you don't remember the Oedipus complex from your own childhood? That lack of memory is exactly Freud's point. These "unacceptable" infantile impulses are repressed or sublimated into more acceptable impulses. The desire to outperform or outearn one's parents can be turned into a positive quality—ambition—through the process of sublimation. Thus for most people, the Oedipus complex is something that is worked through and utterly forgotten. When, however, we fail to work through these impulses or situations, we might feel the compulsion to repeat them, to go over and over a situation again, even an unpleasant or traumatic situation. If the ego copes imperfectly with some event, it tends to resurface in ways that are out of the control of the individual.

So what does this have to do with reading? As we have said, psychoanalysis is a process of interpretation, and it's natural to apply it to literature, because after all, it has been since the beginning a way of understanding narratives, or creative productions. Freud couldn't look at a dream, only at a story someone told about a dream.

Remember that while Freudian psychoanalytic criticism is almost certainly the most widely practiced flavor of psychological criticism, it is by no means the only one. Remarkably, however, there is considerable diversity even among Freudian readings, due partly to the tremendous bulk and diversity of Freud's oeuvre (he was a prolific writer in his own right) and partly to his influence on later theorists—and their influence on how his theories are perceived. What follows is a brief survey of major trends in the practice of psychoanalytic literary criticism; some of the practices are specifically Freudian, and some are not; a couple of other major approaches to psychoanalytic criticism will be addressed as well.

Psychoanalysis and Character

Following Freud's own forays into literary criticism, the earliest psychoanalytic readings tended to focus on psychoanalyzing literary characters. This involves treating the characters as if they are fully realized human beings and analyzing the unconscious motives behind their actions and attitudes. Some theorists object to this practice because literary characters are clearly not human, and their actions and attitudes are determined by their creator, the author, poet, or playwright, not by unconscious anxieties and desires. Others argue, on the other hand, that the characters that seem most compelling and real to us are the most psychologically complex ones, whose words and behaviors suggest a consistent and believable representation of the human psyche. Thus these characters merit psychoanalysis as individuals. The speaker of Robert Browning's "My Last Duchess" could probably be analyzed in this way; his allusion to the statue of Neptune taming the seahorse could be interpreted as an unconscious revelation of his attitude toward his late wife (others would argue that there is nothing unconscious about his attitude at all). Similarly, Charlotte Perkins Gilman provides the speaker of "The Yellow Wallpaper" with enough psychological **verisimilitude** that it is nearly impossible to read the story without trying to psychoanalyze the character, given that one of the story's subjects is the treatment of the mentally ill in that time and place.

Psychoanalysis and the Author

A related approach, also very common in earlier psychoanalytic readings, was the attempt to psychoanalyze the author, treating the text more or less as a symptom or a diagnostic tool, in a process similar to certain kinds of art therapy. While it would be hard to deny a close connection between a given author's psychological makeup and the work of art he or she produces, the nature of that connection must necessarily vary between one author and another to the point where acknowledging the existence of the connection is about as much as we can do. To insist that the literary text transparently has its origins in the author's neuroses—the way a fever is caused by a virus—is essentially to deny the creative process that allows the author to invent characters, motivations, and dilemmas that have nothing to do with his or her own direct experience. When we have access to biographical information (as in the case of Charlotte Perkins Gilman, who, we are told, was subjected to a "rest cure" for hysteria very much as her character is in "The Yellow Wallpaper"), it is very tempting to attribute the story to her experience, almost as a way of explaining it away. But this is no different than saying that *Hamlet* clearly reveals Shakespeare's own Oedipus complex. It can be argued (and has been, by Freud and others) that the character Hamlet suffers from an unresolved

Oedipus complex; whether or not Shakespeare had unresolved Oedipal issues is simply unknowable, though, and probably irrelevant. What is symptom, and what is creativity? There's no way of knowing, but in its most naive form, psychoanalytic criticism sometimes has attributed the psychological peccadilloes a text suggested to the symptoms of its author in a facile way.

Psychoanalysis and the Reader

Another type of psychoanalytic literary criticism considers texts in light of their effect on readers. This mode of psychoanalytic criticism, which came into vogue in the 1960s, is clearly related to *reader-response criticism*, which focuses on the elements of the text that guide its audience's reading experience. In *The Dynamics of Literary Response*, Norman N. Holland describes the relationship between the reader and the text in terms of a psychological interchange. The text exists to be read, and the world of the text only springs into existence when it is being read. In turn, we read because reading fulfills a vital psychological function for us, allowing us to work through our own unresolved psychological issues without ever confronting them as our own. We respond best to works that meet our own particular psychological needs. Like a dream or a daydream, a text allows us to contemplate the unthinkable—our own repressed issues and anxieties—from a safe distance.

This focus on the interaction between the text and its reader is not specifically Freudian; in fact, Jungian literary criticism frequently focuses on the same interrelationship. C. G. Jung was a onetime disciple of Freud's who eventually broke away and founded *analytical psychology*, which views the unconscious as being composed of two parts: the personal and the archetypal, which he termed the *collective unconscious*. An **archetype** is a recurring image, character, or element in literature, art, or myth that is believed to trigger a profound emotional response in the viewer or reader because it resonates mysteriously with something in the collective unconscious. Such an argument could be made, no doubt, regarding the goblins in Christina Rossetti's "Goblin Market." Langston Hughes's poem "The Negro Speaks of Rivers" likewise evokes mythical or archetypal images with its references to the dawn of man and Egyptian monuments.

Psychoanalysis and Language

In recent decades, poststructuralism and psychoanalysis have interacted in dynamic and interesting ways. With the publication of his highly influential collection of lectures and essays *Écrits* (1966), the French psychoanalyst and theorist Jacques Lacan offered a reinterpretation of Freudian thought that suggested that the unconscious itself is structured as a language, applying **semiotics** (literally, the study of signs) to psychoanalysis. In his description of the "mirror stage," when a child recognizes his or her reflection (an image removed from and unattached to the self), Lacan holds that the ego or "I" is ultimately an illusion created by the unconscious. Readers interested in how Lacan's theories can be applied to literary texts will find his influential "Seminar on 'The Purloined Letter'" helpful, as well as commentaries on it by Jacques Derrida and Barbara Johnson, among others.

Psychoanalysis and the Text

Taking a different approach in response to Lacan's application of the structure of language to the unconscious, Peter Brooks, in *Reading for the Plot*, sees a text as a system of internal energies and tensions, compulsions, resistances, and desires and superimposes the model of the functioning of the psychic apparatus on the functioning of the text. According to Brooks, the compulsion to repeat—associated with Freud's concept of repression and return—can manifest itself in texts in very fundamental levels as **rhyme, meter,** or **alliteration** and in more complex ways in terms of **plot**. In human psychology, we repeat unpleasant experiences in order to gain mastery over them. Following Freud and Lacan, Brooks argues that the repetition afforded us by texts answers—though necessarily unsatisfactorily—the compulsive search for the unified self.

Since people write and read using their brains, an understanding of the way the mind works can only contribute to greater understanding of the way texts work. Reading is inherently a psychological process, whether you subscribe to the Freudian model of the unconscious or the Jungian or another. Psychoanalytic literary criticism foregrounds the various relationships between the literary text and the human mind.

RECOMMENDED READING ON PSYCHOANALYTIC CRITICISM

Peter Brooks, *Reading for the Plot: Design and Intention in Narrative*
Sigmund Freud, *Beyond the Pleasure Principle*
---, *The Interpretation of Dreams*
---, *Introductory Lectures on Psychoanalysis*
---, *Jokes and Their Relation to the Unconscious*
---, *The Psychopathology of Everyday Life*
---, *Totem and Taboo*
---, *"The Uncanny"*
Norman N. Holland, *The Dynamics of Literary Response*
John P. Muller and William J. Richardson, eds., *The Purloined Poe: Lacan, Derrida, and Psychoanalytic Reading*
Meredith Anne Skura, *Literary Use of the Psychoanalytic Process*

25.3   DECONSTRUCTION AND POSTSTRUCTURALISM

Introducing students to deconstructionist and poststructuralist theory is extremely challenging for instructors (and textbook writers). In some ways, "deconstruction" is more of a general philosophy in how one should approach the study of a given culture and its various manifestations (like literature) than it is a concise and cohesive method for reading texts critically. As such, it is an incredibly complex system of thought to attempt to define in a short space; in some ways, its amorphous nature defines exactly what it is—which is, in part, the belief that no text can be completely nailed down to one proper reading, interpretation, or explanation. *Poststructuralism, deconstructionism,* and *postmodernism* are often used interchangeably and synonymously, although there are distinct differences between the schools of thought designated by each of these terms. However, in some ways, the last category, postmodernism, may be said in its latest incarnation in the literary lexicon to be an umbrella label encompassing the general theories and methodology shared by deconstructionist and poststructuralist thought.

Many would place the origins of postmodernist thought with the philosophers and cultural theorists working abroad in the 1920s, 1930s, and 1940s, like the German philosopher Walter Benjamin and the Russian theorist Mikhail Bakhtin, whose influence we will discuss at more length later in this chapter. Most scholars, however, note that the pervasive influence of deconstructionist and postmodern thought in critical theory was greatly accelerated when a French philosopher (originally from Algiers) named Jacques Derrida presented a paper titled "Structure, Sign and Play in the Discourse of the Human Sciences" at a 1966 Johns Hopkins University symposium. Although the work of later writers like the Belgian American Paul de Man and the American J. Hillis Miller contributed greatly to Derrida's influence on literary studies, many see Derrida's revolutionary paper as the beginning of the wave of postmodern literary theory that would radically alter the study of literature and culture.

Structuralism and Other Influences

Derrida's theories are in themselves influenced by the German philosopher Martin Heidegger (1889–1976), whose theory of "destruction" stated that people must rid themselves of reductionist thought and the belief that there is one single, unified, stable meaning to any given act, event, occurrence, or text. Rather, in each case, there are a series of unstable variations; the act or event (or text) is open to a multitude of interpretations.

Like the poststructuralists who will follow him, Derrida's theories also are in part derived from (and in part reaction against) the structuralist theories first advanced by the Swiss linguist Ferdinand de Saussure (1857–1913) and the American philosopher Charles Saunders Peirce (1839–1914) in their independently created systems of **semiotics**. In Saussure's linguistic model, first established in his *Course in General Linguistics* (published posthumously in 1916), semiotics dictates that every word in a language is actually composed of two parts that add together and make the third. For example, you have a word, *book*. The actual sound spoken aloud or the letters on the written page mean nothing unless they're actually *signifying* something else.

Therefore, the book itself is *signified*—the referent we intend to speak about or indicate with our written or spoken word—and the linguistic indication of the thing (the written or spoken word *book*) is the *signifier*. When the signifier and signified are combined, we have a *sign*. Although a sign has meaning— you know what we mean when we say "book"—a signifier by itself has no meaning, and there is no way to communicate the idea of something unless there is a referent to be signified. Furthermore, the creation and derivation of the sign are ultimately arbitrary. A book could just as easily be called a *zook*; if we knew that *zook* was the signifier referring to "a collection of pages that you read," it would be just as effective a sign.

Saussure developed these ideas further by noting that all of language is created as a series of differences and binary oppositions (as demonstrated at the most elementary level by the two components of the sign). The word *book* is defined as such because the last letter is a *k* and not an *n*. A *book* and a *boon* are two different things; our interpretation of the sign is deferred until we're sure what the last letter is. Furthermore, culturally and linguistically, we are given to defining words based in part on what they are *not* through evaluation of their dichotomous differences with other words. *Good* is counterbalanced by *evil*, *east* by *west*, *north* by *south*, and so on, with dichotomies like *thin/fat*, *wet/dry*, *hot/cold*, and so on, throughout all language. Furthermore, proclaimed Saussure, all of language is composed of a structural system; the actual utterances and words we speak (which he called *parole*, the French word for "word") mean nothing outside of *langue*, the system and structure of language that surrounds and uses *parole* in order to achieve communication. Language—and by extension, all of human culture—was best analyzed through *synchronic* methods rather than *diachronic* ones. That is, rather than trying to trace the development of a system over the course of time and through mutating traditions (as one would in a diachronic study), the scientist should instead draw all conclusions through an exhaustive analysis of the system as it exists now in all its permutations.

In the decades following World War II, the French anthropologist Claude Lévi-Strauss showed that one could apply the science of semiology and the structuralist techniques of Saussure not only to linguistics but also to other aspects of human culture. Lévi-Strauss argued that certain "mythemes"—or resonating repetitions of certain myths (and certain taboos)—exist across cultures and, like language, are constructed according to a system of oppositions. Structuralist critics would follow Lévi-Strauss's example from the late 1940s through the 1970s.

Early formalist critics were also influenced by Saussure's approaches; just as he asserted that the meaning of language was contingent on a constructed linguistic system, they believed that poetry was better understood through study of its poetic forms—the *system* of poetry—than through the actual content of the poems. As criticism grew more diverse and more varied in its approaches, some formalist critics, like the members of the Prague school in the 1920s and 1930s, including Roman Jakobson, developed different formalist approaches that eventually led to structuralism. A greatly simplified version of their position is this: Jakobson and his contemporaries believed that all of literature was merely a form of advanced linguistics that could be analyzed by understanding its essential semiotic structure. They felt that a given work contained no ultimate meaning beyond what was constructed and that a text could be interpreted in many ways from a number of perspectives. Like the Prague formalists, structuralists showed that texts made use of linguistic and cultural binary oppositions and that once one understood the oppositions in play, one could tease out various meanings from a text. Important later structuralist critics included Roland Barthes in the 1960s (who also would become a leader of poststructuralist thought) and Jonathan Culler, who in the 1970s focused on developing a systematic model not only to analyze the text but also to consider the very act of reading.

Derrida, *Différance*, and Deconstruction

Like the structuralist critics, Derrida and other deconstructionists believe that Western culture and language are based on dichotomous binary oppositions (*wet/dry*, *hot/cold*, and so on, as noted earlier). Derrida argues that a central problem of Western culture is its inherent **logocentrism**, the belief that words and texts have stable, perfectly defined meanings that can point to an ultimate meaning (or exact reading). Furthermore, the binary oppositions used to construct meaning in the Western world are usually constructed in such a way that one side is "privileged" over the other. One of the central binary oppositions that the West has (in Derrida's view) been overly preoccupied with is the distinction between the presence of an ultimate presence (or meaning or authority or God) and its absence. Similarly, logocentric analysts and critics always believe there is one irrefutably correct way to examine a text. Furthermore, Derrida contends that the logocentric West has always privileged the spoken word over the written word, and that philosophers and critics have tacitly assumed that culture exists apart from language and literature and the text. Structuralists believed this too and described the need for a development of a "metalanguage" in order to discuss texts; Derrida, however, contends that all of culture is of one contiguous fabric—or, as he puts it, "there is nothing beyond the text." That is, all the world is a text to be deconstructed and analyzed.

Another key element to deconstructionist theory is Derrida's concept of *différance*. He coined the word as a type of pun on the French word *différer*, which can mean "to defer," as in to put something off for a while, or "to differ," as in to be different from something else. Taking his cues from Saussure's model and advancing further, Derrida agrees that everything in language (and culture) is based on differences; however, like Saussure, he believes that it is essential to remember that meaning is partly derived from deferring as well. After we read the first three letters of *book*, we don't know if we're going to end up with *book* or *boor* or *boon* or *boom*—we *defer* interpretation until the final (or seemingly final) differentiation is made. Derrida points out that language can have *play*, that based on the differences constructed in and around signs, an almost infinite variety of meanings and interpretations can be "supplemented." There is no single correct way to understand a text so long as there are other ways it can be read.

In some ways, deconstructionist readers bear certain similarities to New Critical readers. They both value extremely close readings of texts; they both believe the reader must be well versed in antecedents and tradition. The deconstructionist would also agree that there is no way to comprehend an author's intentions fully. However, the deconstructionist would never argue that a text could be considered a wholly separate artifact that can be divorced from its cultural milieu; a deconstructionist would say that the text *is* a cultural milieu. And the New Critical presumption that there is one significant, appropriate, and "right" way to read a text is utterly refuted by deconstructionist criticism, which contends that any given text can have simultaneously intertwined and contradictory discourses and meanings.

In fact, deconstructionists believe that readings and interpretations of texts may be more interesting when they focus on meanings implicit in a text that were not necessarily intended by the author. Play and supplementation apply to readings just as they do to linguistic variations; a slight shift in perspective when reading a text may reveal a whole new series of meanings. Often deconstructionist readers take a text apart piece by piece in order to search for the **trace**, the missing element that becomes obvious because of its absence. For example, a typical reading of Langston Hughes's poem "The Negro Speaks of Rivers" (included in Part Six) might well discuss how the speaker of the poem seems to represent all African Americans and that his discussion of rivers in a sense tracks the history of racism, slavery, and abuse since the dawn of civilization. A deconstructionist critic, however, might focus on the multiple possibilities represented by the Congo River in the poem. Europeans (most notably the Belgians in the nineteenth century) used the river to move farther and farther into the African continent in their obsessive rush to colonize Africa. At the same time, the Congo was an avenue used by slave traders (both European and African) to raid interior tribes for slaves who would be sent against their will to the New World. Or possibly a deconstructionist would point out that the line about how the narrator "looked upon the Nile and raised the pyramids above it" (7) manages to conflate slavery as practiced by Egyptians (a Semitic African people, as opposed to the sub-Saharan black peoples we are usually referring to when we use the term *African*) with slavery as it was practiced in the American colonies, even though Egyptian slavery was culture- and class-based (non-Egyptians, Jews, black Africans, outsiders, and the poor were made slaves) instead of race-based, as it was in the American continents. These discussions that don't occur in an initial reading of the poem represent in some ways the trace.

Similarly, by following the system of oppositions implicit in a text and realizing that an author is automatically privileging one belief or view or perception over another, we may in a sense see how an author's culture and views are being manifested in a given work. A reading of Edgar Allan Poe's short story "The Fall of the House of Usher" might start by noting that the story takes place in fall, that the house is "scary" because of its black floors and crimson-stained windows, and that the family and the manor house are symbolically related to each other (as implied by the sharing of the appellation "the House of Usher"). Notice the automatic cultural presumptions, however: fall is a "scary" time of year because leaves fall and die and the days grow shorter, and perhaps modern audiences assume so because Halloween is observed in the fall. The black floors and crimson windows are scary because they represent funereal colors and blood, respectively. A deconstructionist critic might interpret these privileged signifiers in any number of ways, just as the deconstructed elements of Hughes's poem might be interpreted through a variety of arguments.

One of the primary goals of the deconstructionist critic is to show, as a given text is further and further unraveled, that instead of there being a proper reading for a text, there *is not* a single proper reading of the text but rather that the meaning of the text is ultimately "undecidable" or indeterminable. Furthermore, many of the threads of meaning pulled from a text may indicate irreconcilable, paradoxical differences; some of these themes or interpretations reflect unstated or unintended agendas on the part of the writer that the careful deconstructionist can reveal and examine. These blind spots—these undecidable, indeterminable contradictory themes or usages or indicators that seem to work against the more overt agendas of a given text—are known as *aporia*.

Poststructuralism

As we stated earlier, deconstructionist theory as a cogent, cohesive approach to the study of literature may not be widely practiced as such, but poststructuralist critics of every stripe have adopted its basic precepts and tenets almost uniformly. The structuralist notions of binary oppositions and systems of differences and semiotics, combined with Derrida's *différance*, recognition of hegemonic privilege, ultimately undecidable texts, and play and supplementation, have influenced theorists and scholars profoundly.

Although Roland Barthes initially wrote as a structuralist theorist in books like *Elements of Semiology* in 1964, before long he became thoroughly identified with poststructuralist criticism. His 1968 essay "The Death of the Author"and his book *The Pleasure of the Text* (1973) discuss how the focus on the author as the central contributor and controlling element of a text, whose beliefs and tactics must be understood if a text is to be understood, is actually a result of Western privileging of the author over the text. Barthes believes that in poststructuralist criticism, reading must be refocused. The author is not the sole creator of the system but merely a vehicle for conveying the system of meanings and differences that make up the text. Barthes also delineates the differences between "readerly" texts, which tend to make use of straightforward narratives, and "writerly" texts, which tend to facilitate interpretation over simple *jouissance*, or reading pleasure.

The pervasive influence of poststructuralist theory is partly exemplified by the French critic Julia Kristeva, author of the important critical text *The Revolution of Poetic Language* (1974), whom we discuss at more length in our examination of **feminist criticism**. Kristeva's poststructuralist understanding of the binary oppositions within modes of Western discourse enlivens her uses of both psychoanalytic and feminist criticism. Similarly, the Marxist historian Michel Foucault uses poststructuralist theory to help initiate cultural studies and criticism, as detailed further later in this chapter.

RECOMMENDED READING ON DECONSTRUCTIONIST AND POSTSTRUCTURALIST CRITICISM

Harold Bloom et al., *Deconstruction and Criticism*

Roland Barthes, *The Pleasure of the Text*

Jonathan Culler, *Structuralist Poetics: Structuralism, Linguistics, and the Study of Literature*

---, *On Deconstruction: Theory and Criticism after Structuralism*

Paul de Man, *Blindness and Insight: Essays in the Rhetoric of Contemporary Criticism*

Jacques Derrida, *Of Grammatology*

---, *Writing and Difference*

Michel Foucault, *The Archaeology of Knowledge and the Discourse on Language*

Julia Kristeva, *The Revolution in Poetic Language*

J. Hillis Miller, *Fiction and Repetition: Seven English Novels*

Christopher Norris, *Deconstruction: Theory and Practice*

Kaja Silverman, *The Subject of Semiotics*

Mark C. Taylor, ed., *Deconstruction in Context: Literature and Philosophy*

25.4   FEMINIST AND GENDER CRITICISM

Like many of the other ways of reading we are surveying in this section, feminism was a broad cultural movement phenomenon first and foremost; it gained significance as a literary theory only within the past few decades. Like most of the theories we are examining, feminism is less a unified, monolithic theory than a multifaceted collection of concepts; not all feminist theorists will agree with each other on issues or on specific texts (if they did, feminism would likely not be a very interesting or vital way to approach literary texts). From a literary standpoint, however, feminism embodies a way of reading that investigates the text's investment in or reaction to the patriarchal power structures that have dominated Western culture. Feminist readings frequently question the canonicity of established writers and the exclusion of others from that elite group; they also question long-held assumptions about the nature of gender itself, arguing that while sex is determined biologically, gender is a cultural construct subject to revision or revolution. We will explore these concepts in some detail by surveying some of the most important contributions to feminist literature and theory and making note of the many ways they intersect with psychoanalytic, Marxist, and poststructuralist theories. At the end of the chapter, we will look at how the underlying assumptions of feminism have been redirected by **gender theory** to examine the implications of all forms of gender construction.

Many accounts of the rise of feminism locate its genesis in Mary Wollstonecraft's 1792 book *A Vindication of the Rights of Woman*. Writing in a period in which revolutionary ideas about human rights ("the rights of man") were being published at an unprecedented rate, Wollstonecraft examined the possibility of women's emancipation through education, arguing effectively that the progress of society depended on education and freedom for women.[2]

Mary Wollstonecraft was certainly not the first to bring to light the neglect of women's art and letters in the male-dominated world of ideas. The Puritan poet Anne Bradstreet had described the phenomenon during the previous century in her 1650 poem "Prologue" (lines 25–30):

> I am obnoxious to each carping tongue
> Who says my hand a needle better fits.
> A Poet's Pen all scorn I should thus wrong,
> For such despite they cast on female wits.
> If what I do prove well, it won't advance,
> They'll say it's stol'n, or else it was by chance.

During the late nineteenth century and early twentieth, women's suffrage movements in Britain and the United States successfully secured women's right to vote, and more women were afforded greater access to education (though certain inequities persisted and, some would argue, persist to the present day). Yet women writers and thinkers were still not taken seriously in the male-dominated world of ideas. Literature by women was still being neglected by the reading public, and many women writers were forced by the marketplace and other considerations to publish their works under male pseudonyms.

Woman as Author

Virginia Woolf's 1929 essay *A Room of One's Own* addressed the predicament of the female artist in the twentieth century by imagining that Shakespeare had a sister, Judith, a Renaissance woman endowed with Shakespeare's socioeconomic background, native abilities, and artistic aspirations. Woolf imagines her furtive attempts at creativity, her resistance to an arranged marriage, and

---

[2]Mary Wollstonecraft's daughter was Mary Wollstonecraft Shelley, author of *Frankenstein*.

her eventual disgrace and suicide as a result of hardship, abuse, and disappointment. A female contemporary of Shakespeare could never have written the plays of Shakespeare, Woolf suggests, not due to a lack of native ability but rather due to a lack of opportunity. In Shakespeare's time, as in Woolf's, most women were denied the time, resources, and private space—quite literally a room of their own—in which to explore their creative impulses and abilities.

But Woolf's argument is about issues much more basic than the consideration of woman as artist, however; it's about poverty and basic human rights. Through most of history—history from which, ironically, they have largely been excluded—women in many societies were prevented, formally or informally, from ownership of property and other rights most of us today would consider inherent in a democratic society. Woolf asserts that in her own experience, financial independence had a greater impact on her freedom than being granted the right to vote. Woolf addresses the success of female novelists in the nineteenth century and the battles they fought to achieve what they did—not the least of which was the battle against internalized self-doubt. The connection Woolf underscores between the personal and the political is one of the fundamental tenets of feminist theory.

Shortly after the publication of *A Room of One's Own*, World War II had an unexpected effect on the role of women in American and European society as male workers were sent to war and replaced by women on the assembly line and at the head of the family. Many women became accustomed to a greater degree of personal and economic autonomy than women had ever experienced before. This created an environment that enabled more questioning of society's basic assumptions about gender construction and the role of women in a patriarchal society.

Woman as Other

In her 1949 book *The Second Sex*, the French theorist Simone de Beauvoir follows Saussure's model of binary oppositions to analyze the very definition of *woman*, finding that in many cases, *woman* is defined negatively as "not man"; women are characterized by the masculine attributes they lack rather than by the traits they have. The human race, often referred to in English as *mankind*, is conceived of as predominantly male. The masculine is considered "subject," and the feminine, "other."

This binary construction of the concept of gender ignores women's individual humanity and subjectivity and focuses on the objectification of women as either ideal, saintly creatures or seductive, corrupting ones. These myths are constructions of the male-dominated social order. The role the Virgin Mary occupies in the Roman Catholic Church (a quintessential patriarchal institution) is an excellent example of the first category. According to scripture and tradition, Eve and Pandora—both women—allowed evil into the world. Feminists argue that both of these conceptions are equally dangerous; the pedestal on which the idealized image of feminine perfection (the Virgin Mary) is elevated can be just as reductive as the conceptual gutter into which the seductress (Pandora) is thrown. As readers, Beauvoir argues, we must work to see through these binary categories.

Politics and Power Structures

By the 1960s, male **hegemony** (leadership, predominant influence, or supremacy) was only one of the prevailing power structures being called into question by theorists, activists, and voters. Kate Millett's *Sexual Politics* (1970) was a radical examination of the role of patriarchy in government, religion, the family, and the academy. Millett defined *politics* as her subject not in the narrow sense of parties and elections but in the Marxist sense as the arrangement of power structures, the means by which people control or are controlled by others; Millett argued that patriarchy as a power structure is based not on nature but on tradition, consensus, and suppression. The patriarchal power structures she identifies and describes function primarily to perpetuate themselves and, by extension, the patriarchy itself. These institutions include not only governments and religious institutions (most of which she feels are transparently patriarchal) but also schools, colleges, and universities, which work in part to promote values that will perpetuate the institutions that sponsor them (again, usually governments or churches).

It would be very difficult to overstate the impact of Millett's *Sexual Politics* on the world of arts and literature, though literary criticism is not the book's primary goal. Instead, Millett examines passages from several representative male writers in order to critique their representation of sex acts as the infliction of male dominance and control as a part of her larger argument about the replication of male hegemony. Patriarchy has been supported for generations by hollow appeals to biology, psychology, and religion, Millett says, but "[p]erhaps patriarchy's greatest psychological weapon is simply its universality and longevity" (58). Millett and her contemporaries are working to create a place outside of the patriarchy and the patterns with which it indoctrinates men and women alike, from which it can be analyzed and invalidated.

Theory and Practice in British and American Feminism

As the cultural phenomenon of feminism became institutionalized in the United States to a degree by attaining deserved credibility in the academy, several important studies demonstrated how feminism worked in practical application to literary texts. Elaine Showalter, in her 1977 book *A Literature of Their Own: British Women Novelists from Brontë to Lessing*, introduced the term *gynocriticism* to denote a specifically female way of reading literature by women in an attempt to define what qualities make such literature feminine. Showalter's title, a clear reference to Virginia Woolf's essay, suggests that the proper focus of feminist literary criticism is the female text. One goal of such reading is the expansion of the canon, not only by including unjustly ignored female writers but also by including a broader range of **genres** than is usually admitted to the canon. Showalter also identified three phases of literature by women during the period with which her study concerns itself: the *Feminine*, during which time female authors adopted and mastered male discourse (the use of male pseudonyms by the Brontë sisters is a part of this attempt); the *Feminist*, during which female writers rejected the comfortable but imposed roles of femininity and used literature to reveal the struggle of women within the confines of a patriarchal society ("The Yellow Wallpaper" by Charlotte Perkins Gilman and *The Awakening* by Kate Chopin would be good examples); and the *Female*, which rejects both imitation of male discourse *and* protest against it in favor of a new and separate mode of expression.

In *The Resisting Reader: A Feminist Approach to American Fiction* (1978), Judith Fetterley begins by acknowledging the political nature of all literature and insisting that the American literature widely believed to embody the "American experience" is dangerously monocultural and exclusionist. Canonical American literature is by and large male, and to participate in it, the reader must attempt to become the texts' implied male reader, accepting male prejudices and male discourse. Fetterley's study, however, is in part an attempt to create "resisting readers," identifying canonical American literature as essentially patriarchal and seeing through its attempts to perpetuate male cultural and intellectual hegemony. Fetterley argues not for the rejection of literature written by men but for the rejection of the value system she believes such literature subliminally imposes on its readers.

In 1979, Sandra Gilbert and Susan Gubar published a highly influential study, *The Madwoman in the Attic*, which addresses the psychology of the female writer in the nineteenth century. The title refers to a character in Charlotte Brontë's novel *Jane Eyre*, the imprisoned, destructive wife of Eyre's employer, Rochester. Invoking a Freudian relationship between desire and suppression, Gilbert and Gubar argue that the "madwoman in the attic" is part of the author's own psyche projected outward as a result of her struggle to participate in literary writing, which was at that time almost exclusively a masculine endeavor. The critics also look at several writers (including Emily Dickinson and Sylvia Plath) whose "madwomen" were made manifest—like the figure behind the wallpaper in Gilman's story—with results that ranged from unhappy to disastrous. Rather than lament the pigeonholing of women into the angel/seductress dichotomy, however, Gilbert and Gubar suggest that these categories are potentially positions of power, though—as is the case with Bertha Rochester in *Jane Eyre*—the power may be destructive or self-destructive (the title of Hélène Cixous's well-known essay on feminine language, "The Language of the Medusa" (1976), suggests the embrace of a traditionally negative mythological representation of female power).

Clearly, there is a remarkable diversity of feminist literary criticism, especially when one notes that the works we have surveyed in this section were written within a span of only a few years. It should go without saying that the kind of applied feminist literary criticism for which British and

American feminist scholars are known is in no way limited to the prominent examples we have surveyed here. Generally, though, these works are identifiable by their close engagement with the literary text. They are theoretical at times, but the goal is usually the implementation of the theory in the interest of examining or reexamining a literary text.

The Practice of Theory in French Feminism

If you are comfortable with the concepts we have introduced in our discussion of the roots of literary feminism so far, be warned that things are about to get much more complicated. As is the case with many other forms of contemporary literary theory, the French practitioners of feminist literary theory tend to be much more, well, theoretical in their approach (this tendency is evident as early as Simone de Beauvoir). The same is true, for instance, of French psychoanalytic and poststructuralist criticism, and French feminism builds on these theories, particularly Jacques Lacan's description of the relationship between language and the unconscious. While they engage less explicitly with literary texts than their American and British counterparts, they are no less important; if you are reading contemporary feminist literary criticism, you are likely to encounter these theorists and their ideas.

The so-called French feminists (more aptly poststructuralist feminists) focus on issues similar to the other theorists we have been discussing, but on the linguistic level. Western culture, according to Lacan, has always been "phallocentric" (centered on men); Derrida advances this idea a step further, noting that Western culture and language are "phallogocentric." The coinage incorporates *phallus* (not in the literal or anatomical sense but rather as a symbol of male power) and *logos*, the divine Word, the rational principle governing the orderly operation of the universe in Greek thought. Lacan and Derrida are referring here not to sexist words and phrases but to the actual structure, syntax, and grammar of language itself. Hélène Cixous and other poststructuralist feminist critics (like Julia Kristeva) have argued that women think and write in ways fundamentally different from male discourse, applying the term *écriture féminine* (literally, "feminine writing") to a way of writing that has its source in the preverbal stage when the child has not yet come to understand that she is an individual, separate from the mother. Unlike phallogocentric language, which is predicated on binary oppositions, logic, and ostensibly objective knowledge, *écriture féminine* operates without rules. In a foray into applied criticism that is nonetheless very theoretical in orientation, Cixous analyzes the language of James Joyce in *Ulysses* and *Finnegans Wake*: often free-associative, often unpunctuated, usually poetic, Joyce's attempts to represent the unconscious have much in common with the language Cixous and other theorists have characterized as *écriture féminine*.

Feminine language for many of these theorists is intimately linked (as indeed it is in Joyce's works) with the body. In *This Sex Which Is Not One* (1985), Luce Irigaray discusses female sexuality as it has been represented in phallogocentric discourse (including, most significantly, Freudian psychology): the female is defined by the *absence* of visible sex organs, and her psychology is therefore defined by her awareness of this absence, which Freud termed *penis envy*. Like most feminist theorists, even those most sympathetic to Freud, Irigaray suggests that female sexuality and female language are intimately connected and not centered on the absence of the literal penis or symbolic phallus; rather, Irigaray discusses the multiplicity of female sexual organs. Female sexual and textual pleasure (Irigaray appropriates the term *jouissance*) is thus similarly decentered.

Like Cixous and Irigaray, Julia Kristeva also focuses on the relationship between language and the body and on the origin of semiotic signification in the earliest stages of development, when the child sees herself as one with the mother. Kristeva argues that all signification or communication of meaning has elements of the semiotic (maternal, prelinguistic, and therefore associated with rhythm, tone, and spatial relationships) as well as the symbolic (paternal, representational, structured, and syntactical). All signification requires both elements, but the masculine and feminine modes of discourse use them in varying degrees.

Gender Theory

By applying the interpretive techniques of feminism to male-oriented texts, Eve Kosofsky Sedgwick produced *Between Men: English Literature and Male Homosocial Desire*, a 1993 study that provided a model for much of the gender criticism that followed it. However, the groundwork for such an application was already in place.

The relationship between feminism and **gender theory** has been the subject of much discussion since gender criticism gained prominence during the 1980s. In its broadest sense, the term applies to the study and critique of the concept of gender. Like feminism, gender theory examines the relationship between biological sex and gender, which is seen not as an absolute but as a social construct replicated and imposed, like all power structures, by the social institutions and cultures that depend on it.

Gender theories can be sorted into two broad categories: essentialist and constructionist. *Essentialist theories* hold that male and female are fundamentally naturally different. *Constructionist theories* maintain that gender is a product of history, education, and acculturation; in other words, gender identification is learned behavior. Most gender critics and theorists subscribe to the latter view, although many feminist critics do not, arguing instead that the masculine and the feminine are utterly separate.

The French historian Michel Foucault (whose work is discussed more fully in section 25.5) addresses gender construction in relation to heterosexuality and homosexuality in his tremendously influential *The History of Sexuality* (1976). Foucault examines in detail the creation of homosexuality as a sexual orientation or identity during the nineteenth century (as opposed to the sex acts with which homosexuality is associated). Foucault's conception of sexuality as a product of history suggests that these categories, along with most others that are used to define people, are social entities rather than natural absolutes. Foucault provides both theory and application, and this text is cited by many as the progenitor of gender criticism and "queer" theory (to be discussed shortly).

Another influential contribution to gender theory is Nancy Chodorow's book *The Reproduction of Mothering: Psychoanalysis and the Sociology of Gender*, which examines the assumption that women are biologically better nurturers—that the act we call "mothering" is women's work. Political and economic developments in the years following the publication of this 1978 study have caused her assertions to be put to the test as more and more Western families come to rely on the dual incomes of two working parents. This reminds us that every theory is to some degree political.

Political considerations also play a role in the common but erroneous equation of gender criticism with gay and lesbian criticism, which focuses on issues of homosexuality in the production and reception of literature. Gay and lesbian criticism that engages with issues of gender construction (as most of it does) certainly falls under the category of gender criticism, but not all gender criticism deals with gay and lesbian gender identity. Many theorists argue against the very categories of heterosexuality and homosexuality, suggesting that rather than a binary opposition, the difference between the two is better understood as a continuum that includes many other variables as well. "Queer theory" is a term used by critics that appropriates and redefines the pejorative slur in order to denote more theoretical approaches to the construction of these gender identities with less application of the theories to specific texts, though occasionally critics refer to the act of reading from these perspectives as "queering" the text (as for instance in a 1995 article by Jonathan Crewe, titled "Queering 'The Yellow Wallpaper'? Charlotte Perkins Gilman and the Politics of Form").

RECOMMENDED READING ON FEMINIST AND GENDER CRITICISM

Simone de Beauvoir, *The Second Sex*

Judith Butler, *Gender Trouble: Feminism and the Subversion of Identity*

Nancy Chodorow, *The Reproduction of Mothering: Psychoanalysis and the Sociology of Gender*

Hélène Cixous, "The Language of the Medusa"

Judith Fetterley, *The Resisting Reader: A Feminist Approach to American Fiction*

Michel Foucault, *The History of Sexuality*

Sandra Gilbert and Susan Gubar, *The Madwoman in the Attic: The Woman Writer and the Nineteenth-Century Literary Imagination*

Luce Irigaray, *Speculum of the Other Woman*

---, *This Sex Which Is Not One*

Julia Kristeva, *Desire in Language: A Semiotic Approach to Literature and Art*

Kate Millett, *Sexual Politics*

Adrienne Rich, *On Lies, Secrets, and Silence*
Eve Kosofsky Sedgwick, *Between Men: English Literature and Male Homosocial Desire*
Elaine Showalter, *A Literature of Their Own: British Women Novelists from Brontë to Lessing*
Mary Wollstonecraft, *A Vindication of the Rights of Woman*
Virginia Woolf, *A Room of One's Own*

25.5   CULTURAL STUDIES AND NEW HISTORICISM

Two of the more prevalent schools of critical theory to emerge from the post-structuralist explosion in literary criticism are **New Historicism** and **cultural studies**. New Historicism is sometimes thought to be a variety of cultural studies (in fact, one of the originators of New Historicism, Stephen Greenblatt, believes that the school of criticism should instead be termed *cultural poetics*), but there are some differences between the New Historicist study of literature and the culturewide project reflected in cultural studies. If nothing else, New Historicism seeks to examine literature mainly (rather than taking the surrounding culture as a whole as its primary focus) and usually concentrates on older texts where the cultural context is more removed from the present. Cultural studies, by contrast, reaches across disciplines, uses a variety of methods to examine culture as a whole, and doesn't necessarily focus on the past.

As a school of literary scholarship, New Historicism is partly descended from and partly a reaction to earlier forms of *historicism*, or historical or biographical criticism. The older form of historical criticism assumed that a basic working knowledge of the historical context of older works would help one to understand the setting, themes, and events transpiring in a text. For example, your understanding of act 3, scene 3 of Shakespeare's *Hamlet*, in which the prince decides not to kill his murderous uncle, Claudius, while he is praying, makes more sense if you possess the Anglo-Catholic knowledge that Shakespeare assumes his audience would have: if Hamlet kills Claudius while he is praying, he will die at a time when his soul is free of sin and will go to heaven. Hamlet's father, on the other hand, was denied the same chance for absolution and now wanders as a ghost whose soul has been damned. Similarly, your appreciation for Frederick Douglass's *Narrative of the Life of an American Slave* might be enriched through knowing something about how slavery started in the American continents, how long it lasted, and what forms it took in Maryland (where Douglass was raised as a slave).

New Historicists would agree that a critic should work toward achieving an understanding of the historical and cultural context of a given work but would first note that a work of historical criticism needs more than a basic understanding of the social and cultural context. Furthermore, they would argue that a truly objective knowledge of history is impossible to achieve. They believe that history is itself a text. Also, like the poststructuralists who have influenced their methodology, New Historicist readers would deny that one could completely reduce a text to a single correct and understandable meaning. They take Derrida's concept that a text is "undecidable" or indeterminable and apply it to history; history, too, is undecidable, and a text is part of that cultural history, not a document that stands apart from it.

Cultural Theorists and Marxist Critics

Although New Historicism may have differences with cultural studies, it is profoundly influenced by the originators and antecedents of cultural studies. To understand New Historicism and cultural studies in general, one first has to be familiarized with some of the philosophers, cultural theorists, scholars, and critics whose doctrines preceded them.

One of the earliest of these influential scholars is the Russian literary critic and philosopher Mikhail Bakhtin. In books like *Problems of Dostoevsky's Poetics* (1929) and *Rabelais and His World* (1940), Bakhtin argues that all of literature, and correspondingly, all of culture, is a series of *discourses*. In Bakhtin, *discourses* refers not only to modes of speech but also to the subtle or overt ideologies conveyed by discourse. Bakhtin argues that books are either **monologic**, containing one voice, series of ideas, or ideology, or **dialogic**, containing divergent or contrary voices or discourses. Novels with multiple dialogic or **polyphonic** ideologies are often more rewarding to the reader than monologic texts. In his study of Rabelais, Bakhtin goes on to show that popular culture sometimes serves as a dissonant voice working against mainstream high culture. He terms this dialogical discourse **carnival**, basing the idea in part on the inherent irony of the Mardi Gras–style celebrations held around the world just before Lent.

As a writer from Soviet Russia, Bahktin is usually counted as a de facto Marxist. Other Marxist scholars have had great influence on cultural studies as well. Readers should remember, however, that Marxism as a theoretical approach in literary criticism is quite different from the communist governments spawned by the political manifestations of its ideologies. Taken at its simplest level, Marxism is **materialism**, the belief that needs and wants dictate all that occurs in society and that, generally speaking, the dominant classes who control the most production of material create an ideology that ensures that they will stay in control. Most Marxist critics, then, work to tease out thematic undercurrents that reflect the discourses of conflicting ideologies.

Foremost among the Marxist scholars who have influenced cultural studies is the antifascist German cultural theorist Walter Benjamin, whose famous 1936 essay "The Work of Art in the Age of Mechanical Reproduction" discusses the ways that societal standards, forms, and rituals are manifested and maintained by "high" culture; he argued for serious consideration of newer "low" forms of popular culture like radio and television as a way of airing diverse voices. The Hungarian-born Soviet writer Georg Lukács argued against the experimentalism of modernist techniques in favor of the content-rich social **realism** of nineteenth-century literature in *The Historical Novel* (1937), and the Italian writer Antonio Gramsci examined the dynamics of dominant, ideology-driven hegemonies in his *Prison Notebooks* (1929–1935).

Gramsci felt that underprivileged peoples could war against the prevailing ideologies of the hegemony by creating their own cultural icons, which would in turn create their own world.

Later influential Marxist theorists and critics include the French scholar Louis Althusser, who rekindled Benjamin and Gramsci's ideas in books like *Lenin and Philosophy, and Other Essays* (1971), in which he argued that the bulk of society was enthralled by a popular culture that reflected only the dominant ideology in order to keep the masses happy and producing. The English theorist Raymond Williams (whom some consider only marginally a Marxist writer) asserts in books like *Culture and Society* (1958) and *The Long Revolution* (1961) that the focus should be less on ideology and belief systems and more on the shared experiences and interactions of a culture at large, including its artistic efforts. Another British writer, Terry Eagleton, rebuts Williams by declaring in *Criticism and Ideology* (1978) that the arts are not merely influenced by culture and society and the dominant ideology of the social milieu but may in turn directly influence and actually help create the dominant belief systems.

Finally, in his books *Marxism and Form* in 1971 and *The Political Unconscious* in 1981, the American critic Fredric Jameson develops what he calls **dialectical criticism** to combine various poststructuralist methodologies with those of Freud, Lacan, and Althusser, among others. Jameson argues that texts reveal the writer's (and by extension, the culture's) repressed desire to confront the dominant ideology. The writers and readers may not be capable of revealing or realizing that the repressed, hidden dialogical discourse is in place, but critics can so long as they realize that they, too, are influenced by ideologies.

Michel Foucault

Possibly the single most important influence on cultural studies has been Michel Foucault, a French historian and philosopher. Foucault's *Discipline and Punish: The Birth of the Prison* (1975) had a gigantic impact on the formation of cultural studies, just as his *History of Sexuality* (1976) greatly informed gender studies.

According to Foucault, no historical event is caused by a single occurrence but is rather the result of an enormous network of interweaving social, economic, cultural, and political components. It is necessary for historians and scholars to remember that they, too, are part of history and part of the dominant and prevalent belief system of their day. As such, scholars should remember that it is particularly difficult to perceive their own culture from a critical perspective and also very challenging to grasp fully the belief systems and ideologies of past times.

Foucault is particularly interested in the dynamics of power—how it is built and how it is applied. In *Discipline and Punish*, Foucault considers the changing paradigms of prisons and the treatment of prisoners and criminals. He notes that once prisoners were dealt with harshly, to the point of torture and execution for minor crimes, and often in public, as a means of controlling the populace. Why did prisoner treatment change? Foucault challenges the common assumption that Western society has evolved to a more humane condition; rather, he notes that the increase in European colonies around the globe meant that prisoners were useful in a way they hadn't been before—as prospective, albeit unwilling, colonists. In each case, we see how power moves through almost subterranean systems. Foucault doesn't perceive power as simply the ability of the cultural controllers (governments, dictators, ruling classes, the wealthy, and other elites) to dominate others; rather, he sees power as a web of interconnected and even sometimes contradictory components. It is visible only through deduction; what occurs in the world reveals where the power actually is, as demonstrated through his study of prisoners and torture. Leaders of a culture don't employ a nebulous "power" in the abstract as much as make use of or take advantage of the various discourses (in the Bakhtinian sense) that enable their dominance.

Foucault argues that history is not **teleological**—straightforward, linear, working in a cohesive and coherent progression. Instead, each given culture (in place and time) has what Foucault terms an **episteme**. An episteme is that culture's held system of beliefs detailing its view of the nature of the world, truth, human nature, codes of conduct, standards of morality, and so on. Each culture uses its episteme to establish criteria to judge what is acceptable and unacceptable, good or evil, worthy or unworthy. With this *epistemological* (as opposed to teleological) model in mind, Foucault believes that the actual act of interpreting history itself reveals a form of power dynamics. Each cultural era contains groups who are able to prevail over the discourses of the day to enforce their own episteme; the "history" left by that culture will reflect that episteme. All history, says Foucault, is completely subjective. Scholars who realize that they, too, are affected by their own epistemes and are products of their culture's own ideological belief systems will have a leg up on those who believe that history can be examined as a more or less objective set of facts. A critic who applies poststructuralist methodology can possibly discern the various inconsistent and possibly contradictory dialogical discourses that reveal the scope and development of an episteme; a scholar could even possibly trace the notions, facts, beliefs, and other elements that were accepted or rejected in creation of the cultural era's episteme.

Cultural Studies and New Historicism in Practice

If we sum up the lessons learned from the various influences we have cited, the basic assumptions of the cultural critics and New Historicists may boil down to something like this: from the Marxists and early cultural theorists like Bakhtin and Benjamin, critics have learned that everything in culture is interconnected and that the arts themselves are as much reflective of a culture and part of it as politics and the economy (as Derrida would put it, "There is nothing outside the text"). The "high" arts aren't necessarily the only arts worthy of study, and in fact the popular arts may speak more about a culture than their rarefied cousins. Furthermore, a culture—or a text—may contain conflicting ideologies and dialogical discourses. With the advent of poststructuralism and Derrida's models of deconstruction, critics learn not only that everything may be indeterminate but also that culture is composed of a set of conflicting, binary oppositions in which one side is always privileged over the other side. We add to this Foucault's portrayal of power dynamics and the dialogical struggles over the episteme and the basic realization that all readers and writers are members of their own particular episteme and must base all reading and interpretations on the knowledge of their own subjectivity.

New Historicists and cultural critics, however, have a different program than deconstructionists; they don't seek merely to unravel a text or culture's assumptions until they can show the various contradictions or *aporia*. Instead, they seek to rediscover a text. By analyzing the social contexts and discourses that have helped create a text and by being able to show where the seams are, they also hope to reveal how the dominant ideology of a given episteme may have worked to smother or ignore other belief systems or divergent interpretations of texts and culture, thereby allowing critics to develop a new reading of a text (or culture).

The leader of New Historicism has been Stephen Greenblatt, a scholar and critic of Renaissance literature. Much New Historicism has been focused on Renaissance literature and Romantic literature, possibly because so much has been written on the texts; works of the Renaissance and **Romanticism** also belong to discrete and remote (from our perspective) cultural time periods. Greenblatt's 1980 book *Renaissance Self-Fashioning: From More to Shakespeare* helped define many of the techniques and objectives of New Historicism.

Greenblatt and his fellow New Historicists argue that critics must always bear in mind that understanding or appreciating a text depends on understanding the dialogical discourses at work in the culture and ideology that any given text is a part of. In a way, the New Historicist critics are diametrically opposed to New Critics because they believe that a study of the text begins with a study of the life of the author and, more important, a study of the sociohistorical, cultural context of the text, as well as any cultural dictates or discourses contained within the text itself. Obviously, no one critic or reader can hope to understand any of those three areas entirely, but investigation into each facet can open new doors and enrich our understanding. In evaluating the cultural context, as well, the critic should take care not to focus solely on the gigantic events so often studied in histories (wars, social unrest, assassinations of famous people) but also to analyze the subtler and more casual aspects of everyday life. Furthermore, Greenblatt reminds critics that challenging historical presumptions and "common knowledge" can be rigorous and difficult and that critics must always be aware that their own texts are merely different works of interpretation, subject to the same prejudices, errors, and valuations that have influenced other interpretations.

For example, a New Historicist scholar analyzing William Shakespeare's *Henry V* or *Julius Caesar* might argue that despite the fact that each of these plays is purporting to be a dramatization of "true" historical events, each actually reveals far more about Elizabethan England than it does early-fifteenth-century England or ancient Rome. The critic would show how the values of Shakespeare's particular era, or his episteme, are reflected in the plays and how Shakespeare consciously rewrites history to suit his own artistic or ideological purposes. Furthermore, the New Historicist might go on to analyze the effect that Shakespeare's restructuring of historical "fact" has on his contemporaries as well as later scholars and historians.

In *Historical Studies and Literary Criticism* and *The Beauty of Inflections: Literary Investigations in Historical Method and Theory*, both published in 1985, the American critic Jerome McGann emphasizes that New Historicists should define history broadly in recognition that the interpretation of history is, in a sense, a social science and that historical critics should follow the Bakhtin school of discourse analysis by taking into account an author's stated intentions. At the same time, the critic should also consider the history of the text's critical evaluations and reviews in order to help understand what discourses have already been automatically and unrecognizably presented to the critic.

Later works in New Historicism have focused more on Romantic literature, particularly the criticism of Marjorie Levinson, who edited *Rethinking Historicism: Critical Readings in Romantic History* (1989). The school was further codified when H. Aram Veeser edited a collection titled *The New Historicism* in 1989 and summed up the New Historicist perspective and methodology. Veeser argued that although New Historicists work in various areas of literary and cultural analysis and are all influenced by different theorists, from Foucault to Benjamin to Bakhtin, they share certain common beliefs: that artistic endeavors (plays, poems, stories, novels, paintings, performance art, and so on) are woven into the very fabric of culture and should not be considered separate artifacts; that the distinction between "popular" and "nonliterary" texts on the one hand and "high art" and "literary" texts on the other is illusory and that popular art can reveal as much (or more) about a culture as high art; that no expression in art or historical interpretation can reveal an "absolute truth" about a time, place, or human nature; and that critics must be aware that their own historical critiques are required to make use of some of the methods they denounce.

The Influence of Cultural Criticism

The advent of cultural criticism, New Historicism, and various poststructuralist and postmodern readings has opened the critical doors wide and has aided the creation of new ways of reading for critics in other schools. For example, the tenets of New Historicism, as expressed here, have contributed to the work of feminist scholars like Janice Radway, whose 1984 book *Reading the Romance: Women, Patriarchy, and Popular Literature* discusses how both reading and writing romance literature become forms of cultural discourse for women.

Cultural studies has also helped spawn a significant school of literary theory called **postcolonialism**. Most critics credit the creation of postcolonial studies to Edward Said, a Harvard-educated Palestinian scholar who grew up in Egypt. His 1978 study, *Orientalism*, describes the struggle that occurs when one culture—or episteme, or ideology—is dominated by another. Said discusses how the West colonized most of the Middle East and other parts of the world and argues that the colonization of a given people, or episteme, in effect separates those people from their cultural history. Said also describes in later texts how in the conflicting discourses between dominant cultures and oppressed cultures, the members of the dominant group always create an *other*, a member of a race, religion, nationality, or other subgroup who doesn't conform to the dominant ideology. Similar to Lacan's "other" but designated culturally rather than psychologically, the other is always forced into a submissive role, relegated to stereotypes, and judged to be inferior due to the differences between the other and the ruling culture.

Homi K. Bhabha further contributes to the development of postcolonial studies in books like *Nation and Narration* (1990) and *The Location of Culture* (1994), in which he notes that what occurs when a dominant culture forces its own epistemology on another culture (as the Belgians did on indigent Africans in the Congo throughout the nineteenth century, for example) is that the members of the colonized or subjugated culture are forced into a position of "unhomeliness." No culture feels like home to them. They are too much a part of the dominant culture to feel connected to their own culture as it was before the cultural invasion of the colonists (even if they could return to a pristine state, culturally), yet they will never belong to the dominant colonial culture either.

Postcolonialism is further explored through collections and works like *The Empire Writes Back: Theory and Practice in Postcolonial Literatures* (1989), by Ashcroft, Griffiths, and Tiffin, and *Past the Last Post: Theorizing Post-Colonialism and Post-Modernism* (1990), edited by Adam and Tiffin. Postcolonial criticism has been further adapted and applied to texts by authors from cultures that are not typically thought of as colonial or post-colonial. Critics writing about Irish literature have shown how the concepts of postcolonial criticism can apply to their studies. The Kenyan-born scholar Abdul Jan Mohamed expanded his studies of literary culture in colonial Africa to also consider African American literature; the African American theorist Henry Louis Gates Jr. describes in books like *Figures in Black: Words, Signs, and the "Radical" Self* (1987) how African American writers draw simultaneously on two discourses, those of both black and white Americans. Cultural studies has, in the least, contributed many diverse and underrepresented voices to the continuing critical and theoretical discourse.

RECOMMENDED READING ON CULTURAL STUDIES AND NEW HISTORICISM

Mikhail Bakhtin, *Problems of Dostoevsky's Poetics*
---, *Rabelais and His World*
Walter Benjamin, "The Work of Art in the Age of Mechanical Reproduction"
Homi K. Bhabha, *The Location of Culture*
Frantz Fanon, *Black Skin, White Masks*
Michel Foucault, *Discipline and Punish: The Birth of the Prison*
---, *The History of Sexuality*
Stephen Greenblatt, *Renaissance Self-Fashioning: From More to Shakespeare*
Marjorie Levinson, ed., *Rethinking Historicism: Critical Readings in Romantic History*
Jerome J. McGann, ed., *Historical Studies and Literary Criticism*
Edward Said, *Culture and Imperialism*
---, *Orientalism*
H. Aram Veeser, ed., *The New Historicism*

25.6   THEORY-BASED READINGS: APPROACHES TO "ARABY"

As we have tried to show throughout this chapter, there are a number of ways
that students can use theory to approach texts and to develop their engagement with texts. Sometimes it may seem that a certain theoretical approach is
naturally fitted to a text. Henry James's *The Turn of the Screw* works very well
with a psychoanalytic reading, while "The Yellow Wallpaper" works well as
a feminist text. A short and fairly straightforward poem like "Desert Places"
might suggest a New Critical approach, whereas *Trifles* perhaps asks in part
for a New Historicist reading.

   However, bear in mind that any text can offer multiple rewarding readings and that the fact that a text seems obviously connected with a particular
school of critical theory doesn't mean that other theories can't be useful in
developing pertinent and engaging interpretations of the text. As we demonstrate in the brief reconsideration of "Araby" that follows, one text can be
rediscovered again and again.

New Criticism

A New Critical approach to "Araby" might be very similar to the short,
explicative reading that we offered in Chapter 5. The critic would not
spend time considering Joyce's Irish childhood or whether other works might
offer any particular agenda but would instead focus on the use of metaphor
and imagery. The New Critical reading would focus on the use of light and
dark throughout the story, examining how, again and again, the boy is in the
dark or in shadow, while Mangan's sister is "defined by the light." The New
Critical approach would also examine the figurative "blindness" of the naive

boy in his foolish desire to win the hand of Mangan's sister, as indicated by such symbols as the "blind" he pulls down to watch her beneath and the fact that he lives on a "blind street."

Psychoanalytic

A psychoanalytic reading might suggest that the narrator is frozen in his development due to the absence of a traditional father figure (and mother figure, for that matter). The many passages referring to the boy's imagination suggest the mysteries of his adolescent sexual awakening, and the narrator's apparent avoidance of the topic, while certainly historically accurate, also suggests the repressive Catholic upbringing and possibly the neuroses it could engender. The dark space of the bazaar at the end represents a feminine space of mystery, of initiation into adulthood, which the boy will have to pierce in order to proceed in his development. The easy substitution of the shop girl for Mangan's sister in the boy's perception indicates an unconscious coping strategy, and the revelatory nature of the story's climax, when he realizes his vanity, suggests the unbidden return of the repressed.

Feminist

A feminist reading of "Araby" might note that the teenage girl, "Mangan's sister," is never really developed as a character, nor is she more than an object to the boy. Her lack of a name in the story reveals that the boy sees her only as a means of satisfying his own needs; her own existence is less important to him than the place she occupies in his life. She is the angelic ideal, and the stairway on which she stands when we first see her is quite literally a pedestal. The saleswoman in the bazaar, her counterpart, might suggest the opposite of a binary pair, the seductive temptress as opposed to the angel. When the shop worker speaks, the narrator may comprehend that he has objectified Mangan's sister through his own preconceived notions; it is only then that he realizes that the object of his infatuation might well have beliefs and feelings of her own.

Cultural Studies

A cultural studies reading might begin by researching Joyce's life and times and would note that Joyce, like the boy in the story, actually lived on Richmond Street until 1896 and that a traveling bazaar similar to the Araby bazaar was in Dublin from May 14 through May 19, 1894. Although we're not sure how old the narrator of the story is supposed to be, Joyce himself would have been twelve years old in 1894, which seems to be around the age of the boy in the story.[3] More important, the cultural studies critic would

---

[3]John Wyse Jackson and Bernard McGinley, *James Joyce's* Dubliners: *An Illustrated Edition with Annotations* (New York: St. Martin's, 1993) 21–23.

note the class and economic elements of the story. The setting of the story clearly depicts the brutal economic conditions of 1890s Dublin. The reader understands the boy's difficulty in acquiring a single florin from his uncle, which leaves him with only eight pence after he pays for his train ride and buys admission to the bazaar. By contrast, we see the vendors of one stall counting stacks of coins on a salver. When he moves to another stall, he hears the voice of a woman "talking and laughing with two young gentlemen," and he "remarks their English accents." The boy is at an economic disadvantage in that he can't afford to purchase a gift that will demonstrate his worth, and at the same time he is at a cultural disadvantage; the English are empowered, the Irish are in a sense the colonized and thus disenfranchised people.

Deconstructionist

Jacques Derrida once said that "[d]econstruction could not have been possible without Joyce."[4] The protagonist's plight at the story's conclusion effectively dramatizes the paralysis of undecidability: are women untouchable ideals, like Mangan's sister, the Virgin Mary, and the boy's absent, unmentioned mother, or are they corrupt, profane moneychangers in the temple like the shopwoman at the bazaar? Yes and no, both and neither—Joyce's text insists on the undecidability of the question. Indeed, the very concept of epiphany that is so important to Joyce's works depends for its imaginative power on the disjuncture between signifier and signified. The cause of the boy's tears is unidentified and unable to be paraphrased.

THINKING EXERCISES

1. Of the various schools of critical theory discussed in Chapter 25, which do you find the most interesting? Why does that particular school interest you?

2. Consider some work of literature you've read in your classes. Which branch of critical theory do you think would be most effective in analyzing the text? Take a few minutes to write a brief outline or paragraph similar to the ones we've written here. Do you think that making use of a theoretical framework has caused you to consider angles you might have otherwise ignored?

3. Do you think it is better to work with one particular kind of theory or to apply multiple theories? Explain your choice and the reasoning behind it in a brief paragraph.

---

[4]"Ulysses Gramophone: Hear Say Yes in Joyce," *James Joyce: The Augmented Ninth*, ed. Bernard Benstock (Syracuse: Syracuse UP, 1988) 27–75.

☙ 26 ❧

Reading a Theory-Based Article

The following article, which appeared in the journal *Literature and Psychology* in 1975, is an accessible example of an article that foregrounds its critical approach to the text. It is, however, traditional literary criticism rather than critical theory; its emphasis is on Rossetti's poem more than on psychoanalytic literary theory. As you read the article, pay attention to the clues the critic provides to the approach itself; some, like the title of the article and the title of the journal in which it appeared, are quite straightforward, while others are much more subtle. We have maintained the critic's original documentation style, which is no longer current MLA style; in your critical reading, you will encounter many such variations, some based on when the article was published and others on the particular style sheet the journal uses.

Untying Goblin Apron Strings: A Psychoanalytic Reading of "Goblin Market"

Ellen Golub

Literature and Psychology 25 (1975): 158–65

Having read Christina Rossetti's "Goblin Market," the reader has the uncanny sense that he has been there before, that he has, in the past encountered goblin-like creatures, been seduced by their charms, and suddenly turned the tide of the relationship to emerge triumphant over them. Such is the experience much fiction offers us. With the safety of aesthetic distance, we meet Captain Hook, the hungry wolf, and our wicked stepmother; we confront our deepest fears with the knowledge that help is on the way, that the poem or the story or the novel will manage our anxieties and we will be restored. For having done battle in the goblin arena, Laura, Lizzie, and their reader will be released from their afflictions; as a reward for confronting and mastering deep anxieties, we receive pleasure and enjoy

A. the heightened self-esteem which is the immediate result of what psychologists call mastery.

A. This, according to much Freudian psychoanalytic criticism, is the appeal of art. Literature allows us to repeat traumatic events in a safe environment in order to gain mastery of them.

Much of the previous criticism of "Goblin Market" is biographical. B. Ifor Evans traces Ms. Rossetti's fondness for wombats back to the favorite books of her childhood.[i] William Michael Rossetti, brother of the poetess, encourages an identification of their sister, Maria, with the character Lizzie, since it was this devoted family member who helped Christina recover from the wounds of an unhappy love affair.[ii] However, to the reader whose interest is in the meaning of the poem itself, these explanations do little to illuminate the text. Closest to accomplishing this task is Lona Packer, who claims that this poem, since it evolved out of Christina's romantic disappointment, derives its theme from "the deprivation of love."[iii]

Temptation, in both its human and theological sense, is the thematic core of "Goblin Market." . . . "Goblin Market" celebrates by condemning sensuous passion . . . the symbolism in which Christina veils her own tribute to eros.[iv]

B. Phrases like this suggest a reader-response approach to analyzing the text; this is consistent with Norman Holland's psychoanalytic approach as detailed in *The Dynamics of Literary Response* (see section 25.2). Golub invokes Holland explicitly in the next paragraph.

According to Packer, the tempting fruit and charming goblins are different aspects of nature, "the core of which is sexual passion."[v]

Rossetti seems to condemn such passion, but in her condemnation she offers much description of it. Eros being very much present, it is the seduction of girls by goblins which

B. engages reader attention. Love is linked with food, with juicy, luscious fruit, and we are drawn to this temptation along with Laura,

C. though it is outlawed.

C. This simultaneous attraction and repulsion, known as ambivalence, is something that psychoanalytic critics tend to make much of in texts, maintaining that these tensions can frequently be traced back to Oedipal ambivalence toward the parents or parental edicts.

Psychoanalytically, this same motion of attraction to and flight from this tempting love relationship may be seen as forming a parallel pattern. To explain the connection between unconscious desires and their conscious expression, Norman Holland has written that

> The libidinal phases of childhood have in them the seeds of the adult clinical entities.[vi] . . . Creative writing follows a pattern like that of the dream. [Quoting Freud:] "A strong experience in the present awakens in the creative writer a memory of an earlier experience (usually belonging to his childhood) from which there now proceeds a wish which finds its fulfillment in the creative work."[vii]

The adult experience of deprivation of love reflects back on an earlier breach of trust so that the lover who fails to deliver his love stands in the same relationship as the mother

D.   who disappointed us as children. Taking as our point of departure the assumption that "literature transforms primitive childish fantasies

E.   into adult, civilized meanings,"[viii] we may see this conflict over yielding to temptation, what Packer polarizes as "the legitimate" versus "the outlawed,"[ix] as an ontogenic but also universally human issue.

The literary transformation of fantasy delineated by Rossetti begins as two maidens hear the goblins hawking their fruit. Both Lizzie and Laura sense the danger which lurks for them should they succumb to this alluring temptation but, nevertheless, Laura is drawn under their spell. As the goblin men, animal-like and seductive, ply their mellifluous wares, she exchanges a lock of hair and a tear to suck the juices of their menu. But Laura is not satisfied. Though she would return to the goblins and have more to eat, she is denied access to them. Sister Lizzie reminds her of Jeanie, another goblin victim now dead, but it is too late for Laura to benefit from her example. Failing to produce fruit even from the kernel stone she has secured from her encounter, Lizzie falls ill. Her imminent demise

D.   This refers implicitly to Freud's theories of infant sexuality and the Oedipus complex.

E.   This is one of the founding assumptions of traditional psychoanalytic criticism and one of the linchpins of Holland's theory of psychological reader response.

causes Lizzie to act, as the wiser sister contacts the sinister figures, resists their seductive charms, and emerges victorious over them. She bears an antidote on her body which, although the same fruit is now distasteful to Laura, brings the suffering sister back to health. Both girls live to tell the tale to their offspring.

The basic story pattern here is not singular. Common to this and other literary fictions are the seduction of young women, the journey from innocence to experience, and the justice of reward and punishment. However, Rossetti's poem offers a fictional experience different from others in that "Goblin Market" frames a unique combination of elements. Most striking is the lushness of language which presents exotic fruit imagery.

F.

> Apples and quinces,
> Lemons and oranges,
> Plump unpecked cherries,
> Melons and raspberries,
> Bloom-down-cheeked peaches,
> Swart-headed mulberries,
> Wild free-born cranberries,
> Crab-apples, dewberries,
> Pineapples, blackberries,
> Apricots, strawberries—
> All ripe together.[x]

Unlike in *Peter Pan*, where Captain Hook is always a character to be feared and fairy dust is always a commodity to be coveted, the fruit of "Goblin Market" alters in function, being sometimes dangerous, sometimes restorative. It is, indeed, as ambivalently charged and equally potent as the fruit in the Garden of Eden which, borne by a woman, was enough to exile mankind from paradise. The fruit, both poison and elixir, is not the poem's only dichotomy. Its "Eve," lecherous and inviting, is the alternately dangerous and impotent goblin group; its "Adam," another dichotomy, consists of two girls, weak and foolish, strong and wise.

G.

Packer explains these elements in terms of the age-old conflict: sexual temptation. The goblins' cry, perceived by the girls, is a love call. Laura's glimpsing of the men and their gifts and

F. This attention to archetypal patterns may seem to suggest a Jungian approach to the text, but the critic is more concerned with the differences between "Goblin Market" and the archetypal patterns than with the similarities they share.

G. The reference to archetypal patterns is particularly interesting in light of the gender reversal.

subsequent involvement with them is her fall into temptation and this experience yields the lesson that "Satiety doesn't come with repletion."[xi] And if the love of the sweet sexual trinkets offered by goblin men is destructive, then sister love, the pure, rational, and untainted love of loyal family members, is redemptive. In its dual function, the fruit symbolizes "the paradox of love:"[xii] according to Packer, it illustrates a discriminatory power which comes to she who is no longer a "youngling."[xiii]

Packer's reading of the poem is a traditional kind of explication, one which directs its attention to the manifest level of the text. It provides excellent answers to the question, "What conscious meaning do we derive from this narrative?" However, to complement such an "above the text" explanation, it may be desirable to plunge beneath the literal level and consider

H. latent meaning. Applied to this poem, it can explain the multiple functions of the fruit and the goblins. And as it charts the relationship between girls and goblins, it clarifies why Laura is forced to pay with precious body parts while Lizzie receives her fruit for free; why Laura is deprived of even viewing the goblins for a second time, while Lizzie is able to encounter and defeat

I. them. Further clarified, using this methodology, is the function of Jeanie in the narrative.

J. Ultimately, both conscious and unconscious themes are the same, but the more essential meaning is the one we derive from an automatic decoding faculty—the unconscious—which

K. encounter during our reading experience.

For instance, Laura and Lizzie are presented in the narrative as two distinct people. As Winston Weathers suggests, they are fragments of a single personality, a literary portrayal of a "divided self."[xiv] And we perceive them as described:

> Golden head by golden head,
> Like two pigeons in one nest . . .
> Like two blossoms on one stem,
> Like two flakes of new-fallen snow . . .
> Cheek to cheek and breast to breast
> Locked together in one nest. (lines 184–98)

H. The term *latent meaning*, comparable to *subtext* in general literary criticism, here suggests meaning that, like the meaning of dreams, becomes clear only when considered in light of the personal meaning of various symbolic elements. This kind of interpretation lies at the heart of the Freudian psychoanalytic process.

I. This series of questions is ultimately this article's reason for existence; they have not, according to the critic, been answered adequately until now.

J. Rather than finding consensus, a poststructuralist critic would probably probe the differences more insistently.

K. Again, this is a basic assumption of traditional psychoanalytic literary criticism.

In recognizing the poem as "a drama that leads from innocence and integration to sickness and fragmentation back to a newer and more mature balance represented in part by the marrying of the sisters and their assumption of marital responsibility,"[xv] Weathers has traced the psychic disorientation resulting from temptation, the ego-split, into two symbolic figures. As Laura leans forward toward temptation, Lizzie stands firm against it; together they form an arch which balances the movement of the poem.

The Laura-Lizzie arch frames the work which, as Norman Holland tells us, is an organic whole radiating out from a center with all elements reflecting its organic unity of

L. organization.[xvi] The imagery, then, is intimately united with the theme. With lush orality wedded to sexual temptation, "Goblin Market," on its most literal level, begins with the temptation
M. to eat, to gratify the first erogenous zone.

The two girls are urged to partake of the fruit and find it threatening because it is connected with goblin men. Lizzie insists, "Their offers should not charm us, / Their evil gifts would harm us" (lines 65–66). The bearers are suspect; on the conscious level, they are sinister male creatures whose attempted seduction of the maidens is adultly sexual and reminiscent of a familiar literary motif. However, on the unconscious level, they represent an equally basic issue of conflict. The lush oral imagery signals the more primitive fantasies of infantile sexuality with the concerns of the first developmental stage: the oral.

The major activity of orality—eating—is prohibited, at first, by both maidens. Even the faculties developed during that stage, seeing and hearing, are restricted, as Laura cautions,

> "We must not *look* at goblin men,
> We must not buy their fruits:
> Who knows upon what soil they fed
> Their hungry thirsty roots?"
> (lines 42–45; emphasis added)

Merely to look is dangerous due to some ambiguous and vague goblin eating habits. Eluding the enticement, Lizzie "thrust a

L. This belief in the essential unity of the work clearly reflects the grounding of Holland's psychoanalytical approach in the structuralist tradition.

M. Golub's analysis here explores the parallels between Rossetti's poem and Freud's theory of the stages of pre-Oedipal sexuality.

dimpled finger / In each ear, shut eyes and ran" (lines 67–68). As in the early stages of childhood, contemplation is magically equated with participation. And refusing to incorporate, Lizzie departs from the scene. Laura remains to confront the basic issues of the oral stage: love and trust.

Typically, the mother is the agent who delivers love to the infant with food. To the child-object of these affections, all of life becomes a taking in with his mouth as the mother's breast and nipple become his sole desires. The oral zone comes to be his—and our—first experience with erogeneity. As the poem deals with the pleasures and pains of orality, it does so with the

N. controlling figure of that stage: the mother.

Packer has designated the goblins as "agents"[xvii] and although they are described as merchant men, it is this function which assigns

O. to them the role of the mother. Always altering in appearance, these goblins are like the child's disjunct perceptions of his mother. She is not a complex person of many moods, but several people: a happy mother, a sad mother, an angry mother. So, too, the goblins are many and changing.

> One had a cat's face,
> One whisked a tail,
> One tramped at a rat's pace,
> One crawled like a snail. (lines 71–74)

Their appearance alters; so too their aural dimension. At first Laura hears the soft sound of doves.

> She heard a voice like voice of doves
> Cooing all together;
> They sounded kind and full of loves
> In the pleasant weather. (lines 77–80)

Just a few lines later, she hears a feline voice as "The cat-faced-purred" (line 109); then a human imitator, "One parrot-voiced and jolly" (line 112); and finally a higher pitched bird, "One whistled like a bird" (line 114).

With the goblins hauling baskets, bearing plates, and lugging dishes full of semi-liquid

N. This is a useful synopsis of Freud's conception of the oral stage.

O. The association of the goblins with the maternal is probably the hardest part of Golub's argument to swallow. Remember, though, that she is referring to the mother from the infant's perspective: the source, like the goblin horde, of food and pleasure. This becomes more evident when Golub later describes Laura as an "incorporating infant."

food, their function and appeal is overwhelmingly material. The poem thus places Laura in the role of the incorporating infant who indulges the infantile wish to take in by submitting to sheer pleasure. She carelessly offers the products of her own body as payment (they mean little to her and she has nothing else to offer); and, with heady thoughts only of that primary erogenous zone, she "sucked their fruit globes fair or red" (line 128). Like the infant, Laura becomes totally dependent; she does not distinguish between life-sustaining and life-threatening. Laura has regressed, and with her the issues of the poem, to a stage of knowing "not was it night or day" (line 139).

The poem presents us with an enormously attractive experience but also with one that is threatening. For though we might all long for that once idyllic human condition of dependence and total gratification of desires, we know that to remain fixated in the oral stage is to be at the mercy of parental figures whose sustenance we would require. Both experience and this poem teach that we dare not trust in such a fate. Jeanie is an example of one who totally trusted and thereby yielded. Having sought her goblin/mother and found them/her not, "she pined and pined away; / . . . [She] dwindled and grew gray" (lines 154–56).

Laura has yielded to the same maternal power as Jeanie, has "sucked and sucked and sucked the more / Fruits which that unknown orchard bore" (lines 134–35). But, as Packer tells us, "Satiety doesn't come with repletion."[xviii]

> I ate and ate my fill,
> Yet my mouth waters still. . . .
>
> *   *   *
>
> You cannot think what figs
> My teeth have met in,
> What melons icy-cold
> Piled on a dish of gold
> Too huge for me to hold.
> (lines 165–66, 173–77)

The imagery, even in its smallest details, promotes the vision of a child at her mother's breast, and thus it incorporates the essential

P. components of the oral stage. First Laura's activity was observation, using her eyes to peep and her ears to hear, to focus on the desirable fruit and to follow it.[xix] Next, her activity became the primary oral one: sucking. But now, Laura has moved into what Erik Erikson terms the later modes of the oral stage.

> To get . . . means to receive and to accept what is given. . . . Now to the second stage, during which the ability to make a more active and directed approach, and the pleasure derived from it grow and ripen. The teeth develop, and with them the pleasure in biting *on* hard things, in biting *through* things, and in biting *off* things. . . . It is now necessary to learn how to continue sucking without biting, so that the mother may not withdraw the nipple in pain or anger. . . . This point in the individual's early history can be the origin of an evil dividedness, where anger against the gnawing teeth, and anger against the withdrawing mother, and anger with ~~h~~e's impotent anger all lead to a ~~c~~eful experience of sadistic and ~~m~~chistic confusion leaving the ~~a~~l impression that once upon a ~~time on~~e destroyed one's unity with ~~mat~~ernal matrix.[xx] (emphasis

from oral passivity to oral ~~i~~t is denied gratification of his ~~log~~ical weaning. Baring her teeth ~~. . . for Laura that same depriva-~~ ~~. . . th~~e infant experiences. As she ~~eye~~-contact the goblins, she is ~~". . .~~" (line 259) . . . "Not for all ~~. . . d~~iscerning even one gob-~~lin, bu~~t, without love, neither ~~can~~ survive. While Lizzie, ~~dep~~endence by resisting ~~wit~~h delight, her disap-~~point~~ent dream . . . sick in

P. Even skeptical readers will admit that the descriptions Rossetti provides do suggest the image of a mother feeding a child.

As Lizzie comes back into prominence, the poem offers the other half of the divided self. **Q.** Regressive Laura is aided by progressive Lizzie. With her alter-ego no longer functioning, Lizzie must free her sister from the goblin's spell. It is that other part of self which must resolve the conflict which Erikson suggested might be anger, and sadistic and masochistic confusion, and which, if unattended, would inevitably cause Laura's demise. Lizzie must compensate for the destroyed maternal matrix by either re-establishing that relationship or advancing to a stage in which one deals differently with such a thing.

Q. Regression and progression suggest the two possible responses to the challenges posed by the maturation process.

The latter option is selected by the poem as Lizzie confronts the issues of the next developmental stage: the anal. **R.** Packer explains that Lizzie is no longer a "youngling" in the contemplation of evil; and her foresight and discriminatory powers clearly indicate a personality more mature than Laura's. On her tongue is Jeanie and the penalties of regressive behavior while on her mind is Laura and her responsibility to produce "life out of death" (line 524). While her sister did not think to bring money and had to part with precious body products, a lock of hair and a tear, Lizzie remembers to "put a silver penny in her purse" (line 324). The Laura-goblin confrontation dealt with the gratification of erogenous desires and the yielding to temptation without regard for its consequences; the Lizzie-goblin confrontation, though still with the intriguing catalogue of fruit very much present, translates into other issues, namely **S.** power, control, and independence.

R. The anal stage follows the oral stage in Freud's theory of infant sexuality.

When Lizzie finally does "Come buy" (line 5), with the accent on actual purchasing, the goblins no longer urge that. Their real desire is "to make her eat" (line 407). Their explanation is

S. The pure physical p... of the oral stage is tra... into less tangible pleas... in the development pr...

> Such fruits as these
> No man can carry:
> Half their bloom would fly,
> Half their dew would dry,
> Half their flavor would pass by.
> (lines 375–79)

The magic of the fruit—its real potency—lies in the conditions of its use. And its demands made clear now, in anal terms, are regression and submission. Recognizing this, Lizzie renounces temptation and executes her plan.

As it previously conveyed the issues of the oral stage through its imagery, the poem now presents the issues of the anal stage with Lizzie's renewed activity. Soothing, plush, and erotic imagery yield to violence, action, and dirt.

> Lashing their tails,
> They trod and hustled her,
> Elbowed and jostled her,
> Clawed with their nails,
> Barking, mewing, hissing, mocking,
> Tore her gown and soiled her stocking,
> Twitched her hair out by the roots,
> Stamped upon her tender feet,
> Held her hands and squeezed their fruits
> Against her mouth to make her eat.

*   *   *

> Though the goblins cuffed and caught her,
> Coaxed and fought her
> Bullied and besought her,
> ˈcratched her, pinched her black as ink,
>   ˌked and knocked her,
>   ˈled and mocked her,
>   ˈ uttered not a word;
>   ˈot open lip from lip
>   ˈ should cram a mouthful in;
>   ˈd in heart to feel the drip
>   ˈt siruped all her face
>   ˈ7, 424–34)

easure
smuted
res later
cess.

gle is latently one between
And while Lizzie accedes to
ˈcoming white and golden,
ˈnsed by the waves which
the goblins become the
e has all along suspected
ˈcture is the child's out-
ˈtworthy mother (with
ˈisbehavior projected
ˈing, soil stockings,
ˈnk, smearing their

ˈce, Lizzie man-
by the foulness
ˈe establishes

T. This is a complicated move on the part of the critic. During, the anal stage of development, the child becomes aware of his or her lack of control over the mother and therefore distrustful of her. The child can only think in a child's terms, however, so that the imagined wrongs of the mother have a distinctly childish flavor.

control over them and refuses to incorporate. Expressing the child's stubborn defiance of the withdrawal of love, she usurps the maternal hierarchy and sends the goblins into oblivion as they writhe on the ground, dive into the brook, and vanish in the distance. Through this Lizzie-goblin confrontation, the poem deals with the more differentiated perception of the goblins as decidedly evil people. Contrasted to them,

> White and golden Lizzie stood,
> Like a lily in a flood—
> Like a rock of blue-veined stone
> Lashed by tides obstreperously—
> Like a beacon left alone
> In a hoary, roaring sea. (lines 408–13)

The anal concern with proper conduct and laws is satisfied by Lizzie's stubborn dominance over the goblins and her deserved success over those who maul and mock her. Also a **U.** part of Lizzie's victory is the retention of her shiny penny while acquiring what the goblins could not retain: their fruit.

U. The choice of the word *retention* here is not accidental, suggesting as it does the phrase "anal-retentive."

With the securing of fruit juices and the obliteration of goblins passed, the ego-split may be healed. We now know that to submit means to die like Jeanie, to ail like Laura, to suffer the withdrawal of a trusted source of love. However, to be strong is to be independent like Lizzie. With her offer to "Eat me, drink me, love me" (line 471), Lizzie encourages the regressive sister to absorb the elixir which she bears and which is **V.** actually Lizzie's experience. As Laura rapidly becomes Lizzie, the poem brings the fragments of self together in better harmony than they have ever been. Maturing even from the infantile "sucked and sucked and sucked" (line 134), Laura now "Kissed and kissed and kissed her" (line 486). Thus, "Swift fire spread through her veins, knocked at her heart, / Met the fire smoldering there / And overbore its lesser flame;" (lines 507–09). The fragments come together as Laura emerges from death to life.

V. This symbolic reading of the juices is particularly interesting.

The fruit, becoming bitter, now changes its function and Laura is no longer threatened by it.

> Both anxiety and functional pleasure
> disappear when the ego is sure of

itself and no longer holds an anxious expectation in readiness. Adults no longer enjoy any special pleasure when they engage in long familiar and automatic activities which made them very proud when first accomplished in their childhood.[xxi]

Lizzie has re-enacted the eating experience but, through an effort of will, has retained autonomy. The reality principle has deposed the pleasure principle as an operational imperative as the poem tells the story of developing ego

W. functions.

The poem's nuclear fantasy, then, is the conflict between regressive oral sadism and the reality-testing anal stage which battles for prominence in normal development. After an immersion in total sensuality and non-responsibility, aggressive impulses are given free access to discharge. By resolving the conflict, the poem also unites warring parts of the self. In addition, it

X. moves briefly to the genital level at which both sisters have matured into wives and mothers.

As it evokes our response, the poem offers

Y. much pleasure. The fruit is hypnotic and mellifluous, appealing and gratifying: it feeds us. When it is maliciously withdrawn, we are martyred by unjust parental figures. But the poem wreaks vengeance on those authority figures and creates a new social order. Through Lizzie's control, we achieve mastery, gain autonomy, and rise to control the actions of others. In her function as alter-ego, she makes us confident that "there is no friend like a sister / In calm or stormy weather" (lines 562–63), that there is an inner resource in ourselves, an internal strength of character capable of raising us from our most regressive personal errors.

For Christina Rossetti, such a poetic exercise might have granted the vicarious experience of mastery which was a rare commodity

Z. for the Victorian woman in her limited social sphere. For her readers, "Goblin Market" dramatizes a basic human conflict and grants the rare opportunity (rare in life, though perhaps not in fiction) to feel heroic. It asserts a comforting concept of autonomy over our own

W. This sentence effectively summarizes the Freudian theory of development figuratively represented, according to Golub, in Rossetti's poem.

X. The genital stage represents the third stage of development in Freud's theory of infant sexuality.

Y. Once again, the word *response* reminds us that we are reading an article focusing on the reader's response to a text that stimulates unconscious echoes of infantile experience; it is also an allusion to Holland's theoretical text *The Dynamics of Literary Response.*

Z. The critic hints at the possibility of historical and feminist readings of the text grounded on these psychoanalytical conclusions, but she does not pursue them.

lives and destinies and tells us that at each stage of development we can find satisfaction. Most of all, however, it indicates that a positive value may be attached to life and suffering, for the fall from innocence is, after all, an ascent into experience.

NOTES

[i] B. Ifor Evans, "The Sources of Christina Rossetti's 'Goblin Market,'" *MLR*, 28 (1933), 156–65.

[ii] William Michael Rossetti in Lona Packer, *Christina Rossetti* (Los Angeles: University of California Press, 1963), p. 150. All subsequent references to this book will refer to this edition.

[iii] Packer, p. 146.

[iv] Packer, p. 142.

[v] Packer, p. 144.

[vi] Norman N. Holland, *The Dynamics of Literary Response* (New York: Oxford University Press, 1968), p. 33.

[vii] Norman N. Holland, "Why Organic Unity?" *CE*, 30 (1968–69), 23.

[viii] Holland, *Dynamics*, p. 32.

[ix] Packer, p. 146.

[x] Christina Rossetti, *Goblin Market and Other Poems* ([n.p.], 1864), lines 5–15. All subsequent reference to this poem will be from this text and will be denoted by line references in the text of this paper.

[xi] Packer, pp. 145–46.

[xii] Packer, p. 149.

[xiii] Packer, p. 148.

[xiv] Winston Weathers, "Christina Rossetti: The Sisterhood of Self," *YP*, 3–4 (1965–66), 85.

[xv] Weathers, p. 82.

[xvi] Holland, *Dynamics*, pp. 6, 31.

[xvii] Packer, p. 144.

[xviii] Packer, pp. 145–46.

[xix] See Erik H. Erikson, *Childhood and Society* (New York: W. W. Norton, 1963), p. 77.

[xx] Erikson, pp. 75–77, 79.

[xxi] Otto Fenichel, *The Psychoanalytic Theory of Neurosis* (New York: W. W. Norton, 1945), p. 45.

✌ Florence ✌
(1949)

Alice Childress

CHARACTERS

Marge

Mama

Porter

Mrs. Carter

PLACE
A very small town in the South.

TIME
The late 1940s.

SCENE
A railway station waiting room. The room is divided in two sections by a low railing. Upstage center is a double door which serves as an entrance to both sides of the room. Over the doorway stage right is a sign "Colored," over the doorway stage left is another sign "White." Stage right are two doors . . . one marked "Colored men" . . . the other "Colored women." Stage left two other doorways are "White ladies" and "White gentlemen." There are two benches, one on each side. The room is drab and empty looking. Through the double doors upstage center can be seen a gray lighting which gives the effect of an early evening and open platform.

At rise of curtain the stage remains empty for about twenty seconds. . . . A middle aged Negro woman enters, looks offstage . . . then crosses to the "Colored" side and sits on the bench. A moment later she is followed by a young Negro woman about twenty-one years old. She is carrying a large new cardboard suitcase and a wrapped shoebox. She is wearing a shoulder strap bag and a newspaper protrudes from the flap. She crosses to the "Colored" side and rests the suitcase at her feet as she looks at her mother with mild annoyance.

MARGE: You didn't have to get here so early, Mama. Now you got to wait!

MAMA: If I'm goin' someplace . . . I like to get there in plenty time. You don't have to stay.

MARGE: You shouldn't wait 'round here alone.

MAMA: I ain't scared. Ain't a soul going to bother me.

MARGE: I got to get back to Ted. He don't like to be in the house by himself. *(She* 5 *picks up the bag and places it on the bench by Mama.)*

MAMA: You'd best go back. *(Smiles.)* You know he misses Florence.

MARGE: He's just a little fellow. He needs his mother. You make her come home! She shouldn't be way up there in Harlem. She ain't got nobody there.

MAMA: You know Florence don't like the South.

MARGE: It ain't what we like in this world! You tell her that.

MAMA: If Mr. Jack ask about the rent, you tell him we gonna be a little late   *10*
on account of the trip.

MARGE: I'll talk with him. Don't worry so about everything. *(Places suitcase
on floor.)* What you carryin', Mama . . . bricks?

MAMA: If Mr. Jack won't wait . . . write to Rudley. He oughta send a little
somethin'.

MARGE: Mama . . . Rudley ain't got nothin' fo himself. I hate to ask him to
give us.

MAMA: That's your brother! If push come to shove, we got to ask.

MARGE: *(places box on bench)* Don't forget to eat your lunch . . . and try to get   *15*
a seat near the window so you can lean on your elbow and get a little rest.

MAMA: Hmmmm . . . mmmph. Yes.

MARGE: Buy yourself some coffee when the man comes through. You'll need
something hot and you can't go to the diner.

MAMA: I know that. You talk like I'm a northern greenhorn.

MARGE: You got handkerchiefs?

MAMA: I got everything, Marge.   *20*

MARGE: *(wanders upstage to the railing division line)* I know Florence is real bad
off or she wouldn't call on us for money. Make her come home. She ain't
gonna get rich up there and we can't afford to do for her.

MAMA: We talked all of that before.

MARGE: *(touches rail)* Well, you got to be strict on her. She got notions a
Negro woman don't need.

MAMA: But she was in a real play. Didn't she send us twenty-five dollars a
week?

MARGE: For two weeks.   *25*

MAMA: Well the play was over.

MARGE: *(crosses to Mama and sits beside her)* It's not money, Mama. Sarah wrote
us about it. You know what she said Florence was doin'. Sweepin' the stage!

MAMA: She was *in* the play!

MARGE: Sure she was in it! Sweepin'! Them folks ain't gonna let her be no
actress. You tell her to wake up.

MAMA: I . . . I . . . think.   *30*

MARGE: Listen, Mama . . . She won't wanna come. We know that . . . but she
gotta!

MAMA: Maybe we shoulda told her to expect me. It's kind of mean to just
walk in like this.

MARGE: I bet she's livin' terrible. What's the matter with her? Don't she
know we're keepin' her son?

MAMA: Florence don't feel right 'bout down here since Jim got killed.

MARGE: Who does? I should be the one goin' to get her. You tell her she   *35*
ain't gonna feel right in no place. Mama, honestly! She must think she's
white!

MAMA: Florence is brownskin.

MARGE: I don't mean that. I'm talkin' about her attitude. Didn't she go to
Strumley's down here and ask to be a salesgirl? *(Rises.)* Now ain't that
somethin'? They don't hire no Colored folks.

MAMA: Others beside Florence been talkin' about their rights.

MARGE: I know it . . . but there's things we can't do cause they ain't gonna let us. *(She wanders over to the "White" side of the stage.)* Don't feel a damn bit different over here than it does on our side. *(Silence.)*

MAMA: Maybe we shoulda just sent her the money this time. This one time.   40

MARGE: *(coming back to the "Colored" side)* Mama! Don't you let her cash that check for nothin' but to bring her back home.

MAMA: I know.

MARGE: *(restless . . . fidgets with her hair . . . patting it in place)* I oughta go now.

MAMA: You best get back to Ted. He might play with the lamp.

MARGE: He better not let me catch him! If you got to go to the ladies' room   45 take your grip.

MAMA: I'll be alright. Make Ted get up on time for school.

MARGE: *(kisses her quickly and gives her the newspaper)* Here's something to read. So long, Mama.

MAMA: G'bye, Margie baby.

MARGE: *(goes to door . . . stops and turns to her mother)* You got your smelling salts?

MAMA: In my pocketbook.   50

MARGE: *(wistfully)* Tell Florence I love her and miss her too.

PORTER: *(can be heard singing in the distance)*

MAMA: Sure.

MARGE: *(reluctant to leave)* Pin that check in your bosom, Mama. You might fall asleep and somebody'll rob you.

MAMA: I got it pinned to me. *(Feels for the check which is in her blouse.)*   55

MARGE: *(almost pathetic)* Bye, Ma.

MAMA: *(Sits for a moment looking at her surroundings. She opens the paper and begins to read.)*

PORTER: *(offstage)* Hello, Marge. What you doin' down here?

MARGE: I came to see Mama off.

PORTER: Where's she going?   60

MARGE: She's in there; she'll tell you. I got to get back to Ted.

PORTER: Bye now . . . Say, wait a minute, Marge.

MARGE: Yes?

PORTER: I told Ted he could have some of my peaches and he brought all them Brandford boys and they picked 'em all. I wouldn't lay a hand on him but I told him I was gonna tell you.

MARGE: I'm gonna give it to him!   65

PORTER: *(Enters and crosses to white side of waiting room. He carries a pail of water and a mop. He is about fifty years old. He is obviously tired but not lazy.)* Every peach off my tree!

MAMA: There wasn't but six peaches on that tree.

PORTER: *(smiles . . . glances at Mama as he crosses to the "White" side and begins to mop)* How d'ye do, Mrs. Whitney . . . you going on a trip?

MAMA: Fine, I thank you. I'm going to New York.

PORTER: Wish it was me. You gonna stay?   70

MAMA: No, Mr. Brown. I'm bringing Florence . . . I'm visiting Florence.

PORTER: Tell her I said hello. She's a fine girl.

MAMA: Thank you.

PORTER: My brother Bynum's in Georgia now.

MAMA: Well now, that's nice.   75

PORTER: Atlanta.

MAMA: He goin' to school?

PORTER: Yes'm. He saw Florence in a Colored picture. A moving picture.

MAMA: Do tell! She didn't say a word about it.

PORTER: They got Colored moving picture theaters in Atlanta.   *80*

MAMA: Yes. Your brother going to be a doctor?

PORTER: *(with pride)* No. He writes things.

MAMA: Oh.

PORTER: My son is goin' back to Howard next year.

MAMA: Takes an awful lot of goin' to school to be anything. Lot of money   *85*
leastways.

PORTER: *(thoughtfully)* Yes'm, it sure do.

MAMA: That sure was a nice church sociable the other night.

PORTER: Yes'm. We raised 87 dollars.

MAMA: That's real nice.

PORTER: I won your cake at the bazaar.   *90*

MAMA: The chocolate one?

PORTER: *(as he wrings mop)* Yes'm . . . was light as a feather. That old train is
gonna be late this evenin'. It's number 42.

MAMA: I don't mind waitin'.

PORTER: *(Lifts pail, tucks mop handle under his arm. He looks about in order to
make certain no one is around and leans over and addresses Mama in a confiden-
tial tone.)* Did you buy your ticket from that Mr. Daly?

MAMA: *(in a low tone)* No. Marge bought it yesterday.   *95*

PORTER: *(leaning against railing)* That's good. That man is real mean.
Especially if he thinks you're goin' north. *(He starts to leave . . . then turns
back to Mama.)* If you go to the rest room, use the Colored men's . . . the
other one is out of order.

MAMA: Thank you, sir.

MRS. CARTER: *(A white woman . . . well dressed, wearing furs and carrying a small,
expensive overnight bag breezes in . . . breathless . . . flustered and smiling. She
addresses the Porter as she almost collides with him.)* Boy! My bags are out
there. The taxi driver just dropped them. Will they be safe?

PORTER: Yes, mam. I'll see after them.

MRS. CARTER: I thought I'd missed the train.   *100*

PORTER: It's late, mam.

MRS. CARTER: *(crosses to bench on the "White" side and rests her bag)* Fine! You
come back here and get me when it comes. There'll be a tip in it for you.

PORTER: Thank you, mam. I'll be here. *(As he leaves.)* Miss Whitney, I'll take
care of your bag too.

MAMA: Thank you, sir.

MRS. CARTER: *(wheels around . . . notices Mama)* Oh . . . Hello there . . .   *105*

MAMA: Howdy, mam. *(She opens her newspaper and begins to read.)*

MRS. CARTER: *(Paces up and down rather nervously. She takes a cigarette from her
purse, lights it and takes a deep draw. She looks at her watch and then speaks to
Mama across the railing.)* Have you any idea how late the train will be?

MAMA: No, mam. *(Starts to read again.)*

MRS. CARTER: I can't leave this place fast enough. Two days of it and I'm
bored to tears. Do you live here?

MAMA: *(rests paper on her lap)* Yes, mam.   *110*

MRS. CARTER: Where are you going?

MAMA: New York City, mam.

MRS. CARTER: Good for you! You can stop "maming" me. My name is Mrs.
Carter. I'm not a southerner really. *(Takes a handkerchief from her purse and
covers her nose for a moment.)* My God! Disinfectant! This is a frightful place.
My brother's here writing a book. Wants atmosphere. Well, he's got it. I'll
never come back here ever.

MAMA: That's too bad, mam . . . Mrs. Carter.

MRS. CARTER: That's good. I'd die in this place. Really die. Jeff . . . Mr. Wiley . . .   *115*
my brother . . . He's tied in knots, a bundle of problems . . . positively in knots.

MAMA: *(amazed)* That so, mam?

MRS. CARTER: You don't have to call me mam. It's so southern. Mrs. Carter!
These people are still fighting the Civil War. I'm really a New Yorker now.
Of course, I was born here . . . in the South I mean. Memphis. Listen . . . am
I annoying you? I've simply got to talk to someone.

MAMA: *(places her newspaper on the bench)* No, Mrs. Carter. It's perfectly alright.

MRS. CARTER: Fine! You see Jeff has ceased writing. Stopped! Just like that!
(Snaps fingers.)

MAMA: *(turns to her)* That so?   *120*

MRS. CARTER: Yes. The reviews came out on his last book. Poor fellow.

MAMA: I'm sorry, mam . . . Mrs. Carter. They didn't like his book?

MRS. CARTER: Well enough . . . but Jeff's . . . well, Mr. Wiley is a genius. He
says they missed the point! Lost the whole message! Did you read . . . do
you . . . have you heard of *Lost My Lonely Way*?

MAMA: No, mam. I can't say I have.

MRS. CARTER: Well, it doesn't matter. It's profound. Real . . . you know.   *125*
(Stands at the railing upstage.) It's about your people.

MAMA: That's nice.

MRS. CARTER: Jeff poured his complete self into it. Really delved into the
heart of the problem, pulled no punches! He hardly stopped for his
meals . . . And of course I wasn't here to see that he didn't overdo. He
suffers so with his characters.

MAMA: I guess he wants to do his best.

MRS. CARTER: Zelma! . . . That's his heroine . . . Zelma! A perfect character.

MAMA: *(interested . . . coming out of her shell eagerly)* She was colored, mam?   *130*

MRS. CARTER: Oh yes! . . . But of course you don't know what it's about do you?

MAMA: No, miss . . . Would you tell me?

MRS. CARTER: *(leaning on the railing)* Well . . . she's almost white, see? Really
you can't tell except in small ways. She wants to be a lawyer . . . and . . .
and . . . well, there she is full of complexes and this deep shame you know.

MAMA: *(excitedly but with curiosity)* Do tell! What shame has she got?

MRS. CARTER: *(takes off her fur neckpiece and places it on bench with overnight bag)*   *135*
It's obvious! This lovely creature . . . intelligent, ambitious, and well . . .
she's a Negro!

MAMA: *(waiting eagerly)* Yes'm, you said that . . .

MRS. CARTER: Surely you understand? She's constantly hating herself. Just
before she dies she says it! . . . Right on the bridge . . .

MAMA: *(genuinely moved)* How sad. Ain't it a shame she had to die?

MRS. CARTER: It was inevitable . . . couldn't be any other way!

MAMA: What did she say on the bridge?   140

MRS. CARTER: Well . . . just before she jumped . . .

MAMA: *(slowly straightening)* You mean she killed *herself?*

MRS. CARTER: Of course. Close your eyes and picture it!

MAMA: *(turns front and closes her eyes tightly with enthusiasm)* Yes'm.

MRS. CARTER: *(center stage on "White" side)* Now . . . ! She's standing on the   145
bridge in the moonlight . . . Out of her shabby purse she takes a mirror . . .
and by the light of the moon she looks at her reflection in the glass.

MAMA: *(clasps her hands together gently)* I can see her just as plain.

MRS. CARTER: *(sincerely)* Tears roll down her cheeks as she says . . . almost!
almost white . . . but I'm black! I'm a Negro! and then . . . *(Turns to Mama.)*
she jumps and drowns herself!

MAMA: *(opens her eyes and speaks quietly)* Why?

MRS. CARTER: She can't face it! Living in a world where she almost belongs
but not quite. *(Drifts upstage.)* Oh it's so . . . so . . . tragic.

MAMA: *(Carried away by her convictions . . . not anger . . . she feels challenged. She*   150
rises.) That ain't so! Not one bit it ain't!

MRS. CARTER: *(surprised)* But it is!

MAMA: *(during the following she works her way around the railing until she crosses*
over about one foot to the "White" side and is face to face with Mrs. Carter) I
know it ain't! Don't my friend Essie Kitredge daughter look just like a
German or somethin'? She didn't kill herself! She's teachin' the third
grade in the colored school right here. Even the bus drivers ask her to sit
in the front seats cause they think she's white! . . . an' . . . an' . . . she just
says as clear as you please . . . "I'm sittin' where my people got to sit by
law. I'm a Negro woman!"

MRS. CARTER: *(uncomfortable and not knowing why)* . . . But there you have it.
The exception makes the rule. That's proof!

MAMA: No such thing! My cousin Hemsly's as white as you! . . . an' . . . an'
he never . . .

MRS. CARTER: *(flushed with anger . . . yet lost . . . because she doesn't know why)*   155
Are you losing your temper? *(Weakly.)* Are you angry with me?

MAMA: *(Stands silently trembling as she looks down and notices she is on the*
wrong side of the railing. She looks up at the "White Ladies room" sign and
slowly works her way back to the "Colored" side. She feels completely lost.) No,
mam. Excuse me please. *(With bitterness.)* I just meant Hemsly works in
the colored section of the shoe store . . . He never once wanted to kill his
self! *(She sits down on the bench and fumbles for her newspaper. Silence.)*

MRS. CARTER: *(caught between anger and reason . . . she laughs nervously)* Well!
Let's not be upset by this. It's entirely my fault you know. This whole
thing is a completely controversial subject. *(Silence.)* If it's too much for
Jeff . . . well naturally I shouldn't discuss it with you. *(Approaching railing.)*
I'm sorry. Let *me* apologize.

MAMA: *(keeps her eyes on the paper)* No need for that, mam. *(Silence.)*

MRS. CARTER: *(painfully uncomfortable)* I've drifted away from . . . What
started all of this?

MAMA: *(no comedy intended or allowed on this line)* Your brother, mam.   160

MRS. CARTER: *(trying valiantly to brush away the tension)* Yes . . . Well, I had to come down and sort of hold his hand over the reviews. He just thinks too much . . . and studies. He knows the Negro so well that sometimes our friends tease him and say he almost *seems* like . . . well you know . . .

MAMA: *(tightly)* Yes'm.

MRS. CARTER: *(slowly walks over to the "Colored" side near the top of the rail)* You know I try but it's really difficult to understand you people. However . . . I keep trying.

MAMA: *(still tight)* Thank you, mam.

MRS. CARTER: *(retreats back to "White" side and begins to prove herself)* Last   165 week . . . Why do you know what I did? I sent a thousand dollars to a Negro college for scholarships.

MAMA: That was right kind of you.

MRS. CARTER: *(almost pleading)* I know what's going on in your mind. . . and what you're thinking is wrong. I've . . . I've . . . eaten with Negroes.

MAMA: Yes, mam.

MRS. CARTER: *(trying to find a straw)* . . . And there's Malcolm! If it weren't for the guidance of Jeff he'd never written his poems. Malcolm is a Negro.

MAMA: *(freezing)* Yes, mam.   170

MRS. CARTER: *(Gives up, crosses to her bench, opens her overnight bag and takes out a book and begins to read. She glances at Mama from time to time. Mama is deeply absorbed in her newspaper. Mrs. Carter closes her book with a bang . . . determined to penetrate the wall Mama has built around her.)* Why are you going to New York?

MAMA: *(almost accusingly)* I got a daughter there.

MRS. CARTER: I lost my son in the war. *(Silence . . . Mama is ill at ease.)* Your daughter . . . what is she doing . . . studying?

MAMA: No'm, she's trying to get on stage.

MRS. CARTER: *(pleasantly)* Oh . . . a singer?   175

MAMA: No, mam. She's . . .

MRS. CARTER: *(warmly)* You people have such a gift. I love spirituals . . . "Steal Away," "Swing Low, Sweet Chariot."

MAMA: They are right nice. But Florence wants to act. Just say things in plays.

MRS. CARTER: A dramatic actress?

MAMA: Yes, that's what it is. She been in a colored moving picture, and a big   180 show for two weeks on Broadway.

MRS. CARTER: The dear, precious child! . . . But this is funny . . . no! it's pathetic. She must be bitter . . . *really* bitter. Do you know what I do?

MAMA: I can't rightly say.

MRS. CARTER: I'm an actress! A dramatic actress . . . And I haven't really worked in six months . . . And I'm pretty well-known . . . And everyone knows Jeff. I'd like to work. Of course, there are my committees, but you see, they don't need me. Not really . . . not even Jeff.

MAMA: Now that's a shame.

MRS. CARTER: Now your daughter . . . you must make her stop before she's   185 completely unhappy. Make her stop!

MAMA: Yes'm . . . why?

MRS. CARTER: I have the best of contacts and *I've* only done a few *broadcasts* lately. Of course, I'm not counting the things I just wouldn't do. Your daughter . . . make her stop.

MAMA: A drama teacher told her she has real talent.

MRS. CARTER: A drama teacher! My dear woman, there are loads of unscrupulous whites up there that just hand out opinions for . . .

MAMA: This was a colored gentleman down here.   190

MRS. CARTER: Oh well! . . . And she went up there on the strength of that? This makes me very unhappy. (*Puts book away in case, and snaps lock, silence.*)

MAMA: (*getting an idea*) Do you really, truly feel that way, mam?

MRS. CARTER: I do. Please . . . I want you to believe me.

MAMA: Could I ask you something?

MRS. CARTER: Anything.   195

MAMA: You won't be angry, mam?

MRS. CARTER: (*remembering*) I won't. I promise you.

MAMA: (*gathering courage*) Florence is proud . . . but she's having it hard.

MRS. CARTER: I'm sure she is.

MAMA: Could you help her out some, mam? Knowing all the folks you do . . .   200
maybe . . .

MRS. CARTER: (*rubs the outside of the case*) Well . . . it isn't that simple . . . but . . . you're very sweet. If only I could . . .

MAMA: Anything you did, I feel grateful. I don't like to tell it, but she can't even pay her rent and things. And she's used to my cooking for her . . . I believe my girl goes hungry sometime up there . . . and yet she'd like to stay so bad.

MRS. CARTER: (*looks up, resting case on her knees*) How can I refuse? You seem like a good woman.

MAMA: Always lived as best I knew how and raised my children up right. We got a fine family, mam.

MRS. CARTER: And I've no family at all. I've got to! It's clearly my duty. Jeff's   205
books . . . guiding Malcolm's poetry . . . It isn't enough . . . oh I know it isn't. Have you ever heard of Melba Rugby?

MAMA: No, mam. I don't know anybody much . . . except right here.

MRS. CARTER: (*brightening*) She's in California, but she's moving East again . . . hates California.

MAMA: Yes'm.

MRS. CARTER: A most versatile woman. Writes, directs, acts . . . everything!

MAMA: That's nice, mam.   210

MRS. CARTER: Well, she's uprooting herself and coming back to her first home . . . New York . . . to direct "Love Flowers" . . . it's a musical.

MAMA: Yes'm.

MRS. CARTER: She's grand . . . helped so many people . . . and I'm sure she'll help your . . . what's her name.

MAMA: Florence.

MRS. CARTER: (*turns back to bench, opens bag, takes out a pencil and an address   215
book*) Yes, Florence. She'll have to *make* a place for her.

MAMA: Bless you, mam.

MRS. CARTER: *(holds handbag steady on rail as she uses it to write on)* Now let's see . . . the best thing to do would be to give you the telephone number . . . since you're going there.

MAMA: Yes'm.

MRS. CARTER: *(writing address on paper)* Your daughter will love her . . . and if she's a deserving girl . . .

MAMA: *(looking down as Mrs. Carter writes)* She's a good girl. Never a bit of trouble. Except about her husband, and neither one of them could help that.   220

MRS. CARTER: *(stops writing, raises her head questioning)* Oh?

MAMA: He got killed at voting time. He was a good man.

MRS. CARTER: *(embarrassed)* I guess that's worse than losing him in the war.

MAMA: We all got our troubles passing through here.

MRS. CARTER: *(gives her the address)* Tell your dear girl to call this number   225
about a week from now.

MAMA: Yes, mam.

MRS. CARTER: Her experience won't matter with Melba. I know she'll understand. I'll call her too.

MAMA: Thank you, mam.

MRS. CARTER: I'll just tell her . . . no heavy washing or ironing . . . just light cleaning and a little cooking . . . does she cook?

MAMA: Mam? *(Slowly backs away from Mrs. Carter and sits down on bench.)*   230

MRS. CARTER: Don't worry, that won't matter to Melba. *(Silence, moves around the rail to "Colored" side, leans over Mama.)* I'd take your daughter myself, but I've got Binnie. She's been with me for years, and I just can't let her go . . . can I?

MAMA: *(looks at Mrs. Carter closely)* No, mam.

MRS. CARTER: Of course she must be steady. I couldn't ask Melba to take a fly-by-night. *(Touches Mama's arm.)* But she'll have her own room and bath, and above all . . . security.

MAMA: *(reaches out, clutches Mrs. Carter's wrist almost pulling her off balance)* Child!

MRS. CARTER: *(frightened)* You're hurting my wrist.   235

MAMA: *(looks down, realizes how tight she's clutching her, and releases her wrist)* I mustn't hurt you, must I.

MRS. CARTER: *(backing away rubbing her wrist)* It's all right.

MAMA: *(rises)* You better get over on the other side of that rail. It's against the law for you to be over here with me.

MRS. CARTER: *(frightened and uncomfortable)* If you think so.

MAMA: I don't want to break the law.   240

MRS. CARTER: *(keeps her eye on Mama as she drifts around railing to bench on her side, gathers overnight bag)* I know I must look a fright. The train should be along soon. When it comes, I won't see you until New York. These silly laws. *(Silence.)* I'm going to powder my nose. *(Exits into "White ladies" room.)*

PORTER: *(singing offstage)*

MAMA: *(Sits quietly, staring in front of her . . . then looks at the address for a moment . . . tears the paper into little bits and lets them flutter to the floor. She opens the suitcase, takes out notebook, an envelope and a pencil. She writes a few words on the paper.)*

PORTER: *(enters with broom and dust pan)* Number 42 will be coming along in nine minutes. *(When Mama doesn't answer him, he looks up and watches her. She reaches in her bosom, unpins the check, smooths it out, places it in the envelope with the letter. She closes the suitcase.)* I said the train's coming. Where's the lady?

MAMA: She's in the *ladies'* room. You got a stamp?   245

PORTER: No. But I can get one out of the machine. Three for a dime.

MAMA: *(hands him the letter)* Put one on here and mail it for me.

PORTER: *(looks at it)* Gee . . . you writing Florence when you're going to see her?

MAMA: *(picks up the shoebox and puts it back on the bench)* You want a good lunch? It's chicken and fruit.

PORTER: Sure . . . thank you . . . but you won't . . .   250

MAMA: *(rises, paces up and down)* I ain't gonna see Florence for a long time. Might be never.

PORTER: How's that, Mrs. Whitney?

MAMA: She can be anything in the world she wants to be! That's her right. Marge can't make her turn back, Mrs. Carter can't make her turn back. *Lost My Lonely Way!* That's a book! People killing theyselves 'cause they look white but be black. They just don't know do they, Mr. Brown?

PORTER: Whatever happened don't you fret none. Life is too short.

MAMA: Oh, I'm gonna fret plenty! You know what I wrote Florence?   255

PORTER: No, mam. But you don't have to tell me.

MAMA: I said "Keep trying." . . . Oh, I'm going home.

PORTER: I'll take your bag. *(Picks up bag and starts out.)* Come on, Mrs. Whitney. *(Porter exits.)*

Mama moves around to "White" side, stares at sign over door. She starts to knock on "White Ladies" door, but changes her mind. As she turns to leave, her eye catches the railing; she approaches it gently, touches it, turns, exits. Stage is empty for about six or seven seconds. Sound of train whistle is heard in the distance. Slow curtain.

✣ The Storm ✣
(1898)

Kate Chopin

I

The leaves were so still that even Bibi thought it was going to rain. Bobinôt, 1
who was accustomed to converse on terms of perfect equality with his little
son, called the child's attention to certain sombre clouds that were rolling with
sinister intention from the west, accompanied by a sullen, threatening roar.
They were at Friedheimer's store and decided to remain there till the storm
had passed. They sat within the door on two empty kegs. Bibi was four years
old and looked very wise.

"Mama'll be 'fraid, yes," he suggested with blinking eyes. 2

"She'll shut the house. Maybe she got Sylvie helpin' her this evenin'," 3
Bobinôt responded reassuringly.

"No; she ent got Sylvie. Sylvie was helpin' her yistiday," piped Bibi. 4

Bobinôt arose and going across to the counter purchased a can of 5
shrimps, of which Calixta was very fond. Then he returned to his perch on the
keg and sat stolidly holding the can of shrimps while the storm burst. It shook
the wooden store and seemed to be ripping great furrows in the distant field.
Bibi laid his little hand on his father's knee and was not afraid.

II

Calixta, at home, felt no uneasiness for their safety. She sat at a side window 6
sewing furiously on a sewing machine. She was greatly occupied and did not
notice the approaching storm. But she felt very warm and often stopped to
mop her face on which the perspiration gathered in beads. She unfastened her
white sacque at the throat. It began to grow dark, and suddenly realizing the
situation she got up hurriedly and went about closing windows and doors.

Out on the small front gallery she had hung Bobinôt's Sunday clothes to 7
air and she hastened out to gather them before the rain fell. As she stepped
outside, Alcée Laballière rode in at the gate. She had not seen him very often
since her marriage, and never alone. She stood there with Bobinôt's coat in her
hands, and the big rain drops began to fall. Alcée rode his horse under the
shelter of a side projection where the chickens had huddled and there were
plows and a harrow piled up in the corner.

"May I come and wait on your gallery till the storm is over, Calixta?" he 8
asked.

"Come 'long in, M'sieur Alcée." 9

His voice and her own startled her as if from a trance, and she seized   10
Bobinôt's vest. Alcée, mounting to the porch, grabbed the trousers and snatched
Bibi's braided jacket that was about to be carried away by a sudden gust of
wind. He expressed an intention to remain outside, but it was soon apparent
that he might as well have been out in the open: the water beat in upon the
boards in driving sheets, and he went inside, closing the door after him. It was
even necessary to put something beneath the door to keep the water out.

"My! what a rain! It's good two years since it rain' like that," exclaimed   11
Calixta as she rolled up a piece of bagging and Alcée helped her to thrust it
beneath the crack.

She was a little fuller of figure than five years before when she married;   12
but she had lost nothing of her vivacity. Her blue eyes still retained their melt-
ing quality; and her yellow hair, dishevelled by the wind and rain, kinked
more stubbornly than ever about her ears and temples.

The rain beat upon the low, shingled roof with a force and clatter that   13
threatened to break an entrance and deluge them there. They were in the dining
room—the sitting room—the general utility room. Adjoining was her bed room,
with Bibi's couch along side her own. The door stood open, and the room with
its white, monumental bed, its closed shutters, looked dim and mysterious.

Alcée flung himself into a rocker and Calixta nervously began to gather   14
up from the floor the lengths of a cotton sheet which she had been sewing.

"If this keeps up, *Dieu sait*[1] if the levees goin' to stan' it!" she exclaimed.   15

"What have you got to do with the levees?"   16

"I got enough to do! An' there's Bobinôt with Bibi out in that storm—if he   17
only didn' left Friedheimer's!"

"Let us hope, Calixta, that Bobinôt's got sense enough to come in out of a   18
cyclone."

She went and stood at the window with a greatly disturbed look on her   19
face. She wiped the frame that was clouded with moisture. It was stiflingly
hot. Alcée got up and joined her at the window, looking over her shoulder.
The rain was coming down in sheets obscuring the view of far-off cabins and
enveloping the distant wood in a gray mist. The playing of the lightning was
incessant. A bolt struck a tall chinaberry tree at the edge of the field. It filled
all visible space with a blinding glare and the crash seemed to invade the very
boards they stood upon.

Calixta put her hands to her eyes, and with a cry, staggered backward.   20
Alcée's arm encircled her, and for an instant he drew her close and spasmodi-
cally to him.

"*Bonté!*"[2] she cried, releasing herself from his encircling arm and retreat-   21
ing from the window, "the house'll go next! If I only knew w'ere Bibi was!"
She would not compose herself; she would not be seated. Alcée clasped her
shoulders and looked into her face. The contact of her warm, palpitating body
when he had unthinkingly drawn her into his arms, had aroused all the old-
time infatuation and desire for her flesh.

[1]"God knows."
[2]"Goodness" or "Gracious."

"Calixta," he said, "don't be frightened. Nothing can happen. The house is   22
too low to be struck, with so many tall trees standing about. There! aren't you
going to be quiet? say, aren't you?" He pushed her hair back from her face that
was warm and steaming. Her lips were as red and moist as pomegranate seed.
Her white neck and a glimpse of her full, firm bosom disturbed him powerfully.
As she glanced up at him the fear in her liquid blue eyes had given place to a
drowsy gleam that unconsciously betrayed a sensuous desire. He looked down
into her eyes and there was nothing for him to do but to gather her lips in a
kiss. It reminded him of Assumption.[3]

"Do you remember—in Assumption, Calixta?" he asked in a low voice bro-   23
ken by passion. Oh! she remembered; for in Assumption he had kissed her and
kissed her and kissed her; until his senses would well nigh fail, and to save her
he would resort to a desperate flight. If she was not an immaculate dove in
those days, she was still inviolate; a passionate creature whose very defense-
lessness had made her defense, against which his honor forbade him to prevail.
Now—well, now—her lips seemed in a manner free to be tasted, as well as her
round, white throat and her whiter breasts.

They did not heed the crashing torrents, and the roar of the elements made   24
her laugh as she lay in his arms. She was a revelation in that dim, mysterious
chamber; as white as the couch she lay upon. Her firm, elastic flesh that was
knowing for the first time its birthright, was like a creamy lily that the sun
invites to contribute its breath and perfume to the undying life of the world.

The generous abundance of her passion, without guile or trickery, was   25
like a white flame which penetrated and found response in depths of his
own sensuous nature that had never yet been reached.

When he touched her breasts they gave themselves up in quivering ecstasy,   26
inviting his lips. Her mouth was a fountain of delight. And when he possessed
her, they seemed to swoon together at the very borderland of life's mystery.

He stayed cushioned upon her, breathless, dazed, enervated, with his heart   27
beating like a hammer upon her. With one hand she clasped his head, her lips
lightly touching his forehead. The other hand stroked with a soothing rhythm
his muscular shoulders.

The growl of the thunder was distant and passing away. The rain beat   28
softly upon the shingles, inviting them to drowsiness and sleep. But they dared
not yield.

The rain was over; and the sun was turning the glistening green world into   29
a palace of gems. Calixta, on the gallery, watched Alcée ride away. He turned
and smiled at her with a beaming face; and she lifted her pretty chin in the air
and laughed aloud.

III

Bobinôt and Bibi, trudging home, stopped without at the cistern to make them-   30
selves presentable.

---

[3]A reference to a Louisiana Parish and to the story "At the 'Cadian Ball." "The Storm" is a sequel to "At
the 'Cadian Ball."

"My! Bibi, w'at will yo' mama say! You ought to be ashame'. You oughtn'   *31*
put on those good pants. Look at 'em! An' that mud on yo' collar! How you
got that mud on yo' collar, Bibi? I never saw such a boy!" Bibi was the picture
of pathetic resignation. Bobinôt was the embodiment of serious solicitude as
he strove to remove from his own person and his son's the signs of their
tramp over heavy roads and through wet fields. He scraped the mud off Bibi's
bare legs and feet with a stick and carefully removed all traces from his heavy
brogans. Then, prepared for the worst—the meeting with an over-scrupulous
housewife, they entered cautiously at the back door.

Calixta was preparing supper. She had set the table and was dripping cof-   *32*
fee at the hearth. She sprang up as they came in.

"Oh, Bobinôt! You back! My! but I was uneasy. W'ere you been during the   *33*
rain? An' Bibi? he ain't wet? he ain't hurt?" She had clasped Bibi and was kiss-
ing him effusively. Bobinôt's explanations and apologies which he had been
composing all along the way, died on his lips as Calixta felt him to see if he
were dry, and seemed to express nothing but satisfaction at their safe return.

"I brought you some shrimps, Calixta," offered Bobinôt, hauling the can   *34*
from his ample side pocket and laying it on the table.

"Shrimps! Oh, Bobinôt! you too good fo' anything!" and she gave him a   *35*
smacking kiss on the cheek that resounded. "*J'vous réponds,*[4] we'll have a feas'
tonight! umph-umph!"

Bobinôt and Bibi began to relax and enjoy themselves, and when the three   *36*
seated themselves at table they laughed much and so loud that anyone might
have heard them as far away as Laballière's.

IV

Alcée Laballière wrote to his wife, Clarisse, that night. It was a loving letter,   *37*
full of tender solicitude. He told her not to hurry back, but if she and the
babies liked it at Biloxi, to stay a month longer. He was getting on nicely; and
though he missed them, he was willing to bear the separation a while longer—
realizing that their health and pleasure were the first things to be considered.

V

As for Clarisse, she was charmed upon receiving her husband's letter. She   *38*
and the babies were doing well. The society was agreeable; many of her old
friends and acquaintances were at the bay. And the first free breath since her
marriage seemed to restore the pleasant liberty of her maiden days. Devoted
as she was to her husband, their intimate conjugal life was something which
she was more than willing to forego for a while.

So the storm passed and every one was happy.   *39*

[4]"I assure you."

✌ The Yellow Wallpaper ✌
(1892)

Charlotte Perkins Gilman

It is very seldom that mere ordinary people like John and myself secure ancestral halls for the summer. 1

A colonial mansion, a hereditary estate, I would say a haunted house, and reach the height of romantic felicity—but that would be asking too much of fate! 2

Still I will proudly declare that there is something queer about it. 3

Else, why should it be let so cheaply? And why have stood so long untenanted? 4

John laughs at me, of course, but one expects that in marriage. 5

John is practical in the extreme. He has no patience with faith, an intense horror of superstition, and he scoffs openly at any talk of things not to be felt and seen and put down in figures. 6

John is a physician, and *perhaps*—(I would not say it to a living soul, of course, but this is dead paper and a great relief to my mind)—*perhaps* that is one reason I do not get well faster. 7

You see he does not believe I am sick! 8

And what can one do? 9

If a physician of high standing, and one's own husband, assures friends and relatives that there is really nothing the matter with one but temporary nervous depression—a slight hysterical tendency—what is one to do? 10

My brother is also a physician, and also of high standing, and he says the same thing. 11

So I take phosphates or phosphites—whichever it is, and tonics, and journeys, and air, and exercise, and am absolutely forbidden to "work" until I am well again. 12

Personally, I disagree with their ideas. 13

Personally, I believe that congenial work, with excitement and change, would do me good. 14

But what is one to do? 15

I did write for a while in spite of them; but it *does* exhaust me a good deal—having to be so sly about it, or else meet with heavy opposition. 16

I sometimes fancy that in my condition if I had less opposition and more society and stimulus—but John says the very worst thing I can do is to think about my condition, and I confess it always makes me feel bad. 17

So I will let it alone and talk about the house. 18

The most beautiful place! It is quite alone, standing well back from the 19
road, quite three miles from the village. It makes me think of English places
that you read about, for there are hedges and walls and gates that lock, and
lots of separate little houses for the gardeners and people.

There is a *delicious* garden! I never saw such a garden—large and shady, 20
full of box-bordered paths, and lined with long grape-covered arbors with
seats under them.

There were greenhouses, too, but they are all broken now. 21

There was some legal trouble, I believe, something about the heirs and 22
co-heirs; anyhow, the place has been empty for years.

That spoils my ghostliness, I am afraid, but I don't care—there is some- 23
thing strange about the house—I can feel it.

I even said so to John one moonlight evening, but he said what I felt was 24
a *draught*, and shut the window.

I get unreasonably angry with John sometimes. I'm sure I never used to 25
be so sensitive. I think it is due to this nervous condition.

But John says if I feel so, I shall neglect proper self-control; so I take pains 26
to control myself—before him, at least, and that makes me very tired.

I don't like our room a bit. I wanted one downstairs that opened on the 27
piazza and had roses all over the window, and such pretty old-fashioned
chintz hangings! but John would not hear of it.

He said there was only one window and not room for two beds, and no 28
near room for him if he took another.

He is very careful and loving, and hardly lets me stir without special 29
direction.

I have a schedule prescription for each hour in the day; he takes all care 30
from me, and so I feel basely ungrateful not to value it more.

He said we came here solely on my account, that I was to have perfect 31
rest and all the air I could get. "Your exercise depends on your strength, my
dear," said he, "and your food somewhat on your appetite; but air you can
absorb all the time." So we took the nursery at the top of the house.

It is a big, airy room, the whole floor nearly, with windows that look all 32
ways, and air and sunshine galore. It was nursery first and then playroom and
gymnasium, I should judge; for the windows are barred for little children, and
there are rings and things in the walls.

The paint and paper look as if a boys' school had used it. It is stripped 33
off—the paper—in great patches all around the head of my bed, about as far
as I can reach, and in a great place on the other side of the room low down. I
never saw a worse paper in my life.

One of those sprawling flamboyant patterns committing every artistic sin. 34

It is dull enough to confuse the eye in following, pronounced enough to 35
constantly irritate and provoke study, and when you follow the lame uncertain curves for a little distance they suddenly commit suicide—plunge off at
outrageous angles, destroy themselves in unheard of contradictions.

The color is repellant, almost revolting; a smouldering unclean yellow, 36
strangely faded by the slow-turning sunlight.

It is a dull yet lurid orange in some places, a sickly sulphur tint in 37
others.

No wonder the children hated it! I should hate it myself if I had to live in   *38*
this room long.

There comes John, and I must put this away,—he hates to have me write a   *39*
word.

*   *   *

We have been here two weeks, and I haven't felt like writing before, since   *40*
that first day.

I am sitting by the window now, up in this atrocious nursery, and there is   *41*
nothing to hinder my writing as much as I please, save lack of strength.

John is away all day, and even some nights when his cases are serious.   *42*

I am glad my case is not serious!   *43*

But these nervous troubles are dreadfully depressing.   *44*

John does not know how much I really suffer. He knows there is no *reason*   *45*
to suffer, and that satisfies him.

Of course it is only nervousness. It does weigh on me so not to do my   *46*
duty in any way!

I meant to be such a help to John, such a real rest and comfort, and here I   *47*
am a comparative burden already!

Nobody would believe what an effort it is to do what little I am able,—to   *48*
dress and entertain, and order things.

It is fortunate Mary is so good with the baby. Such a dear baby!   *49*

And yet I *cannot* be with him, it makes me so nervous.   *50*

I suppose John never was nervous in his life. He laughs at me so about   *51*
this wallpaper!

At first he meant to repaper the room, but afterwards he said that I was   *52*
letting it get the better of me, and that nothing was worse for a nervous
patient than to give way to such fancies.

He said that after the wallpaper was changed it would be the heavy bed-   *53*
stead, and then the barred windows, and then that gate at the head of the
stairs, and so on.

"You know the place is doing you good," he said, "and really, dear, I   *54*
don't care to renovate the house just for a three months' rental."

"Then do let us go downstairs," I said, "there are such pretty rooms there."   *55*

Then he took me in his arms and called me a blessed little goose, and   *56*
said he would go down cellar, if I wished, and have it whitewashed into the
bargain.

But he is right enough about the beds and windows and things.   *57*

It is an airy and comfortable room as any one need wish, and, of course, I   *58*
would not be so silly as to make him uncomfortable just for a whim.

I'm really getting quite fond of the big room, all but that horrid paper.   *59*

Out of one window I can see the garden, those mysterious deep-shaded   *60*
arbors, the riotous old-fashioned flowers, and bushes and gnarly trees.

Out of another I get a lovely view of the bay and a little private   *61*
wharf belonging to the estate. There is a beautiful shaded lane that runs down
there from the house. I always fancy I see people walking in these numerous
paths and arbors, but John has cautioned me not to give way to fancy in

the least. He says that with my imaginative power and habit of story-making, a nervous weakness like mine is sure to lead to all manner of excited fancies, and that I ought to use my will and good sense to check the tendency. So I try.

I think sometimes that if I were only well enough to write a little it would relieve the press of ideas and rest me. 62

But I find I get pretty tired when I try. 63

It is so discouraging not to have any advice and companionship about my work. When I get really well, John says we will ask Cousin Henry and Julia down for a long visit; but he says he would as soon put fireworks in my pillow-case as to let me have those stimulating people about now. 64

I wish I could get well faster. 65

But I must not think about that. This paper looks to me as if it *knew* what a vicious influence it had! 66

There is a recurrent spot where the pattern lolls like a broken neck and two bulbous eyes stare at you upside down. 67

I get positively angry with the impertinence of it and the everlastingness. Up and down and sideways they crawl, and those absurd, unblinking eyes are everywhere. There is one place where two breadths didn't match, and the eyes go all up and down the line, one a little higher than the other. 68

I never saw so much expression in an inanimate thing before, and we all know how much expression they have! I used to lie awake as a child and get more entertainment and terror out of blank walls and plain furniture than most children could find in a toy-store. 69

I remember what a kindly wink the knobs of our big, old bureau used to have, and there was one chair that always seemed like a strong friend. 70

I used to feel that if any of the other things looked too fierce I could always hop into that chair and be safe. 71

The furniture in this room is no worse than inharmonious, however, for we had to bring it all from downstairs. I suppose when this was used as a playroom they had to take the nursery things out, and no wonder! I never saw such ravages as the children have made here. 72

The wallpaper, as I said before, is torn off in spots, and it sticketh closer than a brother—they must have had perseverance as well as hatred. 73

Then the floor is scratched and gouged and splintered, the plaster itself is dug out here and there, and this great heavy bed which is all we found in the room, looks as if it had been through the wars. 74

But I don't mind it a bit—only the paper. 75

There comes John's sister. Such a dear girl as she is, and so careful of me! I must not let her find me writing. 76

She is a perfect and enthusiastic housekeeper, and hopes for no better profession. I verily believe she thinks it is the writing which made me sick! 77

But I can write when she is out, and see her a long way off from these windows. 78

There is one that commands the road, a lovely shaded winding road, and one that just looks off over the country. A lovely country, too, full of great elms and velvet meadows. 79

This wallpaper has a kind of sub-pattern in a different shade, a particularly irritating one, for you can only see it in certain lights, and not clearly then. 80

But in the places where it isn't faded and where the sun is just so—I   81
can see a strange, provoking, formless sort of figure, that seems to skulk
about behind that silly and conspicuous front design.

There's sister on the stairs!   82

*   *   *

Well, the Fourth of July is over! The people are all gone and I am tired   83
out. John thought it might do me good to see a little company, so we just
had mother and Nellie and the children down for a week.

Of course I didn't do a thing. Jennie sees to everything now.   84

But it tired me all the same.   85

John says if I don't pick up faster he shall send me to Weir Mitchell[1] in   86
the fall.

But I don't want to go there at all. I had a friend who was in his hands   87
once, and she says he is just like John and my brother, only more so!

Besides, it is such an undertaking to go so far.   88

I don't feel as if it was worth while to turn my hand over for anything,   89
and I'm getting dreadfully fretful and querulous.

I cry at nothing, and cry most of the time.   90

Of course I don't when John is here, or anybody else, but when I am   91
alone.

And I am alone a good deal just now. John is kept in town very often   92
by serious cases, and Jennie is good and lets me alone when I want her to.

So I walk a little in the garden or down that lovely lane, sit on the   93
porch under the roses, and lie down up here a good deal.

I'm getting really fond of the room in spite of the wallpaper. Perhaps   94
because of the wallpaper.

It dwells in my mind so!   95

I lie here on this great immovable bed—it is nailed down, I believe—   96
and follow that pattern about by the hour. It is as good as gymnastics, I
assure you. I start, we'll say, at the bottom, down in the corner over there
where it has not been touched, and I determine for the thousandth time
that I *will* follow that pointless pattern to some sort of a conclusion.

I know a little of the principle of design, and I know this thing was not   97
arranged on any laws of radiation, or alternation, or repetition, or symme-
try, or anything else that I ever heard of.

It is repeated, of course, by the breadths, but not otherwise.   98

Looked at in one way each breadth stands alone, the bloated curves   99
and flourishes—a kind of "debased Romanesque" with *delirium tremens*—
go waddling up and down in isolated columns of fatuity.

But, on the other hand, they connect diagonally, and the sprawling   100
outlines run off in great slanting waves of optic horror, like a lot of wallow-
ing seaweeds in full chase.

---

[1]Dr. Silas Weir Mitchell, a rest cure advocate.

The whole thing goes horizontally, too, at least it seems so, and I exhaust myself in trying to distinguish the order of its going in that direction. *101*

They have used a horizontal breadth for a frieze, and that adds wonderfully to the confusion. *102*

There is one end of the room where it is almost intact, and there, when the crosslights fade and the low sun shines directly upon it, I can almost fancy radiation after all—the interminable grotesque seem to form around a common center and rush off in headlong plunges of equal distraction. *103*

It makes me tired to follow it. I will take a nap I guess. *104*

* * *

I don't know why I should write this. *105*

I don't want to. *106*

I don't feel able. *107*

And I know John would think it absurd. But I *must* say what I feel and think in some way—it is such a relief! *108*

But the effort is getting to be greater than the relief. *109*

Half the time now I am awfully lazy, and lie down ever so much. *110*

John says I mustn't lose my strength, and has me take cod liver oil and lots of tonics and things, to say nothing of ale and wine and rare meat. *111*

Dear John! He loves me very dearly, and hates to have me sick. I tried to have a real earnest reasonable talk with him the other day, and tell him how I wish he would let me go and make a visit to Cousin Henry and Julia. *112*

But he said I wasn't able to go, nor able to stand it after I got there; and I did not make out a very good case for myself, for I was crying before I had finished. *113*

It is getting to be a great effort for me to think straight. Just this nervous weakness I suppose. *114*

And dear John gathered me up in his arms, and just carried me upstairs and laid me on the bed, and sat by me and read to me till it tired my head. *115*

He said I was his darling and his comfort and all he had, and that I must take care of myself for his sake, and keep well. *116*

He says no one but myself can help me out of it, that I must use my will and self-control and not let any silly fancies run away with me. *117*

There's one comfort, the baby is well and happy, and does not have to occupy this nursery with the horrid wallpaper. *118*

If we had not used it, that blessed child would have! What a fortunate escape! Why, I wouldn't have a child of mine, an impressionable little thing, live in such a room for worlds. *119*

I never thought of it before, but it is lucky that John kept me here after all, I can stand it so much easier than a baby, you see. *120*

Of course I never mention it to them any more—I am too wise,—but I keep watch of it all the same. *121*

There are things in that paper that nobody knows but me, or ever will. *122*

Behind that outside pattern the dim shapes get clearer every day. *123*

It is always the same shape, only very numerous. *124*

And it is like a woman stooping down and creeping about behind that
pattern. I don't like it a bit. I wonder—I begin to think—I wish John would
take me away from here!   *125*

*   *   *

It is so hard to talk with John about my case, because he is so wise, and   *126*
because he loves me so.
    But I tried it last night.   *127*
    It was moonlight. The moon shines in all around just as the sun does.   *128*
    I hate to see it sometimes, it creeps so slowly, and always comes in by one *129*
window or another.
    John was asleep and I hated to waken him, so I kept still and watched the   *130*
moonlight on that undulating wallpaper till I felt creepy.
    The faint figure behind seemed to shake the pattern, just as if she wanted to *131*
get out.
    I got up softly and went to feel and see if the paper *did* move, and when I   *132*
came back John was awake.
    "What is it, little girl?" he said. "Don't go walking about like that—you'll   *133*
get cold."
    I thought it was a good time to talk, so I told him that I really was not   *134*
gaining here, and that I wished he would take me away.
    "Why, darling!" said he, "our lease will be up in three weeks, and I can't   *135*
see how to leave before.
    "The repairs are not done at home, and I cannot possibly leave town just   *136*
now. Of course if you were in any danger, I could and would, but you really
are better, dear, whether you can see it or not. I am a doctor, dear, and I know.
You are gaining flesh and color, your appetite is better, I feel really much
easier about you."
    "I don't weigh a bit more," said I, "nor as much; and my appetite may be   *137*
better in the evening when you are here, but it is worse in the morning when
you are away!"
    "Bless her little heart!" said he with a big hug, "she shall be as sick as she *138*
pleases! But now let's improve the shining hours by going to sleep, and talk
about it in the morning!"
    "And you won't go away?" I asked gloomily.   *139*
    "Why, how can I dear? It is only three weeks more and then we will take   *140*
a nice little trip of a few days while Jennie is getting the house ready. Really
dear you are better!"
    "Better in body perhaps—" I began, and stopped short, for he sat up   *141*
straight and looked at me with such a stern, reproachful look that I could not
say another word.
    "My darling," said he, "I beg of you, for my sake and for our child's sake,   *142*
as well as for your own, that you will never for one instant let that idea enter
your mind! There is nothing so dangerous, so fascinating, to a temperament
like yours. It is a false and foolish fancy. Can you not trust me as a physician
when I tell you so?"
    So of course I said no more on that score, and we went to sleep before   *143*
long. He thought I was asleep first, but I wasn't, and lay there for hours trying

to decide whether that front pattern and the back pattern really did move together or separately.

*   *   *

On a pattern like this, by daylight, there is a lack of sequence, a defiance of law, that is a constant irritant to a normal mind. *144*

The color is hideous enough, and unreliable enough, and infuriating enough, but the pattern is torturing. *145*

You think you have mastered it, but just as you get well underway in following, it turns a back-somersault and there you are. It slaps you in the face, knocks you down, and tramples upon you. It is like a bad dream. *146*

The outside pattern is a florid arabesque, reminding one of a fungus. If you can imagine a toadstool in joints, an interminable string of toadstools, budding and sprouting in endless convolutions—why, that is something like it. *147*

That is, sometimes! *148*

There is one marked peculiarity about this paper, a thing nobody seems to notice but myself, and that is that it changes as the light changes. *149*

When the sun shoots in through the east window—I always watch for that first long, straight ray—it changes so quickly that I never can quite believe it. *150*

That is why I watch it always. *151*

By moonlight—the moon shines in all night when there is a moon—I wouldn't know it was the same paper. *152*

At night in any kind of light, in twilight, candlelight, lamplight, and worst of all by moonlight, it becomes bars! The outside pattern I mean, and the woman behind it is as plain as can be. *153*

I didn't realize for a long time what the thing was that showed behind, that dim sub-pattern, but now I am quite sure it is a woman. *154*

By daylight she is subdued, quiet. I fancy it is the pattern that keeps her so still. It is so puzzling. It keeps me quiet by the hour. *155*

I lie down ever so much now. John says it is good for me, and to sleep all I can. *156*

Indeed he started the habit by making me lie down for an hour after each meal. *157*

It is a very bad habit I am convinced, for you see I don't sleep. *158*

And that cultivates deceit, for I don't tell them I'm awake—O no! *159*

The fact is I am getting a little afraid of John. *160*

He seems very queer sometimes, and even Jennie has an inexplicable look. *161*

It strikes me occasionally, just as a scientific hypothesis,—that perhaps it is the paper! *162*

I have watched John when he did not know I was looking, and come into the room suddenly on the most innocent excuses, and I've caught him several times *looking at the paper!* And Jennie too. I caught Jennie with her hand on it once. *163*

She didn't know I was in the room, and when I asked her in a quiet, a very quiet voice, with the most restrained manner possible, what she was doing with the paper—she turned around as if she had been caught stealing, and looked quite angry—asked me why I should frighten her so! *164*

Then she said that the paper stained everything it touched, that she had 165
found yellow smooches on all my clothes and John's, and she wished we
would be more careful!

Did not that sound innocent? But I know she was studying that pattern, 166
and I am determined that nobody shall find it out but myself!

* * *

Life is very much more exciting now than it used to be. You see I have 167
something more to expect, to look forward to, to watch. I really do eat better,
and am more quiet than I was.

John is so pleased to see me improve! He laughed a little the other day, 168
and said I seemed to be flourishing in spite of my wallpaper.

I turned it off with a laugh. I had no intention of telling him it was 169
because of the wallpaper—he would make fun of me. He might even want to
take me away.

I don't want to leave now until I have found it out. There is a week more, 170
and I think that will be enough.

* * *

I'm feeling ever so much better! I don't sleep much at night, for it is so 171
interesting to watch developments; but I sleep a good deal in the daytime.

In the daytime it is tiresome and perplexing. 172

There are always new shoots on the fungus, and new shades of yellow 173
all over it. I cannot keep count of them, though I have tried conscientiously.

It is the strangest yellow, that wallpaper! It makes me think of all the yel- 174
low things I ever saw—not beautiful ones like buttercups, but old foul, bad
yellow things.

But there is something else about that paper—the smell! I noticed it the 175
moment we came into the room, but with so much air and sun it was not bad.
Now we have had a week of fog and rain, and whether the windows are open
or not, the smell is here.

It creeps all over the house. 176

I find it hovering in the dining-room, skulking in the parlor, hiding in the 177
hall, lying in wait for me on the stairs.

It gets into my hair. 178

Even when I go to ride, if I turn my head suddenly and surprise it—there 179
is that smell!

Such a peculiar odor, too! I have spent hours in trying to analyze it, to 180
find what it smelled like.

It is not bad—at first, and very gentle, but quite the subtlest, most endur- 181
ing odor I ever met.

In this damp weather it is awful, I wake up in the night and find it hang- 182
ing over me.

It used to disturb me at first. I thought seriously of burning the house—to 183
reach the smell.

But now I am used to it. The only thing I can think of that it is like is the *color* of the paper! A yellow smell.   *184*

There is a very funny mark on this wall, low down, near the mopboard. A streak that runs round the room. It goes behind every piece of furniture, except the bed, a long straight, even *smooch*, as if it had been rubbed over and over.   *185*

I wonder how it was done and who did it, and what they did it for. Round and round and round—round and round and round—it makes me dizzy!   *186*

* * *

I really have discovered something at last.   *187*

Through watching so much at night, when it changes so, I have finally found out.   *188*

The front pattern *does* move—and no wonder! The woman behind shakes it!   *189*

Sometimes I think there are a great many women behind, and sometimes only one, and she crawls around fast, and her crawling shakes it all over.   *190*

Then in the very bright spots she keeps still, and in the very shady spots she just takes hold of the bars and shakes them hard.   *191*

And she is all the time trying to climb through. But nobody could climb through that pattern—it strangles so; I think that is why it has so many heads.   *192*

They get through, and then the pattern strangles them off and turns them upside down, and makes their eyes white!   *193*

If those heads were covered or taken off it would not be half so bad.   *194*

* * *

I think that woman gets out in the daytime!   *195*

And I'll tell you why—privately—I've seen her!   *196*

I can see her out of every one of my windows!   *197*

It is the same woman. I know, for she is always creeping, and most women do not creep by daylight.   *198*

I see her in that long shaded lane, creeping up and down. I see her in those dark grape arbors, creeping all around the garden.   *199*

I see her on that long road under the trees creeping along, and when a carriage comes she hides under the blackberry vines.   *200*

I don't blame her a bit. It must be very humiliating to be caught creeping by daylight!   *201*

I always lock the door when I creep by daylight. I can't do it at night, for I know John would suspect something at once.   *202*

And John is so queer now, that I don't want to irritate him. I wish he would take another room! Besides, I don't want anybody to get that woman out at night but myself.   *203*

I often wonder if I could see her out of all the windows at once.   *204*

But, turn as fast as I can, I can only see out of one at one time.   *205*

And though I always see her, she *may* be able to creep faster than I can turn!   *206*

I have watched her sometimes away off in the open country, creeping   *207*
as fast as a cloud shadow in a high wind.

*　　*　　*

If only that top pattern could be gotten off from the under one! I mean to   *208*
try it, little by little.

I have found out another funny thing, but I shan't tell it this time! It does   *209*
not do to trust people too much.

There are only two more days to get this paper off, and I believe John is   *210*
beginning to notice. I don't like the look in his eyes.

And I heard him ask Jennie a lot of professional questions about me. She   *211*
had a very good report to give.

She said I slept a good deal in the daytime.   *212*

John knows I don't sleep very well at night, for all I'm so quiet!   *213*

He asked me all sorts of questions, too, and pretended to be very loving   *214*
and kind.

As if I couldn't see through him!   *215*

Still, I don't wonder he acts so, sleeping under this paper for three months.   *216*

It only interests me, but I feel sure John and Jennie are secretly affected by it.   *217*

*　　*　　*

Hurrah! This is the last day, but it is enough. John is to stay in town over   *218*
night, and won't be out until this evening.

Jennie wanted to sleep with me—the sly thing! But I told her I should   *219*
undoubtedly rest better for a night all alone.

That was clever, for really I wasn't alone a bit! As soon as it was moon-   *220*
light and that poor thing began to crawl and shake the pattern, I got up and
ran to help her.

I pulled and she shook, I shook and she pulled, and before morning we   *221*
had peeled off yards of that paper.

A strip about as high as my head and half around the room.   *222*

And then when the sun came and that awful pattern began to laugh at   *223*
me, I declared I would finish it to-day!

We go away to-morrow, and they are moving all my furniture down   *224*
again to leave things as they were before.

Jennie looked at the wall in amazement, but I told her merrily that I did it   *225*
out of pure spite at the vicious thing.

She laughed and said she wouldn't mind doing it herself, but I must not   *226*
get tired.

How she betrayed herself that time!   *227*

But I am here, and no person touches this paper but me,—not *alive!*   *228*

She tried to get me out of the room—it was too patent! But I said it was   *229*
so quiet and empty and clean now that I believed I would lie down again and
sleep all I could; and not to wake me even for dinner—I would call when I
woke.

So now she is gone, and the servants are gone, and the things are gone,   *230*
and there is nothing left but that great bedstead nailed down, with the canvas
mattress we found on it.

We shall sleep downstairs to-night, and take the boat home to-morrow.   *231*

I quite enjoy the room, now it is bare again.   *232*

How those children did tear about here!   *233*

This bedstead is fairly gnawed!   *234*

But I must get to work.   *235*

I have locked the door and thrown the key down into the front path.   *236*

I don't want to go out, and I don't want to have anybody come in, till John   *237*
comes.

I want to astonish him.   *238*

I've got a rope up here that even Jennie did not find. If that woman does   *239*
get out, and tries to get away, I can tie her!

But I forgot I could not reach far without anything to stand on!   *240*

This bed will *not* move!   *241*

I tried to lift and push it until I was lame, and then I got so angry I bit off   *242*
a little piece at one corner—but it hurt my teeth.

Then I peeled off all the paper I could reach standing on the floor. It sticks   *243*
horribly and the pattern just enjoys it! All those strangled heads and bulbous
eyes and waddling fungus growths just shriek with derision!

I am getting angry enough to do something desperate. To jump out of the   *244*
window would be admirable exercise, but the bars are too strong even to try.

Besides I wouldn't do it. Of course not. I know well enough that a step   *245*
like that is improper and might be misconstrued.

I don't like to *look* out of the windows even—there are so many of those   *246*
creeping women, and they creep so fast.

I wonder if they all come out of that wallpaper as I did?   *247*

But I am securely fastened now by my well-hidden rope—you don't get   *248*
me out in the road there!

I suppose I shall have to get back behind the pattern when it comes night,   *249*
and that is hard!

It is so pleasant to be out in this great room and creep around as I please!   *250*

I don't want to go outside. I won't, even if Jennie asks me to.   *251*

For outside you have to creep on the ground, and everything is green   *252*
instead of yellow.

But here I can creep smoothly on the floor, and my shoulder just fits in   *253*
that long smooch around the wall, so I cannot lose my way.

Why there's John at the door!   *254*

It is no use, young man, you can't open it!   *255*

How he does call and pound!   *256*

Now he's crying for an axe.   *257*

It would be a shame to break down that beautiful door!   *258*

"John dear!" said I in the gentlest voice, "the key is down by the front   *259*
steps, under a plantain leaf!"

That silenced him for a few moments.   *260*

Then he said—very quietly indeed, "Open the door, my darling!"   *261*

"I can't," said I. "The key is down by the front door under a plantain leaf!"   *262*

And then I said it again, several times, very gently and slowly, and said it   *263*
so often that he had to go and see, and he got it of course, and came in. He
stopped short by the door.

"What is the matter?" he cried. "For God's sake, what are you doing!"   *264*

I kept on creeping just the same, but I looked at him over my shoulder.   *265*

"I've got out at last," said I, "in spite of you and Jane. And I've pulled off   *266*
most of the paper, so you can't put me back!"

Now why should that man have fainted? But he did, and right across my   *267*
path by the wall, so that I had to creep over him every time!

↜ Trifles ↝
(1916)

Susan Glaspell

CHARACTERS

George Henderson, *county attorney*

Henry Peters, *sheriff*

Lewis Hale, *a neighboring farmer*

Mrs. Peters

Mrs. Hale

SCENE

The kitchen in the now abandoned farmhouse of John Wright, a gloomy kitchen, and left without having been put in order—unwashed pans under the sink, a loaf of bread outside the breadbox, a dish towel on the table—other signs of incompleted work. At the rear the outer door opens and the Sheriff comes in followed by the County Attorney and Hale. The Sheriff and Hale are men in middle life, the County Attorney is a young man; all are much bundled up and go at once to the stove. They are followed by two women—the Sheriff's wife first; she is a slight wiry woman, a thin nervous face. Mrs. Hale is larger and would ordinarily be called more comfortable looking, but she is disturbed now and looks fearfully about as she enters. The women have come in slowly, and stand close together near the door.

COUNTY ATTORNEY: *(rubbing his hands)* This feels good. Come up to the fire, ladies.

MRS. PETERS: *(after taking a step forward)* I'm not—cold.

SHERIFF: *(unbuttoning his overcoat and stepping away from the stove as if to mark the beginning of official business)* Now, Mr. Hale, before we move things about, you explain to Mr. Henderson just what you saw when you came here yesterday morning.

COUNTY ATTORNEY: By the way, has anything been moved? Are things just as you left them yesterday?

SHERIFF: *(looking about)* It's just the same. When it dropped below zero last night I thought I'd better send Frank out this morning to make a fire for us—no use getting pneumonia with a big case on, but I told him not to touch anything except the stove—and you know Frank.

COUNTY ATTORNEY: Somebody should have been left here yesterday.

SHERIFF: Oh—yesterday. When I had to send Frank to Morris Center for that man who went crazy—I want you to know I had my hands full yesterday. I knew you could get back from Omaha by today and as long as I went over everything here myself—

285

COUNTY ATTORNEY: Well, Mr. Hale, tell just what happened when you came here yesterday morning.

HALE: Harry and I had started to town with a load of potatoes. We came along the road from my place and as I got here I said, "I'm going to see if I can't get John Wright to go in with me on a party telephone." I spoke to Wright about it once before and he put me off, saying folks talked too much anyway, and all he asked was peace and quiet—I guess you know about how much he talked himself; but I thought maybe if I went to the house and talked about it before his wife, though I said to Harry that I didn't know as what his wife wanted made much difference to John—

COUNTY ATTORNEY: Let's talk about that later, Mr. Hale. I do want to talk about that, but tell now just what happened when you got to the house.   10

HALE: I didn't hear or see anything; I knocked at the door, and still it was all quiet inside. I knew they must be up, it was past eight o'clock. So I knocked again, and I thought I heard somebody say, "Come in." I wasn't sure, I'm not sure yet, but I opened the door—this door (*indicating the door by which the two women are still standing*) and there in that rocker— (*pointing to it*) sat Mrs. Wright.

They all look at the rocker.

COUNTY ATTORNEY: What—was she doing?

HALE: She was rockin' back and forth. She had her apron in her hand and was kind of—pleating it.

COUNTY ATTORNEY: And how did she—look?

HALE: Well, she looked queer.   15

COUNTY ATTORNEY: How do you mean—queer?

HALE: Well, as if she didn't know what she was going to do next. And kind of done up.

COUNTY ATTORNEY: How did she seem to feel about your coming?

HALE: Why, I don't think she minded—one way or other. She didn't pay much attention. I said, "How do, Mrs. Wright, it's cold, ain't it?" And she said, "Is it?"—and went on kind of pleating at her apron. Well, I was surprised; she didn't ask me to come up to the stove, or to set down, but just sat there, not even looking at me, so I said, "I want to see John." And then she—laughed. I guess you would call it a laugh. I thought of Harry and the team outside, so I said a little sharp: "Can't I see John?" "No," she says, kind o' dull like. "Ain't he home?" says I. "Yes," says she, "he's home." "Then why can't I see him?" I asked her, out of patience. "'Cause he's dead," says she. "*Dead*?" says I. She just nodded her head, not getting a bit excited, but rockin' back and forth. "Why—where is he?" says I, not knowing what to say. She just pointed upstairs—like that. (*Himself pointing to the room above.*) I got up, with the idea of going up there. I walked from there to here—then I says, "Why, what did he die of?" "He died of a rope round his neck," says she, and just went on pleatin' at her apron. Well, I went out and called Harry. I thought I might—need help. We went upstairs and there he was lyin'—

COUNTY ATTORNEY: I think I'd rather have you go into that upstairs, where you can point it all out. Just go on now with the rest of the story.   20

HALE: Well, my first thought was to get that rope off. It looked . . . *(stops, his face twitches)* . . . but Harry, he went up to him, and he said, "No, he's dead all right, and we'd better not touch anything." So we went back down stairs. She was still sitting that same way. "Has anybody been notified?" I asked. "No," says she, unconcerned. "Who did this, Mrs. Wright?" said Harry. He said it businesslike—and she stopped pleatin' of her apron. "I don't know," she says. "You don't *know?*" says Harry. "No," says she. "Weren't you sleepin' in the bed with him?" says Harry. "Yes," says she, "but I was on the inside." "Somebody slipped a rope round his neck and strangled him and you didn't wake up?" says Harry. "I didn't wake up," she said after him. We must 'a looked as if we didn't see how that could be, for after a minute she said, "I sleep sound." Harry was going to ask her more questions but I said maybe we ought to let her tell her story first to the coroner, or the sheriff, so Harry went fast as he could to Rivers' place, where there's a telephone.

COUNTY ATTORNEY: And what did Mrs. Wright do when she knew that you had gone for the coroner?

HALE: She moved from that chair to this one over here *(pointing to a small chair in the corner)* and just sat there with her hands held together and looking down. I got a feeling that I ought to make some conversation, so I said I had come in to see if John wanted to put in a telephone, and at that she started to laugh, and then she stopped and looked at me— scared. *(The County Attorney, who has had his notebook out, makes a note.)* I dunno, maybe it wasn't scared. I wouldn't like to say it was. Soon Harry got back, and then Dr. Lloyd came, and you, Mr. Peters, and so I guess that's all I know that you don't.

COUNTY ATTORNEY: *(looking around)* I guess we'll go upstairs first—and then out to the barn and around there. *(To the Sheriff.)* You're convinced that there was nothing important here—nothing that would point to any motive.

SHERIFF: Nothing here but kitchen things.   25

The County Attorney, after again looking around the kitchen, opens the door of a cupboard closet. He gets up on a chair and looks on a shelf. Pulls his hand away, sticky.

COUNTY ATTORNEY: Here's a nice mess.

The women draw nearer.

MRS. PETERS: *(to the other woman)* Oh, her fruit; it did freeze. *(To the County Attorney.)* She worried about that when it turned so cold. She said the fire'd go out and her jars would break.

SHERIFF: Well, can you beat the women! Held for murder and worryin' about her preserves.

COUNTY ATTORNEY: I guess before we're through she may have something more serious than preserves to worry about.

HALE: Well, women are used to worrying over trifles.   30

The two women move a little closer together.

COUNTY ATTORNEY: *(with the gallantry of a young politician)* And yet, for all their worries, what would we do without the ladies? *(The women do not*

*unbend. He goes to the sink, takes a dipperful of water from the pail and pouring
it into a basin, washes his hands. Starts to wipe them on the roller towel, turns it
for a cleaner place.)* Dirty towels! *(Kicks his foot against the pans under the
sink.)* Not much of a housekeeper, would you say, ladies?

MRS. HALE: *(stiffly)* There's a great deal of work to be done on a farm.

COUNTY ATTORNEY: To be sure. And yet *(with a little bow to her)* I know there are
some Dickson county farmhouses which do not have such roller towels.

He gives it a pull to expose its full length again.

MRS. HALE: Those towels get dirty awful quick. Men's hands aren't always
as clean as they might be.

COUNTY ATTORNEY: Ah, loyal to your sex, I see. But you and Mrs. Wright   35
were neighbors. I suppose you were friends, too.

MRS. HALE: *(shaking her head)* I've not seen much of her of late years. I've not
been in this house—it's more than a year.

COUNTY ATTORNEY: And why was that? You didn't like her?

MRS. HALE: I liked her all well enough. Farmers' wives have their hands full,
Mr. Henderson. And then—

COUNTY ATTORNEY: Yes—?

MRS. HALE: *(looking about)* It never seemed a very cheerful place.   40

COUNTY ATTORNEY: No—it's not cheerful. I shouldn't say she had the home-
making instinct.

MRS. HALE: Well, I don't know as Wright had, either.

COUNTY ATTORNEY: You mean that they didn't get on very well?

MRS. HALE: No, I don't mean anything. But I don't think a place'd be any
cheerfuller for John Wright's being in it.

COUNTY ATTORNEY: I'd like to talk more of that a little later. I want to get the   45
lay of things upstairs now.

He goes to the left, where three steps lead to a stair door.

SHERIFF: I suppose anything Mrs. Peters does'll be all right. She was to take
in some clothes for her, you know, and a few little things. We left in such
a hurry yesterday.

COUNTY ATTORNEY: Yes, but I would like to see what you take, Mrs. Peters,
and keep an eye out for anything that might be of use to us.

MRS. PETERS: Yes, Mr. Henderson.

The women listen to the men's steps on the stairs, then look about the kitchen.

MRS. HALE: I'd hate to have men coming into my kitchen, snooping around
and criticizing.

She arranges the pans under sink which the County Attorney had shoved out of place.

MRS. PETERS: Of course it's no more than their duty.   50

MRS. HALE: Duty's all right, but I guess that deputy sheriff that came out
to make the fire might have got a little of this on. *(Gives the roller towel a
pull.)* Wish I'd thought of that sooner. Seems mean to talk about her for
not having things slicked up when she had to come away in such a hurry.

MRS. PETERS: *(who has gone to a small table in the left rear corner of the room, and
lifted one end of a towel that covers a pan)* She had bread set.

Stands still.

MRS. HALE:　*(eyes fixed on a loaf of bread beside the breadbox, which is on a low shelf at the other side of the room. Moves slowly toward it.)* She was going to put this in there. *(Picks up loaf, then abruptly drops it. In a manner of returning to familiar things.)* It's a shame about her fruit. I wonder if it's all gone. *(Gets up on the chair and looks.)* I think there's some here that's all right, Mrs. Peters. Yes—here; *(holding it toward the window)* this is cherries, too. *(Looking again.)* I declare I believe that's the only one. *(Gets down, bottle in her hand. Goes to the sink and wipes it off on the outside.)* She'll feel awful bad after all her hard work in the hot weather. I remember the afternoon I put up my cherries last summer.

She puts the bottle on the big kitchen table, center of the room. With a sigh, is about to sit down in the rocking-chair. Before she is seated realizes what chair it is; with a slow look at it, steps back. The chair which she has touched rocks back and forth.

MRS. PETERS:　Well, I must get those things from the front room closet. *(She goes to the door at the right, but after looking into the other room, steps back.)* You coming with me, Mrs. Hale? You could help me carry them.

They go in the other room; reappear, Mrs. Peters carrying a dress and skirt, Mrs. Hale following with a pair of shoes.

MRS. PETERS:　My, it's cold in there.　55

She puts the clothes on the big table, and hurries to the stove.

MRS. HALE:　*(examining her skirt)* Wright was close. I think maybe that's why she kept so much to herself. She didn't even belong to the Ladies Aid. I suppose she felt she couldn't do her part, and then you don't enjoy things when you feel shabby. She used to wear pretty clothes and be lively, when she was Minnie Foster, one of the town girls singing in the choir. But that— oh, that was thirty years ago. This all you was to take in?

MRS. PETERS:　She said she wanted an apron. Funny thing to want, for there isn't much to get you dirty in jail, goodness knows. But I suppose just to make her feel more natural. She said they was in the top drawer in this cupboard. Yes, here. And then her little shawl that always hung behind the door. *(Opens stair door and looks.)* Yes, here it is.

Quickly shuts door leading upstairs.

MRS. HALE:　*(abruptly moving toward her)* Mrs. Peters?
MRS. PETERS:　Yes, Mrs. Hale?
MRS. HALE:　Do you think she did it?　60
MRS. PETERS:　*(in a frightened voice)* Oh, I don't know.
MRS. HALE:　Well, I don't think she did. Asking for an apron and her little shawl. Worrying about her fruit.
MRS. PETERS:　*(starts to speak, glances up, where footsteps are heard in the room above. In a low voice.)* Mr. Peters says it looks bad for her. Mr. Henderson is awful sarcastic in a speech and he'll make fun of her sayin' she didn't wake up.
MRS. HALE:　Well, I guess John Wright didn't wake when they was slipping that rope under his neck.
MRS. PETERS:　No, it's strange. It must have been done awful crafty and still.　65
They say it was such a—funny way to kill a man, rigging it all up like that.

MRS. HALE: That's just what Mr. Hale said. There was a gun in the house. He
says that's what he can't understand.

MRS. PETERS: Mr. Henderson said coming out that what was needed for the
case was a motive; something to show anger, or—sudden feeling.

MRS. HALE: *(who is standing by the table)* Well, I don't see any signs of anger
around here. *(She puts her hand on the dish towel which lies on the table,
stands looking down at table, one half of which is clean, the other half messy.)*
It's wiped to here. *(Makes a move as if to finish work, then turns and looks at
loaf of bread outside the breadbox. Drops towel. In that voice of coming back to
familiar things.)* Wonder how they are finding things upstairs. I hope she
had it a little more red-up[1] up there. You know, it seems kind of *sneaking.*
Locking her up in town and then coming out here and trying to get her
own house to turn against her!

MRS. PETERS: But Mrs. Hale, the law is the law.

MRS. HALE: I s'pose 'tis. *(Unbuttoning her coat.)* Better loosen up your things,   70
Mrs. Peters. You won't feel them when you go out.

*Mrs. Peters takes off her fur tippet, goes to hang it on hook at back of room, stands
looking at the under part of the small corner table.*

MRS. PETERS: She was piecing a quilt.

She brings the large sewing basket and they look at the bright pieces.

MRS. HALE: It's log cabin pattern. Pretty, isn't it? I wonder if she was goin' to
quilt it or just knot it?

*Footsteps have been heard coming down the stairs. The Sheriff enters followed by Hale
and the County Attorney.*

SHERIFF: They wonder if she was going to quilt it or just knot it!

The men laugh; the women look abashed.

COUNTY ATTORNEY: *(rubbing his hands over the stove)* Frank's fire didn't do much
up there, did it? Well, let's go out to the barn and get that cleared up.

The men go outside.

MRS. HALE: *(resentfully)* I don't know as there's anything so strange, our   75
takin' up our time with little things while we're waiting for them to get
the evidence. *(She sits down at the big table smoothing out a block with decision.)* I don't see as it's anything to laugh about.

MRS. PETERS: *(apologetically)* Of course they've got awful important things on
their minds.

Pulls up a chair and joins Mrs. Hale at the table.

MRS. HALE: *(examining another block)* Mrs. Peters, look at this one. Here, this
is the one she was working on, and look at the sewing! All the rest of it
has been so nice and even. And look at this! It's all over the place! Why, it
looks as if she didn't know what she was about!

*After she has said this they look at each other, then start to glance back at the door.
After an instant Mrs. Hale has pulled at a knot and ripped the sewing.*

MRS. PETERS: Oh, what are you doing, Mrs. Hale?

[1]Regional slang for "spruced up."

MRS. HALE: *(mildly)* Just pulling out a stitch or two that's not sewed very good. *(Threading a needle.)* Bad sewing always made me fidgety.

MRS. PETERS: *(nervously)* I don't think we ought to touch things.   80

MRS. HALE: I'll just finish up this end. *(Suddenly stopping and leaning forward.)* Mrs. Peters?

MRS. PETERS: Yes, Mrs. Hale?

MRS. HALE: What do you suppose she was so nervous about?

MRS. PETERS: Oh—I don't know. I don't know as she was nervous. I sometimes sew awful queer when I'm just tired. *(Mrs. Hale starts to say something, looks at Mrs. Peters, then goes on sewing.)* Well, I must get these things wrapped up. They may be through sooner than we think. *(Putting apron and other things together.)* I wonder where I can find a piece of paper, and string.

MRS. HALE: In that cupboard, maybe.   85

MRS. PETERS: *(looking in cupboard)* Why, here's a birdcage. *(Holds it up.)* Did she have a bird, Mrs. Hale?

MRS. HALE: Why, I don't know whether she did or not—I've not been here for so long. There was a man around last year selling canaries cheap, but I don't know as she took one; maybe she did. She used to sing real pretty herself.

MRS. PETERS: *(glancing around)* Seems funny to think of a bird here. But she must have had one, or why would she have a cage? I wonder what happened to it.

MRS. HALE: I s'pose maybe the cat got it.

MRS. PETERS: No, she didn't have a cat. She's got that feeling some people   90
have about cats—being afraid of them. My cat got in her room and she was real upset and asked me to take it out.

MRS. HALE: My sister Bessie was like that. Queer, ain't it?

MRS. PETERS: *(examining the cage)* Why, look at this door. It's broke. One hinge is pulled apart.

MRS. HALE: *(looking too)* Looks as if someone must have been rough with it.

MRS. PETERS: Why, yes.

She brings the cage forward and puts it on the table.

MRS. HALE: I wish if they're going to find any evidence they'd be about it.   95
I don't like this place.

MRS. PETERS: But I'm awful glad you came with me, Mrs. Hale. It would be lonesome for me sitting here alone.

MRS. HALE: It would, wouldn't it? *(Dropping her sewing.)* But I tell you what I do wish, Mrs. Peters. I wish I had come over sometimes when *she* was here. I—*(looking around the room)*—wish I had.

MRS. PETERS: But of course you were awful busy, Mrs. Hale—your house and your children.

MRS. HALE: I could've come. I stayed away because it weren't cheerful—and that's why I ought to have come. I—I've never liked this place. Maybe because it's down in a hollow and you don't see the road. I dunno what it is but it's a lonesome place and always was. I wish I had come over to see Minnie Foster sometimes. I can see now—

Shakes her head.

MRS. PETERS: Well, you mustn't reproach yourself, Mrs. Hale. Somehow we   *100*
just don't see how it is with other folks until—something comes up.

MRS. HALE: Not having children makes less work—but it makes a quiet
house, and Wright out to work all day, and no company when he did
come in. Did you know John Wright, Mrs. Peters?

MRS. PETERS: Not to know him; I've seen him in town. They say he was a
good man.

MRS. HALE: Yes—good; he didn't drink, and kept his word as well as most, I
guess, and paid his debts. But he was a hard man, Mrs. Peters. Just to
pass the time of day with him—*(Shivers.)* Like a raw wind that gets to the
bone. *(Pauses, her eye falling on the cage.)* I should think she would 'a
wanted a bird. But what do you suppose went with it?

MRS. PETERS: I don't know, unless it got sick and died.

She reaches over and swings the broken door, swings it again. Both women watch it.

MRS. HALE: You weren't raised round here, were you? *(Mrs. Peters shakes her*   *105*
head.) You didn't know—her?

MRS. PETERS: Not till they brought her yesterday.

MRS. HALE: She—come to think of it, she was kind of like a bird herself—real
sweet and pretty, but kind of timid and—fluttery. How—she—did—
change. *(Silence; then as if struck by a happy thought and relieved to get back to
everyday things.)* Tell you what, Mrs. Peters, why don't you take the quilt
in with you? It might take up her mind.

MRS. PETERS: Why, I think that's a real nice idea, Mrs. Hale. There couldn't
possibly be any objection to it, could there? Now, just what would I take?
I wonder if her patches are in here—and her things.

They look in the sewing basket.

MRS. HALE: Here's some red. I expect this has got sewing things in it. *(Brings
out a fancy box.)* What a pretty box. Looks like something somebody
would give you. Maybe her scissors are in here. *(Opens box. Suddenly puts
her hand to her nose.)* Why—*(Mrs. Peters bends nearer, then turns her face
away.)* There's something wrapped up in this piece of silk.

MRS. PETERS: Why, this isn't her scissors.   *110*

MRS. HALE: *(lifting the silk)* Oh, Mrs. Peters—it's—

Mrs. Peters bends closer.

MRS. PETERS: It's the bird.

MRS. HALE: *(jumping up)* But, Mrs. Peters—look at it! Its neck! Look at its
neck! It's all—other side *to*.

MRS. PETERS: Somebody—wrung—its—neck.

*Their eyes meet. A look of growing comprehension, of horror. Steps are heard outside.
Mrs. Hale slips box under quilt pieces, and sinks into her chair. Enter Sheriff and
County Attorney. Mrs. Peters rises.*

COUNTY ATTORNEY: *(as one turning from serious things to little pleasantries)* Well,   *115*
ladies, have you decided whether she was going to quilt it or knot it?

MRS. PETERS: We think she was going to—knot it.

COUNTY ATTORNEY: Well, that's interesting, I'm sure. *(Seeing the birdcage.)* Has
the bird flown?

MRS. HALE: *(putting more quilt pieces over the box)* We think the—cat got it.
COUNTY ATTORNEY: *(preoccupied)* Is there a cat?

Mrs. Hale glances in a quick covert way at Mrs. Peters.

MRS. PETERS: Well, not *now*. They're superstitious, you know. They leave.   120
COUNTY ATTORNEY: *(to Sheriff Peters, continuing an interrupted conversation)* No
sign at all of anyone having come from the outside. Their own rope. Now
let's go up again and go over it piece by piece. *(They start upstairs.)* It
would have to have been someone who knew just the—

*Mrs. Peters sits down. The two women sit there not looking at one another, but as if
peering into something and at the same time holding back. When they talk now it is in
the manner of feeling their way over strange ground, as if afraid of what they are saying, but as if they can not help saying it.*

MRS. HALE: She liked the bird. She was going to bury it in that pretty box.
MRS. PETERS: *(in a whisper)* When I was a girl—my kitten—there was a boy
took a hatchet, and before my eyes—and before I could get there—*(Covers
her face an instant.)* If they hadn't held me back I would have—*(catches her-
self, looks upstairs where steps are heard, falters weakly)*—hurt him.
MRS. HALE: *(with a slow look around her)* I wonder how it would seem never to
have had any children around. *(Pause.)* No, Wright wouldn't like the
bird—a thing that sang. She used to sing. He killed that, too.
MRS. PETERS: *(moving uneasily)* We don't know who killed the bird.   125
MRS. HALE: I knew John Wright.
MRS. PETERS: It was an awful thing was done in this house that night, Mrs.
Hale. Killing a man while he slept, slipping a rope around his neck that
choked the life out of him.
MRS. HALE: His neck. Choked the life out of him.

Her hand goes out and rests on the birdcage.

MRS. PETERS: *(with rising voice)* We don't know who killed him. We don't know.
MRS. HALE: *(her own feeling not interrupted)* If there'd been years and years of   130
nothing, then a bird to sing to you, it would be awful—still, after the bird
was still.
MRS. PETERS: *(something within her speaking)* I know what stillness is. When
we homesteaded in Dakota, and my first baby died—after he was two
years old, and me with no other then—
MRS. HALE: *(moving)* How soon do you suppose they'll be through, looking
for the evidence?
MRS. PETERS: I know what stillness is. *(Pulling herself back.)* The law has got to
punish crime, Mrs. Hale.
MRS. HALE: *(not as if answering that)* I wish you'd seen Minnie Foster when
she wore a white dress with blue ribbons and stood up there in the choir
and sang. *(A look around the room.)* Oh, I *wish* I'd come over here once in a
while! That was a crime! That was a crime! Who's going to punish that?
MRS. PETERS: *(looking upstairs)* We mustn't—take on.   135
MRS. HALE: I might have known she needed help! I know how things can
be—for women. I tell you, it's queer, Mrs. Peters. We live close together
and we live far apart. We all go through the same things—it's all just a

different kind of the same thing. *(Brushes her eyes; noticing the bottle of fruit, reaches out for it.)* If I was you I wouldn't tell her her fruit was gone. Tell her it *ain't.* Tell her it's all right. Take this in to prove it to her. She—she may never know whether it was broke or not.

MRS. PETERS: *(takes the bottle, looks about for something to wrap it in; takes petticoat from the clothes brought from the other room, very nervously begins winding this around the bottle. In a false voice)* My, it's a good thing the men couldn't hear us. Wouldn't they just laugh! Getting all stirred up over a little thing like a—dead canary. As if that could have anything to do with—with—wouldn't they *laugh!*

The men are heard coming down stairs.

MRS. HALE: *(under her breath)* Maybe they would—maybe they wouldn't.

COUNTY ATTORNEY: No, Peters, it's all perfectly clear except a reason for doing it. But you know juries when it comes to women. If there was some definite thing. Something to show—something to make a story about—a thing that would connect up with this strange way of doing it—

The women's eyes meet for an instant. Enter Hale from outer door.

HALE: Well, I've got the team around. Pretty cold out there.   140

COUNTY ATTORNEY: I'm going to stay here a while by myself. *(To the Sheriff.)* You can send Frank out for me, can't you? I want to go over everything. I'm not satisfied that we can't do better.

SHERIFF: Do you want to see what Mrs. Peters is going to take in?

The County Attorney goes to the table, picks up the apron, laughs.

COUNTY ATTORNEY: Oh, I guess they're not very dangerous things the ladies have picked out. *(Moves a few things about, disturbing the quilt pieces which cover the box. Steps back.)* No, Mrs. Peters doesn't need supervising. For that matter, a sheriff's wife is married to the law. Ever think of it that way, Mrs. Peters?

MRS. PETERS: Not—just that way.

SHERIFF: *(chuckling)* Married to the law. *(Moves toward the other room.)* I just   145
want you to come in here a minute, George. We ought to take a look at these windows.

COUNTY ATTORNEY: *(scoffingly)* Oh, windows!

SHERIFF: We'll be right out, Mr. Hale.

Hale goes outside. The Sheriff follows the County Attorney into the other room. Then Mrs. Hale rises, hands tight together, looking intensely at Mrs. Peters, whose eyes make a slow turn, finally meeting Mrs. Hale's. A moment Mrs. Hale holds her, then her own eyes point the way to where the box is concealed. Suddenly Mrs. Peters throws back quilt pieces and tries to put the box in the bag she is wearing. It is too big. She opens box, starts to take bird out, cannot touch it, goes to pieces, stands there helpless. Sound of a knob turning in the other room. Mrs. Hale snatches the box and puts it in the pocket of her big coat. Enter County Attorney and Sheriff.

COUNTY ATTORNEY: *(facetiously)* Well, Henry, at least we found out that she was not going to quilt it. She was going to—what is it you call it, ladies?

MRS. HALE: *(her hand against her pocket)* We call it—knot it, Mr. Henderson.

᧼ Those Winter Sundays ᧽
(1962)

Robert Hayden

Sundays too my father got up early
and put his clothes on in the blueblack cold,
then with cracked hands that ached
from labor in the weekday weather made
banked fires blaze. No one ever thanked him.   5

I'd wake and hear the cold splintering, breaking.
When the rooms were warm, he'd call,
and slowly I would rise and dress,
fearing the chronic angers of that house,

Speaking indifferently to him,   10
who had driven out the cold
and polished my good shoes as well.
What did I know, what did I know
of love's austere and lonely offices?

❧ Hills Like White Elephants ❧
(1927)

Ernest Hemingway

The hills across the valley of the Ebro were long and white. On this side there 1
was no shade and no trees and the station was between two lines of rails in the
sun. Close against the side of the station there was the warm shadow of the
building and a curtain, made of strings of bamboo beads, hung across the open
door into the bar, to keep out flies. The American and the girl with him sat at a
table in the shade, outside the building. It was very hot and the express from
Barcelona would come in forty minutes. It stopped at this junction for two minutes and went on to Madrid.

"What should we drink?" the girl asked. She had taken off her hat and put it 2
on the table.

"It's pretty hot," the man said. 3

"Let's drink beer." 4

"*Dos cervezas*," the man said into the curtain. 5

"Big ones?" a woman asked from the doorway. 6

"Yes. Two big ones." 7

The woman brought two glasses of beer and two felt pads. She put the felt 8
pads and the beer glasses on the table and looked at the man and the girl. The
girl was looking off at the line of hills. They were white in the sun and the country was brown and dry.

"They look like white elephants," she said. 9

"I've never seen one," the man drank his beer. 10

"No, you wouldn't have." 11

"I might have," the man said. "Just because you say I wouldn't have doesn't 12
prove anything."

The girl looked at the bead curtain. "They've painted something on it," she 13
said. "What does it say?"

"Anis del Toro. It's a drink." 14

"Could we try it?" 15

The man called "Listen" through the curtain. The woman came out from the 16
bar.

"Four reales." 17

"We want two Anis del Toro." 18

"With water?" 19

"Do you want it with water?" 20

"I don't know," the girl said. "Is it good with water?" 21

"It's all right." 22

"You want them with water?" asked the woman. 23

"Yes, with water." 24

"It tastes like licorice," the girl said and put the glass down. 25

"That's the way with everything." 26

"Yes," said the girl. "Everything tastes of licorice. Especially all the things 27
you've waited so long for, like absinthe."

"Oh, cut it out." 28

"You started it," the girl said. "I was being amused. I was having a fine time." 29

"Well, let's try and have a fine time." 30

"All right. I was trying. I said the mountains looked like white elephants. 31
Wasn't that bright?"

"That was bright." 32

"I wanted to try this new drink: That's all we do, isn't it—look at things 33
and try new drinks?"

"I guess so." 34

The girl looked across at the hills. 35

"They're lovely hills," she said. "They don't really look like white ele- 36
phants. I just meant the coloring of their skin through the trees."

"Should we have another drink?" 37

"All right." 38

The warm wind blew the bead curtain against the table. 39

"The beer's nice and cool," the man said. 40

"It's lovely," the girl said. 41

"It's really an awfully simple operation, Jig," the man said. "It's not really 42
an operation at all."

The girl looked at the ground the table legs rested on. 43

"I know you wouldn't mind it, Jig. It's really not anything. It's just to let 44
the air in."

The girl did not say anything. 45

"I'll go with you and I'll stay with you all the time. They just let the air in 46
and then it's all perfectly natural."

"Then what will we do afterward?" 47

"We'll be fine afterward. Just like we were before." 48

"What makes you think so?" 49

"That's the only thing that bothers us. It's the only thing that's made us 50
unhappy."

The girl looked at the bead curtain, put her hand out and took hold of two 51
of the strings of beads.

"And you think then we'll be all right and be happy." 52

"I know we will. You don't have to be afraid. I've known lots of people that 53
have done it."

"So have I," said the girl. "And afterward they were all so happy." 54

"Well," the man said, "if you don't want to you don't have to. I wouldn't 55
have you do it if you didn't want to. But I know it's perfectly simple."

"And you really want to?" 56

"I think it's the best thing to do. But I don't want you to do it if you don't 57
really want to."

"And if I do it you'll be happy and things will be like they were and you'll 58
love me?"

"I love you now. You know I love you."   59

"I know. But if I do it, then it will be nice again if I say things are like   60
white elephants, and you'll like it?"

"I'll love it. I love it now but I just can't think about it. You know how I   61
get when I worry."

"If I do it you won't ever worry?"   62

"I won't worry about that because it's perfectly simple."   63

"Then I'll do it. Because I don't care about me."   64

"What do you mean?"   65

"I don't care about me."   66

"Well, I care about you."   67

"Oh, yes. But I don't care about me. And I'll do it and then everything   68
will be fine."

"I don't want you to do it if you feel that way."   69

The girl stood up and walked to the end of the station. Across, on the   70
other side, were fields of grain and trees along the banks of the Ebro. Far
away, beyond the river, were mountains. The shadow of a cloud moved across
the field of grain and she saw the river through the trees.

"And we could have all this," she said. "And we could have everything   71
and every day we make it more impossible."

"What did you say?"   72

"I said we could have everything."   73

"We can have everything."   74

"No, we can't."   75

"We can have the whole world."   76

"No, we can't."   77

"We can go everywhere."   78

"No, we can't. It isn't ours any more."   79

"It's ours."   80

"No, it isn't. And once they take it away, you never get it back."   81

"But they haven't taken it away."   82

"We'll wait and see."   83

"Come on back in the shade," he said. "You mustn't feel that way."   84

"I don't feel any way," the girl said. "I just know things."   85

"I don't want you to do anything that you don't want to do—"   86

"Nor that isn't good for me." she said. "I know. Could we have another   87
beer?"

"All right. But you've got to realize—"   88

"I realize," the girl said. "Can't we maybe stop talking?"   89

They sat down at the table and the girl looked across at the hills on the   90
dry side of the valley and the man looked at her and at the table.

"You've got to realize," he said, "that I don't want you to do it if you don't   91
want to. I'm perfectly willing to go through with it if it means anything to you."

"Doesn't it mean anything to you? We could get along."   92

"Of course it does. But I don't want anybody but you. I don't want any   93
one else. And I know it's perfectly simple."

"Yes, you know it's perfectly simple."   94

"It's all right for you to say that, but I do know it."   95

"Would you do something for me now?"   96

"I'd do anything for you."   97

"Would you please please please please please please please stop talking?"   98

He did not say anything but looked at the bags against the wall of the station. There were labels on them from all the hotels where they had spent nights.   99

"But I don't want you to," he said, "I don't care anything about it."   100

"I'll scream," the girl said.   101

The woman came out through the curtains with two glasses of beer and put them down on the damp felt pads. "The train comes in five minutes," she said.   102

"What did she say?" asked the girl.   103

"That the train is coming in five minutes."   104

The girl smiled brightly at the woman, to thank her.   105

"I'd better take the bags over to the other side of the station," the man said. She smiled at him.   106

"All right. Then come back and we'll finish the beer."   107

He picked up the two heavy bags and carried them around the station to the other tracks. He looked up the tracks but could not see the train. Coming back, he walked through the barroom, where people waiting for the train were drinking. He drank an Anis at the bar and looked at the people. They were all waiting reasonably for the train. He went out through the bead curtain. She was sitting at the table and smiled at him.   108

"Do you feel better?" he asked.   109

"I feel fine," she said. "There's nothing wrong with me. I feel fine."   110

ᕽ The Negro Speaks of Rivers ᕽ
(1925)

Langston Hughes

I've known rivers:
I've known rivers ancient as the world and older than the flow of human blood
  in human veins.

My soul has grown deep like the rivers.

I bathed in the Euphrates when dawns were young.
I built my hut near the Congo and it lulled me to sleep.   5
I looked upon the Nile and raised the pyramids above it.
I heard the singing of the Mississippi when Abe Lincoln went down to New
  Orleans, and I've seen its muddy bosom turn all golden in the sunset.

I've known rivers:
Ancient, dusky rivers.

My soul has grown deep like the rivers.   10

✤ Theme for English B ✤
(1949)

Langston Hughes

The instructor said,
    Go home and write
    a page tonight.
    And let that page come out of you—
    Then, it will be true.   5

I wonder if it's that simple?
I am twenty-two, colored, born in Winston-Salem.
I went to school there, then Durham, then here
to this college on the hill above Harlem.
I am the only colored student in my class.   10
The steps from the hill lead down into Harlem,
through a park, then I cross St. Nicholas,
Eighth Avenue, Seventh, and I come to the Y,
the Harlem Branch Y, where I take the elevator
up to my room, sit down and write this page: 15

It's not easy to know what is true for you or me
at twenty-two, my age. But I guess I'm what
I feel and see and hear, Harlem, I hear you:
hear you, hear me—we two—you, me, talk on this page.
(I hear New York, too) Me—who?   20
Well, I like to eat, sleep, drink, and be in love.
I like to work, read, learn, and understand life.
I like a pipe for a Christmas present,
or records—Bessie, bop, or Bach.[1]
I guess being colored doesn't make me *not* like   25
the same things other folks like who are other races.
So will my page be colored that I write?
Being me, it will not be white.
But it will be
a part of you, instructor.   30

---

[1]Bessie Smith was a well-known blues singer; bop refers to the kind of jazz developed in the 1940s by musicians like Charlie Parker and Dizzy Gillespie; Bach was a famous German composer in the 18th century.

You are white—
yet a part of me, as I am a part of you.
That's American.
Sometimes perhaps you don't want to be a part of me.
Nor do I often want to be a part of you.   35
But we are, that's true!
As I learn from you,
I guess you learn from me—
although you're older—and white—
and somewhat more free.   40

This is my page for English B.

✄ Araby ✄
(1914)

James Joyce

North Richmond Street, being blind, was a quiet street except at the hour when   1
the Christian Brothers' School set the boys free. An uninhabited house of two
storeys stood at the blind end, detached from its neighbours in a square ground.
The other houses of the street, conscious of decent lives within them, gazed at
one another with brown imperturbable faces.

    The former tenant of our house, a priest, had died in the back drawing-   2
room. Air, musty from having been long enclosed, hung in all the rooms, and the
waste room behind the kitchen was littered with old useless papers. Among
these I found a few paper-covered books, the pages of which were curled and
damp: *The Abbot*, by Walter Scott, *The Devout Communicant* and *The Memoirs of
Vidocq*. I liked the last best because its leaves were yellow. The wild garden
behind the house contained a central apple-tree and a few straggling bushes
under one of which I found the late tenant's rusty bicycle-pump. He had been a
very charitable priest; in his will he had left all his money to institutions and the
furniture of his house to his sister.

    When the short days of winter came dusk fell before we had well eaten our   3
dinners. When we met in the street the houses had grown sombre. The space of
sky above us was the colour of ever-changing violet and towards it the lamps of
the street lifted their feeble lanterns. The cold air stung us and we played till our
bodies glowed. Our shouts echoed in the silent street. The career of our play
brought us through the dark muddy lanes behind the houses where we ran the
gauntlet of the rough tribes from the cottages, to the back doors of the dark dripping gardens where odours arose from the ashpits, to the dark odorous stables
where a coachman smoothed and combed the horse or shook music from the
buckled harness. When we returned to the street light from the kitchen windows
had filled the areas. If my uncle was seen turning the corner we hid in the
shadow until we had seen him safely housed. Or if Mangan's sister came out on
the doorstep to call her brother in to his tea we watched her from our shadow
peer up and down the street. We waited to see whether she would remain or go
in and, if she remained, we left our shadow and walked up to Mangan's steps
resignedly. She was waiting for us, her figure defined by the light from the half-
opened door. Her brother always teased her before he obeyed and I stood by the
railings looking at her. Her dress swung as she moved her body and the soft rope
of her hair tossed from side to side.

    Every morning I lay on the floor in the front parlour watching her door. The   4
blind was pulled down to within an inch of the sash so that I could not be seen.
When she came out on the doorstep my heart leaped. I ran to the hall, seized my

books and followed her. I kept her brown figure always in my eye and, when we came near the point at which our ways diverged, I quickened my pace and passed her. This happened morning after morning. I had never spoken to her, except for a few casual words, and yet her name was like a summons to all my foolish blood.

Her image accompanied me even in places the most hostile to romance. On Saturday evenings when my aunt went marketing I had to go to carry some of the parcels. We walked through the flaring streets, jostled by drunken men and bargaining women, amid the curses of labourers, the shrill litanies of shop-boys who stood on guard by the barrels of pigs' cheeks, the nasal chanting of street-singers, who sang a *come-all-you* about O'Donovan Rossa,[1] or a ballad about the troubles in our native land. These noises converged in a single sensation of life for me: I imagined that I bore my chalice safely through a throng of foes. Her name sprang to my lips at moments in strange prayers and praises which I myself did not understand. My eyes were often full of tears (I could not tell why) and at times a flood from my heart seemed to pour itself out into my bosom. I thought little of the future. I did not know whether I would ever speak to her or not or, if I spoke to her, how I could tell her of my confused adoration. But my body was like a harp and her words and gestures were like fingers running upon the wires.   5

One evening I went into the back drawing-room in which the priest had died. It was a dark rainy evening and there was no sound in the house. Through one of the broken panes I heard the rain impinge upon the earth, the fine incessant needles of water playing in the sodden beds. Some distant lamp or lighted window gleamed below me. I was thankful that I could see so little. All my senses seemed to desire to veil themselves and, feeling that I was about to slip from them, I pressed the palms of my hands together until they trembled, murmuring: "*O love! O love!*" many times.   6

At last she spoke to me. When she addressed the first words to me I was so confused that I did not know what to answer. She asked me was I going to *Araby*. I forgot whether I answered yes or no. It would be a splendid bazaar, she said; she would love to go.   7

"And why can't you?" I asked.   8

While she spoke she turned a silver bracelet round and round her wrist. She could not go, she said, because there would be a retreat that week in her convent. Her brother and two other boys were fighting for their caps and I was alone at the railings. She held one of the spikes, bowing her head towards me. The light from the lamp opposite our door caught the white curve of her neck, lit up her hair that rested there and, falling, lit up the hand upon the railing. It fell over one side of her dress and caught the white border of a petticoat, just visible as she stood at ease.   9

"It's well for you," she said.   10

"If I go," I said, "I will bring you something."   11

What innumerable follies laid waste my waking and sleeping thoughts after that evening! I wished to annihilate the tedious intervening days. I   12

---

[1]An Irish nationalist who was imprisoned in 1865 for revolutionary activities, was banished to the United States in 1870, and returned to Ireland in the 1890s.

chafed against the work of school. At night in my bedroom and by day in the classroom her image came between me and the page I strove to read. The syllables of the word *Araby* were called to me through the silence in which my soul luxuriated and cast an Eastern enchantment over me. I asked for leave to go to the bazaar on Saturday night. My aunt was surprised and hoped it was not some Freemason affair. I answered few questions in class. I watched my master's face pass from amiability to sternness; he hoped I was not beginning to idle. I could not call my wandering thoughts together. I had hardly any patience with the serious work of life which, now that it stood between me and my desire, seemed to me child's play, ugly monotonous child's play.

On Saturday morning I reminded my uncle that I wished to go to the bazaar in the evening. He was fussing at the hallstand, looking for the hatbrush, and answered me curtly: *13*

"Yes, boy, I know."   *14*

As he was in the hall I could not go into the front parlour and lie at the window. I left the house in bad humour and walked slowly towards the school. The air was pitilessly raw and already my heart misgave me.   *15*

When I came home to dinner my uncle had not yet been home. Still it was early. I sat staring at the clock for some time and, when its ticking began to irritate me, I left the room. I mounted the staircase and gained the upper part of the house. The high cold empty gloomy rooms liberated me and I went from room to room singing. From the front window I saw my companions playing below in the street. Their cries reached me weakened and indistinct and, leaning my forehead against the cool glass, I looked over at the dark house where she lived. I may have stood there for an hour, seeing nothing but the brown-clad figure cast by my imagination, touched discreetly by the lamplight at the curved neck, at the hand upon the railings and at the border below the dress.   *16*

When I came downstairs again I found Mrs. Mercer sitting at the fire. She was an old garrulous woman, a pawnbroker's widow, who collected used stamps for some pious purpose. I had to endure the gossip of the tea-table. The meal was prolonged beyond an hour and still my uncle did not come. Mrs. Mercer stood up to go; she was sorry she couldn't wait any longer, but it was after eight o'clock and she did not like to be out late, as the night air was bad for her. When she had gone I began to walk up and down the room, clenching my fists. My aunt said: *17*

"I'm afraid you may put off your bazaar for this night of Our Lord."   *18*

At nine o'clock I heard my uncle's latchkey in the halldoor. I heard him talking to himself and heard the hallstand rocking when it had received the weight of his overcoat. I could interpret these signs. When he was midway through his dinner I asked him to give me the money to go to the bazaar. He had forgotten.   *19*

"The people are in bed and after their first sleep now," he said.   *20*

I did not smile. My aunt said to him energetically: *21*

"Can't you give him the money and let him go? You've kept him late enough as it is."   *22*

My uncle said he was very sorry he had forgotten. He said he believed in the old saying: "All work and no play makes Jack a dull boy." He asked me where I was going and, when I had told him a second time he asked me did I know *The Arab's Farewell to His Steed*. When I left the kitchen he was about to recite the opening lines of the piece to my aunt.   *23*

I held a florin tightly in my hand as I strode down Buckingham Street   *24*
towards the station. The sight of the streets thronged with buyers and glaring
with gas recalled to me the purpose of my journey. I took my seat in a third-
class carriage of a deserted train. After an intolerable delay the train moved out
of the station slowly. It crept onward among ruinous houses and over the twin-
kling river. At Westland Row Station a crowd of people pressed to the carriage
doors; but the porters moved them back, saying that it was a special train for
the bazaar. I remained alone in the bare carriage. In a few minutes the train
drew up beside an improvised wooden platform. I passed out on to the road
and saw by the lighted dial of a clock that it was ten minutes to ten. In front of
me was a large building which displayed the magical name.

I could not find any sixpenny entrance and, fearing that the bazaar would   *25*
be closed, I passed in quickly through a turnstile, handing a shilling to a
weary-looking man. I found myself in a big hall girdled at half its height by a
gallery. Nearly all the stalls were closed and the greater part of the hall was in
darkness. I recognised a silence like that which pervades a church after a service. I walked into the centre of the bazaar timidly. A few people were gathered about the stalls which were still open. Before a curtain, over which the
words *Café Chantant* were written in coloured lamps, two men were counting
money on a salver. I listened to the fall of the coins.

Remembering with difficulty why I had come I went over to one of the   *26*
stalls and examined porcelain vases and flowered tea-sets. At the door of the
stall a young lady was talking and laughing with two young gentlemen. I
remarked their English accents and listened vaguely to their conversation.

"O, I never said such a thing!"   *27*

"O, but you did!"   *28*

"O, but I didn't!"   *29*

"Didn't she say that?"   *30*

"Yes. I heard her."   *31*

"O, there's a . . . fib!"   *32*

Observing me the young lady came over and asked me did I wish to buy   *33*
anything. The tone of her voice was not encouraging; she seemed to have spoken to me out of a sense of duty. I looked humbly at the great jars that stood like
eastern guards at either side of the dark entrance to the stall and murmured:

"No, thank you."   *34*

The young lady changed the position of one of the vases and went back   *35*
to the two young men. They began to talk of the same subject. Once or twice
the young lady glanced at me over her shoulder.

I lingered before her stall, though I knew my stay was useless, to make my   *36*
interest in her wares seem the more real. Then I turned away slowly and
walked down the middle of the bazaar. I allowed the two pennies to fall against
the sixpence in my pocket. I heard a voice call from one end of the gallery that
the light was out. The upper part of the hall was now completely dark.

Gazing up into the darkness I saw myself as a creature driven and   *37*
derided by vanity; and my eyes burned with anguish and anger.

✄ Goblin Market ✄
(1859)

Christina Rossetti

Morning and evening
Maids heard the goblins cry:
"Come buy our orchard fruits,
Come buy, come buy:
Apples and quinces,   *5*
Lemons and oranges,
Plump unpecked cherries,
Melons and raspberries,
Bloom-down-cheeked peaches,
Swart-headed mulberries,   *10*
Wild free-born cranberries,
Crab-apples, dewberries,
Pine-apples, blackberries,
Apricots, strawberries;—
All ripe together   *15*
In summer weather,—
Morns that pass by,
Fair eves that fly;
Come buy, come buy:
Our grapes fresh from the vine,   *20*
Pomegranates full and fine,
Dates and sharp bullaces,
Rare pears and greengages,
Damsons and bilberries,
Taste them and try: *25*
Currants and gooseberries,
Bright-fire-like barberries,
Figs to fill your mouth,
Citrons from the South,
Sweet to tongue and sound to eye;   *30*
Come buy, come buy."

Evening by evening
Among the brookside rushes,
Laura bowed her head to hear,
Lizzie veiled her blushes: *35*
Crouching close together
In the cooling weather,

With clasping arms and cautioning lips,
With tingling cheeks and finger tips.
"Lie close," Laura said,   40
Pricking up her golden head:
"We must not look at goblin men,
We must not buy their fruits:
Who knows upon what soil they fed
Their hungry thirsty roots?"   45
"Come buy," call the goblins
Hobbling down the glen.
"Oh," cried Lizzie, "Laura, Laura,
You should not peep at goblin men."
Lizzie covered up her eyes,   50
Covered close lest they should look;
Laura reared her glossy head,
And whispered like the restless brook:
"Look, Lizzie, look, Lizzie,
Down the glen tramp little men.   55
One hauls a basket,
One bears a plate,
One lugs a golden dish
Of many pounds weight.
How fair the vine must grow   60
Whose grapes are so luscious;
How warm the wind must blow
Thro' those fruit bushes."
"No," said Lizzie: "No, no, no;
Their offers should not charm us,   65
Their evil gifts would harm us."
She thrust a dimpled finger
In each ear, shut eyes and ran:
Curious Laura chose to linger
Wondering at each merchant man.   70
One had a cat's face,
One whisked a tail,
One tramped at a rat's pace,
One crawled like a snail,
One like a wombat prowled obtuse and furry,   75
One like a ratel tumbled hurry skurry.
She heard a voice like voice of doves
Cooing all together:
They sounded kind and full of loves
In the pleasant weather.   80

Laura stretched her gleaming neck
Like a rush-imbedded swan,
Like a lily from the beck,[1]

[1] A brook.

Like a moonlit poplar branch,
Like a vessel at the launch   85
When its last restraint is gone.

Backwards up the mossy glen
Turned and trooped the goblin men,
With their shrill repeated cry,
"Come buy, come buy."   90
When they reached where Laura was
They stood stock still upon the moss,
Leering at each other,
Brother with queer brother;
Signalling each other,   95
Brother with sly brother.
One set his basket down,
One rear'd his plate;
One began to weave a crown
Of tendrils, leaves, and rough nuts brown   100
(Men sell not such in any town);
One heav'd the golden weight
Of dish and fruit to offer her:
"Come buy, come buy," was still their cry.
Laura stared but did not stir,   105
Long'd but had no money:
The whisk-tail'd merchant bade her taste
In tones as smooth as honey,
The cat-faced purr'd,
The rat-faced spoke a word   110
Of welcome, and the snail-paced even was heard;
One parrot-voiced and jolly
Cried "Pretty Goblin" still for "Pretty Polly";
One whistled like a bird.

But sweet-tooth Laura spoke in haste: 115
"Good folk, I have no coin;
To take were to purloin:
I have no copper in my purse,
I have no silver either,
And all my gold is on the furze   120
That shakes in windy weather
Above the rusty heather."
"You have much gold upon your head,"
They answer'd all together:
"Buy from us with a golden curl."   125
She clipp'd a precious golden lock,
She dropp'd a tear more rare than pearl,
Then suck'd their fruit globes fair or red:
Sweeter than honey from the rock,
Stronger than man-rejoicing wine,   130

Clearer than water flow'd that juice;
She never tasted such before,
How should it cloy with length of use?
She suck'd and suck'd and suck'd the more
Fruits which that unknown orchard bore;   135
She suck'd until her lips were sore;
Then flung the emptied rinds away
But gather'd up one kernel stone,
And knew not was it night or day
As she turn'd home alone.   140

Lizzie met her at the gate
Full of wise upbraidings:
"Dear, you should not stay so late,
Twilight is not good for maidens;
Should not loiter in the glen   145
In the haunts of goblin men.
Do you not remember Jeanie,
How she met them in the moonlight,
Took their gifts both choice and many,
Ate their fruits and wore their flowers   150
Pluck'd from bowers
Where summer ripens at all hours?
But ever in the noonlight
She pined and pined away;
Sought them by night and day,   155
Found them no more, but dwindled and grew grey;
Then fell with the first snow,
While to this day no grass will grow
Where she lies low:
I planted daisies there a year ago   160
That never blow.
You should not loiter so."
"Nay, hush," said Laura:
"Nay, hush, my sister:
I ate and ate my fill,   165
Yet my mouth waters still;
To-morrow night I will
Buy more"; and kiss'd her:
"Have done with sorrow;
I'll bring you plums to-morrow   170
Fresh on their mother twigs,
Cherries worth getting;
You cannot think what figs
My teeth have met in,
What melons icy-cold   175
Piled on a dish of gold
Too huge for me to hold,

What peaches with a velvet nap,
Pellucid grapes without one seed:
Odorous indeed must be the mead   180
Whereon they grow, and pure the wave they drink
With lilies at the brink,
And sugar-sweet their sap."

Golden head by golden head,
Like two pigeons in one nest   185
Folded in each other's wings,
They lay down in their curtain'd bed:
Like two blossoms on one stem,
Like two flakes of new-fall'n snow,
Like two wands of ivory   190
Tipp'd with gold for awful kings.
Moon and stars gaz'd in at them,
Wind sang to them lullaby,
Lumbering owls forbore to fly,
Not a bat flapp'd to and fro   195
Round their rest:
Cheek to cheek and breast to breast
Locked together in one nest.

Early in the morning
When the first cock crowed his warning,   200
Neat like bees, as sweet and busy,
Laura rose with Lizzie:
Fetched in honey, milked the cows,
Aired and set to rights the house,
Kneaded cakes of whitest wheat,   205
Cakes for dainty mouths to eat,
Next churned butter, whipped up cream,
Fed their poultry, sat and sewed;
Talked as modest maidens should:
Lizzie with an open heart,   210
Laura in an absent dream,
One content, one sick in part;
One warbling for the mere bright day's delight,
One longing for the night.

At length slow evening came: 215
They went with pitchers to the reedy brook;
Lizzie most placid in her look,
Laura most like a leaping flame.
They drew the gurgling water from its deep;
Lizzie plucked purple and rich golden flags,   220
Then turning homewards said: "The sunset flushes
Those furthest loftiest crags;
Come, Laura, not another maiden lags,

No wilful squirrel wags,
The beasts and birds are fast asleep."   225
But Laura loitered still among the rushes
And said the bank was steep.

And said the hour was early still,
The dew not fall'n, the wind not chill:
Listening ever, but not catching   230
The customary cry,
"Come buy, come buy,"
With its iterated jingle
Of sugar-baited words:
Not for all her watching   235
Once discerning even one goblin
Racing, whisking, tumbling, hobbling;
Let alone the herds
That used to tramp along the glen,
In groups or single,   240
Of brisk fruit-merchant men.

Till Lizzie urged, "O Laura, come;
I hear the fruit-call but I dare not look:
You should not loiter longer at this brook:
Come with me home.   245
The stars rise, the moon bends her arc,
Each glowworm winks her spark,
Let us get home before the night grows dark:
For clouds may gather
Though this is summer weather,   250
Put out the lights and drench us through;
Then if we lost our way what should we do?"

Laura turned cold as stone
To find her sister heard that cry alone,
That goblin cry,   255
"Come buy our fruits, come buy."
Must she then buy no more such dainty fruit?
Must she no more such succous pasture find,
Gone deaf and blind?
Her tree of life drooped from the root: 260
She said not one word in her heart's sore ache;
But peering thro' the dimness, nought discerning,
Trudged home, her pitcher dripping all the way;
So crept to bed, and lay
Silent till Lizzie slept;   265
Then sat up in a passionate yearning,
And gnashed her teeth for baulked desire, and wept
As if her heart would break.

Day after day, night after night,
Laura kept watch in vain   270
In sullen silence of exceeding pain.
She never caught again the goblin cry:
"Come buy, come buy";
She never spied the goblin men
Hawking their fruits along the glen: 275
But when the noon waxed bright
Her hair grew thin and gray;
She dwindled, as the fair full moon doth turn
To swift decay and burn
Her fire away.   280

One day remembering her kernel-stone
She set it by a wall that faced the south;
Dewed it with tears, hoped for a root,
Watched for a waxing shoot,
But there came none;   285
It never saw the sun,
It never felt the trickling moisture run:
While with sunk eyes and faded mouth
She dreamed of melons, as a traveller sees
False waves in desert drouth   290
With shade of leaf-crowned trees,
And burns the thirstier in the sandful breeze.

She no more swept the house,
Tended the fowls or cows,
Fetched honey, kneaded cakes of wheat,   295
Brought water from the brook:
But sat down listless in the chimney-nook
And would not eat.

Tender Lizzie could not bear
To watch her sister's cankerous care   300
Yet not to share.
She night and morning
Caught the goblins' cry:
"Come buy our orchard fruits,
Come buy, come buy":   305
Beside the brook, along the glen,
She heard the tramp of goblin men,
The voice and stir
Poor Laura could not hear;
Longed to buy fruit to comfort her,   310
But feared to pay too dear.
She thought of Jeanie in her grave,
Who should have been a bride;
But who for joys brides hope to have

Fell sick and died   315
In her gay prime,
In earliest winter time,
With the first glazing time,
With the first snow-fall of crisp winter time.

Till Laura dwindling   320
Seemed knocking at Death's door:
Then Lizzie weighed no more
Better and worse;
But put a silver penny in her purse,
Kissed Laura, crossed the heath with clumps of furze   325
At twilight, halted by the brook:
And for the first time in her life
Began to listen and look.

Laughed every goblin
When they spied her peeping: 330
Came towards her hobbling,
Flying, running, leaping,
Puffing and blowing,
Chuckling, clapping, crowing,
Clucking and gobbling,   335
Mopping and mowing,
Full of airs and graces,
Pulling wry faces,
Demure grimaces,
Cat-like and rat-like,   340
Ratel- and wombat-like,
Snail-paced in a hurry,
Parrot-voiced and whistler,
Helter skelter, hurry skurry,
Chattering like magpies,   345
Fluttering like pigeons,
Gliding like fishes,—
Hugged her and kissed her,
Squeezed and caressed her:
Stretched up their dishes,   350
Panniers, and plates:
"Look at our apples
Russet and dun,
Bob at our cherries,
Bite at our peaches,   355
Citrons and dates,
Grapes for the asking,
Pears red with basking
Out in the sun,
Plums on their twigs;   360

Pluck them and suck them,
Pomegranates, figs."—

"Good folk," said Lizzie,
Mindful of Jeanie:
"Give me much and many":   365
Held out her apron,
Tossed them her penny.
"Nay, take a seat with us,
Honour and eat with us,"
They answered grinning: 370
"Our feast is but beginning.
Night yet is early,
Warm and dew-pearly,
Wakeful and starry:
Such fruits as these   375
No man can carry;
Half their bloom would fly,
Half their dew would dry,
Half their flavour would pass by.
Sit down and feast with us,   380
Be welcome guest with us,
Cheer you and rest with us."—
"Thank you," said Lizzie: "But one waits
At home alone for me:
So without further parleying,   385
If you will not sell me any
Of your fruits though much and many,
Give me back my silver penny
I tossed you for fee."—
They began to scratch their pates,   390
No longer wagging, purring,
But visibly demurring,
Grunting and snarling.
One called her proud,
Cross-grained, uncivil;   395
Their tones waxed loud,
Their looks were evil.
Lashing their tails
They trod and hustled her,
Elbowed and jostled her,   400
Clawed with their nails,
Barking, mewing, hissing, mocking,
Tore her gown and soiled her stocking,
Twitched her hair out by the roots,
Stamped upon her tender feet,   405
Held her hands and squeezed their fruits
Against her mouth to make her eat.

White and golden Lizzie stood,
Like a lily in a flood,—
Like a rock of blue-veined stone   410
Lashed by tides obstreperously,—
Like a beacon left alone
In a hoary roaring sea,
Sending up a golden fire,—
Like a fruit-crowned orange-tree   415
White with blossoms honey-sweet
Sore beset by wasp and bee,—
Like a royal virgin town
Topped with gilded dome and spire
Close beleaguered by a fleet   420
Mad to tug her standard down.

One may lead a horse to water,
Twenty cannot make him drink.
Though the goblins cuffed and caught her,
Coaxed and fought her,   425
Bullied and besought her,
Scratched her, pinched her black as ink,
Kicked and knocked her,
Mauled and mocked her,
Lizzie uttered not a word;   430
Would not open lip from lip
Lest they should cram a mouthful in:
But laughed in heart to feel the drip
Of juice that syruped all her face,
And lodged in dimples of her chin,   435
And streaked her neck which quaked like curd.
At last the evil people
Worn out by her resistance
Flung back her penny, kicked their fruit
Along whichever road they took,   440
Not leaving root or stone or shoot;
Some writhed into the ground,
Some dived into the brook
With ring and ripple,
Some scudded on the gale without a sound,   445
Some vanished in the distance.

In a smart, ache, tingle,
Lizzie went her way;
Knew not was it night or day;
Sprang up the bank, tore thro' the furze,   450
Threaded copse and dingle,
And heard her penny jingle
Bouncing in her purse,

Its bounce was music to her ear.
She ran and ran   455
As if she feared some goblin man
Dogged her with gibe or curse
Or something worse:
But not one goblin skurried after,
Nor was she pricked by fear;   460
The kind heart made her windy-paced
That urged her home quite out of breath with haste
And inward laughter.

She cried "Laura," up the garden,
"Did you miss me?   465
Come and kiss me.
Never mind my bruises,
Hug me, kiss me, suck my juices
Squeezed from goblin fruits for you,
Goblin pulp and goblin dew.   470
Eat me, drink me, love me;
Laura, make much of me:
For your sake I have braved the glen
And had to do with goblin merchant men."

Laura started from her chair,   475
Flung her arms up in the air,
Clutched her hair:
"Lizzie, Lizzie, have you tasted
For my sake the fruit forbidden?
Must your light like mine be hidden,   480
Your young life like mine be wasted,
Undone in mine undoing
And ruined in my ruin,
Thirsty, cankered, goblin-ridden?"—
She clung about her sister,   485
Kissed and kissed and kissed her;
Tears once again
Refreshed her shrunken eyes,
Dropping like rain
After long sultry drouth;   490
Shaking with aguish fear, and pain,
She kissed and kissed her with a hungry mouth.

Her lips began to scorch,
That juice was wormwood to her tongue,
She loathed the feast: 495
Writhing as one possessed she leaped and sung,
Rent all her robe, and wrung
Her hands in lamentable haste,
And beat her breast.

Her locks streamed like the torch   *500*
Borne by a racer at full speed,
Or like the mane of horses in their flight,
Or like an eagle when she stems the light
Straight toward the sun,
Or like a caged thing freed,   *505*
Or like a flying flag when armies run.

Swift fire spread through her veins, knocked at her heart,
Met the fire smouldering there
And overbore its lesser flame;
She gorged on bitterness without a name: *510*
Ah! fool, to choose such part
Of soul-consuming care!
Sense failed in the mortal strife:
Like the watch-tower of a town
Which an earthquake shatters down,   *515*
Like a lightning-stricken mast,
Like a wind-uprooted tree
Spun about,
Like a foam-topped waterspout
Cast down headlong in the sea,   *520*
She fell at last;
Pleasure past and anguish past,
Is it death or is it life?

Life out of death.
That night long Lizzie watched by her,   *525*
Counted her pulse's flagging stir,
Felt for her breath,
Held water to her lips, and cooled her face
With tears and fanning leaves:
But when the first birds chirped about their eaves,   *530*
And early reapers plodded to the place
Of golden sheaves,
And dew-wet grass
Bowed in the morning winds so brisk to pass,
And new buds with new day   *535*
Opened of cup-like lilies on the stream,
Laura awoke as from a dream,
Laughed in the innocent old way,
Hugged Lizzie but not twice or thrice;
Her gleaming locks showed not one thread of gray,   *540*
Her breath was sweet as May
And light danced in her eyes.

Days, weeks, months, years
Afterwards, when both were wives
With children of their own;   *545*

Their mother-hearts beset with fears,
Their lives bound up in tender lives;
Laura would call the little ones
And tell them of her early prime,
Those pleasant days long gone   *550*
Of not-returning time:
Would talk about the haunted glen,
The wicked, quaint fruit-merchant men,
Their fruits like honey to the throat
But poison in the blood   *555*
(Men sell not such in any town);
Would tell them how her sister stood
In deadly peril to do her good,
And win the fiery antidote:
Then joining hands to little hands   *560*
Would bid them cling together,—
"For there is no friend like a sister
In calm or stormy weather;
To cheer one on the tedious way,
To fetch one if one goes astray,   *565*
To lift one if one totters down,
To strengthen whilst one stands."

✑ Oranges ✑
(1985)

Gary Soto

The first time I walked
With a girl, I was twelve,
Cold, and weighted down
With two oranges in my jacket.
December. Frost cracking   5
Beneath my steps, my breath
Before me, then gone,
As I walked toward
Her house, the one whose
Porch light burned yellow   10
Night and day, in any weather.
A dog barked at me, until
She came out pulling
At her gloves, face bright
With rouge. I smiled,   15
Touched her shoulder, and led
Her down the street, across
A used car lot and a line
Of newly planted trees,
Until we were breathing   20
Before a drugstore. We
Entered, the tiny bell
Bringing a saleslady
Down a narrow aisle of goods.
I turned to the candies   25
Tiered like bleachers,
And asked what she wanted—
Light in her eyes, a smile
Starting at the corners
Of her mouth. I fingered   30
A nickel in my pocket,
And when she lifted a chocolate
That cost a dime,
I didn't say anything.
I took the nickel from   35
My pocket, then an orange,
And set them quietly on

The counter. When I looked up,
The lady's eyes met mine,
And held them, knowing   *40*
Very well what it was all
About.

      Outside,
A few cars hissing past,
Fog hanging like old
Coats between the trees.   *45*
I took my girl's hand
in mine for two blocks,
Then released it to let
Her unwrap the chocolate.
I peeled my orange   *50*
That was so bright against
The gray of December
That, from some distance,
Someone might have thought
I was making a fire in my hands.   *55*

✧ Glossary ✧

Aesthetic   As an adjective, the artistry, beauty, or pleasing elements of a given work of art; as a noun, a philosophy of art production that an artist holds.

Affective Fallacy   As defined by the New Critics, the focus on how a work of literature affects one emotionally rather than on how a text works at a more elemental level.

Allegory   A narrative work that makes sense on the literal level but also suggests a reasonably coherent system of meaning on another level through use of **symbols**, **figurative language**, and the like. Common examples of allegories are *Everyman* and *The Pilgrim's Progress*.

Alliteration   The repetition of initial consonant sounds (usually in accented syllables, often but not always the first syllables in a word). For example, from the first two lines of Jean Toomer's poem "Reapers," "Black reapers with the sound of steel on stones / Are sharpening scythes."

Allusion   A comparison that draws a brief connection between the writer's subject and some other literary or historical person, object, or event.

Antagonist   A character who works against the **protagonist**.

Aporia   A deconstructionist term for themes or interpretations uncovered by careful readings that reflect unstated or unintended agendas (possibly imposed by the writer's cultural or historical milieu) that seem to work against the more overt agendas of a given text. See also **Deconstructionism**.

Apostrophe   A **rhetorical device** in which a speaker addresses somebody or something that isn't present, for rhetorical effect.

Archetype   A recurring image, character, or element in literature, art, or myth that evokes a profound emotional response in the audience because of its resonance with something in the collective unconscious or shared belief systems of the audience.

Aside   A brief speech by a character in a play directly to the audience, usually to reveal the character's inner thoughts; typically, the other characters on the stage cannot hear the aside spoken to the audience.

Assonance   The repetition of vowel sounds in the stressed syllables of words that end differently, often occurring in poetic verse using *slant* or *imperfect rhyme*. See **Rhyme**.

Authorial Intention   The actual, original intention of an author of a literary work. Numerous scholars and theorists have argued that readers can never presume that they truly understand an author's intentions. See also **Intentional Fallacy**.

Ballad   A narrative poem that was originally written to be sung.

Bildungsroman   A German term for a story of apprenticeship and initiation in which a young character sets out on a road of trials and is initiated into adulthood with the help of one or more mentor figures. Examples include *Great Expectations* by Charles Dickens and *The Adventures of Huckleberry Finn* by Mark Twain.

Biographical Criticism   Criticism that makes use of writers' life stories and attempts to show how writers' lives have influenced their work.

Blank Verse   Lines of verse that follow an established, formal **meter** but not a regular **rhyme** scheme.

Canon   The collection of works judged by literary scholars, readers, and writers of the current culture and past cultures to be worthy of study and continual rediscovery. As suggested in this book, many factors—some of them controversial, political, or topical—contribute to whether a work becomes part of the canon or not.

Carnival   As used by the theorist Mikhail Bakhtin, a kind of discourse created when popular culture works as a dissonant voice against the beliefs and intents of mainstream high culture. He derives the term from the Mardi Gras–style celebrations held around the world just before Lent, which he perceives as ironic or dissonant when one considers the somber, religious reasons for Lent.

Catharsis   As defined by Aristotle, the effect that occurs when a work (he specifically refers to **drama**) evokes such a powerful response that the audience experiences an emotional renewal through vicarious participation in the events depicted.

Characterization   The strategies employed by an author to depict characters in their various forms that help guide readers' perceptions and attitudes toward those characters. In *The Aspects of the Novel* (1927), E. M. Forster suggested the term *round characters* for characters who seem idiosyncratic and who change and grow over the course of a narrative and are therefore more believable and interesting; he suggested the term *flat characters* for stereotypical characters who are never really fleshed out.

Chiasmus   A **rhetorical device** in which the word order in similar phrases is reversed, as in this passage from the end of James Joyce's story "The Dead": "His soul swooned slowly as he heard the snow falling faintly through the universe and faintly falling. . . ."

Chicago School   A group of critics, directly influenced by the New Critics, who applied formalist techniques to Aristotelian principles of rhetoric and the arts. One of the foremost critics in the Chicago School is Wayne Booth.

Chronicle Play   See **History Play**.

Climax   In narrative, the moment when the various lines of the **plot** intersect and are in some way resolved.

Close Reading   Carefully and analytically considering every component of a text from a variety of angles. Particular attention is paid to the form and **structure** of the piece, as well as any use of internal **symbols** and **figurative language**.

Closet Drama   A play written to be read rather than performed.

Comedy   **Drama** that is intended to amuse. Plotlines are resolved happily, and irreversible tragedies usually do not occur.

Conceit   Either an intricate, elaborate, and sustained **metaphor** (like the ones used by John Donne in his metaphysical poems) or any elaborate convention of a given **genre** form.

Connotative Meaning   An implied meaning derived from cultural context, which may be distinct from the literal meaning. "White House" in the United States doesn't mean only a house painted white; its cultural connotation implies the place where the president resides and operates.

Couplet   A group of two lines whose terminal sounds rhyme; usually the two rhyming lines are of equal metrical length.

Creative Nonfiction   A work of narrative prose that brings the techniques of fiction writing—**characterization, figurative language, dialogue**, and so on—to nonfiction pieces such as memoirs and narrative histories. *Angela's Ashes* by Frank McCourt and *The Liar's Club* by Mary Karr are examples of creative nonfiction.

Critical Theory   A loose name for the various kinds of philosophical, aesthetic, cultural, and historical perspectives critics employ when considering literature and other forms of culture. At its simplest level, if criticism is attempting to analyze and evaluate various works, critical theory is the method used to develop an analytical or evaluative critique. **New Criticism, cultural studies, deconstructionism, feminist criticism**, and **psychoanalytic criticism** are all kinds of critical theory.

Cultural Studies   A form of **critical theory** that became influential in the 1970s and 1980s, influenced by Marxist studies and by cultural critics from the earlier part of the twentieth century like Bakhtin, Benjamin, and Lukács. Closely connected to **New Historicism**, cultural studies assumes that all the various practices of a given culture—not just the production of art—are connected, and popular and low arts are as worthy of study as "high" arts; furthermore, critics following the cultural studies model are wary of the intrinsic ideologies of a given text.

Deconstructionism   A way of reading that is predicated on the belief that there is no definitive or stable interpretation of a text. Deconstructionist readers often take a text apart piece by piece to search for the **trace**, the missing element that becomes obvious because of its absence. See also *Aporia* and *Différance*.

Denotative Meaning   The literal, dictionary definition of a word, without any extra cultural or contextual shading. The denotative meaning of the phrase "white house" is a house that is painted white.

Denouement   The resolution that occurs at the end of a narrative after the **climax**.

Dialectical Criticism   An approach to literary and cultural studies initiated by Fredric Jameson that argues that texts reveal the writer's (and by extension, the culture's) repressed desire to confront the dominant ideology of a given culture.

Dialogic Discourse   As opposed to **monologic discourse**, writing or expression that contains divergent or contrary views.

Dialogue   Any conversation between characters. Dialogue often serves as a way for authors to convey information about characters or **plot** not directly but through the mouths of their characters.

Didactic   Preachy or lesson-oriented; a text that puts its message before its art or **verisimilitude** can be said to be didactic.

Différance   A term coined by the French philosopher and theorist Jacques Derrida as a pun on the French word *différer*, which can mean "to defer," as in to put something off for a while, or "to differ," as in to be different from something else. Influenced by Ferdinand de Saussure, Derrida notes that everything in language (and culture) is based on differences; like Saussure, he believes that it is essential to remember that meaning is partly derived from deferring as well. Derrida argues that the *signs* making up languages have an almost infinite variety of meanings and interpretations that can be "supplemented," implying that there is no single correct way to understand a text so long as there are other ways it can be read. Thus the term *différance* incorporates language's mutability and variations and multiple, almost inexhaustible interpretations. See also **Deconstructionism** and **Semiotics**.

Donnée   A French term applied to literature by Henry James, meaning a shared, given assumption or starting point that all readers have in common for a work of literature; the term may also refer to the apparent **theme** of a work.

Drama   Any work intended to be performed on the stage by actors; one of the oldest literary forms. Modern times have given rise to new forms of drama, such as "teledramas" and screenplays.

Dramatic Monologue   A poem that reveals the thoughts of a single speaker (a character who is not the poet) in an identifiable dramatic context; typically, the goal of the poem is to reveal the inner thoughts and character of the speaker through the speech alone.

Ego   The Freudian term for the conscious mind.

Elegy   Originally, any poem that used the elegiac **meter**, including love poems; however, modern readers generally assume an elegy to be a comparatively long lyrical meditation on a serious **theme** such as death or loss.

Epic   In poetry, a long narrative poem that usually tells of a hero (often someone of divine or noble birth) and the hero's mission or quest; frequently the epic begins *in medias res*, in the middle of the story.

Epiphany   A religious term appropriated for literature by James Joyce to describe the moment when a character gains a sudden insight into her or his situation and circumstances.

Episteme   As defined by Michel Foucault, a culture's shared system of beliefs detailing its view of the nature of the world, truth, human nature, codes of conduct, standards of morality, and so on.

Epistolary   Written in the form of correspondence or a letter or, more broadly construed, in the form of a journal or diary. Samuel Richardson's *Pamela* (1740) is an epistolary **novel**.

Exegesis   An explanation or interpretation of a given text, originally applied to **explications** of passages from the Bible.

Explication   A close or thorough reading and interpretation of a given text. In some cases, an explication may be no more than a paraphrase of a difficult text; in others, the word may represent a line-by-line interpretation of symbolic language.

Exposition   Information that is provided to the reader about the **plot**, **setting**, or characters in a work of literature. Exposition is often introduced directly in the narrative or by character **dialogue** (especially in the case of **drama**).

Farce   A literary work that accomplishes its goals—whether to be merely humorous or to assert a thematic point—through gags and crude or slapstick humor.

Feminist Criticism   A way of reading that investigates the text's investment in or reaction to the partriarchal power structures that have dominated Western culture. Feminist readings frequently question the canonicity of established writers and the exclusion of others from that elite group; they also question long-held assumptions about the nature of gender itself, arguing that while sex is determined biologically, gender is a cultural construct subject to revision or revolution.

Figurative Language   Writing or speech that makes use of **imagery**, **metaphors**, **similes**, **symbols**, and the like to broaden, deepen, and enrich our understanding of a description, place, person, or turn of phrase. Often it is the figurative elements in a work that subtly convey the **theme**.

Figure of Speech   A type of **figurative language** in which the words expressed connote more than their obvious or **denotative meaning**, often in order to compare dissimilar things.

First Person   The **point of view** of a narrator who is actually a participant in the events of the narrative, either as a **protagonist** or as a side character observing the action from a distance, and who refers to himself or herself as "I." For example, Mark Twain's *The Adventures of Huckleberry Finn* is narrated in the first person.

Foot   In poetic **meter**, the fundamental repeating unit of **rhythm**. Most of these units consist of two or three syllables and are distinguished by the number and placement of stressed syllables within them.

Formal Verse   Verse that follows a consistent **rhyme** scheme and makes use of a consistent **meter**.

Formalists   In a general sense, critics who see the study of the form of the literary work as more important than the consideration of its content; these critics would argue that in the best literary works, form influences content. One of the first schools of formalism was composed of the Russian formalists, who directly influenced the Prague Circle formalists; these groups in turn influenced the New Critics. The Russian formalists particularly believed that the **figurative language** and **rhetorical devices** of literary discourse separated it from other forms of discourse and that to engage literature, one had to study these divergent, distinguishing devices, **tropes**, and techniques.

Fourth Wall   In realistic **drama**, the invisible wall through which the audience watches the action of the play. The actors pretend that the wall exists, and the audience pretends to believe that the wall exists for the characters.

Frame Story   A narrative that contains an exterior story and an interior story, or a story within a story. Usually the frame or outer story provides an introduction to a secondary story that might be told. At its more sophisticated levels, the interior narrative's *themes* might have some bearing on characters in the frame. One of the most famous frame stories, told in verse, would be Chaucer's *Canterbury Tales*; in modern cinema, the movie *Titanic* makes use of the frame **structure**.

Free Verse   Verse without regular metrical form or an overall, uniform **rhyme** scheme. A poem may still make use of inconsistent **meter**, cadence, and rhymes and be free verse. Line and **stanza** breaks take on greater formal attributes in works of free verse.

Freytag's Pyramid   A visual depiction of **plot structure** in **drama** devised by the German writer and playwright Gustav Freytag (1816–1895).

Gender Theory   The study and critique of the concept of gender in culture. Gender theory examines the relationship between biological sex and gender as social constructs imposed by the dominant culture. Gender theory generally falls into two broad categories, *essentialist* and *constructionist*. Essentialist theories hold that male and female are fundamentally naturally different. Constructionist theories maintain that gender is a product of history, education, and acculturation; in other words, gender identification is learned behavior. Most gender critics and theorists subscribe to the latter view, although many feminist critics do not, arguing instead that the masculine and the feminine are utterly separate.

Genre   Category of writing. Literature may be broken into various genres: fiction, **creative nonfiction**, poetry, **drama**, and so on. At the same time, different genres may be divided into subgenres; fiction may be divided into science fiction, detective fiction, horror fiction, and literary fiction. Poetry may be divided into **blank verse** poems, **free verse** poems, **sonnets**, **villanelles**, confessional school poems, New York school poems, and the like. The term *genre fiction* usually implies fiction that falls into the various subgenres of fiction that are not considered literary fiction.

Gothic   Describing a work of fiction intended primarily to scare the reader; so called because the early horror **novels** were set in scary, medieval castles, monasteries, and ruins featuring Gothic architecture. Many critics consider Horace Walpole's *The Castle of Otranto* (1764) the first gothic novel; the form was further popularized by books like *The Mysteries of Udolpho* by Ann Radcliffe (1794) and *The Monk* by M. G. Lewis (1796).

Haiku   A Japanese verse form that is made up of three lines; the first line contains five syllables, the second seven, and the third five. Haiku are usually meant to evoke brief and powerful images.

Hamartia   A Greek term commonly understood as "tragic flaw," more accurately translated as "missing the mark." The term refers, in **drama**, to the tragic hero's erroneous decision that eventually brings about his or her downfall.

Hegemony   The predominant culture's supremacy over other cultural traditions.

History Play   A dramatic work that draws on historical chronicles for its source and often encompasses the reign of a single monarch. Shakespeare's *Henry V* is a history play.

Hyperbole   A **rhetorical device** that uses intentional overexaggeration to achieve a desired effect. Shakespeare uses hyperbole in Sonnet 18 ("Shall I compare thee to a summer's day?") when the speaker argues throughout that the subject of a poem is more wonderful than a summer's day; he then mocks the standard use of hyperbole in sonnets in Sonnet 130 ("My mistress' eyes are nothing like the sun").

Iamb   A poetic **foot** composed of two syllables, an unstressed syllable followed by a stressed syllable: ˘ ´. Note the iambs in Emily Dickinson's line "Bĕcaúse Ĭ coúld nŏt stóp fŏr deáth. . . ."

Id   Freud's term for the part of the human consciousness that is the source of our primal instincts and libido.

Imagery   **Figurative language** that specifically appeals to the senses, usually consisting of a vivid, concrete representation of some kind of sensory perception or perceptible object.

Implied Author   As first defined by Wayne Booth, the creative consciousness suggested by a literary work. Generally, readers have no problem assuming that the author Mark Twain is a separate entity from the character Huckleberry Finn, in that *The Adventures of Huckleberry Finn* is a **first-person** work told from Huck's **point of view**; however, they may make the erroneous assumption that narrative discourse in a third-person work necessarily reflects the author's own thoughts and attitudes. Instead, readers should still acknowledge that the author may well have created a distinctive persona to narrate a given work of literature. Thus when Jane Austen's novel *Pride and Prejudice* begins, "It is a truth universally acknowledged, that a single man in possession of a good fortune must be in want of a wife," we don't assume that this perspective is actually Austen's opinion (although it might be) but rather that of the implied author.

Intentional Fallacy   The mistaken belief that readers can know exactly what an author's intention in a work is; the intentional fallacy argues that the reader can never know exactly what the author's intention is, nor, ultimately, does the author's intention matter.

Interior Monologue   Narrative discourse that purports to reproduce the so-called **stream of consciousness**, the uninterrupted and often unorganized flow of ideas, thoughts, impressions, and sensations that pass through a character's conscious mind. Although the terms are often used interchangeably, some critics differentiate them by using *stream of consciousness* to denote the flow of ideas and *interior monologue* to denote the literary representation of that flow.

Irony   The practice of saying something other than what is literally meant, generally for rhetorical effect. *Verbal irony* refers to a spoken statement that implies its opposite either through **tone** or through situation. *Structural irony* is a more involved form of irony in which the whole work is designed to convey two parallel meanings; successful interpretation of such works depends on the reader's ability to see past what is being literally conveyed by the narrative persona to what seems to be intended. *Dramatic irony* is found in narratives when the audience knows something that a character does not know.

Literary Present Tense   The convention in critical writing of referring to the events or assertions of a literary work in the present tense rather than the past tense.

Logocentrism   The belief that words and texts have stable, perfectly defined meanings that can point to an ultimate meaning. Most schools of poststructuralist theory maintain that language works differently, that the meanings of words are understood in terms of what they are not.

Lyric Poem   A short poem, generally nonnarrative, that expresses the thought or emotion of a single speaker.

Magical Realism   A literary movement characterized by narrative that is realistic in most respects but altered by the intrusion of elements of the fantastic, supernatural, or mythic. Many of Gabriel García Márquez's works are classified as magical realism.

Marxist Literary Theory   Criticism predicated on the belief that needs and wants dictate all that occurs in society and that generally speaking, the dominant classes who control the most production of material create an ideology that ensures that they will stay in control. Most Marxist critics, then, work to tease out thematic undercurrents that reflect the discourses of conflicting ideologies and the tensions and power struggles between and among them.

Materialism   The principle that matter matters and that human social development is based on issues pertaining to the production and control of material goods. Materialism is a principle associated with **Marxist literary theory**.

Metaphor   A comparison in which something is referred to as something else, ascribing qualities associated with the term for artistic or rhetorical effect. The practice of referring to famous actors as "stars" is a simple example: stars are luminous, beautiful, and distant. A metaphor need not always be a noun, however; sometimes the metaphor is an adjective (a reference to the "epidemic proliferation of cellular phones" suggests that they are comparable to a disease). Sometimes, in fact, a metaphor is sustained throughout a literary work.

Meter   A poem's overall pattern of **rhythm**, characterized by the recurrence of similar groups of stressed and unstressed syllables (**feet**). In most metrical English poetry, meter is described by identifying the type of recurring **foot** (an **iamb**, for instance, is an unstressed syllable followed by a stressed one) and the number of **feet** in the line. *Iambic pentameter*, therefore, refers to verse in which there are five **iambs** per line.

Metonymy   The substitution, for rhetorical or artistic effect, of the name of an associated object or idea in place of the name of the object or idea itself. A newscaster who refers to the executive branch of the United States government as "the White House" is using metonymy.

Milieu   Environment or **setting**; background or circumstances.

Mise en Scène   French for "placed on the stage"; in **drama** and film studies, the actual arrangement of visual elements in a scene, including actors, scenery, props, and lighting. The term is also used in film studies to describe the composition of a film frame.

Monologic Discourse   As opposed to **dialogic discourse**, writing that suggests or contains only one voice, series of ideas, or ideology. Literary language, according to Mikhail Bakhtin, is most commonly dialogic.

Morality Play   A type of **drama** developed during the Middle Ages in which allegorical representations of abstract concepts (Temptation, for instance, or Temperance) appear as characters and struggle for control of the human soul.

Motif   A conventional or recurring element, **plot** device, or **figure of speech**. Many kinds of elements can function as motifs; what they all have in common is that they recur, either culturally, within an author's **oeuvre**, or within a specific work.

Mystery Play   A medieval play based directly on biblical events.

New Criticism   A school of literary criticism originated in the 1930s that maintains that the work of literature is to be taken on its own terms as a discrete object and that literary language is a kind of discourse completely distinct from other types of language. The practice of New Criticism involves **close reading** of the text, with minimal reference to its author or cultural **milieu**.

New Historicism   A literary theory that views literature as a dynamic part of history. For New Historicists, history is text, not context, not a **donnée** against which a literary work can be measured; rather, literary texts and other kinds of cultural artifacts (artistic and utilitarian, "high" and "low" culture) are considered as a web of texts that comment dynamically on each other.

New Humanism   A school of literary theory that flourished briefly in the early twentieth century and focused on the moral and ethical qualities of literature, affirming human free will in the face of scientific and psychological assertions of determinism.

New Journalism   Highly stylized nonfiction reportorial prose characterized by a subjective voice and perspective, as opposed to the impersonal and supposedly objective presentation of traditional journalism.

Novel   A long work of prose fiction. Novels are usually associated with the realistic representation of characters and events, and it is generally assumed that some organizing principle, **theme**, or **plot** holds a novel together. In *The Rise of the Novel*, Ian Watt maintains that characters in novels must be individuals rather than types, operating in particular circumstances rather than generic situations determined by stale literary convention.

Novel of Manners   A **novel** that primarily deals, usually satirically, with social customs, social status, and the mores of a particular social class. Usually, though not always, the novel of manners focuses on the middle or upper classes.

Novelette   A work of prose fiction longer than a **short story** and shorter than a **novel**. See **novella**.

Novella   Originally, any tale or short story; today, a **novelette**, any work of prose fiction longer than a **short story** but shorter than a **novel**.

Occam's Razor   The axiom that entities should not be complicated beyond necessity. This is usually translated into the principle that all things being equal, the simplest acceptable answer to a problem is the best. While it may be true that all things are never equal, Occam's razor can often be fruitfully applied to literary interpretations.

Ode   A poetic form defined by the seriousness of its subject matter and an internal consistency of **stanza** form. The *Pindaric ode* is characterized by the alternation of three different stanza types. The *Horatian ode* (named after the Roman poet Horace) consists of one stanza type, which can take almost any form as long as it is consistent throughout the poem. The stanzas of the *irregular ode* can vary in length, **rhyme**, and **meter**.

Oeuvre   A body of work, usually the life's work of an author, artist, or composer.

Onomatopoeia   The use of words that mean what they sound like (*buzz*, for instance, or *bang*); in a broader sense, the term can also mean verse or prose passages that suggest, via auditory means, what they describe.

Ottava Rima   A **stanza** form with eight lines of iambic pentameter rhyming *abababcc*. The form originated in Italy and was later adopted by English and American poets.

Personification   A **rhetorical device** that involves the imposition of human features, attributes, or qualities on nonhuman entities.

Picaresque   An episodic story of a rogue's adventures. Picaresques are considered by some to be precursors to the **novel** and by others to be early examples of the form. The picaresque does not generally demonstrate character development or narrative structure, attributes associated with the novel. Many novels do, however, feature picaresque elements, *Don Quixote* being an example.

Plot   The sequence of events described in a narrative, chosen and arranged for a particular artistic effect.

Point of View   The standpoint of the speaker who is telling a narrative or through whose mind the narrative is filtered. A story is in the **first person** if the narrator speaks of himself or herself as "I" and is somehow a part of the story. A *third-person* narrator remains outside the story. The point of view of the *omniscient* narrator is not limited to one character's perspective, but the *limited* point of view is restricted to what one character knows, thinks, or experiences.

Polyphonic Discourse   In the theory of Mikhail Bakhtin, a narrative containing multiple voices, perspectives, or ideologies, often in conflict with each other. Negotiating the tensions among these multiple voices is one of the goals of Bakhtin's mode of literary analysis.

Postcolonialism   A mode of literary and cultural analysis that focuses on countries of the so-called Third World that are former colonies of European nations. Some critics apply postcolonial theory even to the literature of countries that were separated from the British Empire much earlier in history, including Canada, New Zealand, Ireland, and Australia.

Poststructuralism   An umbrella label encompassing the general theories and methodology shared by deconstructionist and postmodern thought. Post-structuralism purports to go beyond structuralism in its attention to the self-deconstructing nature of the text and to the impossibility of discussing language without using language—inherently flawed, infinitely decentered—to do so.

Prosody   The analysis of *versification*, examining three different qualities of poetry: **meter**, **rhyme**, and **stanzas**.

Protagonist   The main or central character in a narrative.

Psychoanalytic Criticism   A group of related methods of literary analysis predicated on the work of theorists such as Sigmund Freud, C. G. Jung, and Jacques Lacan. Psychoanalytic criticism frequently focuses on the significance of **symbols** and apparently accidental utterances that reveal the deeper intentions of the unconscious mind. Some critics attempt to explain the behavior of characters based on their supposed unconscious motivations, while others treat the literary text as a reflection of the author's own desires.

Quatrain   A four-line **stanza**.

Realism   A literary movement associated with the **novel** in the nineteenth century. Realistic fiction attempts to portray life as it is, focusing on specific details rather than broad literary types, allowing the representation of the raw material of everyday life to guide the course of the novel rather than preconceived notions of **plot**. The term is often used interchangeably with **verisimilitude**.

Rhetorical Device   Any of several identifiable **figures of speech** that use language in ways that are to some degree nonliteral. The *rhetorical question*, a question for which no answer is expected, is an example.

Rhyme   Words rhyme when they end with the same sounds. *Masculine rhyme* refers to a rhyme formed by the stressed concluding syllables of rhyming words (as in *fat, pat*); *feminine rhyme* occurs when the rhyming stressed syllables are followed by identical unstressed syllables (as in *fatten, Patton*). *Near rhyme* (also known as *slant* or *imperfect rhyme*) occurs when either the vowel sounds or the consonant sounds of the corresponding end syllables are the same, but not both.

Rhythm   In **prosody**, the pattern of stressed and unstressed syllables in lines of verse. See also **Meter**.

Roman à Clef   Literally a "**novel** with a key," a narrative in which the characters and **plot** scenarios actually refer to real people, living or dead, and "true" situations (as defined by that particular author). Often character and place names are thinly veiled references to recognizable figures; in Robert McLiam Wilson's novel *Eureka Street*, for instance, the real-life Irish political figure Gerry Adams is represented by a character named Jimmy Eve.

Romance   A narrative, the typical style of which has changed over the course of several centuries. The *medieval romance* is a tale, in prose or verse, of the age of chivalry, frequently focusing on courtly love and high manners. Later the term was used to signify a type of narrative distinct from the **novel**: the romance portrayed ideals, while the novel portrayed reality.

Romanticism   A literary movement in the late eighteenth and early nineteenth centuries distinguished by its reaction against the formal and rational philosophies of the Neoclassical period, which preceded it.

Scansion   A method of describing **rhythms** in poetry by grouping, counting, and marking accented and unaccented syllables.

Semiotics   The analysis of signs, based on the theory that every word in a language is composed of two parts—the *signifier* (the linguistic indication, either spoken or read, that represents an object or idea) and the *signified* (the object or idea that is being represented)—that combine to make a third, the *sign*. Also known as *semiology*.

Setting   The place, time, or situation in which the events in a narrative occur. The term can also refer to the (often merely implied) circumstances in which a **lyric poem** is uttered.

Short Story   A work of prose fiction ranging in length from a few hundred to twenty thousand words.

Simile   An explicit comparison for artistic effect, usually signaled by the use of the word *like* or *as*. The first line of Byron's "Destruction of Sennacherib" contains a famous simile: "The Assyrian came down like the wolf on the fold. . . ."

Soliloquy   The dramatic convention of a character speaking aloud to himself or herself in order to express inner thoughts to the audience.

Sonnet   Both the English (Elizabethan or Shakespearean) sonnet and the Italian (Petrarchan) sonnet generally have fourteen lines of iambic pentameter. The English sonnet usually consists of three **quatrains** (groups of four lines) and a **couplet** (a group of two lines) with a **rhyme** scheme of *abab, cdcd, efef, gg*. The Italian sonnet, by contrast, is divided into an *octave* (a group of eight lines) and a *sestet* (a group of six lines). Typically, the Italian sonnet's rhyme scheme uses only five rhymes: *abba, abba, cdecde*. Although each sonnet is a complete poem unto itself, it is often also part of a *sonnet cycle* or *sequence*, a group of sonnets on a similar **theme**.

Stanza   A sequence of lines in a poem, set off typographically and sometimes distinguished by a recurring pattern of **rhyme**.

Stereotype   A collection of traits attributed to characters with certain things in common. In real life, we are correctly taught that stereotypes are deceptive at best and harmful at worst. In literary **characterization**, however, writers sometimes use stereotypes as a kind of shorthand to sketch out flat characters.

Stock Characters   Characters in fiction or **drama** who are drawn from the conventions of a literary form. The Wacky Neighbor is a stock character in the situation comedy.

Stream of Consciousness   The unprocessed flow of ideas, impressions, and thoughts passing through the mind of the conscious human being. **Interior monologue** is frequently the literary device chosen to represent this flow.

Structure   The form a piece of literature takes: its plan, outline, **stanza** framework, or other applicable distinction.

Subtext   The web of underlying points or **themes** that is implied in a work of literature through use of **symbol**, **metaphor**, **imagery**, and other literary devices.

Superego   Freud's term for the conscience, which works to temper the often antisocial impulses of the **id**.

Symbol   An element in a work of literature—an item, a character, or some other thing—that is a concrete entity within the world of the text and at the same time the suggestion or representation of some other, often more abstract, idea.

Synecdoche   A **trope** in which an object or concept is referred to by the name of one of its parts.

Teleological   Foucault's term for describing a naive conception of history that is straightforward, linear, and moving in a cohesive and coherent progression.

Tercet   A **stanza** of three lines, in which all of the lines rhyme.

Terza Rima   A three-line **stanza** used by Dante in *The Divine Comedy* with a **rhyme** scheme that links the stanzas: *aba bcb cdc ded efe* . . .

Theater of the Absurd   **Drama** that abandons **verisimilitude** to underscore the essential emptiness and meaninglessness of the human condition. Isolation and disconnectedness are common **themes**.

Theme   The central idea of a work of literature—not the subject or topic but the idea, usually abstract, that it addresses. The theme of a work is not necessarily a moral or lesson.

Thesis   The main idea that an essay is attempting to promote or prove.

Tone   The attitude of the speaker or narrator of a work of literature toward the subject, implied largely by the diction the speaker employs.

Trace   In deconstructionist criticism, a missing element that becomes obvious because of its absence. See also **Deconstructionism**.

Tragedy   A play chronicling the fall of a person from a position of honor or privilege for the purpose of evoking fear and pity leading to **catharsis**. Often the tragic hero's very virtues lead him or her to a disastrous decision or **hamartia**. *Classical tragedy* refers to plays that conform most strictly to the rules set forth by Aristotle, which state implicitly that a tragedy should be the story of a character of noble stature brought low by that character's virtues, flaws, and an often cruel fate. The *domestic tragedy* differs from other forms of tragedy by concentrating not on the highborn or noble protagonist but on a person of common birth. The *revenge tragedy* takes as its subject the quest for revenge.

Trope   A **figure of speech** or thought in which words are used to signify ideas other than their literal meanings.

Verisimilitude   The appearance of truth in a work of literature, frequently achieved through the use of concrete details. Sometimes also called *realism*.

Villanelle   A poem of nineteen lines, in which two of the lines repeat in a set pattern, alternating as the last line of each of the following three-line **stanzas**. They also form the concluding **couplet**.

✣ Credits ✣

Faith Bafford, "Life or Death" (student essay). (Pages 203–6)

Robert Browning, "My Last Duchess." (Pages 59–60)

Alice Childress, *Florence*. Copyright © 1950, renewed © 1978 by Alice Childress. Used by permission of Flora Roberts, Inc. (Pages 258–67)

Kate Chopin, "The Storm" from *The Complete Works of Kate Chopin* edited by Per Seyersted. Baton Rouge: Louisiana State University Press, 1970. Copyright (c) 1969, 1997 by Louisiana State University Press. Reprinted by permission of the publisher. (Pages 268–84)

Robert Frost, "Desert Places" and "The Road Not Taken" from *The Poetry of Robert Frost* edited by Edward Connery Latham. New York: Henry Holt, 1969. Copyright © 1936 by Robert Frost, renewed © 1964 by Lesley Frost Ballantine, and © 1969 by Henry Holt and Company, LLC. Reprinted by permission of the publisher. (Pages 35 and 36–37)

Charlotte Perkins Gilman, "The Yellow Wallpaper." (Pages 272–84)

Susan Glaspell, *Trifles*. (Pages 285–94)

Ellen Golub, "Untying Goblin Apron Strings: A Psychoanalytic Reading of 'Goblin Market'" in *Literature and Psychology* 25 (1975): pp. 158–65. Ellen Golub is a professor of communications at Salem State College and a research associate at the Hadassah-Brandeis Institute. (Pages 244–57)

Robert Hayden, "Those Winter Sundays" from *Angle of Descent: New and Selected Poems* by Robert Hayden. New York: Liveright Publishing Corporation, 1962. Copyright © 1966 by Robert Hayden. Used by permission of the publisher. (Page 295)

Ernest Hemingway, "Hills Like White Elephants" from *Men Without Women* by Ernest Hemingway. New York: Scribner, a division of Simon & Schuster, 1955. Copyright © 1927 by Charles Scribner & Sons, renewed © 1955 by Ernest Hemingway. Reprinted by permission of the publisher. (Pages 296–300)

Langston Hughes, "The Negro Speaks of Rivers" and "Theme for English B" from *Collected Poems of Langston Hughes*. New York: Alfred A. Knopf, a division of Random House Inc., 1994. Copyright © 1994 by The Estate of Langston Hughes. Used by permission of the publisher. (Pages 301–2)

James Joyce, "Araby." (Pages 303–6)

Stanley Renner, "Moving to the Girl's Side of 'Hills Like White Elephants'" in *The Hemingway Review* 15.1 (Fall 1995), pp. 27–42. Copyright © 1995 by The Ernest Hemingway Foundation. All rights reserved. (Pages 167–86)

Christina Rossetti, "Goblin Market." (Pages 307–19)

William Shakespeare, Sonnet 18 and Sonnet 130. (Pages 39 and 41)

Gary Soto, "Oranges" from *New and Selected Poems* by Gary Soto. San Francisco: Chronicle Books, 1995; visit ChronicleBooks.com. Copyright © 1995. Used by permission of the publisher. (Pages 320–21)

✧ Index ✧